Bob Marley FAQ

Bob Marley FAQ

All That's Left to Know About the King of Reggae

Brent Hagerman

Backbeat
Books

An Imprint of Hal Leonard LLC

Published in 2018 by Backbeat Books
An Imprint of Hal Leonard LLC
7777 West Bluemound Road
Milwaukee, WI 53213

Trade Book Division Editorial Offices
33 Plymouth St., Montclair, NJ 07042

Printed in the United States of America

Book design by Snow Creative

Library of Congress Cataloging-in-Publication Data is available upon request.

ISBN 978-1-61713-665-8

www.backbeatbooks.com

For Kate, Avalon, Raven, and Devon.
This book proves that all the time I spent listening to Bob Marley records was, in fact, for work, and not just for pleasure (though it was that too).

Contents

Introduction

How Many Bob Marleys
Are There?

W ho is your favorite Bob Marley? Athletic soccer jock? Herb aficionado? "One Love" superhero? Subversive revolutionary? Sexy ladies man? Political activist? Dreadlocked bohemian? Peace broker? Rastafarian natural mystic? Third-world theologian? Streetwise ghetto rude boy? International pop star? Folksy troubadour? Reggae guitarist? Loving family man? Shrewd businessman?

A quick perusal of his song titles and life story will tell you that Bob Marley was multidimensional. Dig a bit deeper into what Bob Marley means for his fans, and you will find that he has become a universal symbol through which diverse peoples can see their own concerns reflected. In the sixties, he and his band were aligned with the defiant Kingston youths known as "rude boys," but his songs also spoke of restraint, spirituality, morality, love, and carnal pleasure. He was marketed in the early seventies by Island Records as a Rastafarian outlaw, capitalizing on the popularity of Jimmy Cliff's reggae Robin Hood character in the film *The Harder They Come*. His rebel anthems such as "I Shot the Sheriff" cemented his credentials as a revolutionary. His leading role in quelling politically motivated gang violence on the streets of Kingston in the late seventies earned him the respect of social activists worldwide. His attempted assassination in 1976 demonstrated that the life he lived and the life he sang about were inseparable. He is remembered as a natural mystic whose concerts opened with Rastafari blessings, and whose stages were adorned with pictures of the man he believed to be the living Black God, Haile Selassie. Rastafari communities around the world routinely cite him as the reason they adopted the faith. He is an icon of peace for many, with an essential message of "One Love." And as the man who penned lyrics that have been turned into children's books, he is also a roots family man. In life and in death, Bob Marley has represented different ideals to different groups of people.

Don Taylor, his manager since 1973, captured the difficulty of trying to sum up Bob Marley when he said that Bob was three persons in one: the "Tuff Gong" revolutionary, the meek and kind family man and lover, and the world-traveling reggae superstar.

Bob Marley statue in Kingston, Jamaica, sculpted by Alvin Marriott.   *Photo by Avda, Creative Commons license*

Bob Marley FAQ captures these many sides of Bob Marley. Divided into four parts—the Man, the Music, the Mystic, and the Myth—the book probes each aspect of his character and representation, giving readers a well-rounded look at the singer whom Bono called "Dr. King in dreads."

Boundaries Crossed, Bridges Built

Bob Marley was a boundary crosser, a hybrid human, a musician and a thinker. Perhaps because he knew so well the lines that divide us—racially, politically, musically—he was able to be an effective bridge-builder. For instance, to much of the world, Bob Marley was an African Jamaican musician. But in his hometown of Nine Mile, with a white father and black mother, he was seen as mixed race, not fully black. His music was a form of racial activism speaking directly to the discrimination of people of African descent and a legacy of colonialism that included the transatlantic slave trade. But his message transcended race. In his memoir, Don Taylor quotes Marley as saying, "Unity is the world's key, and racial harmony. . . . All the people on earth are just one family." Boundaries crossed, bridges built.

As a Rastafarian, Marley was keenly aware of living in Babylon, the land of exile, and saw Africa as his spiritual home. He trod through Babylon but did not accept it. He was always mindful of his true African identity, which he spoke passionately of in his songs, retelling the legacy of slavery and using reggae music to "chant down Babylon." But his message transcended one religion: Babylon came to mean not just the non-African world—the land of slavery and exile for the African diaspora—but all oppressive systems of the world. We can all get behind chanting down global oppression. Boundaries crossed, bridges built.

He was the ghetto superstar born and raised in poverty, first on a rural farm and then in a concrete jungle, who grew up to become a jet-setting millionaire. But he never forgot the ghetto. He provided financial assistance to a steady stream of outstretched hands at his compound on Hope Road, and he gave money to causes he believed in. He outright refused to exploit Jamaicans as he gained international recognition, ensuring that many of his concerts on home soil were free, to allow the poorest to attend. He even cautioned hangers-on against trying to build walls around his uptown residence in an attempt to keep out the poor. Boundaries crossed, bridges built.

Great artists do not mimic the work of others, they blaze new pathways, and, as a musician, Bob Marley did this through his fusion of genres. The musicians that sparked new subgenres in the twentieth century did so by breaking down musical barriers and combining diverse musical cultures. Chuck Berry and Elvis Presley were among a group of musicians in the early fifties that brought country and R&B together to form rock 'n' roll. Bob Dylan amalgamated the poetry and quest for an original voice from the romantic literary tradition with folk and rock. The Beatles expanded rock's horizons by turning it into art; San Francisco bands made it psychedelic; Black Sabbath made it heavy; and the punks made it matter again. Ray Charles, Aretha Franklin, Sam Cooke, Otis Redding, and James Brown married the spiritual and the secular to produce soul. Kool Herc and Grandmaster Flash deconstructed funk, soul, and R&B to create the hybrid genre hip-hop. Run-DMC and the Beastie Boys were at the vanguard of rap by slamming together rock samples underneath dope rhymes.

Bob Marley fits easily with this crowd. Like them, he crossed musical boundaries, bringing together Jamaican rhythms with rock and soul. Like the #1 song in the US the month he was born—the Andrews Sisters' "Rum and Coca

Cola"—Bob Marley merged Caribbean and American culture. But unlike this bowdlerized cover of a Trinidadian calypso, which keeps little of the original's rhythmic complexity and soul, Marley's hybrid music maintained its soulful heart. He expanded the sound of reggae without pruning the roots of reggae.

The Struggles of the Third World and the Ears of the First World

Bob Marley FAQ is a lively and entertaining book answering many questions both casual and hardcore fans might have about the King of Reggae, and offering new facts and perspectives. This book will not only give readers an engaging overview of Marley's life, music, and legacy, it will contextualize Marley's career in a musical and religious mission that successfully saw him spread both reggae music and the Rastafari religion globally. Marley was more than just a rock star; as a political activist, black nationalist, sage, lover, and theologian, his impact has been felt in arenas far removed from the music industry. *Bob Marley FAQ* presents the singer as an unparalleled twentieth-century artist who, in the turbulent and often violent postcolonial era, took the struggles of the third world to the ears of the first world using a new subgenre of music that forged African-Jamaican rhythms and song craft with American popular music.

Bob Marley FAQ unpacks the reasons behind Marley's rise to fame and enduring global appeal, which accounts for sales of up a quarter of a million copies of the *Legend* greatest-hits package per year, and his ranking as the sixth-highest-earning dead celebrity in 2016, according to *Forbes Magazine*. While his Jamaican contemporaries like Toots and the Maytals, Desmond Dekker, Peter Tosh, Bunny Wailer, Big Youth, and Burning Spear continued to rule the charts at home, Marley was exceptional in his ability to transcend the local music business to become the third world's first superstar. Some of this has to do with his musical genius in crafting songs that bridged local and universal concerns, couched in addictive layers of polyrhythms and anthemic melodies. But the triumph of Bob Marley was as much about the savvy marketing and crossover appeal that presented him as an exotic and prophetic protest singer to audiences for whom reggae had previously been little more than exotic novelty music.

Countercultural Icon

In a world of plastic celebrities, reality television, and virtual reality, Bob Marley remains unique. A meta-superstar/shaman, he has transcended the kind of commercial cult of celebrity that lionizes the prepackaged pop-star elites of today. Bob Marley has become as much myth as man, and in this way he stands

Since his death in 1981, Bob Marley's global popularity has steadily grown. Here he is depicted in a mural on San Francisco's Haight Street.   *Franco Folini*

among the greats of twentieth-century countercultural personalities: Muddy Waters, Elvis, Bob Dylan, the Beatles, Johnny Cash, Jimi Hendrix, Malcolm X, Martin Luther King Jr., Marcus Garvey, Tupac Shakur, and Che Guevara.

What makes Bob Marley so special in the pantheon of lionized musicians is that his music tangibly made the world a better place. I don't think anyone has put it better than Jo Thomas, who wrote in a *New York Times* report on Marley's funeral in May 1981, "It is not that he changed the landscape—the ghetto where he grew up is still scarred by violence—but he turned the despised dialect of that place into songs that transformed the way people saw themselves."

Speaking prophetically, as he often did, Marley knew his songs would endure. Near the beginning of his international stardom in 1973, he told Fikisha Cumbo, "My music will go on forever. Maybe it's a fool say that. But when me know facts me can say facts, you know. My music go on forever."

Bob Marley FAQ

Part 1

The Man

Captain and Ciddy

Bob Marley's Parents

Nesta Robert Marley was born on February 6, 1945, a fatherless child. He did have a father, of course, but you'd hardly know it. Captain Norval Marley, the white man who sired the King of Reggae, was by most accounts a sickly polygamist—a bed-wetting, deadbeat dad. Bob was raised by his mother, Cedella "Ciddy" Malcolm; his grandfather, Omeriah Malcolm; and his maternal great-grandmother, Katherine "Yaya" Malcolm. These were the most important influences in his early life.

Ciddy was born in Nine Mile on July 23, 1926. Her mother, Alberta Willoughby, or "Miss B.," died when Ciddy was just ten, leaving her father, Omeriah, to raise her and her eight brothers and sisters: Enid, Ivy, Jonathan, David, Solomon, Amy, Surgeon, and Gibson. Omeriah—like his famous grandson later in life—enjoyed the comforts of many women outside the marriage bed. According to Ciddy, he had "a dozen or more women in the district, who bore him between twenty and thirty children." By comparison, the adult Bob Marley would go on to sire between ten and fourteen kids with nine different women.

Omeriah was a comparatively well-off farmer, bush doctor, and storeowner. He wasn't rich by white Jamaican standards, but he was well off enough to own several fields and two houses, one where he met his mistresses. He owned one of the only cars—a luxury DeSoto—and generators in the village. The generator allowed him to listen to the radio on Sundays with his friends and neighbors—an uncommon occurrence among rural Jamaicans in the days when radios were an extravagant expenditure.

The full extent of Omeriah's livelihood is murky. In her memoir, Rita Marley writes that he was successful in business. Besides farming and renting out land, some of the other business ventures that have been attributed to him include a bakery, a grocery store, a dry goods store, a coffee factory, and a repair service for shoes and machinery. Whatever the truth, he had a lot of irons in the fire, and he was prosperous enough to be able to employ farm laborers to help with his crops, which included coffee, bananas, yam, cocoa bean, sugarcane, corn, and pimento.

The Mysterious Captain Norval Sinclair Marley

There is a recurring theme in biographies of Bob Marley concerning the facts, or lack thereof, of his early life. Exact dates, events, occupations, parentage, and even names, in some cases, are contested or lost to history. In some instances, the misinformation seems to be purposeful. Cedella Malcolm, for instance, was eighteen years old when she got married and had Nesta, yet she put her age as twenty on her marriage register in Saint Ann. Norval Marley was by some accounts sixty, by others sixty-three or sixty-four, though he is listed as fifty in the marriage register. It is doubtful that Ciddy even knew his real age. The only fact that seems to have been verified about Norval Marley—Bob's father—is that he existed. Even his date of birth, nationality, race, occupation, and middle name (sometimes listed as Sinclair, at others St. Clair) are up for debate.

Bob's absentee father didn't stick around long enough to see the boy raised. He never took pride in young Nesta's work ethic (Bob's mother always called him Nesta) in helping in his grandfather's fields, or the way he helped his struggling single mother by cooking and shopping, or even as his love of music took root and blossomed.

Whatever love he might have had for the child, or for Ciddy, is difficult to ascertain, because he left Nine Mile the day after his wedding, on June 9, 1944. As his son told *Melody Maker* in 1973, "I only remember seeing him twice, when I was small."

We could think the best of him and assume that unfortunate circumstances kept him from supporting this family with financial and emotional assistance, but what record does remain paints a much different picture. Shortly before Norval died, in 1955—and the last time Bob saw him—he gave his abandoned son a few pennies; Ciddy has called this the only birthright he received from his father.

The Bob Marley we know was born poor and only gained material wealth and celebrity through sheer determination and hard work. But in a different time and place, he might have grown up wealthy. His father was a somewhat privileged white Jamaican. Norval's family owned a construction company called Marley and Plant, and his father, Robert Marley, was a businessman and an attorney. When Bob was an infant, his paternal grandmother, Edith Bloomfield, lived in a nice part of Kingston, near Hope Road.

Norval was the less successful of his mother's two sons. His elder brother, Robert, was an engineer and cricketer of some renown who died in 1938. Norval's nephews—Bob's paternal cousins—were prosperous, too, with one becoming a lawyer and the other the CEO of a concrete plant. Yet despite this privileged upbringing and family connections, Norval never really succeeded at anything—and, to make matters worse, he was reportedly disinherited when

The house that Captain Marley paid for, and Bob Marley grew up in, in Nine Mile. Today, it is a tourist destination and part of the Bob Marley Mausoleum compound. *Brent Hagerman*

his mother found out he had married a black woman. Given the location, era, and history of racial prejudice, this is certainly plausible. There's more, though. It has been suggested by biographers and recently confirmed by one member of her family that Edith was mixed race herself, but her complexion was light enough that she passed for white. If she did indeed disinherit her son because of his black bride, she was also paying a tremendous insult to her own ancestry. Such was the internalization of her racial hatred and/or her attempt to conceal her own bloodline.

Bob had little to no contact with the white Marleys, but he told friends that the Marley and Plant construction company was owned by the same Marleys he was related to, and he also once tracked down some of these relatives to ask for money. In his autobiography, Bob's manager, Don Taylor, claims that Bob told him he had asked an uncle—a Duke Street lawyer by the name of Cecil Marley—for £300 to produce a record. Cecil kicked him out and called the constabulary. In Kevin MacDonald's excellent *Marley* documentary, Wailers artistic director Neville Garrick says the money was to be used to buy a car to deliver records, while Rita adds of this attempt for family financing, "They told us to go away. They knew nothing about Norval having a baby."

Bob was used to rejection, however, and turned the experience into the song "Corner Stone," which positions him as "the stone that the builder refused," the stone that would become the "head corner stone." Just as the song predicts, Bob would eventually ascend from the Kingston ghetto of Trench Town to Hope Road, a stone's throw away from the prime minister's residence, and he would make the Marley name famous around the world, earning wealth that far outstripped that of his white relatives. But he had to do it without his paternal family's support and influence.

So how did a well-to-do white Jamaican end up fathering a child with a black farmer's daughter in a backwater country town? Norval seems to have been a bit of a misfit—he is even called a ne'er-do-well by some—and had more than a touch of wanderlust. He took a roundabout way of getting to Nine Mile. Born between 1880 and 1885 in Clarendon Parish, Jamaica, he seems to have been a restless sort. Trying to make his way in the world, he worked for a time in Cuba, at a cement plant, and at another point he traveled to South Africa, where he worked on a boat. In fact, the story goes that he got this job while out fetching butter for his mother, and simply didn't come back! She received a postcard months later, explaining that he had bumped into a friend who said there was work available on a ship. He left without even saying goodbye.

When World War I broke out, Norval attempted to make his mark on the world by enlisting in the Liverpool Scottish infantry battalion. Military records show that he enlisted on August 12, 1916, and record his height as five feet five inches; he evidently passed his small stature on to his son. His occupation was listed on this document as construction engineer, his birthplace as Crowborough, East Sussex, England, and the year of his birth as 1885. (Christopher Farley, who has painstakingly researched Norval, disputes these details, claiming that Norval probably fudged the data to appear younger and British-born.)

It was generally accepted by his family and by early biographers that Captain Marley's rank was bestowed upon him during the war, when in reality he was discharged a private and never rose to the rank of captain. In fact, there is no evidence to suggest he ever became captain of anything. Norval's army tenure, like the rest of his life, was largely unexceptional, outside of his siring of Jamaica's most famous son. Whereas his battalion saw extensive service on the Western Front during the war, Norval himself had complained of sickness a month after enlisting and never made it off British soil. Instead, he was sent to the infirmary, where medical reports describe him as a "neurotic type of man" who claimed incontinence of urine and said that he had (non-attributed) rheumatism.

Some have suggested that these ailments were the symptoms of shell shock, though Norval never served on the frontlines. He underwent an unspecified operation and ended up serving out the war in England in a support battalion known as the Labour Corps. Historian Keith Pybus told BBC News that these Labour Corps essentially did the work of laundry and sanitation: "If you're unfortunate enough in the army to be wetting the bed, that does not especially make you look as if you're of heroic status." Norval did receive a military pension, and after the war he served in Lagos, in the British colony of Nigeria. It was probably there that the title of captain was either earned (if indeed it actually was) or adopted.

Norval eventually made his way back to Jamaica in the early forties, but his actual occupation after that has also been debated. He is often said to have been a superintendent overseeing the settlement of crown land in the areas around Nine Mile; Ciddy remembers him as an impressive and important man with tall boots riding a white horse around the countryside. To her, he was an army officer in charge of parceling out government lands to old soldiers. But even this is shrouded in mystery. On his marriage license, he listed his occupation as "clerk." Farley reasons that he probably had a much less prestigious position—possibly as a surveyor's assistant. In research undertaken by Christopher Marley, one of the white Marleys, and published by Roger Steffens in 2017, Norval is listed as a "ferro-cement engineer" who was overseeing the conversion of rural land to housing for war vets in Saint Ann Parish.

While in Nine Mile, Norval rented a room in a house belonging to Ciddy's grandmother, Yaya. Ciddy soon caught his eye, and he made many unsuccessful attempts to woo her. He was in his late fifties or early sixties at the time, and she in her mid-teens. She finally relented when she was sixteen, and the two started a clandestine relationship under the noses of her father and grandmother.

It's hard to keep these sorts of things a secret, though, especially with everyone living in such close quarters. Ciddy shared a bedroom in the small house with her siblings, and one night one of them saw her sneak out to visit the Captain and informed Omeriah. Imagine his surprise when he found his teenage daughter in bed with a man nearly his own age—in the house of his own mother! Tempers flared, and Ciddy ran away in the heat of the moment. She moved in with an aunt in the next town for a while, but she returned when emotions had cooled. Omeriah eventually gave his consent to the relationship, and, in Ciddy's words, she then became "the Captain's girl."

Ciddy Catches Religion

The romance almost ended when Ciddy caught religion of the Pentecostal variety at the Shiloh Apostolic Church. Pentecostalism puts great emphasis on moral character, and the Shiloh Apostolic Church, according to its website, instructs all members to "abstain from sinful habits such as smoking, taking of drugs, alcoholic beverages, gambling, attending public places where sin is practiced: nightclubs, dancehall, parties, theatres and any such places."

Jamaican Pentecostals, like their American cousins, are strictly against fornication. And, in the Jamaican context, the importance of keeping proper sexual relations within the bonds of marriage became a central concern for the church. This is because marriage had been illegal among enslaved Africans in Jamaica until 1826, and as such was not considered particularly desirable by many of their descendants. Still today, the vast majority of Jamaicans are not married; they prefer common-law or "visiting" unions. With 80 percent of adult Jamaicans never having been wed, the island's marriage rate ranks as one of the lowest in the world. This troubled the Christian missionaries to the island, and, in an attempt to combat what they saw as African permissiveness and promiscuity, they tried in vain to promote the idea of marriage. For the missionaries, marriage was a symbol of civilization and Christian values. This influenced the upper classes, to whom marriage came to represent respectability, and Jamaican Pentecostals, to whom it became linked to the very idea of holiness.

Inspired by these teachings, Ciddy cut off coital relations with the Captain, citing respect for her eternal soul as the reason. Norval didn't take this well; he already hated the church, and he complained to Ciddy's father. Omeriah, who has been described as religious but not churchgoing, had a stern talk with his daughter. If she was the Captain's girl, Omeriah said, she had duties to perform, adding that a woman shouldn't withhold sex from her man. Ciddy held off for a while, but eventually she agreed to share the Captain's bed again, and, in May 1944, Nesta was conceived.

Marriage and Departure

Once Ciddy told the Captain she was pregnant, he arranged to marry her, though whether he had any intention of sticking around at the time is unknown. They were married on Yaya's porch on June 9, 1944.

This relationship between a sexagenarian and a teenage girl is difficult to understand from the perspective of seventy years later. Certainly, the yearning for sexual companionship is not hard to understand, but Norval's matrimonial record is puzzling. Ciddy herself has said that she later found out that he had

had a child with his mother's maid—Bob's half-sister, Constance—though the Captain didn't marry her. Then, years after his marriage to Ciddy, he got married again—perhaps twice—without ever divorcing Ciddy. Ciddy had hunted him down a long time after he abandoned them and found him living with another woman. She promptly took him to court for bigamy. He was represented in court by his nephew, Cecil Marley—the same lawyer who allegedly told Bob he had no knowledge of Norval fathering a child—and the charges were dismissed after he was found to be senile.

To make matters worse, the day after his marriage to Ciddy, Norval left Nine Mile to work in Kingston. His excuse was that he had a hernia that made it too painful for his work on a horse, so he took a less physical job overseeing the construction of bridges in the city. He returned a few times after Nesta was born. During the first visit, he tried to convince Ciddy to let his nephew (presumably Cecil again) adopt the boy, but she flatly refused. He seems to have only spent a few scant weeks with his young family in his entire life. He initially wrote to Ciddy often and sent money back home to her—enough to build the house where Ciddy and Bob lived. This same house still stands in the mausoleum complex where Bob is buried. But over time Norval failed to return her letters.

The Death of Norval Marley

The last time Nesta saw his father was shortly before the old man died, probably in 1955, though some sources say 1957. Ciddy took him to visit his absentee father, and this is when he received his penny inheritance. Ciddy faced Norval in court one last time after this, primarily so that she could get divorce papers and be freed of him. He died soon after. She made sure to get a copy of the death certificate to authenticate her widowhood.

The facts of the Captain's death are as sketchy as those of his life. Some sources, including Christopher Marley, say he died of a heart attack; others state that he died in a motorcycle accident. Ciddy herself thought it was cancer or malaria.

2

Nice Time in Nine Mile

Early Life

When Bob Marley was born, he was first known to the world as Nesta Robert Marley. Norval gave his son his first and his middle names. While the name Robert was after Norval's brother, it is not known why Norval named him Nesta. Ciddy didn't like the name initially, thinking people would mistakenly call him Lester. In fact, people did call him Lester, and Bob even introduced himself to band member Beverley Kelso in the early sixties using this very name.

Until his late teens, then, Bob Marley's friends and family knew him as Nesta. Then, in 1963, while trying to secure a passport in Kingston so that he could travel to America, he abruptly changed his name from Nesta Robert Marley to Robert Nesta Marley. Why? Because the passport clerk—the person who had the power to issue or withhold this key to freedom—told him that Nesta sounded like a girl's name, and that he should switch them. Without that passport clerk, we might today be listening to Nesta Marley, not Bob Marley.

Marley's youth was typical by the standards of country life in Jamaica. By typical, I mean that it was a mix of hard work and hard play under crude living conditions, yet in the midst of exceptional beauty and bounty. Bob's childhood was spent on a hillside farm, surrounded by forests, plentiful fruit trees, and his mother's loving family. He had no electricity or running water, and he often had to hike to a nearby stream to collect water. But the setting was truly idyllic. Compared with the heat and scorching concrete of Kingston, Nine Mile seems like a cool oasis of lush green hills and quaint shacks. It is only fifty-five miles from Kingston, but the drive can take several hours over the narrow road of Mount Diablo. It is doubtful any tourist would make that trek to see the place from Kingston, or even the thirty miles from Ocho Rios, if it didn't boast Bob Marley as its most famous son.

During the forties, Nine Mile was worlds away from the thriving metropolis of Kingston. Whereas Kingston was a collection of ghetto shantytowns, government-built low-cost cement tenements, and, further up the hill, middle- and upper-class neighborhoods, Nine Mile was a hamlet set among the green mountains of Saint Ann, the "Garden Parish." There is one road running through the village; if you drive one mile west, you come to the town of Eight Miles. If you continue to drive seven more miles west, you come to the town of Alexandria. Nine Mile takes its name from this measurement.

Football and Farm Chores

Nesta Marley grew up barely knowing his father. Captain Norval Marley had run off to Kingston a day after marrying Ciddy, and had virtually nothing to do with the family. Without a husband's support, Ciddy supported herself and her child by working in grocery shops in and around Nine Mile. Growing up without a father meant Nesta had to take on responsibility early in his life and help his mother out. He had to do chores such as drawing water from the tank in times of drought, or sometimes from a mountain spring further away. He learned to cook at an early age and routinely made meals for his family. He also did the shopping. When he was old enough, he accompanied his grandfather to his fields to help with sowing and harvesting. He preferred farm work to school, and he would often run barefoot or travel up and down the hilly fields on a donkey named Nimble. These experiences stayed with him; later in life, he told Neil Spencer of the *New Musical Express*, "Me love farming. Me want to live upon a farm later. Me no really want to live in a flat and go to a club every night and come back, then do it again."

While Bob is generally described as a bright child, like most rural boys he preferred farming and sports to his schoolbooks. His lifelong love of sports and physical activity took hold early in life, when he would play cricket or football with anything round or ball-like—most often fruit. Later in life, he would often be photographed playing football and/or dressed in his football kit. He continued to play the game almost daily.

Grandfather Omeriah's talents weren't limited to business, produce, and women. He was something of a big man in the village, even earning the nickname "Custos." Officially, this meant magistrate, but as a peasant landowner it would be like being called "boss" as a term of respect. The reasons for this respect probably had to do with more than his business acumen and proven virility. When Nesta was still an infant, he became sick and unresponsive. Ciddy writes that her father was "renowned through the district as a bush doctor and herbalist," and pronounced that the young child was possessed by evil spirits. As a bush doctor or Myalman, Omeriah was able to make an herb bag to cure and protect him.

Many people, including his mother, have attested that Bob Marley had a sort of natural mystical power. When he was around five, Nesta would go to work with her and began reading the palms of his customers. Ciddy thought it was nonsense, but some of the villagers swore by the youth's readings.

Taken to Kingston

Nesta's days as a carefree country kid were numbered. Having been absent for years, Norval showed up in Nine Mile and told Ciddy that he'd arranged for Nesta to attend school in Kingston. So, when he was five or six years old—in around 1950 or 1951—Nesta traveled with his father, a man he didn't remember ever seeing before, on a bus to Kingston. Ciddy regularly wrote to Norval to inquire about her son, but he responded to none of her letters. Several months went by without her hearing from either of them. She began to get worried. Eventually, providence intervened when a friend from Nine Mile happened to see Nesta in the Trench Town area of Kingston while she was selling her goods at the market. She reported this back to Ciddy, remembering only that Nesta said he lived on Haywood Street. Ciddy jumped on a bus and trekked up and down Haywood Street until she was reunited with her boy, nearly a year after she'd seen him last.

Captain Marley has left very little to history except mystery. It has been said that he wanted to put Nesta in a city school, yet he never actually did this, and no one knows why. Instead, Norval deposited Nesta at the house of an elderly lady named Miss Gray, whom Nesta ended up caring for. Ciddy never found out the reason for this, but it has been charitably suggested by some that Norval felt guilty about not giving his child an inheritance, so had arranged with Miss Gray to enlist Nesta's help in return for having him inherit her house upon her death. This is conjecture, though, and to this day it is unknown why Bob Marley spent almost a year in Trench Town looking after a mysterious ailing lady while his mother was beside herself with worry, wondering what had become of him.

Back in Nine Mile

After this foray into city life, Nesta went back to Nine Mile with his mother. The two had no contact with the Captain for several years. Ciddy found it difficult to make ends meet in the hamlet, and, as a young single mom, eventually longed for a livelier setting. Periodically, she left Nesta in the care of relatives—Omeriah or various aunts—and tried her hand at work in the big city. After a failed attempt at "higgling" (selling country-grown produce at market) in Kingston, she worked as a domestic servant. She lived between the houses of several siblings, and her life in Kingston meant that she would sometimes go without seeing her son for months at a time.

Meanwhile, Nesta added a new hobby to his list of pastimes. His cousin built him a guitar out of goatskin and bamboo, and he began to sing. Then, when Nesta was eleven or twelve, another musical boy moved from Kingston to Nine

Mile. His name was Neville "Bunny" Livingston. The two became friends, and Bunny told Nesta all about the vibrant music scene in Kingston—its calypso and mento bands—and about the radio signals that carried American jazz and R&B over the ocean from Miami and New Orleans. They would both move back to Kingston eventually, when Ciddy became involved with Bunny's father, Taddeus Livingston, or "Mr. Taddy." Later, when Ciddy had a baby, Pearl, by Mr. Taddy, Nesta and Bunny would become half-brothers. And, by the early seventies, they would go on to turn the world onto a new music called reggae with their band, the Wailers.

Nine Mile: Home of Bob Marley

Bob Marley lived away from Nine Mile for most of his life. By his early teens he had moved to Kingston, and the city would be his base of operations until he died in 1981. But he always considered Nine Mile his home, and he returned often. He eventually inherited Omeriah's property, and he even farmed it for a time when he and Rita relocated there from the winter of 1967 to the spring of 1968. He had just returned from working in Wilmington, Delaware, where he composed the song "Nice Time," in which he thinks about his new wife back

The beautiful hills of Nine Mile, near where Bob Marley was born.
Photo by Nic from Stevenage, United Kingdom, Creative Commons license

in Kingston. He and Rita were living with her aunt in Trench Town, and they wanted to get out on their own. They figured they could save money by moving out of Kingston and taking up residence in Omeriah's old house, where they could grow their own food and still make occasional trips to Kingston when the need arose. The house was still without running water and electricity, but this didn't faze them.

Throughout Bob's life, Nine Mile served as a place where he could go to when he wanted to get away from the demands of fame and the music industry and get back in touch with his love of nature and working on the land. When he died, the property was converted into a mausoleum, and it is there in the green hills of Saint Ann that his remains rest.

3

Can Anything Good Come Out of Trench Town?

The Birth of Reggae

On Bob Marley's last album, *Confrontation*, there is a song called "Trench Town," referring to the Kingston ghetto in which he lived for much of his life. He sings defiantly, mockingly, "They say, 'Can anything good come out of Trench Town?'" The song then answers the question by assuring us that Trench Town can free people with music. The power of music, and reggae music specifically—to heal, to bring people together, to fight oppression, to spark revolution—is at the heart of Marley's philosophy. And for him, the epicenter of this power was Trench Town, a place Wailers percussionist Seeco Patterson told Kevin MacDonald carried a "heavy vibration." But when Marley moved to Trench Town in the late fifties as a boy, the world had not yet heard of Trench Town, nor of its musical potential. Yes, good things come from Trench Town. Bob Marley is one of them. Reggae is another.

Nine Mile to Trench Town

Trench Town started out as a squatter's settlement called Trench Pen, where many country folk landed when they arrived in Kingston in search of a better life. By the fifties, however, the government had torn down makeshift shacks and built concrete tenements: basic, low-cost housing where a group of buildings shared plumbing and cooking facilities in an adjacent open yard. Trench Town is home to several communities, such as Wilton Gardens (a.k.a. "Rema") and Arnette Gardens (a.k.a. "Jungle"). When Bob Marley later sang of the Concrete Jungle, this was this area he was speaking about, though the implication is of all inner-city ghettos.

By the sixties, Trench Town had gained a reputation as the Motown of Jamaica, because so many ska, rocksteady, and reggae artists had started out there. Its current designation as the birthplace of reggae stems from this and the fact that Bob Marley, the King of Reggae, spent his early musical career there. Other notable musical talents from Trench Town include fellow Wailers Bunny Livingston and Peter Tosh; their vocal coach and local hit-maker, Joe Higgs; and celebrity musicians Delroy Wilson, Hortense Ellis, and her elder brother Alton Ellis.

Ciddy and Nesta moved around quite a bit when he first got to Trench Town, often living with his aunts and uncles. When Nesta was fourteen, Ciddy was able to secure a government-build tenement at 19 Second Street. These low-rent cement complexes were hard to come by, and Ciddy only got this one because her elder brother, Solomon, passed it on to her.

Marley also attended a few different schools while living in Trench Town, and his single mother worked several jobs to support the two of them, including as a domestic laborer, barmaid, and restaurateur. It was here that Bob really developed the ambition to become a singer. Eventually, he'd enter talent competitions at the Queen's Theatre, singing the first song he wrote, "Fancy Curls." Sometimes he'd win, sometimes not.

While his mother called him Nesta, Bob's friends in his Trench Town days remember calling him either Robbie or Lester. By this time, Ciddy had taken up with Bunny Livingston's father, Mr. Taddy. They had a child together, Pearl, in 1962, and had a slightly messy domestic situation: Mr. Taddy was already married to another woman. Sometimes he and Bunny lived at 19 Second Street with the Marleys, but not always. This at least gave Bob and Bunny ample opportunity to dream about going professional.

While in her autobiography Ciddy portrays her role during the Trench Town days as that of a loving mother struggling to make ends meet under harsh conditions, others have remembered this time differently. Joe Higgs told Roger Steffens that, in fact, Bob was treated like an outcast, and that Ciddy didn't even want people to know she was his mother.

Joe Higgs's Trench Town Conservatory of Music

Bob and Bunny couldn't afford music lessons, but they found something of equal value: a mentor. Local celebrity Joe Higgs had already had a few hits of his own. Edward Seaga (who later became prime minister) had produced one, called "Manny-O," in 1960, as released by the duo Higgs and Wilson. Higgs lived on Third Street, around the corner from Bob and Bunny, and in the evenings his yard became a sort of impromptu music school for the youth of the community. All the original Wailers attended these sessions, and this is where Bob and Bunny met Peter Tosh, as well as the other three singers that would make up the original Wailers lineup: Junior Braithwaite, Beverley Kelso, and Cherry Green.

Higgs taught his charges about group harmony singing, arrangements, and proper breath control. He inspired them thematically, too, having already

Today, the creative learning initiative known as the Trench Town Reading Centre occupies an old rehearsal room on First Street in Trench Town. Bob Marley often sang about this ghetto, and, in doing so, he helped it gain international acclaim as the birthplace of reggae.   *Brent Hagerman, 2008*

written songs about ganja and Rastafari almost a decade before it became fashionable to do so. It was in Joe Higgs's Trench Town yard (and in others like it) that reggae music was born. And it was here that Bob and his friends learned to sing like professionals, play guitar, write songs, and carry themselves like a group. They still had a long way to go—and much more schooling would take place once they signed on to work with Jamaica's leading hit-maker, Studio One—but Higgs set the foundation. From here, they would enter amateur song contests and talent shows under various names, including the Teenagers and the Wailing Rudeboys.

Cold Ground Was My Bed Last Night

Ciddy immigrated to the United States when Bob was seventeen. She had been living on and off with Mr. Taddy, and when she left for the States she allowed him and his wife to move into 19 Second Street with Bob. As you can imagine, this wasn't exactly a positive environment for the teenager. Eventually, after a series of run-ins with the wife of his mother's former lover, he moved out.

Bob didn't have a permanent place to go. For a time, he slept on the kitchen floor of his friend Vincent "Tata" Ford. Money was tight, and the pair often went hungry. Ford would later be rewarded for his generosity when Marley put his name down as the songwriter of "No Woman, No Cry" and "Roots, Rock, Reggae." This was apparently in a bid to outsmart his publishing company, which took a percentage of all songs attributed to Bob Marley. (That company, Cayman Music, took Marley's estate to court in the mid-eighties, claiming that songs like "No Woman, No Cry" were in fact written by Bob Marley, and that as such it was owed a share of the royalties. The estate won the case.)

As the Wailers began to have success at Studio One, their producer, Coxsone Dodd, took a special interest in Bob and helped him out when he was essentially homeless by allowing him to sleep in a shed behind the studio. This temporary arrangement changed after Bob met his future wife, Rita Anderson. At first,

The entrance to the Trench Town Culture Yard, a national heritage site and museum, where Vincent "Tata" Ford once lived. During his teenage years, Bob Marley was often virtually homeless and at times slept in Ford's kitchen. Later, he would honor Ford by attributing songwriting credits to him, including "No Woman, No Cry."   *Brent Hagerman, 2008*

Rita snuck him into her bedroom at her aunt Viola's house, until Bob formally received permission to move in with her.

Bob would remain connected to Trench Town for the rest of his life. He and Rita lived there for much of the sixties into the early seventies. And, even after he moved uptown to 56 Hope Road, he always remembered his roots, praising Trench Town and its people in his songs, visiting almost daily for a game of soccer, and supporting many of his old friends.

4

Night Shift

Bob's Nonmusical Jobs

When perusing the Internet's repository of factoids and trivia about Bob Marley, popular information aggregate sites like Wikipedia list his occupation as "singer, songwriter, and musician." You could probably add freedom fighter, national hero, and King of Reggae to this list. These things aside, Bob Marley had very few traditional jobs. He worked alongside his grandfather on the farm in Nine Mile as a child, and he periodically returned to the farm to grow his

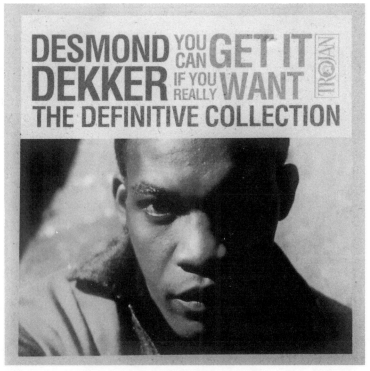

Desmond Dekker was instrumental in helping Bob Marley get an audition at Beverley's. Dekker worked alongside Bob as an apprentice welder, until both found success in the local music industry. *Author's collection*

own food and ganja, though this doesn't really qualify as a paid position. As a teenager, he was briefly apprenticed to an electrical welder, and he later made periodic trips to Delaware, where he would join other Caribbean migrant workers earning money to send back home at various manual labor positions. Bob saw this labor as a stepping-stone to a better life: the money he earned helped kick-start various musical ventures, including setting up a record shop and record label.

Welding a Wha' De Young Gal Want

In Caribbean music, double meanings abound. The Starlights had a hit in 1972 called "Soldering," which features the line, "Soldering a wha' de young gal want," and, well, it didn't refer to joining together inanimate metal objects. The subtext was probably quite animated. Similarly, "welding" in Jamaican parlance can refer to sex, and a "welding torch" to a big penis. The authors of *Reggae Bloodlines* wondered about this when they interviewed Bob Marley for the book. He told them with a laugh that before he got into music, he was a welder. Aware of the double entendre, they didn't know if he was joking or not.

In fact, Bob Marley *was* an apprentice welder in Trench Town. He left school at fourteen or fifteen, for reasons that vary depending on who you ask. His mother has said that he came home one day with his school books and told her the school closed down and the headmistress had moved to the country. Others say that Bob simply didn't want to go to school anymore. Either way, his mother insisted he learn a trade.

As with a lot of the details of Bob's early life, the exact road to him briefly working at a welding shop had many side footpaths. Either Mr. Taddy secured the apprenticeship at a firm he was familiar with on Hagley Park Road, or Ciddy asked one of the customers at the bar where she worked for suggestions as to where her son could learn a trade, and was told about a shop on South Camp Road. Either way, Bob wasn't happy about this career choice. What he really wanted to do was sing. But working in the welding shop put him alongside a youth four years older than him who had already recorded a song called "Honour Your Father and Your Mother" at a professional studio. Desmond Dekker and Bob Marley became friends and began jamming together in Bob's bedroom. And it was Dekker who made the necessary introductions to get Bob his first recording contract at Beverley's.

Bob's tenure as a welder didn't last long. Welding while not wearing goggles resulted in a shard of metal becoming lodged in his eye, and he had to go to the hospital to have it removed. This proved the opportunity he needed: he told his mother the accident would never have happened if he had been singing, not welding. She took pity on him and gave him her blessing to pursue a music career. From that moment on, he devoted his time to making it in the music business.

Delaware Jobs

Bob sang successfully with the Wailers from 1964 to 1966, earning a string of locally charting hits. But successful by Jamaican standards meant that he was still living hand-to-mouth. To make ends meet, Peter Tosh continued to work at a dry cleaner, and Bunny Livingston for his father, even while the band had Top 10 hits locally. Jamaican producers tended to get the lion's share of the profits, leaving the Wailers struggling financially. They desperately wanted to get from under the yolk of these producers and establish their own label, but they needed capital to do it.

Bob had a plan. Two days after marrying Rita Anderson in February 1966, he moved to the United States temporarily, as a migrant laborer. He wanted to make enough money to buy some musical equipment, which he would take back to Kingston. While he was in the US he lived with his mother and her new husband, Edward Booker, at 2313 Tatnall Street in Wilmington, Delaware. He had started to grow dreadlocks at this time, reflecting his interest in Rastafari, but his mother suggested he trim them to look more presentable to employers. He obeyed.

Bob's first attempt to get a job in Wilmington was unsuccessful. He applied to be a stevedore on the docks, but his small stature made him unsuitable. He eventually found other work, though, and he spent nine months in the city before returning to Jamaica in October.

Bob used his American connections to return several times—the next was 1968—for short-term work that would provide him with good money to support his family and music career back home. He and his young family would also live there periodically in the early seventies, traveling back and forth to Jamaica. He invested the money he made the first time in setting up the Wailers' own record label, Wail'n Soul'm, and a record store of the same name that was essentially one room of Aunt Viola's house at 18A Greenwich Park Road in Trench Town. Later, his Delaware money would enable him to establish a new Wailers label called Tuff Gong in 1970.

Biographers differ as to what jobs Bob had and when. Some seem farfetched, such as his supposed role as a lab assistant at the DuPont Chemical Company. Others are more believable: janitor at the Dupont Hotel, laborer at the Chrysler Plant in Newark. He has been credited with a variety of positions at the Chrysler plant: working in the body shop; driving a forklift on the nightshift, where the song "Night Shift" is said to have originated; working on the assembly line, putting fenders and back doors on station wagons, sedans, or trucks; working in the spare parts section; and transporting supplies to the assembly line crews.

Supplemental Income

Even with the periodic influx of American cash and hits back home, until Bob signed to Island Records in 1973 and released *Catch a Fire*, his musical future was insecure and his financial situation poor. When bassist Familyman first started working with Bob circa 1969–1970, "Fams" was an established session player with his own car, whereas Bob only had a bicycle. The Wailers were able to take control of their own music thanks in part to Bob's investment, but the late sixties and early seventies were not lucrative for them. They sold their own records from their own record store and delivered them to other stores and jukeboxes—sometimes on bicycle—around Kingston, but they still had to supplement their income. Tosh was able to find work as a session musician, and Bob, according to Fams, used to travel to the country and bring back brooms on the roof of his car to sell in the city.

5

Love and Affection

Bob's Marriage to Rita Marley

Bob Marley had many women but only one wife. Sometimes cast as the jealous, jilted wife, only in it for the money, Rita Marley is at other times portrayed as the anchor that supported Bob in good times and bad, held the family together even while he took advantage of the benefits fame afforded him, and kept the Marley name alive after he died. She was also the muse for some of his greatest songs: "Stir It Up," "No Woman, No Cry," "Nice Time," and "Chances Are."

Their marriage was a complicated one, and no doubt had its share of happiness and hardship, particularly for Rita, who had to put up with her husband's very public philandering. They had three children together, but they raised many more from extramarital affairs (mostly his, but one hers). They went from young lovers to working parents to international rock stars, and finally to a sort of platonic partnership. Rita's marriage to Bob suffered, and survived, poverty, physical abuse, distrust, broken hearts, and even an assassination attempt. Yet despite this hardship, she rose to become the matriarch of the Marley estate, the guiding hand behind the Marley brand and Marley Foundation, a recipient of both an honorary doctorate from the University of West Indies and the Order of Distinction from the Jamaican government, and one of the richest women in Jamaica.

To think of Rita as only Bob's wife is to reduce not only the role she played in supporting his career but also her own musical contribution. You see, Bob and Rita were romantically and professionally linked from the beginning. Rita sang alongside Bob for much of his career, and she is credited with writing or co-writing many of his songs (including "Johnny Was," "Crazy Baldheads," "Natty Dread," and "So Jah Seh"). She also led her own sixties group, the Soulettes, dubbed the "Supremes of the Caribbean"; she ran the Wailers' record shops and distributed their albums on bicycle. She had a successful solo career after Bob died, too, including the infectious international hit "One Draw"—the first reggae song to top *Billboard*'s Disco Singles chart.

Born Alpharita Constantia Anderson in 1956, Rita was the daughter of a Cuban mother and a Jamaican father. Some sources, including Bob's mother, have claimed that she was born in Cuba, but Rita has insisted that she was born in Kingston.

Rita Marley's 1991 Grammy-nominated solo album. Rita began her music career as a member of the Soulettes at Studio One in 1965. She sang alongside Bob Marley as part of the backing trio the I-Threes in the 1970s, and released several solo albums following his death. *Author's collection*

Rita's mother abandoned the family at a young age and eventually moved to Toronto. Her father, a musician, left the island, like a lot of young men, to find work. He bounced between Stockholm, London, and New York; after Bob died, he came home to Kingston to help Rita run the estate.

One Love at Studio One

Rita heard Bob on the radio before ever meeting him. They both lived in the same Kingston neighborhood of Trench Town, where his band, the Wailers, were local heroes. The Wailers had to pass by her house on the way to Studio One, where they recorded. She was studying to become a nurse at the Bethesda School of Practical Nursing at the time, but she had her own musical ambitions, too. Gradually Rita caught the band's attention, and in 1964 or 1965 she urged Wailer Beverley Kelso to set up an audition with Coxsone for her own group, the

Soulettes. To the surprise of the rest of the Wailers, the Soulettes were signed to Studio One. Bob Marley was given the job of writing and arranging songs for them. He also started to take a special interest in Rita.

With no parents to look after her, Rita was raised by her very strict aunt, Viola Britton, known simply as Aunty. Rita already had a baby, Sharon, with another man. This didn't seem to faze Bob (who already had a baby of his own, though this is generally not acknowledged). Bob would later adopt and raise Sharon as his own. Aunt Viola took to Bob after seeing him care for Sharon, but she later counseled Rita to divorce him when he had two sons born with two different women one month after the birth of his son with Rita, Stephen.

Marriage and Signs of Trouble

The story of Bob and Rita's marriage has many sides. They were married by the Justice of the Peace on either February 10 or 11, 1966, a few days after Bob's twenty-first birthday. Rita was nineteen at the time. He saved up for a ring, and Coxsone Dodd, a father figure to the young man, reportedly purchased a black wedding suit and fancy shoes for him to wear, though Bunny Wailer has suggested that Bob got married in his stage suit (also purchased by Dodd). Aunt Viola made a wedding dress for Rita. Love didn't stand in the way of work, though, and, according to Rita, that night the Wailers had a gig at the National Stadium—their biggest show yet. Rita remembers that Bob left the next day for Delaware to work, but others suggest that it wasn't so soon, though he did eventually leave her alone in Jamaica, possibly while pregnant.

Rita says that it was a combination of Bob's love for her and his possessiveness that led him to propose to her and them to get hitched in quick succession. He feared that Rita would find another boyfriend while he was away. Ciddy wanted Bob to emigrate and live with her in Delaware, where there was more opportunity for work than could be found in Jamaica. The original plan was for him to get established in the US, and then sponsor Rita and Sharon to join him there.

Rita's accounts of their early years together are of a young couple very much in love, struggling to make ends meet. They had their fights, but love won out every time. She was Bob's muse; he penned love songs in tribute to her. It wasn't until later—once Bob started to get some success and began enjoying the extra-marital carnal opportunities that this presented him with—that the troubles started.

Bob had a different story—or at least the people who are left to speak for him do. This story goes that he didn't want to get married in the first place. He didn't even tell his mother he was getting married, and he didn't invite Peter or Bunny to the wedding. Sometimes he claimed he was tricked into it, blaming Coxsone Dodd for this chicanery. In this telling, Dodd pushed him into getting married before he left for Delaware, thereby ensuring his hit-maker put down family roots and making it more probable that he would return home to continue recording. He did, after all, return nine months later, though by that time his relationship with Studio One had soured.

Ciddy, meanwhile, would supply a supernatural explanation for Bob's resistance to the marriage, claiming that he thought an Obeah woman performed a curse on him to get him to marry Rita. (Obeah is an African-Jamaican religious tradition that, like Haitian Vodou, has more half-truths and negative stereotypes associated with it in popular culture than actual facts. Practitioners of these religions see them as wholesome, African-derived healing traditions.) And his later manager, Don Taylor, remembers that Bob said he was "Obeah'd" by Aunty, though another source recounts that an Obeah woman from Greenwich Farm had hexed him by kissing his hand. The next thing Bob knew, he was married to Rita, with no recollection of the ceremony.

Many aspects of Bob's life suggest that he would rather have been single, and that he felt marriage was a burden. He was angry at Rita's use of the Marley surname, and he argued with her about this, charging that the marriage had merely been an arrangement to allow her to get a green card, which would make it easier for his kids to find a better life in the US.

On the recommendation of his then record label, JAD, he routinely told the American media in early seventies that Rita was his sister. In 1973, a *Melody Maker* article assured fans that "Rita Marley is known as Bob's wife, but they aren't actually married—it was just an idea to get some publicity for one of her records." And Bob himself told the Caribbean *Times* in 1975, "Me never believe in marriage that much . . . marriage is a trap to control men; Woman is a coward, man stronger." When asked by the *L.A. Free Press* in December 1973 if he had an "ol' lady" or kids, he replied, "My kids are by different girls," and "No really a one lady yet." He told *People Magazine* the following year, "Married people are chained. . . . You can't live by strenuous rules other people make. Check out people who are married—weird."

Mix-Up Family: Bob's Affairs

Perhaps he was happily married for a time, but things certainly changed. Bob began to spend more and more time away from Rita and their three kids— Sharon, Cedella, and Ziggy—and these absences were a source of conflict. He told her he was working on his music, but eventually she realized he was working on his mojo, too.

While Rita was pregnant with Stephen, she moved to Delaware for work and lived there with Ciddy. After the child was born in April 1972, she wanted to move home to be with Bob, but he surprised her by telling her to stay put in Delaware. Growing suspicious, she came home to find out that, days after Stephen was born, Bob had had two other sons, Robbie and Rohan, with two different women.

Jilted, humiliated, and angry, Rita had some hard decisions to make. Her trust in her husband was shattered, and, at age twenty-five, she knew that the wellbeing of their four children was on her shoulders. Aunty's advice was to divorce the philanderer, who in her eyes had neither money nor a real job. Beverley Kelso later told Roger Steffens that Rita had been serious about divorce at one time. Instead, after a period of self-examination, she decided that this would not set a good example for her children, so she resigned herself to staying strong for them.

Living Worlds Apart in the Same City

Bob Marley acquired 56 Hope Road from Island Records head Chris Blackwell in 1975, as part of a renegotiation of his record contract, and it became his musical and personal headquarters: a rehearsal hang-out for the band, and a bachelor pad for Bob. This house became a thorn in their marriage. Rita would show up at Hope Road most days, but she felt out of place, especially with all the women hanging around: Esther Anderson, Cindy Breakspeare, Diane Jobson. These women were lighter-skinned and skinnier than Rita, showing Bob's preference for more "European" beauty standards, and they were all upper-middle-class.

56 Hope Road, Bob's personal and professional headquarters in the 1970s. It now houses the Bob Marley Museum.
Photo by Dubdem sound system, Creative Commons license

But the experience only made the defiant Rita tougher. As she states in her autobiography, "What else could I be but black and proud around all the light-skinned 'book pretty' girls?"

While Bob was happily ensconced in his love nest, entertaining his many admirers, Rita was still living with Aunt Viola and four children in Trench Town. Bob asked Rita and the kids to join him at Hope Road, but Rita was no fool, even though Bob took her for one often. As a girl born in the ghetto who knew poverty and hunger, she understood that Bob provided well for her and the kids, but she wasn't about to pretend to turn a blind eye to his many love affairs. She was eager to get out of Trench Town, but not if it meant losing her dignity.

Rita didn't want her children living around such an immoral scene, so she decided to get some independence. She applied for, and received, a government-built house at 15 Windsor Lodge in Bull Bay, a half-hour by car from Kingston. So, while Bob was living the life of a rock star, Rita kept the home fires burning in government housing, in what she termed the "family house."

Rita and the kids moved into a house that initially had no running water or electricity—government houses came unfinished—but one that was hers for the first time in her life. Bob paid all the bills—and never balked at doing so. At first, he would spend time there—he would come "home" after tours, play with the kids, sleep with Rita. And he kept his clothes there, too. But he would also disappear for months at a time, and Rita wouldn't know where he was.

On Her Own Two Feet

Instead of retreating to Bull Bay and staying out of sight, Rita was far from idle. She worked daily, minding Bob's local business interests. She took care of the Tuff Gong store on Beeston Street, selling Wailers records; stocked jukeboxes around the city; and dealt with the record pressing plants. She went to 56 Hope Road often, too, and she also opened up a shop there to sell Ital food (adhering to the Rastafari diet) to the hangers-on. In her "free" time, she put in a lawn and garden at the Bull Bay house, mixed cement, and built a veranda on the house and a wall around the property. All this while raising several kids—and pregnant with another.

While Bob's star was rising, Rita also decided to get back into singing. She teamed up with old friends Marcia Griffiths and Judy Mowatt, both of whom had had their own successful music careers, to form the I-Threes. By the time of the 1974 recording sessions for the album *Natty Dread*, original Wailers Peter Tosh and Bunny Wailer had left the group, but Bob still wanted rich harmonies in his songs. He needed only to look to his wife's group to provide them. The

The I-Threes, performing at a Bob Marley concert at Dalymount Park, Dublin, Ireland, on July 6, 1980. *Left to right*: Judy Mowatt, Rita Marley, and Marcia Griffiths.
Photo by Eddie Mallin, Creative Commons license

I-Threes joined the Wailers in the studio for the album, and they continued as Bob's backing singers for the rest of his career. In addition to the stipend Bob paid Rita for the children and upkeep of the family house, he also paid her a musician's salary.

Fussing and Fighting

When Johnny Nash and Danny Sims of JAD Records signed Bob Marley in 1968, Rita had gotten a taste of "Babylon life"—and she didn't like it. She would watch as Nash entertained groupies in one room while his wife was in another. Rita thought this was scandalous and immoral, yet this is what she eventually saw in her own husband, too. And as his philandering grew bolder, Bob would flaunt his women in Rita's face.

Rita had had enough, and in 1973 she cut Bob off. In her autobiography, she writes, "I told him plain, straight out, if you're going to be doing this, we will not have a sexual relationship." How did Bob take this? Not well. Used to having his own way with women, he told her, "You're my wife and I want you." In her book she states, "I was almost raped," describing how he insisted they have sex and she relented. However, on the tour promoting her book in 2004, she told the *Mirror*, "Bob wouldn't take no for an answer. . . . He said to me, 'No, you're my wife and you're supposed to.' So he forced himself on me, and I call that rape."

From then on, Rita decided that the only way she could cope with the strange living arrangement they found themselves in was to train herself to see Bob just as "loving father and friend." He was a "good loving brother more so than a real husband.... Let all those women turn him on, I'm just gonna love my children, love myself, and see what comes out of it." With this new detachment, Bob's affairs felt less threatening to her. Rita's role changed from miserable wife to a sort of sister/partner/guardian/friend who "had more responsibility than just that of a wife." This attitude sustained her in the more difficult times, when Bob was romancing other women very publicly.

Harmonica player Lee Jaffe's account of the relationship also suggests Bob had a mean streak with Rita. He saw them arguing once while Rita was "very pregnant"; Bob "started physically to go after her," but Jaffe and Marley confidant Skill Cole stopped him. Trench Town friend Segree Wesley told Roger Steffens that Bob could be rough with Rita, while manager Don Taylor later wrote that he saw Bob "beat Rita mercilessly" in a hotel room in Germany when she complained about the money he was spending on child support for his daughter Karen.

Rita Finds Love Again, but Not with Bob

With Bob living his Babylon life and Rita shut out of a romantic relationship with him, she drifted toward the arms of another man. Owen Stewart, a.k.a. "Tacky" or "Ital," was a Rastafarian soccer player and accountant with whom she found comfort. Many sources say that Tacky, who was a friend of Bob's, is also the father of her daughter, Stephanie, though Rita's own memoir lists Bob as the father. Bob himself suspected as much about Stephanie's parentage, and this angered him greatly, despite the fact he already had three extramarital children of his own. He confronted Rita about this several times and complained to his mother that he wanted to divorce her over it. Ciddy, always ready to muddy the waters where Rita is concerned, writes that Bob was heartbroken at Rita's infidelity, after all he'd done to raise her out of the ghetto. He had even claimed Rita gave him cancer—perhaps due to heartbreak or stress—and exclaimed to his mother, "Me left Rita and gone go work in England fe her, and when me gone Rita breed fe me friend." When Rita heard about this, her response, according to Ciddy, was that Jah had given him cancer "because of his wickedness to her." Ouch.

Obviously, all of this put further strain on their relationship. Bob was very possessive of Rita, and extremely jealous. He'd check her hotel phone bills while they were out on tour to see who she'd called. When he suspected Tacky was having an affair with Rita, he confronted him angrily. Tacky replied that he didn't realize Rita was Bob's wife because he had read in the press that they were siblings. All Bob could do was laugh.

Bob was so unhappy with the marriage that during one stay in Delaware he smashed a wedding photo. Another time he dragged Rita into a car and drove her to the Palisadoes in Kingston, where he demanded his ring back and then tossed it in the ocean.

Despite this acrimony, he raised Stephanie as his biological daughter. After his death, Rita rekindled her relationship with Tacky, with whom she had her daughter Serita in 1985.

Throughout the seventies, Bob's stature on the international stage grew. As he toured worldwide, Rita, as one of the I-Threes singers, was still at his side. Don Taylor made sure to book her a hotel room on a separate floor to Bob, so as to avoid contact between Bob's wife and his many mistresses. Late in the evenings, however, Bob would often send for Rita and have her wash his locks. The relationship between the two of them, bittersweet as it was, was deep-rooted and enduring.

At some point, Rita admits, they ended up in a romantic relationship again, but the pain of Bob's infidelities never completely left her. In the winter of 1977, during the recording of *Exodus* in London, Rita and Judy Mowatt boycotted some of the sessions because of Bob's behavior. The remaining I-Three, Marcia Griffiths, often voiced all three parts in their absence. On tour, Bob would flirt constantly, and he seemed to have a woman in every city. He didn't even try to hide his women from Rita, but eventually she resigned herself to just taking care of him. When a newspaper in Paris carried a front-page photo of Bob dancing with Jamaican beauty queen Sandra Kong at an after-party at Chez Regine, her only thought was that he shouldn't be dancing with his injured toe, because a soccer injury was causing him a lot of pain.

Marley Matriarch

Despite the continual emotional discomfort of being married to a man who kept many women, Rita made peace with several of his extramarital children. Bob and Rita recognized five children as their own, including Rita's daughters Sharon and Stephanie. As Bob's brood grew, though, Rita accepted responsibility for raising many of them, and she has claimed she wanted to make sure the children were looked after. In addition to her own children, she also raised Robert, Rohan, and Karen. Others, like Julian and Ky-Mani, spent holidays with their siblings but were raised by their birth mothers.

Looking at her today—with her money, awards, respect, and control of the Marley legacy—it seems that Rita has had the last laugh. She appears to have come to terms with Bob's failings, too, telling Matt Roper in 2013, "He was corrupted by show business, by the girls who would throw themselves at him. This is what I've come to understand."

6

Blame It on Rita

The Yoko Ono of Reggae?

Remember Yoko Ono? She was an annoying, clingy, talentless intruder that broke up the greatest band in rock history, right? Not really. Not even close. But that's how rock historians have remembered her.

In a blog post for the *Curvature*, Cara Kulwicki examines the Yoko Ono stereotype. According to Kulwicki, since Ono wasn't what journalists deemed a "proper" band wife—meaning "a doting doormat" who looked the other way while her man was trysting—she was tagged as "a mentally unbalanced, scheming, money-grubbing, castrating bitch." In other words, because Ono actually had a backbone and opinions of her own, she posed a threat to the circle of male dominance in the Beatles.

This stereotype is continually applied to other strong women. Kulwicki writes, "Any woman who dates a male band member and expects to be treated like a person, or any woman who is seen to in some way cause a change in a male artist of any kind, is particularly at risk of being called 'Yoko.'" Didn't Courtney Love get Cobain hooked on heroin and scheme to make her own band famous? A Yoko Ono.

And, of course, there's Rita Marley. Chris Farley, in his book *Before the Legend*, writes about how he feels that Rita has suffered the Ono yoke. And he's right. Rita has been accused of tricking Bob into marry her, holding him back when he was about to break internationally, fooling around behind his back, deviously laying claim to his wealth when he died intestate, and worse. However, these accusations are little more than misogynistic and slanderous ravings meant to question her foundational role in Bob Marley's life and career to discredit her from benefitting from it.

The Marriage Was a Sham

First, there is the odd rumor that Rita somehow *made* Bob marry her before he decamped for the United States in 1966. How this supposedly took place changes depending on who is telling the story. She either faked being pregnant so that Bob would marry her out of a sense of duty, used malevolent supernatural forces, or simply tricked him. The common thread here is that Bob did not marry Rita for love. And this goes a long way toward disgracing her. In 2012, Bunny Wailer posted the following to tuffgongrecords.blogspot.ca: "How could Rita be involved in any of Robert Marley's business when she Rita wasn't even a Marley?"

Even Bob played up the story that he and Rita weren't really married. Remember when the White Stripes planted the rumor that Jack and Meg White were siblings (or was it spouses?)? This worked well to drum up interest in a band that was either brother and sister or husband and wife or both. (It turns out they weren't related by blood, but by marriage. Then they got a divorce.) Bob opted for a similar tack, though probably to drum up interest among the single ladies. On JAD's recommendation, he told the press on his early tours abroad that Rita was his sister. The ruse was successful enough that even the Jamaican press was confused as to the exact nature of the relationship. When the *Gleaner* reported on the assassination attempt that left both Bob and Rita injured, they called her his common-law wife.

The Breeding Ball and Chain

Not only was the marriage supposedly not a real marriage, Rita was also the "ball and chain" keeping Bob from flying free. This attitude was voiced by one of Bob's younger, lighter-skinned (weren't they all lighter-skinned?), prettier flings, Esther Anderson. Rita often visited 56 Hope Road, the uptown house where Bob kept his musical and extramarital affairs away from the family home. She once had a run-in with Anderson there, when the mistress wouldn't let the wife talk to her pop-star husband. According to Rita's memoir, Anderson said to her, "Why don't you leave him alone? Why don't you stop breeding? All you do is breed! Bob needs a career, and you need to stop breeding and let him have a life."

So there you have it, folks. Rita Marley was holding Bob back because she kept having his children, and looking after them, and trying to maintain some kind of normality in her life, while her husband cavorted with half the female population of Jamaica, getting a good number of them pregnant.

A Harlot with Questionable Sexual Leanings

Remember the rock-star trope that a man can sow his wild oats but his wife must be true to him alone, else she be known as a harlot? Of course, Rita has been subjected to this one as well. Bob's mother, in her tell-all autobiography, takes pains to point out to readers that Rita wasn't a very good singer, and that she was the cause of many of the fights between her and Bob. Oh, and Bob's many, many, many affairs are fine in her book, but Rita's one documented affair is a cause for ire. Okay, so she had an affair. Can you blame her?

On top of that, rumors also spread that Rita was sexually promiscuous in another way—that she and her friend Minnie were supposedly lesbians, because they spent so much time together in the seventies. This is a further example of how Rita's legitimacy to the Marley legacy has been undermined, by attempting to call into question her sexuality and thereby position Bob as some sort of victim of deceit.

Satan's Disciple—In It for the Money

Fights over the estate continued for years after Bob's death, with various parties vying for a stake in his considerable wealth, and Rita accused of selfishness and greed. When I interviewed Wailers bassist Aston "Familyman" Barrett in 2003, he had nothing good to say about Rita or her eldest child with Bob, Cedella. "I show you how evil they are against Familyman and the Wailers, Rita Marley and Cedella Marley especially," he told me, recounting how six US Marshalls showed up at a concert in L.A. to seize any merchandise that had Bob's likeness on it. "They are cruel people—they all love the name Marley but none of them think like Bob. They are the devil's disciples, Satan's disciples."

Bob's manager, Don Taylor, was also part of the crowd that interpreted Rita's interest in her husband's estate as an attempt to gain wealth unscrupulously. Like others, he has repeated the notion that they were married in name only, and that Bob chided her for insisting on using his surname, even while he rubbed his affairs in her nose. According to Taylor, we know that Bob, too, thought she was greedy, because he supposedly wrote "Want More" about her: "Now you get what you want / do you want more?"

Instead of sheepishly accepting the humiliating, subservient role Bob restricted her to, Rita, we are told, dishonestly tried to wrangle millions from the estate, defrauding it through tricks like forging Bob's signature, attempting to sideline his "baby-mothers" (whom she supposedly referred to as the "big pussy girls") and alienating those parties that once were close to Bob.

"In the wake of Bob's death," Taylor writes, "Rita played the role of queen and tried to dismiss everyone, including the Wailers, and establish her own private court. She insisted on being addressed by her employees as 'Mrs. Marley.'" She even purported to benefit from Marley's death by going on tour in 1983 to exploit the publicity drummed up by the release of *Legend*. Sounds suspiciously like a Yoko Ono.

Peter's and Bunny's Toxic Hatred of Rita

After Bob's death, Peter and Bunny did not withhold their hatred of Rita, whom they claimed was trying to steal Bob's money. Well, she was married to him. That's not exactly stealing, is it? I believe that's called inheritance.

In a blog post, Bunny Wailer called Rita a "dark, abusive Jezebelic character." It is interesting that he uses the term *Jezebelic* here. This is a favorite of conservative Christians and Rastas alike, who have turned the biblical character Jezebel into a symbol of promiscuity and idolatry. Jezebel was a foreign queen whose sexual wiles supposedly made the otherwise pious King Ahab of Israel turn away from the one true god. You know the cliché: the guy couldn't keep it in his pants, but he blames the woman for seducing him.

What could Rita Marley possibly have in common with this? Well, Jezebel was sort of a Yoko Ono figure, too. She is blamed for her influence over a male leader, and, ultimately, for trying to break up Israel. Rita stood in the way of Bunny and Peter taking control of Bob's legacy after he died. In her autobiography, she states that in the months after Bob's death, his two former partners tried to wrest control of the business from her, even becoming angry enough to pull pictures of Bob from the walls of the Tuff Gong office. Their grievances with Bob and the way he effectively captured the Wailers name and legacy for himself, manifested in their animosity toward Rita. Like Jezebel and Yoko, Rita was an outsider to the circle of male leaders. And as a woman in that patriarchal Jamaican culture, it was felt she had no right to the fruits of her husband's labors.

Bunny's vitriol regarding Rita knows no bounds. In a series of blog posts in 2012, he accused her of several unseemly behaviors that fit the Ono stereotype. Characterizing her as dishonorable and promiscuous, he wrote that she "seemingly prostituted herself" by trying to hook up with the Wailers, "indulged Peter of the Wailers into her unholiness of actually having a sexual affair with him," and then started a relationship with Bob. Rita's wicked influence over Bob was compounded when Peter and Bunny were not invited to the wedding of their best friend, nor even told firsthand about the marriage.

There are a few key issues here. First, Bunny states repeatedly that Rita acted shamefully by being sexually active when "she had Sharon as a suckling on her breast." This is clearly an attempt at moral regulation, an age-old pattern whereby a conservative man attempts to control the body and actions of a woman. It's rife in Jamaican culture, and in Rastafari especially.

Second, Bunny alleges that Rita had a sexual relationship with Peter. However, in a rare interview with Roger Steffens published in 2017, fellow Wailer Beverley Kelso recalled that Bob and Peter had had a competition over who could bed Rita first. In his enthusiasm (that's putting it generously) to win,

Peter reportedly attempted to force himself on her. Kelso walked in on them in the back room of Studio One to see Peter holding Rita down while she tried to push him off her. Kelso didn't tell anyone at the time, but she felt it utterly unfair that Bunny and Peter had subsequently accused her of seduction.

Third, Bunny positions Rita as a wedge between the original Wailers. In his idyllic retelling, the three singers lived in a heroic man's world and adhered to an all-for-one, one-for-all code—until a morally corrupt woman came between them. Rita, using her sexual wiles, tried to dismantle this union. As far back as 1990, Bunny told Roger Steffens that her intention from the beginning was to break up the band. Next, he cast doubt on whether Cedella—Bob and Rita's first child together—was truly fathered by Bob. He alludes to rumors that he himself was the father (without elaborating), or even that the child belonged to Bob's spiritual advisor, Mortimo Planno. ("Cedella was not accepted as Robert's child but was imposed under Jezebelic emotional confusion," he wrote, "which can be seen in Cedella's non-Marley behavior.") Again, he is simply playing on sexist stereotypes to call into question Rita's integrity without offering a shred of evidence to support his outlandish claims.

Finally, and you need to hold on to your seat for this one, Bunny has actually accused Rita of killing Bob Marley and Peter Tosh. He insists that Chris Blackwell received "Radio Active Ash" from the CIA for the express purpose of killing Bob. Blackwell and Rita worked together, he adds, with Rita adding the poison to Bob's food. The conspiracy to kill Peter Tosh in 1987 took an apparently more violent route. Rita, again according to Bunny, hired a killer to shoot up Peter's home while he and his guests were in it. Tosh, "Doc" Brown, and radio deejay Jeff "Free I" Nixon were shot to death in a botched robbery at Peter's home, while Marlene Brown and "Santa" Davis sustained bullet wounds but survived.

Dennis "Leppo" Lobban was found guilty of the murders, and while there are several conspiracy theories about Tosh's death—most of them having to do with it being a targeted assassination—there is no evidence Rita Marley had anything to do with it. Not even Yoko was accused of orchestrating her husband's death, so perhaps from now on, if the wife of a male star is really, really annoying, and especially if she's implicated in his death, we just call her a Rita Marley. (Just kidding.)

Bunny has also claimed that Rita robbed the Wailers and stole the Studio One name, and hinted that she may have killed others (including her aunt and an unnamed Japanese warrior). He was left feeling that he should watch his back: "It is quite obvious that Rita having killed two members of 'The Wailers' would [also] try and do the same to the survivor 'Bunny Wailer.'"

This whole Rita-killed-Bob thing doesn't just come from Bunny. Cedella Booker, Bob's mom, has also implicated Rita in a roundabout way. In her memoir, she relays the idea that Bob thought Rita gave him cancer. She doesn't bother to speculate how she might have done so; it is enough for her to suggest that Bob believed his, compounding the smearing of Rita to discredit any claim to his legacy and money.

So, if you've been paying attention, Rita is a greedy, bloodthirsty, murdering, talentless intruder who broke up the greatest band in reggae history. I wonder if the hatred and sexism directed toward her would have been different had she just raised the kids quietly, stayed in the background, ignored Bob's indiscretions, and been at his beck-and-booty call once in a while? Probably, but that's not what "Yoko Onos" do.

7

Playboy

Bob's Love Interests

Bob once told the *New York Amsterdam News* that his only weakness was women: "My only vice is plenty women. Other than that I am a saint." As a global superstar, he had his pick, and he picked often. One of these trysts was even with Miss World 1976. Bianca Jagger planted a kiss on him backstage. Princess Caroline of Monaco had her eyes on him.

Once Bob acquired 56 Hope Road, it became his professional residence and his love-pad, where he would make himself available to the many women who wanted to sleep with him. Most of the women that hung out there were not dark-skinned and voluptuous like his wife, but instead were closer to the European beauty standards that privileged lighter skin tones and slimmer builds. Most of Bob Marley's women were passing flings, a few had children with him, and at least one in particular became a serious love interest.

The Workers

Bob Marley surrounded himself with men in his professional life—other than backing singers, the musicians in his band were exclusively men—and in keeping with Jamaican and Rasta cultural norms, he believed in a hierarchy of gender roles in which men were dominant. He even told the Caribbean *Times* in 1975, "Woman is a coward. Man is stronger." But while he tended to treat women as conquests, and his wife as a doormat, he did include a select number of women in his business circle.

Besides being his wife and mother to some of his kids, Rita was also Bob's business partner during their early life together, and she remained involved professionally with him as a backing singer even as his affairs increased in the seventies. However, she was eventually sidelined by being kept out of his business decisions and made to live in the family house while Bob enjoyed the fruits of his celebrity at Hope Road.

Another woman with whom Marley had a work/romance relationship was Yvette Morris-Anderson Crichton. Yvette's exact trajectory is murky, partly because she is listed variously as Yvette Morris, Yvette Anderson, and Yvette Crichton, whom some write of as three separate people. However, one Yvette Morris-Anderson Crichton is listed as the copyright holder for a 1993 recording called "All That" under her pseudonym, Tabanca Lady. (*Tabanca*, by the way, means lovesickness in Trinidad.) This suggests that all three women are, in fact, the same person.

Assuming all the Yvettes in Bob's life refer to this one person, her connection to Bob looks like this: she was the former girlfriend of Johnny Nash, had worked at Chelsea Records, and produced a show titled *Bay Leaf*, which consisted of music and poetry "to praise the glory of life," at the community radio station KPFA in Berkeley. She met Bob through the radio station, probably when she became its director of third-world content, which allowed her to spend time in Jamaica. At some point the two commenced a romantic relationship.

Bob's mother, Ciddy, picks up the story in her book, telling us that Yvette would visit Bob at her house in Delaware when he was there, through which she developed a close relationship with Ciddy. Yvette eventually fell out with Bob romantically, but she remained in contact with Ciddy. Through this, she ended up managing Bob's fan club, the Movement of Jah People, out of Ciddy's house in Miami.

Other sources, including her profile at KPFA, list Yvette as an employee at Tuff Gong. According to Rita, Yvette worked on Bob's publishing and toured with him on occasion, the insinuation being that their connection was more than professional. When Don Taylor became Bob's manager, Yvette played a part in helping Bob set up the publishing scam that involved listing alternate names as songwriters of many of his songs in order to skirt around paying publishing dividends to Cayman Music. As such, she was privy to many of Bob's business decisions. They resumed a sexual relationship the year before Bob died, and Yvette gave birth to his last child, Makeda, soon after he passed.

With only a few exceptions, most of the women Bob Marley was close to had romantic relationships with him. But there's one woman that he allowed into the center of his professional life—his lawyer, Diane Jobson—with whom his relationship may have simply been platonic. Jobson was a light-skinned uptown Rasta convert—evidence that the religious sect from the hills and ghettos of Jamaica was making inroads among the "planter" class. She was the sister of Chris Blackwell's best friend and business partner, Dickie Jobson.

As Bob's dreadlocked lawyer, Jobson was his steady business companion, and Don Taylor suggests that the three of them were the only ones with full knowledge of his business dealings. There's some speculation—particularly from Bob's wife and mother—that Jobson was more than just his lawyer, but this could simply be because he spent so much time with her.

The Flings

Several girlfriends are mentioned in passing in sources on Bob's life, as women he was enthused about for a brief period. While he was in Stockholm for two months in 1971 to work on a film soundtrack, he hooked up with a girl and didn't mention to his musical companions that he had a wife back home. This kind of "band wife" lifestyle continued when he and the Wailers set up shop at the Chelsea Hotel in New York for a week in 1973, and Bob wiled away the hours with a Danish girl called Mooskie. Don Taylor makes mention of sisters that Bob was dating, Virginia and Nancy Burke, at the same time as he was courting Cindy Breakspeare. Ciddy also talks of a Jennifer who got pregnant but lost the baby, and another girl named Winnie.

The "Baby-Mothers"

Besides his flings, Bob had many well-documented girlfriends who bore him children. Before he married Rita, he had a child with Cheryl Murray (Imani Carole) in 1963. Not much is known about Trench Town resident Pat "Lucille" Williams, mother of Robbie, other than that Bob was inspired to write "Midnight Ravers" after spending the night with her at Hope Road. He also had kids with Janet Hunt of Jamaica (Rohan), Janet Bowen of England (Karen), Lucy Pounder of Barbados (Julian), Anita Belnavis of Jamaica (Ky-Mani), Cindy Breakspeare of Jamaica (Damian), and Yvette Morris-Anderson Crichton of the United States (Makeda).

The African Princesses

Bob sure wasn't born into royalty, but he became the King of Reggae, and being a monarch has its privileges. Bob was involved with not one but two African princesses. While Bob was spending time in exile in London after the assassination attempt of 1976, the daughter of the Libyan oil minister, known as Princess Yashi to Bob's circle, was attending boarding school there, and she became an expensive girlfriend. On a trip to Miami she ordered a $35,000 bottle of wine and had Bob pay for it.

The other princess was Pascalene Bongo, daughter of Omar Bongo, the president of Gabon (1967–2009). At times she joined Bob on tour, where she would follow the bus in her limousine. She would fly with her entourage in her private jet to Jamaica to spend a few days with Bob on occasion.

The Actress

Between 1972 and 1974, Esther Anderson was Bob's main romantic interest. The pair of them spent a lot of time, along with harmonica player Lee Jaffee and Bob's cousin Sledger, enjoying life between Hope Road and the cabin Bob and Esther built in nearby Negril. Anderson was a Jamaican actress, filmmaker, model, and photographer of African, Welsh, and East Indian descent who had dated Marlon Brando and starred alongside Sidney Poitier in *A Warm December*. She came from a well-to-do family and was connected to Island Records as an investor and former girlfriend of Chris Blackwell, which is how she ended up at Hope Road. When Rita saw the group of them together, Bob instructed Lee to tell her that Esther was with him. Rita, of course, soon found out otherwise.

Esther collaborated with Bob in a few different ways. Her photos of the Wailers appear on the albums *Catch a Fire*, *Burnin'*, and *Natty Dread*. She has

Esther Anderson starred in *A Warm December* alongside Sidney Poitier.

also said that she co-wrote "Get Up, Stand Up" on a flight with him, and that she and Lee Jaffee both contributed to "I Shot the Sheriff," though she is not credited on either song. Esther was in the car when the group were stopped at a roadblock coming back from Negril one night, an event that was immortalized in "Rebel Music (3 O' Clock Roadblock)."

In 2011, Esther made the documentary film *Bob Marley: The Making of a Legend*, based on footage she shot in the early seventies.

The Beauty Queens

One woman who held a special place in Bob's heart was Cindy Breakspeare, mother of Damian and muse for the love songs on *Kaya* ("Is This Love") and *Exodus* ("Waiting in Vain" and "Turn Your Lights Down Low"). In fact, Bob wooed her with the latter song by singing it outside her room, and Rita later refused to sing it on tour.

Born in Toronto to Jamaican parents in 1954, Cindy was white and upper-middle-class. When she was four, her family moved back to Kingston, where she attended a Roman Catholic convent from age ten, and she watched Bob's star rise before meeting him when both were tenants of Chris Blackwell at 56 Hope Road. Cindy worked at Dizzi Disco in the evenings and Bob went there often to court her. Initially, she wasn't interested in him, and this may have been the spark that ignited his passion for her. His manager figures this is the only woman Bob truly ever loved, and the only woman he ever witnessed Bob continue to pursue after she walked away.

When Bob received the deed to Hope Road in 1975 as part of the renegotiation of his contract with Island Records, Cindy and her brother, Stephen, became his tenants. After the assassination attempt she flew to meet him in Nassau, where he would spend time with her at her hotel in between visits with Rita and the kids.

Their romance was not a secret, least of all to Rita, and it was widely resented in some camps. According to Bob's mother, "Everyone in Kingston was talking about their love affair. Public opinion was heatedly against it," she writes, because of the differences in race and class. The upper classes were against the union because Bob was nothing but a dirty Rasta. The Rastas couldn't believe that Bob would fall for a white(ish), bikini-clad Barbie. What happened to black power? Peter Tosh felt that, as a Rasta, Bob shouldn't take up with a white woman. Others were of the opinion that Bob was selling out—a black ghetto revolutionary living uptown with his white girlfriend. According to Don Taylor's memoir, Bob's response was, "Me a carry Rasta uptown."

Cindy, like Bob, was a vegetarian and an athlete. But there were some major differences in their values. Whereas the Wailers were tapped into black-nationalist rhetoric around the beauty of African heritage and all that colonization had done to destroy pride in black culture, Cindy was a white beauty queen—the epitome of European beauty and commercial culture. Makeup, nail polish, and shaven legs were a long way from the Ital lifestyle practiced by Rastafarian women, and this is something that left Bob's detractors stymied, wondering how he could rationalize the cognitive dissonance.

Incidentally, Cindy was not the only beauty queen girlfriend Marley had. He was also romantically involved with a running mate of hers, Sandra Kong, who went on to place seventh in the 1979 Miss Jamaica World competition.

Cindy had won bodybuilding competitions, and in 1976 she was sweeping up beatify contests at home and abroad. She took the title of "Miss Jamaica Body Beautiful" and won the Miss Universe bikini contest in London. Her measurements that year, according to a *Gleaner* article, were 35–24½–36½. She wanted to attend the Miss World competition in London that December, but the Manley government, with its socialist bent, was against such competitions, and refused to fund her attendance. Bob paid for her to go, though, and she won. Bob also supported Cindy in a startup venture by giving her $100,000 in seed money for her Ital Craft Company. Once she became pregnant, he also bought her a house in the posh Cherry Gardens district.

Of all Bob's women, Cindy was the one that Rita was most jealous of; in her memoir, she calls her "one of Chris Blackwell's kittens." She couldn't understand why Bob was attracted to her, and resented the fact that Bob was very public about this affair with a lighter-skinned woman. Cindy, too, was jealous of Rita. According to Ciddy, when Bob bought Rita a BMW, Cindy complained, "And here my VW Beetle is barely running." That BMW, to Rita's mind, was consolation for his affair with Cindy. Cindy initially didn't know that Bob was married, until Ciddy told her when she was pregnant with Damian. After this, Cindy apparently was led on by Bob to think that he would divorce Rita and marry her. This, of course, did not happen. After Bob passed away in 1981, Cindy married Jamaican senator and attorney Tom Tavares-Finson.

8

Shame and Scandal in the Family

Bob's Many Children

Timothy White quotes Bob as saying that he wanted to have "as many children as dere were shells on de beach." He didn't make it that far, but he sure deserves an *A* for effort. How many children did Bob Marley have? As with many of the facts of his life, the answer depends on who you ask, but the number is usually somewhere between nine and fourteen. According to his mother, Bob and his wife Rita only had three legitimate children together—Cedella, Ziggy, and Stephen—though by Rita's count they had four (these three plus Stephanie), and she has said that if Bob had lived they would have had a few more. Her views on birth control, which Bob shared, help account for this, and go some way to explaining Bob's own attitude concerning the products of his affairs. In her book, she writes, "As a strict Rastafarian, I did not use birth control or believe in abortion; it's our belief that such practices are intended to kill the black race."

So where did the other children come from? Bob's eldest child, Sharon, was actually the daughter of Rita and a previous lover, but Bob adopted her. It's not widely known, but many people surmise that Bob had already had a child with another woman by the time he met Rita. His mother, meanwhile, has claimed that his daughter Stephanie was not his biological child but the result of an affair between Rita and one of Bob's friends. Of course, Bob had many extramarital relationships, and many of those resulted in children born out of wedlock.

Bob's daughter Cedella has said that there are nine siblings in total, and told www.celebs.com that they "all lived in the same house at the same time at one time or another," but his mother counts eleven recognized heirs, from seven different mothers. Other sources put the number higher, at thirteen or fourteen. One author has said that there are relatives who estimate Bob had up to twenty-two children.

By my count, there are thirteen known children. Some of them are officially recognized as Bob's children, but a few are not. Here they are, in birth order.

1. Imani Carole Anne

Born on May 22, 1963, Imani Carole Anne is Bob's first child, born to a native of Boston, Massachusetts, Cheryl Murray, who reportedly was eighteen at the time. Imani has remained out of the limelight, and she is not officially acknowledged on the Marley website. In a conversation, she told me that she is a graduate of the University of the Virgin Islands and a charter member of the Alpha Kappa Alpha Sorority, and that she currently lives in the United States. She is married with two children. A very private person, she volunteers her time to many organizations rooted in the Virgin Islands and donates to the Diabetes Foundation, AIDS research, the Cancer Foundation, and others. She remembers her father visiting her every time he played in Boston.

Only a few biographers have mentioned the existence of Marley children from before Bob's marriage to Rita. Chris Salewicz reports that Murray's brother James insisted she break off the relationship because of Bob's "white blood" or mixed-race background. Yet in an earlier biography by Stephen Davis, a similar story is told about an affair Bob had during the same period with a fourteen-year-old neighbor named Esther. (Bob would have been seventeen at the time.) In this account, Esther's brother is said to have ended the love affair by saying, "We don't want no white man in our breed."

It is possible that these stories have more to do with positioning Bob as an outcaste due to his mixed race, rather than the actual events. And it seems most probable that both have become conflated in Bob Marley mythology, making it difficult to gauge the truth of either tale. For her part, Imani doubts

Bob's eldest child, Imani Carol.   *Courtesy of Imani Carol*

that this story has any relation to her mother. "My mom is of American Indian, Caucasian, and African American descent," she states, "so the accounts of 'white blood' is totally outlandish."

2. Sharon Marley

Born on November 23, 1964, Sharon was Rita's child from a previous relationship. Her father's name is not publicly known. Rita does not mention him by name in her autobiography, stating only that they had been in love and the boy was eager to be a father. After she became pregnant at age seventeen, the boy's mother sent him away to England.

Rita was pressured to abort the child, but she chose not to. When she first met Bob, she concealed the fact that she had a daughter, but once he found out, when Sharon was about five months old, Bob was very supportive of Rita's responsibilities as a parent. He also insisted that Rita break off correspondence with Sharon's biological father. When they married in 1966, Bob adopted Sharon. So, while she was not his biological child, she is legally recognized as his.

Sharon was previously married to Peter Prendergast, a Jamaica football official, but in 2014 she married Ghanaian sunlife singer Ekow Alabi Savage (sunlife being a mix of reggae and highlife). Her nonmusical activities include being the curator of the Bob Marley Museum and the managing director of a Montessori childcare center, the Total Care Learning Centre (TCLC), both of which are in Kingston, Jamaica.

Sharon Prendergast contributed to the soundtrack for *The Mighty Quinn* and had bit parts in the movie.

3. Cedella Marley

Born on August 23, 1967, Cedella is the first biological child of Bob and Rita, and was named after Bob's mother. She was conceived soon after Bob arrived home from working in Delaware, and was born in Kingston after the couple had spent six months living at Bob's childhood home in Nine Mile. He recorded a song at Studio One around this time called "Nice Time" about returning home to his wife Rita, and when Cedella was born later that year, she was given the nickname "Nice Time." Cedella's nonmusical activities include acting in the Denzel Washington vehicle *The Mighty Quinn* alongside her sister, Sharon. She has continued the family legacy by authoring children's books based on her father's songs and life (*One Love, Every Little Thing, The Boy from Nine Mile, 56 Thoughts from 56 Hope Road*). She has also published a ganja cookbook, *Cooking with Herb: 75 Recipes for the Marley Natural Lifestyle*. As a clothing designer, she established the Catch a Fire women's clothing line (www.cedellamarleydesign.com), and has designed collections for Zion Rootswear (the family's apparel company) and the Jamaica track-and-field team's uniforms for the 2012 Olympics, as worn by athletes including Usain Bolt. She also oversees the family's philanthropy as director of the Bob Marley Foundation, a nonprofit charitable organization.

4. David Nesta "Ziggy" Marley

Rita and Bob's first son, Ziggy, was born on October 17, 1968, in Kingston, Jamaica. He was named for King David but was given the pet name Ziggy when he was three years old. Bob said he had football legs, meaning he would be a good player, zigging and zagging around rivals on the field. Bob himself once had the nickname Ziggy too.

Like the rest of the clan, Ziggy has branched out from music. He has a few acting credits, voicing Dog Gnarly in *Pup Star* and Ernie the Rastafarian jellyfish in *Shark Tale*, as well as appearing in season six of *Hawaii Five-o*. And, like his dad, he loves his ganja, going so far as to publish a graphic novel and web series called *Marijuanaman* based on characters he conceived. When I interviewed him about its release, he said, "The idea was to kind of take away the stigma of the plant by portraying the plant as a superhero. The hero is a metaphor for the plant. This superhero is from another planet and he comes here to seek a solution for the problems his planet is having, some environmental problems. And he finds out when he lands in this pot field that he feels a connection to the plant. And his DNA starts to change and he gains these superpowers."

Ziggy Marley, Savannah, 2007.   *Photo by Bruce Tuten, Creative Commons license*

Stephen Marley, Vancouver, 2007.   *Photo by David Koppe from Kyoto, Japan,*
Creative Commons license

Like his sister Cedella, Ziggy has penned a children's book, *I Love You Too*, based on a song from his children's album *Family Time*. Other business endeavors include the *Ziggy Marley and Family Cookbook* (2016) and Ziggy Marley Organics, through which he sells hempseed snacks, Hemp Rules Caribbean Crunch cereal, and Coco'Mon flavored coconut oils.

5. Stephen Robert Nesta "Raggamuffin" Marley

Bob's third child with Rita, Stephen was born in Wilmington, Delaware, on April 20, 1972. Rita had moved with Ziggy to Delaware in 1971, leaving Bob in Kingston and their older children in the care of her aunt Viola. Stephen was born while in the United States but came to live in Kingston shortly after.

6. Robert Nesta "Robbie" Marley II

Rita had a double shock when she arrived back from working in Delaware with newborn Stephen in tow in 1972 to find not only that Bob had had two affairs but also that both had produced children. Less than a month after Rita gave birth to Stephen, Pat "Lucille" Williams gave birth to his second child born out of wedlock, Robbie, on May 16, 1972. Maureen Sheridan, in her book *Soul Rebel*, says that Williams seduced the musician while he was eating breadfruit naked in the moonlight at 56 Hope Rd (as one does, apparently). Like many of Bob's "outside children," Robbie was brought to live with Rita, so he grew up around his brothers and sisters in the financial security of the Marley fold. Unlike many of his siblings, though, he has not sought a career in music. Instead, he has run the Vintage Marley clothing store in Miami, led the motorcycle club Miami Warriors, and had a bit part in *2 Fast 2 Furious*.

7. Rohan Anthony Marley

Rohan was born May 19, 1972—three days after Robbie—to Janet Hunt. Bob had children with two women named Janet, and they are often distinguished by their nationality. Rohan's mother is "Janet from Jamaica," as opposed to Karen's mother, who is "Janet from England." Like Robbie, Rohan was raised by Rita and Bob, but he later went to live in Miami with Ciddy, who has said that she adopted him. Taking after his father in his love of sports, Rohan made a name for himself in football, playing for the University of Miami and later the Canadian Football League's Ottawa Rough Riders. He also co-founded the Tuff Gong clothing line and the Marley Coffee business.

Rohan Marley shows off House of Marley audio equipment at the Consumer Technology Association trade show, 2012.
Photo by pop culture geek from Los Angeles, CA, USA, Creative Commons license

8. Karen Marley

Born in England in 1973 to Bob Marley and Janet Bowen ("Janet from England"), Karen lived for a time with her maternal grandmother in Harbour View, Jamaica. She was then taken to live with Rita when she was four or five and grew up with her brothers and sisters. Karen graduated with a degree in psychology from the University of Western Ontario before getting involved in the family entertainment business empire.

9. Stephanie Marley

Born on August 17, 1974, Stephanie is either the last child of Rita and Bob or the lovechild of Rita Marley and Jamaican soccer star Owen Stewart, a.k.a. Tacky or

Ital, who was also a friend of Bob's. Ciddy Booker insists that she could tell by looking at the baby that she was not Bob's, and she believed Rita had an affair while Bob was in Britain. However, in her autobiography, Rita states that she thinks she became pregnant with Stephanie after having sex with Bob when he almost raped her after she refused to sleep with him. Ciddy Booker supports her own claim, though, by relaying that Tacky supposedly told her the child was his. She also states that Bob wanted a blood test and threatened divorce, and that Rita eventually admitted her infidelity to Bob when Stephanie was three. Whatever the truth, Stephanie was part of the Marley family, and she is accepted as an official heir of Bob Marley.

While not a performer, Stephanie has worked in the family business as concert promoter for Tuff Gong Productions, and as managing director of several Marley businesses: the Bob Marley Foundation, Tuff Gong International, the Bob Marley Museum, Tuff Gong recordings, URGE, and the Rita Marley Foundation. She is also the director of the Marley Resort and Spa at Cable Beach in Nassau, Bahamas (www.marleyresort.com), and founded the B'uniqk Modeling Talent Agency (pronounced "be unique") in Kingston in 2015.

10. Julian "Ju Ju" Marley

Julian is the son of Bob and Lucy Pounder, who lived in Barbados. Julian was born in London on June 4, 1975, and was the first of Bob's acknowledged children not to be raised by Rita. Instead, he was raised by his mother in London, though he visited his Jamaican family often. He even recorded his first demos at age five at the Marley family home in Kingston.

11. Ky-Mani Marley

Born on February 26, 1976, in Falmouth, Jamaica, Ky-Mani is the son of Anita Belnavis, a Caribbean table-tennis champion. Like Julian, he was raised mostly outside the Marley fold, though he spent summers with Bob and Rita. He spent his early years in Falmouth before moving, at age nine, to inner-city Miami, where his life stood in contrast to the privileged upbringing of many of his siblings, as he shared a two-bedroom home with an eight-member family. He moved back to Jamaica in 1992, and while he was initially not interested in a music career, he released his debut in 1996. Besides his music career, he has starred in two Jamaican films, *Shottas* and *One Love*.

Julian Marley, 2010.   *Photo by Alessio Del Regno
from Livorno, Italia,
Creative Commons license*

Ky-Mani Marley has enjoyed
a successful film career and
starred in this Jamaican
gangster film *Shottas*.
Author's collection

Ky-Mani Marley at the Festival des Vieilles Charrues, 2014.
Photo by Thesupermat, Creative Commons license

12. Damian Robert Nesta "Jr. Gong" Marley

Bob's youngest son, Damian, was born in Kingston on July 21, 1978, to Cindy Breakspeare, Miss World 1976 and Bob's muse for songs such as "Waiting in Vain" and "Turn Your Lights Down Low." His "Jr. Gong" nickname refers to Bob's own nickname, "Tuff Gong."

13. Makeda Jahnesta Marley

Born in Miami on May 30, 1981, only weeks after Bob died, Makeda is the daughter of Yvette Crichton (sometimes listed as Yvette Morris), a radio deejay from Philadelphia. Makeda shares her name with the Ethiopian name for the Queen of Sheba, who, according to the *Kebra Nagast*, is the mother of the Ethiopian dynasty, as Haile Selassie traced his lineage back to Menelik I, the son of Queen Makeda and King Solomon. Doubt has been cast on Makeda's paternity, and Bob's manager, Don Taylor, has called her mother a troublemaker for claiming Bob as the father. After a paternity test proved inconclusive, Rita refused to sign a paternity document, but Bob's mother, Cedella, supported Yvette's bid to have Makeda included as an official offspring, and she is now recognized as one of Bob's heirs by the Marley estate. She was not raised alongside the other children, growing up instead in Pennsylvania.

Damian Marley at the Smile Jamaica concert, 2008.

Photo by AlfredMoya.com for Jamaica MAX

Unlucky 14

There was once a hopeful fourteenth child but, alas, it was not meant to be. Fabian Marley, born Othneil Stanford on July 27, 1968, to mother Raphie Munroe, had claimed that Bob Marley was his father. The singer, who also goes by the nickname Gong Kid, told the *Jamaica Observer,* "I know I am a true Marley." It turns out, though, that he is not. He had a DNA test after the Marley family's lawyers, Michael Hylton and Associates, served him with a cease-and-desist order, requesting that he refrain from using the Marley name. The results of that test show that he is not, in fact, Bob's son.

9

Melody Makers

The Musical Careers of Bob's Children

I t seems like every day there's a new Marley releasing music, especially now that Bob's grandchildren have entered the fray. The array of companies carrying the Marley name is dizzying—some sell clothing, others food, still others marijuana—and even trying to keep track of all the family music ventures is difficult as the second generation has released music on many different family-owned labels.

Not all of Bob's sires have become professional musicians, but generally speaking, the ones who have followed the musical path have found success. Thanks, at least in part, to their last name, the Marley children have been recognized by the Grammy establishment for their many accomplishments. To see a breakdown of all their Grammys, head over to the next chapter. In the meantime, here is an overview of the music careers of Bob's children, starting with the Melody Makers, who went on to international success in the eighties.

Melody Makers: Sharon, Cedella, Ziggy, and Stephen

Many of Bob's children have had successful solo music careers, but the oldest of them—Sharon, Cedella, Ziggy, and Stephen—started out in a family band called the Melody Makers. These kids grew up together at their mother's house in Bull Bay. Every day after school they would be driven to Hope Road to hang out with their dad, and often to watch him play football. They would also encounter the musicians who played with him, and at times they were even allowed to sit in on recording sessions.

With this kind of upbringing, it's no wonder the children started putting on family concerts in the basement of their home. They officially formed a band in 1979 to record "Children Playing in the Streets," with the Wailers as their backing band. Bob wrote the song for the United Nations' "International Year of the Child," and all proceeds from the single went to UNICEF. The band's name was derived from the British music magazine *Melody Maker*, the cover of which Bob had graced in April 1978. The kids thought the name referred to their father—a melody maker—and felt it fit well for a Marley family band.

One of the Melody Makers' first live performances was actually at their father's funeral in May 1981, where they sang and danced onstage with the Wailers and I-Threes. It seemed natural that they would continue as a band after their father's passing, and Rita Marley believed that her husband wanted the family to continue his legacy. Ziggy told the *Daily Beast* in 2011 that Bob's final message to his son was a song that went, "On your way up, take me up / On your way down, don't let me down." Ziggy later turned that into his own song, "Won't Let You Down." They performed at the 1981 Reggae Sunsplash festival soon after. In the tumultuous years after Bob died, when the estate was in turmoil, Rita kept the Marley name alive by ensuring the I-Threes, Melody Makers, and Wailers were touring.

The Melody Makers released a few singles on Tuff Gong before Bob died (as well as "Children Playing in the Streets," they issued "Sugar Pie" and "Trodding" in 1980) and sporadically in the intervening years until they put their first album out in 1985. Despite their acrimonious relationship, Rita hired Bob's former manager, Don Taylor, to get the Melody Makers a record deal. He secured one with EMI, which released *Play the Game Right*. For their second album, *Hey World*, they changed their name to Ziggy Marley and the Melody Makers. They went on to release ten albums in total over their career, garnered several Grammy wins, and became MTV staples with the hit single "Tumblin' Down" in 1988.

Perhaps it is appropriate that since they started out as a child band, they would also record some kid-themed material. They contributed a version of "Give a Little Love" to Disney's *For Our Children*, while the reggae theme song to *Arthur* ("Believe in Yourself") is a cover by Ziggy Marley and the Melody Makers. They also appeared on *Sesame Street*.

The Melody Makers had wound down by the early 2000s, finally disbanding in 2002. Ziggy and Stephen have since launched successful solo careers.

Sharon Marley

Unlike the Marley boys, the Marley girls have not been musically prolific. Besides being a member of the Melody Makers, Sharon appeared as an actress in *The Mighty Quinn*, and her cover of her father's "I'm Hurting Inside" with Sheryl Lee Ralph and Cedella Marley is featured in the film. Along with sister Cedella and Erica Newell, Sharon recorded one song as the Marley Girls ("Unbelievable") in 1997, which is on Island Records' *Dancehall Queen* soundtrack.

Cedella Marley

A member of the Melody Makers and the Marley Girls, Cedella's musical career has since been reduced to a few one-off singles for major corporations. In 2003, she and siblings Stephen, Julian, Damian, and Ky-Mani sang "Master Blaster" on *Conception: An Interpretation of Stevie Wonder Songs.* "Master Blaster," incidentally, was the song Stevie Wonder wrote about Bob Marley. In 2010, she was featured on the *Disney Reggae Club* album with a cover of the *Lion King*'s "Can You Feel the Love Tonight." In 2013, she teamed up with Starbucks to cover the Wailers' "Get Up, Stand Up" for the *Every Mother Counts Volume 2* compilation. As a business-woman, though, she is a powerhouse, and at the helm of many Marley family musical ventures, including Hope Road Merchandising and House of Marley. She is the CEO of Tuff Gong International, the family's record label.

Ziggy Marley

An eight-time Grammy winner (three with the Melody Makers), Bob's eldest son has certainly done his father proud. In 2003, he released his first solo album, *Dragonfly*, which was a departure from the pop-reggae material of the

After leading the Melody Makers until 2002, Ziggy Marley embarked on a prolific and successful solo career.   *Author's collection*

Melody Makers. Since then, he has established his own label, just like his dad, called Tuff Gong Worldwide. All his subsequent releases have been through this imprint, and he's also used it to pay respect to the roots of Jamaican music with the "Ziggy Marley Presents" series. Speaking about the first release in the series, *Ziggy Marley Presents Dancehall Originators, Volume 1,* he told me, "What I want to focus on is the history of the music. That is something I'm interested in because I think especially in Jamaica the younger generation [is not] exposed enough to the history of the music. I want to pay respect to that."

He hasn't felt weighed down by trying to live up to his father's legacy, though. When I interviewed him in 2011, he told me, "My father is a world-wide known. Because him was such a significant individual, there would still be certain expectations of me—this is how it works. But it is a positive, never negative." Despite going solo, he still collaborates with his siblings, including on the documentary film *Marley African Road Trip* with half-brothers Rohan and Robbie. He and brothers Stephen, Damian, and Julian set up the Ghetto Youths International record label to release Marley family material. Out of the entire Marley clan, Ziggy feels closest to his brother Stephen, as they are close in age and share both parents. "We live separate lives, but me and Stephen is the closest, and Rohan. Damian is the youngest one. He's a little closer to Stephen than to me because I'm the oldest boy, you know?"

Stephen Marley

A songwriter, singer, and producer, Stephen has racked up eight Grammy Awards, and, along with Ziggy and Damian, has had the most international success of the Marley brood. Originally part of the Melody Makers, Stephen performed onstage with his dad and Ziggy when the Wailers played in Zimbabwe's independence celebrations in 1980. He moved into music production in the late nineties, and has worked with family members (producing debut albums by brothers Julian and Damian), other reggae artists (Capleton, Michael Franti, Inner Circle), and hip-hop stars (the Fugees, Nelly, Erykah Badu). He was in the production chair for Damian Marley's first three records—*Mr. Marley, Halfway Tree,* and *Welcome to Jamrock*—and won Grammys for the latter two. He also oversaw the popular *Chant Down Babylon* remix album in 1999. As the Marley Boyz, Stephen, Damian, and Ky-Mani released *Educated Fools* in 2003 on Ghetto Youths International. He began releasing solo material in 2007 with the critically acclaimed *Mind Control.*

Julian, Damian, and Ky-Mani

Unlike the kids in the Melody Makers, Julian, Damian and Ky-Mani didn't grow up in the family home, though they all spent time there. Almost two decades after the Melody Makers formed, these three sons from different mothers began to release their own brand of Marley family reggae.

Julian grew up in England but benefitted from his father's name by studying music under some of the Wailers when he was in Jamaica, many of whom performed on his debut album, *Lion in the Morning*. As a teenager, he formed a reggae band called Uprising and opened for the Melody Makers and the Wailers.

At age thirteen, Damian (a.k.a. Jr. Gong) joined the offspring of reggae artists Freddie McGregor and Third World's Cat Coore to form the Shepherds. This band performed at Sunsplash in 1992.

Julian Marley in Portugal, 2010.   *Pedro Alves*

In the early nineties, Julian moved to Jamaica, and he and Damian teamed up with Ziggy and Stephen to form the collaborative group Ghetto Youth Crew. Both he and Damian appeared on the 1997 Lollapalooza tour. He also played guitar on Lauryn Hill's Jamaica-recorded and highly acclaimed project *The Miseducation of Lauryn Hill* in 1998. (Hill, by the way, has another Marley connection. She has five children with Rohan Marley, but they are no longer together.)

Damian, in particular, has achieved commercial and critical success, notably with his 2001 Grammy-winning album *Halfway Tree* and the massive 2005 single "Welcome to Jamrock." He made forays into the urban music scene in the United States when he collaborated with Nas on an album called *Distant Relatives* in 2010. The following year, Damian diversified his sound and audience once again by joining Mick Jagger, Eurythmics' Dave Stewart, Joss Stone, and Indian composer A.R. Rahman in the supergroup SuperHeavy.

Damian Marley, Colombia, 2011.   *Juan Santacruz*

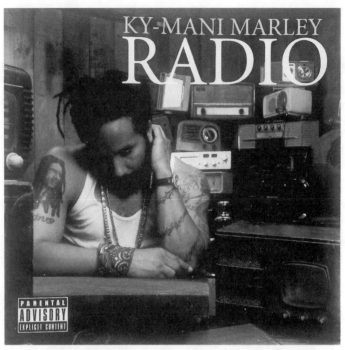

Ky-Mani Marley's 2007 release *Radio*.   *Author's collection*

Ky-Mani was based in Miami in his teens, and he grew up largely outside of the Marley fold. His 1996 debut, *Like Father Like Son*, included covers of some of his father's music, including "Judge Not" and "Who the Cap Fit." A year later, he released a cover of Eddy Grant's "Electric Avenue" with Pras of the Fugees. He's gone on to collaborate with family members and release seven solo albums.

Generation Three: Marley's Musical Grandchildren

No doubt we'll see releases from a growing list of grandchildren in the years to come as the Marley family sticks to the family business. As of now, there are six grandchildren in the music industry: Stephen's sons Jo Mersa and Yohan; Ziggy's son Daniel Bambaata Marley; Sharon's son Matthew Prendergast, also known as Biggz General; Ky-Mani's son Ky-Mani Marley Jr., known as K. J. Marley; and Cedella's son Skip Marley.

10

Marley Get the Grammy

The Controversial Reggae Award

There is a standing joke in the reggae world that if you are a reggae artist and you want to win the reggae Grammy, you need to change your name to Marley. Other reggae artists have complained bitterly that the Marley name counts more than talent when it comes to this prestigious prize. Take a look at the Grammy stats below and decide if this really is a joke.

Bob Marley never received a Grammy award in his lifetime. This is because the Grammys have only included a reggae category since 1985, four years after he passed. But that doesn't mean the Marley name does not hold sway over pop music's highest honor.

Original Wailer Bunny Wailer earned Grammy awards for two tribute records to Bob Marley. *Author's collection*

From 1985 until 1991, the award was called "Best Reggae Recording," before changing to "Best Reggae Album" in 1992. In the thirty-three years from its inception to the writing of this book, eighteen "Best Reggae Album" awards have been given to artists connected with the Marley brand. Just to be clear, more than half of the reggae Grammys have gone to Marley-related artists, meaning his wife and offspring, former band members and their offspring, and producers. Thirteen of those were given to Marley children. If we include the few awards given to Marleys outside of the reggae category, the total number increases to twenty-two. And it goes up considerably, to forty-one, when you factor in all the times people associated with the Marley brand were nominated for a Grammy. Total Grammys for Marley family members alone amount to sixteen: five awards for Ziggy Marley (2007, 2009, 2014, 2015, 2017), three for Stephen Marley (2008, 2010, 2012), three awards for Ziggy Marley and the Melody Makers (1989, 1990, 1998), three awards for Damian Marley (2002, two awards in 2006, 2018), and one for Bob Marley himself, who won a Grammy "Lifetime Achievement Award" in 2001.

Marley's former bandmates have also picked up Grammys: three for Bunny Wailer (1991, 1995, 1997), who won twice with tribute albums to Bob; and one for Peter Tosh (1988). Tosh's son Andrew, by the way, was nominated twice. The

Stephen Marley won two Grammy awards for two versions of the same album.   *Author's collection*

Wailers, as a standalone band, were also nominated in 1990 for their album *I.D*; and the Original Wailers, a band that includes two of Marley's former guitarists, Al Anderson and Junior Marvin, were nominated in 2013.

The Marley name is so powerful among members of the Recording Academy that, in 2010, Stephen Marley beat out Buju Banton and won the Grammy for *Mind Control Acoustic*—an acoustic version of an album he had previously won a Grammy for in 2008. Really—he won two Grammy awards for the same record. Okay, one was a bit different, but did I mention that they were the same record?

How many records do you think you would need to sell to garner a Grammy nomination? In the same year that Stephen won his second Grammy (SECOND GRAMMY!) for *Mind Control*, his half-brother

Bob's children have seemed to dominate the "Best Reggae Album" category since its inception. This is their 1991 album, for which they were nominated for a Grammy.

Author's collection

brother Julian was nominated for *Awake*, despite the fact that his album had only sold thirty thousand copies as of the nomination date. Oh, did I mention that Julian's last name is Marley?

In the thirty-three-year history of the award, only three artists have won the reggae Grammy when a Marley was also nominated. Jimmy Cliff beat out one Marley (Ziggy Marley and the Melody Makers) and one Marley associate (Judy Mowatt) in 1986; Shabba Ranks won against two Marleys (Rita Marley, and Ziggy Marley and the Melody Makers) and one Marley associate (Bunny Wailer) in 1992; and Inner Circle beat out Ziggy Marley and the Melody Makers in 1994. Since 1998, every year a Marley was nominated, a Marley has won (and twice in that period, more than one was nominated).

Why does this matter? The Grammy Awards are pop music's most prestigious scale of achievement, and all artists prize getting the nod from the Recording Academy. Because of this, they provide legitimacy to reggae— a musical genre that sees itself as embattled against mainstream genres, with Jamaican artists only creeping into the international charts on occasion.

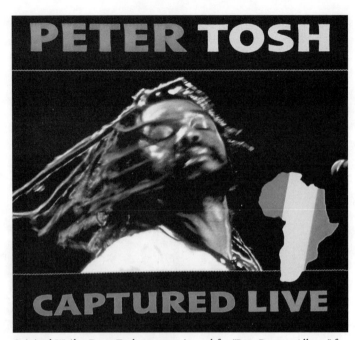

Original Wailer Peter Tosh was nominated for "Best Reggae Album" for *Captured Live* in 1985.   *Author's collection*

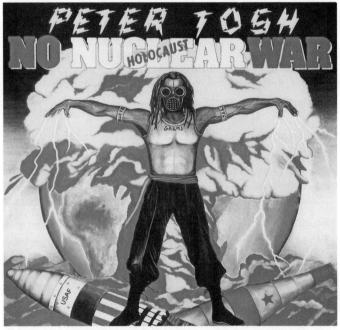

Peter Tosh won the Grammy in 1988 for his solo album *No Nuclear War*.
Author's collection

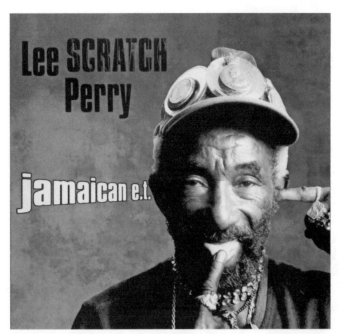

Wailers producer and Bob Marley collaborator Lee "Scratch" Perry has enjoyed his share of reggae Grammy nominations and won for *Jamaican E.T.* in 2003.   *Author's collection*

Ziggy Marley has earned five Grammys for solo records, including one in the "Best Musical Album for Children" category for *Family Time* in 2009.   *Author's collection*

Here is a list of all the Marley and Marley-related Grammy nominees and recipients, organized by year:

- 1982: *Reggae Sunsplash '81: A Tribute to Bob Marley* nominated for "Best Ethnic or Traditional Folk Recording"
- 1985: Peter Tosh nominated for *Captured Live*
- 1986: Ziggy Marley and the Melody Makers nominated for *Play the Game Right*; I-Threes singer Judy Mowatt nominated for *Working Wonders*
- 1988: Peter Tosh won for *No Nuclear War*
- 1989: Ziggy Marley and the Melody Makers won for *Conscious Party*
- 1990: Ziggy Marley and the Melody Makers won for *One Bright Day*; Bunny Wailer nominated for *Liberation*; Wailers Band nominated for *I.D.*
- 1991: Bunny Wailer won for *Time Will Tell: A Tribute to Bob Marley*; Andrew Tosh (Peter Tosh's son) nominated for *Make Place for the Youth*
- 1992: Rita Marley nominated for *We Must Carry On*; Ziggy Marley and the Melody Makers nominated for *Jahmekya*
- 1994: Ziggy Marley and the Melody Makers nominated for *Joy and Blues*
- 1995: Bunny Wailer won for *Crucial! Roots Classics*
- 1996: Ziggy Marley and the Melody Makers nominated for *Free Like We Want 2 B*

Despite poor sales, Julian's album *Awake* earned him a nomination for "Best Reggae Album."   *Author's collection*

- 1997: Bunny Wailer won for *Hall of Fame: A Tribute to Bob Marley's 50th Anniversary*
- 1998: Ziggy Marley and the Melody Makers won for *Fallen Is Babylon*
- 2001: Bob Marley won a Grammy "Lifetime Achievement Award"
- 2002: Damian Marley won for *Halfway Tree*; Ky-Mani Marley, nominated for *Many More Roads*
- 2003: Lee "Scratch" Perry (Wailers producer) won for *Jamaican E.T.*
- 2006: Damian Marley won for *Welcome to Jamrock*; he also won the Grammy for "Best Urban/Alternative Performance" for the same album
- 2007: Ziggy Marley won for *Love Is My Religion*
- 2008: Stephen Marley won for *Mind Control*; Lee Perry nominated for *The End of an American Dream*
- 2009: Ziggy Marley won "Best Musical Album for Children" for *Family Time*; Lee Perry nominated for *Repentance*
- 2010: Stephen Marley won for *Mind Control—Acoustic*; Julian Marley nominated for *Awake*
- 2011: Lee Perry nominated for *Revelation*; Andrew Tosh nominated for *Legacy: An Acoustic Tribute to Peter Tosh*
- 2012: Stephen Marley won for *Revelation Pt. 1: The Roots of Life*; Ziggy Marley nominated for *Wild and Free*
- 2013: The Original Wailers nominated for *Miracle*
- 2014: Ziggy Marley won for *In Concert*
- 2015: Ziggy Marley won for *Fly Rasta*; Lee Perry nominated for *Back on the Controls*
- 2017: Ziggy Marley won for *Ziggy Marley*
- 2018: Damian Marley, won for *Stony Hill*

11

Wages of Love

Bob's Views on Women

Bob Marley is often lauded for his views on racial and economic equality—the champion of the underclasses. Gender equality, though, is a different story. A select few women worked alongside him in the music business, but Bob was very much a macho, domineering figure when it came to his relationships with, and views on, women.

Keeping Women in Their Place

As other chapters in this book have already shown, Bob treated Rita as a subordinate, tolerated because she was the mother of some of his children. He began cheating on her even before they were wed. She knew that he had other women while he was dating her, but believes that he kept them out of Rita's way in a strange show of respect. Rita has said that a girl named Cherry accosted her after their wedding, once Bob had left for Delaware, claiming that Bob was her man.

Sometimes he would attempt to rationalize his affairs by saying they were really a benefit to her. In her book, Rita writes that if she complained about his other children, Bob would tell her, "Baby, you couldn't have all the babies that I feel I should have. I don't want to get you pregnant every year. So some of that is really just taking the burden off your body."

The reverse, of course, was not true. When he suspected daughter Stephanie to be the product of an affair he thought Rita had, he was livid. When Rita was worried that Bob was going to leave her and marry Yvette, he countered that he was angry that she had been "breeding" with someone else while they were married. Bob could sleep around as he wished, it seemed, but according to Ciddy's memoir, "Once another man had entered a woman of his, Nesta would drop her forever. That was the way he was with Pat, Robbie's mother; that was how he was with Rita."

Bob's ideas of gender roles were conservative to say the least. He once complained to his mother that Rita shirked her proper domestic duties, like washing his clothes, cooking him dinner, and making him a cup of tea. He felt he had brought her from the ghetto to uptown, but that she showed no gratitude for it. (Interestingly, Rita's account of this is that, in the early days, she had to wash Bob's single pair of underpants every night.)

Bob also felt his women should be "natural," insisting they not use makeup or hair products. Even the beauty queen Cindy Breakspeare took off her makeup before visiting him. Despite his preference for a natural appearance, however, he didn't feel the same about the completely natural act of breastfeeding, at least in public. He once admonished Rita for feeding infant Ziggy in an airport.

Bob was also physically violent with Rita, as more than one source attests. And she told a British tabloid in 2004 that he raped her when she refused to sleep with him, and that he claimed he had a right to do so as her husband. So Bob might have been all "One Love" sometimes, but he was also very much a chauvinist who believed women were subservient to him.

The Pleasures of Fallen Women

Reggae is a man's game. The vast majority of reggae artists over the years have been men, and the point of view in their songs is overwhelmingly male-dominated and often downright misogynistic. Women in reggae songs are often likened to the biblical Jezebel (as in Justin Hinds's "Carry Go Bring Home" or Maxi Priest's "Close to You"), which in Jamaican/Rastafari culture is translated as duplicitous and wanton; or the biblical Eve, who, after all, caused the fall of humankind (as in Bob Marley's "Adam and Eve").

Women are also depicted as greedy. Ian McCann quotes Bob's own words from 1975, drawn from a Jamaican proverb, which speak to this: "If the money's done, you may not have a woman either." Elsewhere, women are typically viewed as conquests, sexual objects to be acted upon by a man. Bob's own "Kinky Reggae," with its wish to "hit and run," insinuates this.

For a man with hundreds of songs to his name, Bob wrote about love sparingly. When he did, his depictions of women were typical by both Jamaican and pop-music standards. In his love songs, he often portrayed himself as a comforter ("No Woman, No Cry"), an enduring lover trying to do the right thing ("Is This Love"), a well-intentioned suitor ("Baby We've Got a Date (Rock It Baby)"), or a man pining for the attention of a new lover by sweet-talking her ("Mellow Mood," "Turn Your Lights Down Low," "Waiting in Vain"). He also celebrated the beauty of spending time with his lover in "Nice Time," "Satisfy My Soul," and "Stir It Up."

In these songs, he hardly comes across like a chauvinist. However, according to cultural critic Carolyn Cooper, who has written a lot on reggae, there are also hints of conservative Rastafarian gender politics that frame women in the Garden of Eden narrative as fallen, in league with Satan, and entrappers of men. We see this in "Adam and Eve," which, though not written by Marley, was covered by him in 1970, and contains the lyric, "Woman is the root of all evil."

For Cooper, though, the song that best demonstrates his views is one from a decade later. In her book *Sound Clash*, she calls "Pimper's Paradise," "the classic example in Bob Marley's repertoire of that ambiguous Rastafari response to 'fallen women' as temptress, both attraction and repulsion, condemnation and empathy. It is the woman who allegedly initiates the fall, which the man himself thoroughly enjoys."

Bob Marley, with his many girlfriends, certainly enjoyed this kind of "fall." For a singer who is often equated with love songs—thanks in part to his greatest-selling album, *Legend*, being heavily weighted with them, and the enduring popularity of "One Love" (itself not actually a love song)—it is interesting to discover that behind some of his talk of love is the idea that women are the untrustworthy, weaker counterparts to men.

12

Ambush in the Night

The Assassination Attempt

Many celebrated musicians never made it to their thirtieth birthday—Jimi Hendrix, Janis Joplin, Jim Morrison, Brian Jones, Jacob Miller, Kurt Cobain, and Amy Winehouse were all part of the "27 club," while Tupac, the Notorious B.I.G., Buddy Holly, Ian Curtis, and Otis Redding didn't even make it that far. Others slid from their malcontented teens and twenties into corporate shills as they hit their thirties. Case in point: at age thirty-one, the once vital and independent Elvis Presley was pandering to his corporate bosses, shooting his twenty-second film in Hollywood, and releasing dull soundtrack albums (three in that year alone). He also built a snowman on the lawn of Graceland, leased a house in Palm Springs, became interested in horses, and proposed to Priscilla. Oh, and he was the tenth highest paid star in show business.

By comparison, at the same age, Bob Marley's mind was not on reaping the material fruits of fame and frolicking around like a country-club prig. Rather, he was trying to affect social change. By the fall of 1976, Bob was carrying the weight of the country on his shoulders and trying to figure out a way to avert a civil war between opposing political factions that was spilling out into the street and manifesting in gang warfare.

Marley had become a key political figure in Jamaica—not in the sense of party politics but as a visionary who had the inclination and popular appeal to unite people. But while he was a celebrity at home and abroad, he had enemies. On the night of Friday, December 3, 1976, these enemies almost took his life in a brash, bullet-strewn invasion of home.

Protected by His Majesty

On the evening in question, the Wailers were rehearsing in the music room on the main floor of Hope Road with the Zap Pow horn section. Taking a break, Bob went to the kitchen at the back of the house and started peeling a grapefruit. With him were Don Taylor and guitarist Don Kinsey. Rita had just left and was walking to her VW Beetle in the driveway. She had offered a lift to two youths, Shanty and Senior, back to Bull Bay, and as she stepped into the car she noticed strangers with guns on the steps of the house—the steps she'd just left. When she started the car, the noise startled the gunmen. Some began shooting at the house, while others chased after Rita's car as she sped down the driveway. Shots smashed the back window, but Shanty and Senior were already on the floor, so luckily they were not hit.

Rita wasn't so lucky. She felt blood on her neck and, realizing she'd been struck in the head with a bullet, thought she was dying. She stopped the car before she got to the gate—the getaway car was blocking it—and lay her head on the steering wheel. A gunman came to her window and put his gun to her head, but then shouted to the others, "Everybody dead," walking away as sirens pierced the night.

Meanwhile, when the shots started, those in the kitchen thought someone had let off firecrackers, since it was almost Christmas. Don Taylor recounts the incident, and Bob's reactions, in his book. "Who the blood claat a bus firecracker in mi yard?" shouted Bob. But then they were met with the sound of machine-gun fire and bullets flying through the back windows. Don was hit five times, one bullet nicking his aorta and another coming to rest in his spine. He fell on to Bob, who exclaimed, "Selassie I Jah Rastafari."

Shots were fired into the band room as well, but the only person hit was Louis Griffiths, who was standing near the soundboard. According to a *Sunday Gleaner* article in the wake of the shooting, he was a band assistant. Bob was shot in the arm and another bullet grazed his chest, but he wasn't seriously injured. Rita, meanwhile, had a bullet lodged near her brain. She underwent a successful operation, and has since attributed her survival to her dreadlocks—they stopped the bullet from going deeper into her head, either by mystical force or woolen density.

Bob would later put these events into song, most obviously in "Ambush in the Night," with the lyric, "They opened fire on me now," but also in "Jamming," which defiantly asserts his autonomy: "No bullet can stop us now."

Don Taylor was by far the worst off. In the aftermath of the shooting there was a period of uncertainty in the kitchen. The Rastas present thought Taylor was dead and refused to touch his corpse. Their revulsion was derived from the Nazirite vow—a Hebrew code that informs Rasta practice around dreadlocks, diet, and aversion to death. For instance, Numbers 6:6–8 states, "Throughout the period of their dedication to the Lord, the Nazirite must not go near a dead body. Even if their own father or mother or brother or sister dies, they must not make themselves ceremonially unclean on account of them, because the symbol of their dedication to God is on their head. Throughout the period of their dedication, they are consecrated to the Lord."

In the end, it was Bob, wounded himself, who lifted up Taylor and helped the police set him in a car bound for the hospital. Taylor was taken to the hospital, where he was actually pronounced dead before an intern realized the error. He underwent surgery in Jamaica but remained paralyzed by the bullet in his spine. He was then airlifted to Miami, where he was successfully operated on by Dr. William Bacon. Taylor was soon able to walk and remained grateful to Dr. Bacon. He would remember this man a few years later, when Bob Marley wanted a second opinion on his cancer diagnosis, and it would be Dr. Bacon that initially cut out the cancer in Bob's toe.

Smile Jamaica

In order to understand why someone would want to kill Bob Marley, it is helpful to look at the political climate in Kingston at the time, and in particular the Smile Jamaica concert, a free event organized by Marley's people in conjunction with the government and intended to heal political division. The assassination attempt came two days before the concert was scheduled to take place.

For Marley, the concert was a way to help heal a nation divided by political violence. Kingston's ghettos—which were historically aligned with one of the two government parties—were on the verge of war with each other. Prime Minister Michael Manley called a state of emergency to try to protect citizens through measures like imposed curfews, and any songs deemed inflammatory—including Bob's "War," "Crazy Baldheads," "Who the Cap Fit," and "Rat Race," which made up nearly half of his recent *Rastaman Vibration* album— were banned from the radio.

Bob hoped to lift the country's spirits and relieve some of the pressure. The concert was also an opportunity for him to repay the support of the Jamaican people over the previous decade. To this end, he didn't want to charge admission, and in his memoir, Don Taylor recalls him stating, "We nuh need nuh more money out of we Jamaican people." He was inspired by Stevie Wonder's generosity in donating half of his payment for a Jamaican concert to a local school for the blind the year before.

Michael Manley, Jamaican prime minister 1972–1980.   *Public Domain*

Bob's celebrity meant he had the ear of the prime minister, and the day he thought of the concert he called up Michael Manley and almost immediately was granted an audience at his office at Jamaica House, which happened to be a ten-minute walk from 56 Hope Road.

The two even spoke of Marley writing a song—not a tourist song, but a song affirming Jamaica. The result was two versions of the same song, one fast, one slow, with slightly different lyrics: "Smile Jamaica Part 1" and "Smile Jamaica Part 2." Lee Perry recorded them both, but the fast one was done at Black Ark and the slow one at Harry J.'s. Bob wanted to perform at the concert with the original Wailers, so he invited Peter and Bunny to play with him. They hadn't shared the stage in over a year, since reuniting to open for Stevie Wonder. Neither, however, was interested in the Smile Jamaica project.

Marley was adamant that he didn't want the concert to be in support of any political party, though at the press conference after the meeting, he and Don Taylor billed it as a joint production by Bob Marley and the government. They had also arranged to hold it at Jamaica House. In the diametrical partisan world of domestic politics, this made it look to many as though Bob had officially thrown his support behind Manley.

These optics were compounded shortly thereafter when Manley's party, the People's National Party (PNP), exploited Marley's goodwill and announced a new election for December 20, just two weeks after the concert. This did not please the Bob Marley camp, who were angered that, despite Marley's official relative neutrality in politics, people would now think he was Manley's stooge. With this in mind, Bob moved the venue to Heroes Park Circle and paid for the production costs himself.

If the shooting was supposed to scare him away from performing—or, indeed, finish him off—it didn't work. Lying low for two days, Bob rejected calls to cancel the show, even though some of the Wailers refused to play. Then, on Sunday, December 5, 1976, the Smile Jamaica concert went ahead as scheduled, in front of an estimated fifty-to-sixty-thousand concertgoers. Many in Bob's inner circle took to the stage with him, creating a buffer between him and any potential attackers. Rita dramatically appeared onstage with her head bandaged. Bob danced ecstatically, and near the end of the performance he opened his shirt to show those present the wound on his chest and pointed to his bandaged elbow.

The entire show all but dared the assailants to try and take him down. His set, which opened with "War / No More Trouble" and lasted over an hour, began with an address to the crowd about recent events that made it clear Bob was above the partisan political fray: "When mi decide to do dis ya concert two and a half months ago, me was told dere was no politics, I just wanted to play fe de love of the people."

In Exile

It was obvious that the political climate was too hot for the King of Reggae. After the concert he was ferreted away into hiding in the Blue Mountains at Chris Blackwell's Strawberry Hills resort, where he had been staying since the shooting, guarded by members of Rastafarian group the Twelve Tribes. He left the island the next day on Blackwell's private plane and began an eighteen-month self-imposed exile. He first went to Nassau, in the Bahamas, where Rita and the kids joined him. Soon, the old entourage of band members, Diane Jobson, and even Cindy Breakspeare appeared—sort of like a Hope Road transported to Compass Point. "Everybody cooked and wrote songs and got a little exercise," Cindy is quoted as saying in Goldman's *Book of Exodus*. "Things didn't change that radically from one place to another. Just different geography."

After three weeks of recuperating and hanging out, Marley flew to London, where he and the band continued work on new material they had started in Jamaica. These recordings would later be released as *Exodus* and *Kaya*.

Why Was Bob Marley Shot?

Depending on who you ask, Bob was shot by one of the two political parties in Jamaica, either by the ruling party (the PNP) as a political martyr, or by the opposition Jamaica Labour Party (JLP) because he was thought to be cozying up to the PNP. Or, he and/or his entourage simply had enemies.

In 1972, Bob Marley stayed in this flat at 34 Ridgemount Gardens in Bloomsbury, London, during his self-imposed exile from Jamaica after the shooting.   *Emanuel Berglund*

That's pretty much the scope of a declassified State Department report on the shooting. The once-confidential document cites three different rumors surrounding the shootout. First, it could have been "an attempt by JLP gunmen to halt the concert which would feature the 'politically progressive' music of Marley." Second, it was "a deep-laid plot to create a progressive, youthful Jamaican martyr—to the benefit of the PNP. Those holding the latter view note that of the four persons shot, three of them—including Marley—suffered only minor wounds." Third, "The assailants may simply be enemies of Marley or one of his associates." Theories floated to support this include the suggestion that these enemies could have targeted Bob because his best friend Skill Cole was implicated in fixing a horse race, so perhaps the attack on Bob was retribution for Cole's alleged transgressions, or that the gunmen were after Don Taylor, a noted gambler.

Notice there's no mention of a CIA-backed plot here, yet that is one of the longest-standing conspiracy theories concerning the assassination. As the chapter on Bob Marley's death explains, there have been recurring rumors of CIA involvement in his ultimate demise. One of the first Marley biographies to be published, Timothy White's *Catch a Fire*, all but preaches this as truth, even providing CIA missives as evidence, though evidence of *what* is left up to the imagination of the reader.

Many believe the shooting was orchestrated by the CIA, which was allegedly working to destabilize the ruling party because of its socialist inclinations—values that Marley shared and appeared to support publicly. Conspiracy theorists point to reports of mystery visitors at Hope Road before the shooting as evidence of CIA operatives scouting the place.

The CIA theory hinges on the American intelligence community's reported dislike of the PNP government's socialism. The idea here is that the American government tried to undermine the PNP—and getting rid of Marley would aid in this—by backing the much more capitalist- and American-friendly JLP. JLP opposition leader Edward Seaga even gained a new nickname on the streets, such was the traction in these rumors: "CIA-ga." A June 1976 *Chicago Tribune* article about the political violence reported, under the headline "Jamaicans See CIA Behind the Bullets," that "CIA-ga" graffiti could be found around Kingston. Rumors of CIA involvement on the island also no doubt led to the line, "Rasta don't work for no CIA," in Bob's own "Rat Race."

The CIA conspiracy theories gained further traction when it was discovered that former agency head William Colby's son, Carl, was a cameraman in the crew set to film the Smile Jamaica concert. Carl had landed in Kingston on the day of the shooting—perhaps he was working for the US intelligence agency? Alas, probably not. In an interview with Roger Steffens in 2001, he denied these outlandish accusations, adding that he wasn't even aware that he had been implicated in these conspiracy theories.

Tuff Gong: Bob and the Gangsters

CIA plot or not, Marley was no stranger to the Jamaican criminal underground. In fact, known political thugs were regulars at Hope Road. Rita remembers that Bob commanded more respect that the prime minister among murderers and gunmen, who would insist on meeting with him at all hours of the day and night. Some of these characters included JLP enforcers Claudie Massop (the leader of the Phoenix gang and the don of Tivoli Gardens) and Tek Life. In an obituary for Massop—who died in a shootout with the police in February 1979—the *Gleaner* wrote that, while he was never convicted, his rap sheet was lengthy, with charges of perjury, armed robbery, and murder to his name. In fact, he had been charged with eleven murders, but the only thing he was ever convicted of was illegal possession of a firearm.

From the PNP side, gangsters like Bucky Marshall and Tony Welch hung out at Hope Road, too. The shady characters around Bob were, no doubt, used as muscle—having gunmen around for bodyguards should have been good for security. But it might have also made sense in Kingston's climate of near warfare. Bob attempted to steer clear of political patronage by remaining apolitical, and maintaining ties to both sides could certainly have helped him to play it safe.

When people inquired about these characters, Bob would say he was letting them live at Hope Road because he was reforming them. He was authentically interested in bringing together all of Kingston's slum-dwellers because he felt they should all work together against the real enemy: Babylon. So, reforming gangsters, and helping them find common ground, could certainly have been part of his plan.

Political Affiliations

Bob's own political affiliations leaned toward the PNP. And, as a musician in Kingston, being aligned with a political party was the norm, not the exception. The Jamaican music industry has deep connections to the island's politics. Edward Seaga, Jamaica's fifth prime minister (1980–1989), was once a record producer. Michael Manley used Delroy Wilson's "Better Must Come" for his successful campaign song in the 1972 election, and he wielded a staff—the Rod of Correction—given to him by Selassie himself. This and the fact that he intimated he might look favorably toward decriminalization of ganja and assist repatriation to Africa meant that Rastas like Marley generally held him in high regard.

Musicians were often aligned with the political party that represented their neighborhood. Trench Town, where Marley grew up, was affiliated with the PNP, though Saint Ann—the parish of his birth—was staunchly JLP. The Wailers had aided Manley's PNP campaign, performing on the PNP Musical Bandwagon in 1971 and 1972. This would seem to indicate clear support for the PNP, though Bunny Wailer told Roger Steffens that they did it for the money, and that just because they performed on a political campaign tour didn't mean they supported the candidate.

The Wailers also performed at a Marvin Gaye benefit for the Trench Town Sports Complex organized by PNP MP Tony Spaulding—the same politician behind the Smile concert. Based on this, manager Don Taylor has said that Marley supported the PNP, though it is doubtful that the man who once sang, "Never let a politician grant you a favor / He will always want to control you forever" ("Revolution") would have put it in those blunt terms. Bob was friends with supporters of both parties—Cindy Breakspeare, for instance, was a JLP supporter—and the men who hung around his home were from both sides of the political divide. And, by the middle of the decade, Marley was not about to throw public support behind any one party when the country was so violently divided.

A Dangerous Life

Bob Marley was living a dangerous life. In the political quagmire of Jamaica, he was seen to be affiliated with the ruling party, despite his efforts otherwise, and he had no qualms about housing enforcers from both sides at his residence, mere steps away from Jamaica House. He brought international attention to Jamaica, which was good, but he also brought attention to its domestic problems, which was not so good. So, in the lead-up to the Smile Jamaica concert, both parties were nervous, and both were eyeing him suspiciously.

Don Taylor has summed up the quandary this way: PNP gunmen began to fear that Bob was disloyal, playing both sides in case Seaga managed to win the next election, while JLP operatives Claudie Massop and Tek Life had warned Bob not to do the show because they saw it as an endorsement for Manley. Rita alleges that JLP thugs threatened to kill Bob if he refused to cancel the show. The tensions grew to the point that I-Threes singer Marcia Griffiths left for New York because of the death threats.

One Love Peace Concert

The attempted murder of Bob Marley was traumatic for the island. Vivien Goldman, who covered the shooting in 1976, later articulated the effect of the event on the Jamaican psyche in *Book of Exodus*: "More than just a favorite son, Bob had become the island's hope. Articulating Jamaica's aspirations, Bob had virtually single-handedly shattered the country's rigid class structure and united a population whose national motto was 'Out of many, one people,' but whose color-conscious inhabitants, still haunted by the British class system, rarely acted out that ideal."

In the wake of near tragedy, the Smile Jamaica concert did little to quell the violence. People wanted Bob home, and until he came there would be no peace.

Perhaps Bob's attempt at reforming gunmen was working, however, because the ghetto gangsters themselves seemed to have realized by the end of 1977 that the bloodshed had to stop. The key moment came when top JLP warlord Claudie Massop found himself sharing a jail cell with a PNP thug named Bucky Marshall. Both men were good friends of Marley's, and they began talking about how they could instigate a ceasefire between the gangs. Claudie's idea was a peace concert. Both Massop and Marshall met with Bob at the Keskidee Centre in London to ask him to call off his self-imposed exile and return to the country to host a peace concert. One peace concert had sent him into exile, and now another would bring him home.

What is remembered as the One Love Peace Concert in April 1978 was a triumphant return for Bob Marley. It was truly a reggae/Rasta/ghetto homecoming, with plenty of dreadlocked reggae heavyweights gracing the stage: Culture, Big Youth, Dennis Brown, the Meditations, Jacob Miller and Inner Circle, Beres Hammond, Peter Tosh, and Ras Michael and the Sons of Negus. But the crowning achievement was when Bob brought onstage Prime Minister Michael Manley and opposition leader Edward Seaga and made them shake hands in a gesture of peace. This was seen as a major coup, and one thought to be nearly impossible in the world of Jamaica's zero-sum politics.

What Happened to the Gunmen?

The police investigation into the attempted killing of Jamaica's biggest star did not turn up any solid names and did not result in any convictions. Various names of alleged gunmen have been printed in books on Bob; though none provide solid evidence as to who the culprits were, they are generally thought to have met with ghetto justice. Bob did not see his attackers, but he sensed that he probably knew them; perhaps they had been among those looking for handouts at Hope Road.

Don Taylor has provided ambiguous information about the shooters. At one point, he implicated JLP organizer and Marley confident Claudie Massop. According to Taylor, Bob predicted that the attacker would die by the same amount of bullets fired—fifty-six. Massop, Taylor said, was shot fifty-six times (though the *Gleaner* reported forty). However, this is unlikely, as Massop was in jail at the time of the assassination attempt.

Taylor's other information about the identities and fate of the shooters suggests that Massop actually helped apprehend them. In his recounting of the events, Bob's manager writes that he and Bob were invited to a sort of ghetto court near MacGregor Gully in June 1978—a year and a half after the incident— where three men were tried for the attempted murder of Bob Marley. All were found guilty. Two were hanged and one shot in the head, as witnessed by both Marley and Taylor. A fourth suspect was said to have died soon after of a drug overdose.

This version of events contrasts with the one given by journalist Vivien Goldman in her *Book of Exodus*. Based on interviews with people close to the events, including Massop's widow, Goldman writes that Massop phoned Bob from jail to warn him that JLP henchmen were going to try to kill him. Specifically, the danger was from Massop's rival for leadership of the JLP-affiliated Phoenix Gang, Lester Coke, a.k.a. Jim Brown. Laurie Gunst's history of Jamaican gang culture, *Born Fi' Dead: A Journey Through the Jamaican Posse Underworld*, claims that Bob had indeed seen his attacker, and that he told Trevor Phillips of the Central Peace Council it was Coke. Coke, like Massop, was a JLP henchman, but, unlike Massop, he was more interested in drug trafficking and his own rise to power than toeing any party line. Coke was not apprehended on this charge, however, and he went on to rule the Tivoli Garden area of Kingston as leader of the Shower Posse throughout the eighties. His organization subsequently emerged as a notorious North American cocaine trafficking gang. He died in custody in 1992, while awaiting extradition to the US.

Incidentally, Coke's son, Christopher "Dudus" Coke, later took over the Shower Posse and was the subject to a US extradition request in 2009. The Jamaican government initially refused, but when it finally agreed to enforce the extradition in May 2010, it set off violent protests among Coke's supporters that resulted in a state of emergency being called and seventy-four people losing their lives. Coke is currently serving a twenty-three-year sentence in the United States.

13

Duppy Conqueror

Sickness and Death

Cancer carried Bob Marley away in Miami on May 11, 1981, after an eight-month battle. In death, he has commanded as much attention as he did in life. As noted already, his death has been the subject of conspiracy theories (some wild, some tame) involving the CIA, and it led some to believe that the reggae industry itself would crumble. This chapter looks at the events leading up to his death and surveys the various conspiracy theories.

Did Bob Marley Die of a Soccer Injury?

Bob Marley loved soccer and played the game daily. Sometimes, his death is even attributed to it. Bob died of cancer, but the cancer began as a malignant melanoma on the skin under the nail of the big toe on his right foot. The melanoma metastasized, eventually spreading to his internal organs, including his brain.

While soccer didn't cause the initial cancer, he had injured his toe several times while playing the game, unknowingly aggravating the malignant lesion. He first hurt it in September 1975, when a soccer cleat ran over it. Dismissing it as a routine sports injury, he didn't seek medical attention, even though the toe continued to hurt and refused to heal. Rita subsequently insisted that he stop playing soccer, but of course he didn't, and he injured the toe again in May 1977, during a game in Paris while touring *Exodus*. This time, Rita demanded that Bob show his foot to Don Taylor, who had a doctor examine it at the hotel. The doctor removed the nail and bandaged the toe, but that was the extent of the treatment. According to Taylor's memoir, "From that day, Bob was never completely healthy again."

The wound still festered. Soon after this incident, Bob was examined by a second doctor in London and diagnosed with melanoma. He was given an ultimatum—either the toe or the tour—although his physician, Carl "Pee Wee" Fraser, later told Roger Steffens that the London doctors actually wanted to amputate his leg. Being a Rasta, Bob was suspicious of Western medicines, preferring natural medicines and depending instead on the healing properties of marijuana. When he heard about the plan to remove his toe, Timothy White writes in *Catch a Fire*, he reportedly stated, "Rasta no abide amputation. I and I don't allow a mon ta be dismantled. Jah, de living God, His Imperial Majesty Haile Selassie I, Ras Tafari, Conquering Lion of the Tribe of Judah, two hundred twenty-fifth ruler of the t'ree-t'ousand-year-old Ethiopian empire, Lord of Lords, King of Kings, Heir to the Throne of Solomon, He will heal me wit' de meditations of me ganja chalice, me cutchie, or He will tek me as a son inta His Kingdom. No scalpel shall crease me flesh! Dem cyan't kill Jah, cyna kill Rasta. Rastamon live out."

Bob outright rejected these Babylonian prognoses, refusing to even believe that he could have cancer, especially because, like both Rita and Don Taylor, he believed that melanoma was a disease of white people. Skin cancer, they surmised, usually occurs as a result of sun damage on white skin. There was also the possibility that, because he was of mixed racial heritage, his skin would be more susceptible to the sun's UV rays, but still this seemed pretty far-fetched.

What they didn't know at the time was that the kind of skin cancer Bob had was not the result of sun exposure. Acral lentiginous melanoma (ALM) is a rare form of melanoma and can occur in people of African descent. In fact, at the time of Marley's death it was not yet documented as a distinct melanoma. According to Jamaican podiatrist Angela Davis, ALM accounts for just over a third of all skin cancers found in people of color. ALM commonly infects hairless—or acral—skin, the kind found under the nails and on the palms and soles of feet. It is a fast-growing cancer and can cross into the dermis, where it is able to spread throughout the body. Whereas other forms of skin cancer are attributed to UV radiation, ALM is likely genetic. Despite some sources suggesting the soccer injury gave Bob cancer, then, this is not how melanoma develops. Early detection increases the chance of survival, but in Marley's case the lesion was initially thought to have resulted from the soccer injury, not cancer, so was not attended to.

First Treatments

On Taylor's recommendation, Bob sought a second opinion from Dr. Bacon, the black Miami physician who had operated on Taylor after the assassination attempt. Bacon was originally skeptical of the melanoma diagnosis, as it was indeed rare in darker skinned people, but after running tests he confirmed it. The cancer diagnosis confused Bob, who according to Stephen Davis told his mother, "Why Jah let me have cancer, momma? I never do anybody anything that is bad."

It also caused uproar within the Twelve Tribes of Israel, whose leader, Prophet Gad, flew to Miami to tell Bob that a Rasta can't have cancer, so the diagnosis must be an error. (Or, perhaps he was insinuating that if Bob did have cancer, he wasn't a real Rasta?) Bob sought a third opinion from his Rastafarian doctor, Pee Wee Fraser, who confirmed what the other two doctors had already found. The American leg of the *Exodus* tour was canceled to allow Bob to get treatment, but the official story was that he was suffering from exhaustion.

According to Rita Marley, Dr. Bacon told her he could stop the spread of the cancer if Bob allowed him to remove the toe. Bob was unwilling to undergo the amputation, though, fearing that it could leave him unable to stand and dance onstage and might end his performing career. In the end, he allowed Dr. Bacon to surgically remove the lesion on the toe and graft new skin over the area.

Bob convalesced for a few months and was then given a clean bill of health. After that, of course, he went back to his daily regime of soccer and planning the 1978 world tour for *Kaya*.

The Beginning of the End

Bob was very active in the wake of his first surgery, releasing three albums and touring extensively in 1978, 1979, and 1980, even venturing further afield to Japan, Australia, New Zealand, Hawaii, Gabon, and Zimbabwe. But the surgery was ultimately not successful, and the cancer spread to his liver, lungs, and brain. This wasn't discovered until September 1980, but according to Davis's *Conquering Lion of Reggae*, Bob's bandmates had noticed that he seemed ill earlier in the summer, while Bob had told guitarist Al Anderson, "I got a pain in my throat and my head, and it's killing me. It's like somebody's trying to kill me. I feel like I've been poisoned. And something wrong with me voice. I've never felt this before in my life."

After the Wailers opened for the Commodores for two nights at Madison Square Garden, New York, in mid-September, Bob played soccer and went jogging in Central Park with Skill Cole and Pee Wee. It was a Sunday morning, September 21. He collapsed while exercising, complaining that his body had frozen up. Skill Cole told Malika Lee Whitney that he saw Bob twist and shake and unable to talk: "Foam start to come out his mouth and a bredren come and hold him hand and squeeze it and he was getting speechless and him color start to change. That go on for almost a minute, it come like a man have epileptic fits." They took him to the hospital, and then the following day Pee Wee took him to see a neurologist, who determined that the collapse was due to a stroke and, worse, that the cancer had returned vigorously as a brain tumor. Bob was given two or three weeks to live.

Second Treatments

The rest of the tour had to be canceled, but Bob played one final show, at Pittsburgh's Stanley Theatre, on September 23. That night's events were recounted thirty years later in the *Pittsburgh Post-Gazette*. A booking agent reportedly told the promoter, "I would be surprised if he plays," but play Bob did, telling the promoter, "I wasn't going to, I'm going to for my band and everybody. It's a sold-out show," adding, "The guys need the money."

Bob was taken to the Cedars of Lebanon Hospital in Miami for further tests, and then to the Memorial Sloan Kettering Cancer Center in New York. He underwent radiation therapy and then, after another stroke, chemotherapy. The treatment caused his mighty dreadlocks to fall out, and he became paralyzed temporarily from the waist down.

Third and Final Treatments

Some in Bob's circle were urging him to try alternative, nontoxic treatments, as the chemotherapy seemed to be having little effect. Pee Wee and Skill Cole managed to track down Dr. Josef Issels who was lecturing in New York. Issels was a holistic doctor shunned by the medical community—the American Cancer Society had deemed his treatments ineffective. He specialized in terminal cancer patients at his Sunshine House clinic in Bad Wiessee, Bavaria, Germany. He agreed to take Bob on as a patient, and Bob was flown by Concorde to London before arriving in the Bavarian Alps on November 9, 1980.

Issels's practice is known as Integrative Immuno-Oncology and focuses on treatments that enhance the body's natural defenses while destroying cancer cells. His methods included a strict diet, tonsillectomy, hyperthermia, blood transfusions, removal of any unhealthy teeth, ultraviolet light therapy, and injections of Interferon. Bob was supposed to avoid ganja too, but a friend smuggled some in every fortnight.

During this time, the press and fans were kept in the dark. The official word was that Bob was suffering from exhaustion, until newspapers broke the story in mid-November that Bob had cancer.

The Issels clinic kept Bob alive for longer than the American doctors had predicted, but the treatment was ultimately unsuccessful. Surrounded by friends and family in the Alps, Bob endured his treatment over the winter months. His weight dropped but his hair began to grow back. In March, he gave an optimistic interview to London's *Daily Mail*, but by May he was down to seventy pounds and too weak to eat. Dr. Issels discharged him from the clinic, effectively to go home to die.

Bob asked Chris Blackwell to charter a plane so that he could fly home to Jamaica, but he never made it. His journey ended in Miami, where Ciddy lived, and where he asked his whole family to join him. He was admitted to the Cedars of Lebanon Hospital on May 9, where he died two days later, at the age of thirty-six. He left no will.

Conspiracy Theories

Elvis disappeared; he didn't die. Tupac faked his own death. Paul McCartney was killed in a car accident in 1966, and the bloke that's been posing as him ever since is just a *doppelganger*. The US government killed John Lennon because he was critical of American foreign policy. Kurt Cobain was killed by his wife.

Sometimes fans can't accept the death of the stars they adore, so they turn to conspiracy theories for comfort. Bob Marley's death is no different. There are many stories about how he died, and some even point the finger at the CIA.

Was Bob Marley Killed by the CIA?

Investigative journalist Alex Constantine believes the CIA was behind the assassination attempt on Bob before the Smile Jamaica concert and his paranoid book, *The Covert War Against Rock*, charges that they were ultimately successful. How did they try and kill him? First, through a hail of bullets and then, apparently, it was a case of "death by shoe."

In the December 1976 attempt on Bob's life at his Hope Road residence, it is alleged that there were shady characters hanging around on the day of the shooting, believed to be CIA operatives. According to Constantine, one of these—Carl Colby, the son of former CIA director William Colby—was pretending to be part of the camera crew at the Smile Jamaica concert. He allegedly gave a gift to the singer: a pair of boots. These were no ordinary shoes, however, but "assassin shoes" containing cancerous cells on a copper wire that would stick into the toe of the wearer. According to *The Covert War Against Rock*, an American cinematographer who witnessed this claimed, "He put his foot in and said, 'Ow!'" Then, when he looked in the boot, he "pulled a length of copper wire out—it was embedded in the boot." The theory goes that Bob pricked his right big toe on the wire and contracted cancer. Six months later, he was diagnosed with cancer in London.

As far-fetched as this sounds, that the CIA might be interested in Bob Marley is not all that hard to believe. After all, they had kept tabs on John Lennon, who, like Marley, was an outspoken left-wing artist and a counterculture hero. In

Jamaica, Bob Marley was a powerful man with great political clout. Rumors swirled that the CIA wanted the socialist-leaning and Castro-loving Manley government out and had thrown its weight behind opposition leader Edward Seaga. Michael Manley writes in his memoirs that the CIA denied any attempt to destabilize his government in the seventies, but that he and the heads of the Jamaican security forces (the police and the army) believed that the CIA was behind many malicious events, including three assassination attempts on Manley himself.

But even if the CIA's interest in Manley and Marley's careers seems to contain some truth, the wire theory does not. Cancer cannot be contracted in this way. And, for his part, Colby has denied any knowledge of or participation in such a nefarious plot. But then he would, wouldn't he?

Lasers, Lead Poisoning, and Nazis

A few other theories have been floated that bear similarities to the one that Bob caught cancer from some cells on a copper wire. These include Bob being poisoned, submitted unknowingly to cancer-causing rays in his hotel rooms (or at home), or ultimately succumbing to lead poisoning from the bullets that grazed his skin in the botched 1976 assassination attempt. Another suggests that lasers were hidden in the stage lights of his shows to burn through to his brain, presumably causing the tumor. Some believe that Dr. Issels intentionally killed Marley in Bavaria, even alleging that Issels worked for the S.S. during World War II, and that he practiced alongside the "Angel of Death," Dr. Joseph Mengele, at Auschwitz. As a Nazi doctor, he would have been steeped in Fascist racial doctrines, and would have welcomed the chance to finish off the man he allegedly called "one of the most dangerous black men in the world."

Rita Marley and Chris Blackwell, Unlikely Assassins

Bunny Wailer was Bob's half-brother and bandmate, and one of his oldest friends. He was hit hard by the passing of Marley, and in the intervening years he has concocted some astonishing accusations, completely devoid of evidence. These center around his duel hatred of Rita Marley—the woman he says tricked Bob into marrying her, and then conspired to steal all his money—and Chris Blackwell, a man he has likened to a slave owner in the context of the Wailers' career.

As noted in chapter 6, Bunny vented his anger publicly on his blog at tuff-gongrecords.blogspot.ca, stating that the two conspired to kill Bob Marley using a "drug" he calls "Radio Active Ash." It is not clear what this is, or how this occurred, but he has insinuated that they were in league with the CIA.

14

Come to the Burial

The Three Funerals

Marley was large in life, no doubt. And he was also large in death—so large, in fact, that one funeral was not enough to effectively send him on his way to Zion. Bob died on May 11, 1981, and was memorialized three times in the days that followed before finally being laid to rest. His official public funeral was also his third, during which Jamaica ground to a halt for a day of mourning. The government even postponed the tabling of its budget, and Prime Minister Seaga delivered the eulogy at the National Stadium. Afterward, Marley's body was carried in the back of a pickup truck some fifty-five miles along country roads lined with mourners to his final resting place in Nine Mile.

First Funeral: Miami, Wednesday, May 13

Even though Don Taylor had been dismissed from Bob's services in early 1979, his name remained on many of Bob's business ventures. Bob had called him shortly before he died and asked him to make sure that his money went to his children. In hindsight, it seems as though it would have been simple enough for Bob to make a will to that effect, but he told Taylor that he was being pressured to sign wills by various interests—Rita, the Twelve Tribes of Israel, and Diane Jobson among them. Curiously, he refused them all, so it fell to Taylor to try to make sense of the financial quagmire left behind.

This is how Taylor happened to be in town when Bob died in Miami: he had planned to meet Bob to work on the details of succession, but he was too late. Instead, he found himself taking on a managerial role again as he asked the Grange Funeral Parlor to prepare the body for burial and made arrangements for funerals in Florida and Jamaica.

The first funeral was held at the house Bob had asked Don Taylor to purchase for his mother—"a big one like she used to clean for white people"—on Vista Lane in Miami. Rita flew friends in from all over, and the procession of guests lasted all day. Rasta symbols abounded; the Ethiopian flag stretched out from the roof of the

Bob Marley's casket, from the liner notes to Alan Greenberg's *Land of Look Behind* DVD.

Author's collection

house, and Rasta drummers played in the yard as they passed the chalice among them. There was a short service, and Ciddy sang "Redemption Song."

Coxsone Dodd, Bob's producer at Studio One, was one of the mourners who approached the bronze casket where the superstar was laid, a wig made of his own dreadlocks adorning his head. In his hands was a Bible turned to the twenty-third Psalm. Ciddy urged mourners to talk to Bob, to testify to him. In the liner notes to the DVD *Land of Look Behind*, filmmaker Alan Greenberg provides his recollections from the day. He describes how Dodd spoke to the body, saying, "Bob, I'm sure you remember your first public concert, in Spanish Town it was. You know I grabbed you after the show, and over and over and over I shouted, 'First you sing the song, Bob and *then* you dance!'"

Jimmy Cliff, the onscreen outlaw of *The Harder They Come* and one of Jamaica's foremost reggae stars, stepped up to the casket and remembered the first day he met Bob at Beverley's: "You know it was I who gave you your first break. I helped you get off the street."

During the wake, Diane Jobson told mourners that Marley had just appeared to her and asked to have his guitar laid in the casket with him. She fetched the turquoise Ovation from the singer's bedroom and placed it in his arms. She added that Marley also wanted Jobson to prevail upon Alan Greenberg, who was present, to make a film to "protect his legacy."

Greenberg, a friend of Marley's who had met him while growing up in Miami, had some film experience but had never actually made one of his own. He had worked, uncredited, as a "glass transporter" on Werner Herzog's 1976 film *Heart of Glass*, and he would subsequently write about this experience in a book of the same name. Despite his lack of experience, however, the Marley family seemed content with Bob's instructions from beyond and agreed to enlist Greenberg's services.

The resulting film's working title was *Marley Nuh Dead*, but it was eventually released as *Land of Look Behind*. It contains footage of both Jamaican funerals and a reggae tribute to Bob at the Kingston concert venue Skateland with Gregory Isaacs and Lui Lepki.

Second Funeral: Kingston Maxfield Park Ethiopian Orthodox Church, Thursday, May 21, 8:00 a.m.

Bob's body was flown home to Jamaica on Tuesday, May 19. Edward Seaga had finally beaten Michael Manley and formed a JLP government in October 1980. In what some have called an attempt to defuse Bob Marley's revolutionary legacy by making him a government-sanctioned national hero, the JLP had awarded him the Jamaican Order of Merit for his outstanding contribution to the country's culture a month before his death, and had offered to give him a state funeral. Seaga called Marley shortly before his death to say that his gov-

ernment was being petitioned by the people to confer this award on him, and that he hoped Bob would approve. As recounted by the *New York Times* in 1981, Bob's response was, "Big man, if you can do it, do it." (Cynics point out that these strategic moves effectively allowed the new prime minister to exploit Marley's death for his government's benefit, just as the Manley government had exploited his celebrity during the Smile Jamaica concert fiasco.)

On Wednesday, May 20, Marley's body lay in state at Kingston's National Stadium. The JLP called off a budget vote and announced a national day of mourning so that thousands of fans could file past his body. Conservative estimates suggest forty thousand people showed up to the viewing, while more liberal counts peg the number at more than one hundred

Alan Greenberg's documentary *Land of Look Behind*, which includes footage of Bob Marley's funeral. The documentary's working title was *Marley Nuh Dead*.

Author's collection

thousand. As the mourners waited at the gates, the ever-present higglers hocked refreshments, and when the lines dissolved and people surged forward, the police used tear gas to stop people rushing the arena gate.

On May 21, Marley's body was moved to the Kingston Maxfield Park Ethiopian Orthodox Church for a semi-private service at 8:00 a.m. Abouna Yesehaq, Archbishop of the Ethiopian Orthodox Church in the Western Hemisphere, officiated, speaking in Geez, Amharic, and English. Film crews captured priests chanting, burning incense, and preaching. After the service, the body was carried via motorcade past 56 Hope Road and onto the National Arena.

Third Funeral: National Stadium, Thursday, May 21, 11:00 a.m.

The official funeral of Bob Marley was a public ceremony held at the National Arena, attended by government officials, reporters, international film crews, and, of course, everyday Jamaicans. It was significant not only because it was a celebration of the life of Jamaica's most famous son but also as the largest state funeral in Caribbean history. It was a funeral fit for a head of state—or, indeed, a king.

The funeral showed the boundaries that Marley bridged in life and death: the Christian and the Rastafarian, the Jamaican and the African, the pop star and the revolutionary, the celebrity and the holy man, the social elite and ghetto dweller, the political agitator and political pawn. Marley's casket was draped in two flags, Jamaica's and Ethiopia's, with the latter's colors of red, gold, and green representing both Rastafari and the country of Ras Tafari's birth. Edward Seaga gave the eulogy at the funeral, explaining that Marley "translated into music, in a remarkable style, the aspirations, pain and feeling of millions of people throughout the world." Michael Manley shared the stage with him, calling Marley a "genius" who turned a folk art into "a part of the universal language of the arts of the world." The fact that both these men spoke is symbolic, making clear Marley's political clout and importance to the state.

Marley's complex religious beliefs were represented by both Christian and Rastafarian delegates, though the tension between them was palpable. The liturgy was led by Ethiopian Orthodox priests, the sanctioned officiants of the event, but filmmaker Alan Greenberg remembers that the Twelve Tribes of Israel delegation—dressed in the white robes and wearing red, gold, and green tams, or banners—greeted every mention of Jesus Christ with "irate catcalls and fiery protestations."

The Twelve Tribes were incensed that they had been largely left out of the funerary rites, even though there was no precedent for a Rasta funeral, as Rastas didn't even believe in the existence of death and thus avoided the dead. The tension came to a head when Skill Cole, asked to read scripture, took the opportunity to make a statement on behalf of the Twelve Tribes, including in it a proclamation of Selassie's divinity. In what would later be called the "capture of the ceremonies," Cole read, "We the twelve Tribes of Israel, that are scattered abroad, greet each and every one of you in the name of our Lord and Savior Jesus Christ, who is this day revealed in the personality of His Imperial Majesty, Emperor H. Selassie I, the First! We also preach to you through Faith, which is a function of the heart, acquired through a mystic incorporation, or unity in One. Knowing that, man's body is the temple of the Living God–Selassie I!"

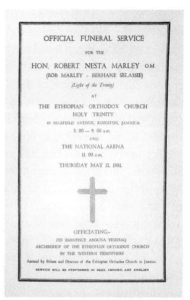

The funeral program, from the liner notes to Alan Greenberg's *Land of Look Behind* DVD.   *Author's collection*

The funeral also included a performance by the Wailers, who backed up Bob's sons, Ziggy and Stephen, while they danced next to their father's casket. The I-Threes sang "Natural Mystic" and "Rastaman Chant," bidding farewell to their patriarch with a lyric derived from the gospel favorite "I'll Fly Away": "Fly away home to Zion."

The motorcade carrying Marley's casket traveled from Kingston to his childhood home in Nine Mile along roads lined with mourners. Nine Mile itself hosted thousands more people, who watched the graveside ceremony and the sealing of the tomb.

Wait, a Rasta Funeral?

As explained later in this book, in the chapter on the attempt to move Bob's body to Ethiopia, there is a longstanding belief among Rastas that they are somehow immune to death as long as they remain faithful to Haile Selassie. When it was reported in the media in 1975 that Selassie had died, Rastas greeted the news as false, because God can't die, as Marley's own "Jah Live" attests.

Going along with this denial of death is an aversion to anything associated with death, including corpses, animal-based food products, and funeral rites. This aversion can be traced to the fear of contamination by dead things held traditionally by Jamaican peasants, but whereas they developed elaborate death rites to ensure the spirit of the deceased made the transition from this world smoothly, Rastas have regarded these practices as superstition. Instead, they steer clear of any funeral rites. Given this, then, Marley's elaborate funeral (all three of them) was highly exceptional.

For many, a Rasta funeral would be an oxymoron, yet Marley had three. His state funeral—and the annual celebrations of his death held first in Nine Mile—have also contributed to the normalizing of death rituals and commemoration among Rastafarians. Other prominent Rastas who have since passed away, such as Prophet Gad and Mortimo Planno, have also had large public funerals. Peter Tosh—the man who sang, "I no go no one burial," and refused to go to Bob's—was also given a state funeral, and is interred in a mausoleum of his own, open to fans.

The death of such a prominent Rastafarian in 1981 forced the movement to revisit their beliefs surrounding death, sin, and even funerals. Its followers had to confront for the first time the need for tradition-specific burial rites. It seems, then, that thanks to Bob Marley, the traditional Rasta belief of everlasting life and repatriation to Zion in this lifetime has shifted to make room for the contingency of death.

15

Mighty Dread Can't Dead

Bob's Posthumous Financial Power

In 2013 the Kings of Pop, Rock, and Reggae ranked as the #1, #2, and #3 highest-earning dead musicians, in that order. John Lennon, by the way, occupied the fourth position. Bob, in other words, was in excellent company.

Rita Marley has said that Bob didn't die a millionaire, but his manager disputes this, saying that the estate had $17 million in overseas accounts, with a total of $30 million in the band's, at the time. At the time of his death, Bob owned several properties, including 56 Hope Road and Ian Fleming's Golden Eye estate, and several companies, like Bob Marley Music and Media Aides Limited, which

Released in 1984, the career retrospective *Legend* still sells up to a quarter of a million albums annually and has been certified platinum fifteen times in the United States. *Author's collection*

One Drop Coffee, one of the many products that utilize the Marley
name.   *Photo by Mike Mozart, Creative Commons license*

House of Marley leverages the musical legacy of Bob Marley to
entice consumers into buying products such as these natural wood
speakers.   *Photo by Jason Cipriani, Creative Commons license*

The number of products featuring Marley's image is astonishing.
Feel like an aromatic reggae candle? Try this "Positive Vibration
Patchouli."   *Author's collection*

administered a growing music empire. Chris Blackwell subsequently purchased the publishing rights to his songs for $12 million.

Since his death, Bob has only become richer—much richer. To give you an example of just how wealthy the estate is, Bob is the only Caribbean artist ever to find himself in the *Forbes* list of top-earning celebrities, dead or alive. The current value of the Marley name is pegged at around $130 million. When you put his worth up against nonmusical celebrities, he drops a bit in the *Forbes* ranking. In 2017, the magazine estimated his income at $23 million, making him the fifth-highest-earning dead celebrity, beat out only by Elvis Presley (#4, with $35 million), Charles Schulz (#3, with $38 million), Arnold Palmer (#2, with $40 million), and Michael Jackson (#1, with $75 million). That makes him the third-highest-paid dead musician. In 2016, the magazine ranked him as the sixth-highest-earning dead celebrity and fourth-highest-paid dead musician, with an annual income of $21 million. He was beaten by Prince (#5, with $25 million), Elvis Presley (#4, with $27 million), Arnold Palmer (#3, with $40 million), Charles Schulz (#2, with $48 million), and Michael Jackson (the top earner, with a stunning $825 million). Still, that makes him the fourth-highest-paid dead musician. He was even higher up the ladder in 2015, due to the fact that neither Palmer nor Prince had joined the list yet, though his earnings remained constant, at $21 million.

In 2014, Marley was again the third highest-paid dead musician, but the fifth dead celebrity, with Michael Jackson, Elvis, Charles Schulz, and Elizabeth Taylor outranking him. His earning power has been steadily increasing, too; in 2002–2003, he pulled in $9 million.

So where does all this money come from? Well, he's sold over seventy-five million albums, so that's a good start, while 1984's *Legend* moves up to a quarter of a million units annually, more than thirty years after its release. To date, it has been certified platinum twenty times in New Zealand, fifteen times in the US, and eleven times in the UK. In total, seven of Marley's albums have been certified gold in the US, four in the UK.

Marley's popularity has only increased since his death. He may have a paltry 62,074 YouTube subscribers, but his fan base increases when looking at other social-media platforms. With over 73 million Facebook fans, and more than 1.4 million Twitter followers, Starcount, which tracks users on eleven digital platforms, including those previously mentioned, estimates that he has currently the second-highest social-media following of any dead celebrity (after Michael Jackson). His total social-media following amounts to 42.6 million people, just beating out Tupac Shakur and easily defeating John Lennon, Elvis Presley, Whitney Houston, Jimi Hendrix, and the Notorious B.I.G.

There are lots of ways to leave money in Marley's—or his heirs'—pockets. You can't leave Kingston or Montego Bay without passing a Marley/Tuff Gong

Trading Store, and, if you are so inclined, you could try to book a recording session at Kingston's Tuff Gong Recording Studios, which is one of the largest in the Caribbean. You could also drop money at the Bob Marley Museum in Kingston, or the Bob Marley Mausoleum in Nine Mile, both of which house Marley-branded gift shops and restaurants.

Of course, the bottom line is helped immensely by the aggressive branding by his heirs as part of a portfolio that includes the Marley Beverage company, Marley Coffee, House of Marley audio products, Hope Road Merchandising, Zion Rootswear, the Marley Resort and Spa in Nassau, Marley Natural marijuana and accessories, Tuff Gong Pictures, and numerous licensing deals to put Bob's name and image on products ranging from musical instruments to stationary. When the man sang, "You a go tired fe see me face," in "Bad Card," he wasn't kidding.

Part 2

The Music

16

Do the Reggae

Telling the Difference Between Ska, Rocksteady, and Reggae

You probably already know that Bob Marley is the King of Reggae. But what even is reggae? Did he invent it? No. Did he play music besides reggae? Yes. Is all Jamaican music called reggae? No. Is ska reggae? No. And what the heck are rocksteady, dub, and dancehall?

Like most genres, reggae has become an umbrella term for numerous styles of music. It generally refers to the popular music of Jamaica from about 1968 onward, and it consists of several subgenres such as roots reggae, lover's rock, dancehall, and dub. Some people make a division between dancehall, which they see as a modern derivative akin to rap, and reggae, which connotes the music artists like Bob Marley made in the seventies and continued on in full-band vocal music by bands like Black Uhuru, Steel Pulse, and Aswad.

Dancehall came to prominence in the late seventies and early eighties and was characterized, initially, by deejays and singers voicing over rhythms played by a sound system at a live dance. Bob Marley did not record any music that could be considered dancehall, although deejays like U-Roy did toast over Wailers rhythms. The music that Bob Marley is most associated with internationally, by the way, is usually called roots reggae, or conscious reggae.

Reggae as a term was first applied in 1968, and, depending on who you talk to, was coined either by Toots and the Maytals' "Do the Reggay" or Don Tony Lee's "Regay Time." Before that, Jamaican popular music was called rocksteady (1966–1968), which was itself preceded by ska (circa 1960–1965). The origins of the word date back to the Yoruban term *rege-rege*, meaning rough, and also to Tobago, where it meant uncultured. It was also known in Jamaica to mean untidy. The implication is compelling: the rich cultural heritage of reggae, flowing from what the elites would consider the rough, uncultured people of Kingston's poorest neighborhoods.

Whereas reggae is sometimes used now to refer to all Jamaican popular music since the early sixties, more accurately its predecessors—rocksteady and ska—are not reggae. Here's how to tell the difference between them all.

Mento was a precursor to ska, rocksteady, and reggae, influencing Jamaican popular music in theme, rhythm, and lyrics. Bob Marley would have heard mento bands as a child in Nine Mile.

Author's collection

Ska (1960–1965)

When the British groups the Specials and the Selecter released the double-A-side single "Gangsters" / "The Selecter" on Coventry's 2 Tone label in 1979, they sparked a second wave of ska, known as 2 Tone. Both these bands were steeped in Jamaican music history and included members born in Jamaica. "Gangsters" was even a reworking of a 1964 ska classic called "Al Capone" by Prince Buster. But by 1979, ska had long been replaced by reggae back on Jamaican soil.

The original ska music came out of Kingston's studios in the early sixties. Studio One, established in October 1963 as the Jamaican Recording and Publishing Studio, was the island's most important ska label, and many of the best examples of early ska come from Studio One's house band from 1964 to 1965, the Skatalites.

In the fifties and very early sixties, Jamaica bands played jazz, Trinidadian calypso, its close Jamaican cousin, *mento*, American R&B, and a *Jamaicanized* form of R&B. When Jamaica was granted independence from Britain in 1962, Jamaicans rejoiced in an independent country and culture. A few culturally minded and enterprising producers and musicians put their heads together to come up with an indigenous form of music. This resulted in ska, which kept the horn sections from American jazz and some of the rhythmic patterns, melodies, and themes from mento, religious revival music, and burru drumming, and married these to the chord progressions, vocal styles, and overall aesthetic of R&B.

Session pianist Richard Ace (born Evan Lloyd Richards) places the break between the earlier Jamaican R&B and ska with a song he played on, Toots and the Maytals' "Sixth and Seventh Books of Moses," released in 1963. Others say it was Clue J. and the Blues Busters' 1960 adaption of big-band standard "Little Brown Jug," which they called "Shufflin' Jug," and which was led and arranged by guitarist Ernest Ranglin.

The term *ska* is often attributed to onomatopoeia—the sound guitarists make when they play scratchy staccato chop chords on the offbeat—but saxophonist Tommy McCook has said it comes from the greeting "skavoovie." New Orleans musicians like Fats Domino were an important influence on ska. Domino was a rock 'n' roll piano player who adapted the boogie-woogie form. His typical style emphasized a walking bass with his left hand and choppy offbeat chording with his right, forming a *jump* beat. You can hear a good example of this in his song "Be My Guest." This syncopation appealed to Jamaicans because they shared the same musical ancestry—African polyrhythms.

Jamaican musicians like guitarist Ernest Ranglin adopted this syncopation and gave the offbeat dominance over the downbeat by playing muted chords on the upstroke. This upstroke became known as the *skank* (also called the *ska stroke*, *chank*, or *skengay*) and became one of the defining features of Jamaican popular music.

By emphasizing the upstroke, ska seems like it has an opposite rhythmic structure to most Western popular music, particularly R&B and the rock 'n' roll of the era. In fifties R&B and its derivatives, as in early rock 'n' roll, the drummer plays what is known as a backbeat. This means that, in a four-beat bar, the kick drum hits on the first beat of the bar (the downbeat) and the third beat of the bar, while the snare hits each backbeat (the two and the four). This is a mild form of syncopation (syncopation simply meaning an emphasis on non-dominant beats). Ska, meanwhile, puts the emphasis in between these beats, on what is known as the offbeat or afterbeat. If there are four beats in a bar (one-two-three-four) then musicians count the offbeats as "and" (one-*and*-two-*and*-three-*and*-four-*and*). In a typical ska song, the guitars, keyboards, and horns play staccato chords on each "and," and their rhythm comes to dominate the song. When the horns are not riffing or soloing, they honk along on individual notes, emphasizing the afterbeat.

Ska is typically faster than R&B, and more ecstatic, thanks in part to the horn players, who were a defining feature of its development. Thanks to the Skatalites' powerhouse horn section, ska came to be characterized by brassy horn music, and there are many classic ska instrumentals that attest to this. Even with vocal ska, if there is a solo in a song, it is usually performed by a saxophone, trombone, or trumpet, not a guitar or piano. The Latin grooves of Cuban-born percussionist and composer Mongo Santamaria were a major influence on the Skatalites, who either covered or renamed several of his songs, turning them into the raw material for own ska instrumentals: "Tear Up" was based on "Fatback," "Hammer Head" became "Phoenix City," and "El Pussy Cat" kept its title.

Another defining role is taken by the piano. In American R&B, the pianist's left hand plays in the bass register, but session pianist Gladstone Anderson found that when he did that, it muddied up the bassist's part. He switched to playing both hands in the treble register, focusing on chords instead of riffs, giving a more toppy feel to the piano, which, along with the brass, made the music brighter.

Ska singers of the era were often shouters, trying to get above the musical fray. Delroy Wilson, Derrick Harriott, Alton Ellis, Lord Creator, and the Wailers all had success with this, and their short vocal verses were often interspersed with enthusiastic solos from the jazz-trained horn players. Early Wailers ska songs include "Simmer Down," the first version of "One Love," "Ska Jerk," "Love and Affection," "Shame and Scandal," and "Hooligans."

Unlike the 2 Tone artists mentioned above, Bob Marley didn't feel the need to revisit past musical styles. After the end of the ska era, he, like most Jamaican artists, moved on to the next thing. When he did revisit songs from this era (rarely), he did so in the updated style, as with "One Love."

The Wailers also recorded a lot of Jamaicanized doo-wop and soul at Studio One, so their output during this period wasn't exclusively ska. If it's an up-tempo, horn-driven track, though, it is most likely in the ska style.

Part of ska's allure and success with Jamaican audiences in the era of independence was that it was a music of their own, not something imported. So much of popular culture was American-based, and US R&B dominated music tastes in Jamaica. But ska songs like the Wailers' "Simmer Down" used Jamaican patois, not fake American accents, and sang about Jamaican issues, not foreign teenage situations involving bobbysocks, drive-in movies, and V8 Fords.

Ska is now remembered as the sound of Jamaica in the early days of independence, but it was only the sound of downtown, not uptown. Middle-class tastes were still focused on American pop and soul. The radio, jukeboxes, and clubs catered to this demographic, as did many Jamaican bands like Byron Lee and the Dragonniares, Lynn Taitt and the Comets, and the Mighty Vikings.

Rocksteady (1966–1968)

The name *rocksteady* was first established around 1967, but many 1966 hits, such as Alton Ellis and the Flames' "Cry Tough," have a rocksteady feel. Anecdotal histories of Jamaican music say that 1966 was a scorching hot summer, and that because of this the music slowed down, so that the dancers wouldn't get so hot dancing to ska. There's probably some truth in this. Rocksteady generally has a slower feel than ska, but there are a few other important differences, too.

First, the hit-power moved from Studio One to the Treasure Isle studio owned by Duke Reid. This probably had to do with the fact that when the Skatalites split up in August 1965, they splintered into a few groups, one of which became Treasure Isle's studio band, the Supersonics.

Second, the horns took a backseat. There were often horns in the music, but they didn't dominant it. Instead, rocksteady songs tend to have fewer solos, and, with less emphasis on ska's jumpy pace and zealous energy, the singers stepped forward to croon love songs over the top of more melodic and elegant accompaniment. Dawn Penn's excellent "You Don't Love Me (No, No, No)," The Paragon's "Tide Is High," Stranger Cole's "Love Me Today," and the Wailers' "Nice Time" are good examples of this.

The biggest change from ska to rocksteady occurred with the bass and drums. Instead of the walking bass lines commonly associated with ska, in rocksteady the bassist plays repeated melodic figures, known in musical parlance as ostinatos. While a walking bass line tends to play on every quarter-note or eighth-note of a bar, a rocksteady bass line is more rhythmically diverse, using rests and syncopation to, in effect, accentuate the spaces in between the notes, thereby creating a more exciting melody. This use of melodic bass ostinatos became one of the hallmarks of reggae.

Another innovation had to do with technology. In ska bands, a standup bass was typical; in rocksteady, the use of the electric bass allowed the low end more dominance in the music—something that would be crucial to later reggae. The Ethiopians' "Train to Skaville" is a good example of the transition between ska and rocksteady. Its tempo is slow, and the bass plays a two-bar melodic ostinato characteristic of rocksteady, but the guitar and piano play a choppy afterbeat, as in ska.

Along with the more prominent role of the bass in rocksteady, the beat the drummer played went a long way to giving the music a new, mellower feel. Eventually, this beat would become the *one drop* favored by Bob Marley's drummer, Carlton Barrett, and immortalized in Marley's song "One Drop." Leonard Dillon of the Ethiopians told David Katz that "rock steady is the one drop," and rocksteady session drummers Winston Grennan and Hugh Malcolm are often credited as the first to use the beat. So called because the downbeat (the "one" in a four-beat bar) is omitted or dropped, the one drop changes the feel of the backbeat by playing it in half-time, placing the emphasis on beat three, instead of beats two and four. This essentially makes the music feel slower, even if the tempo doesn't change, by extending one measure over two measures. Whereas rocksteady is often thought to be slower than ska, both genres have fast and slow songs.

The one drop can be heard in songs like Alton Ellis's "Rock Steady," Derrick Morgan's "Tougher Than Tough," the Uniques' "People Rocksteady," the Techniques' "Queen Majesty," the Melodians' "Last Train to Expo '67," and much of the Wailers' Wail'n Soul'm material from 1967 (including the original "Stir It Up," "Bend Down Low," "Nice Time," "Hypocrites," and "Fire Fire").

Like ska, rocksteady kept the afterbeat skank played on the guitar and keys. The main guitarist associated with rocksteady was Trinidadian Lynn Taitt. One of the developments he brought to the music that continued on in reggae was the doubling of the bass line on the bottom strings of an electric guitar. This enabled the bass melody to be more conspicuous, especially when the music is played through small speakers that don't have the dynamic range to broadcast booming low tones. This trend helped push the bass line further to the center of the arrangements.

Versions and Riddims

By 1968, the feel of the music gradually began to change again to what would eventually be called reggae, but the links between rocksteady and reggae are multiple. Not only were there musical and thematic changes afoot, the production methods of rocksteady had a fundamental impact on Jamaican music. As far back as 1965, producers realized that they could save money if they recycled backing tracks already recorded by a studio band. Coxsone did this with Lee Perry and the Dynamites' "Hold Down," which was used as the backing track for Roland Alphonso's "Rinky Dink." As this trend grew, another one followed: rival studios re-recording a popular backing track—soon to become known as a *riddim*, or rhythm—for their own use.

By the rocksteady period, recording a new version of an existing backing track had become popular. When the Ethiopians had a hit with their self-produced "Train to Skaville" in 1966, the Beverley's studio had its own band record a new version of the riddim, but the song Toots and the Maytals sang over it was entirely different. Their "54-46" uses the same bass line as "Train to Skaville" but updates the arrangement to better fit the rocksteady feel of 1967. Similarly, Studio One recorded its own version of the riddim, and Marcia Griffiths had a hit with "Feel Like Jumping" over the top of it.

This practice became part of what is known as *versioning*, which also led to the inclusion of instrumental versions of hit songs on the B-sides of 7-inch records, as well as the practice of toasting over these instrumentals live in the dancehall, one-off records called dub plates (made for sound systems), and the entire subgenre of dub. By the seventies, it was common practice in reggae to base new songs on existing hit records, either from one's own studio or a rival's. In fact, many of the artists who left Coxsone would re-record their same hits for rival producer Bunny Lee. He put out new versions of Studio One riddims with different singers voicing new songs over the top, and was integral to the development of versioning by putting several singers over a track like the Uniques' "My Conversation."

Even after the ever-creative Jamaican musicians shifted from rocksteady to reggae, the practice of versioning ensured that the sound of rocksteady remained alive in all subsequent reggae. The bass lines, in particular, of the rocksteady era form a storehouse of standard riddims that are continually versioned today. This is due, in a large way, to deejay U-Roy, who released a group of records during the period 1969–1970 featuring him toasting over instrumental rocksteady riddims from a few years before, most notably the Paragons' "Wear You to the Ball" and Alton Ellis's "Girl I've Got a Date" from 1967, the latter of which was versioned as "Wake the Town" in 1969 and became a big hit for U-Roy.

Remember "Train to Skaville"? Its bass line was rejuvenated in 1986 on Super Cat's hit "Boops," and again in 2010 on Assassin's "History Book." It is common for popular riddims to undergo hundreds of iterations in reggae, and it is quite normal for a modern hit to be based on a riddim that started life in the rocksteady or even ska days.

Reggae

Lyrically and thematically, reggae shares a lot of ground with American funk and soul, because, like soul, it was the sonic expression of pride in black culture. And while a lot of seventies reggae is thematically no different to any American pop music, many black Jamaicans suffered harsh living conditions in the seventies, and reggae became one of the Caribbean's most potent vehicles of social critique against the ongoing legacies of colonialism. It was also closely aligned with the African-Jamaican religion of Rastafari, and artists like Bob Marley, Burning Spear, and Black Uhuru became known around the world during this time for their fiery condemnations of Babylon (Rastafarian-speak for all oppressive systems of the world).

Listening to reggae in the seventies has been likened to watching documentary footage—it dealt with real life in gritty detail. Thematically, then, one of the changes between rocksteady and reggae is that the new genre became closely associated with protest music.

Musically, you can usually tell a reggae song from a few things. The prominent bass ostinatos and the one drop beat remain from the rocksteady era, but they are, simply put, heavier. Lloyd Bradley called his 2001 history of Jamaican music *Bass Culture* for a reason. Any reggae session worth its salt should mean you can hear the bass from five blocks away, and when you leave you should be humming a bass line.

Studio One engineer Sylvan Morris devised a way to get bigger bass frequencies from Coxsone's rudimentary 2-track Ampex tape recorder and Lang board: he used an Electro-Voice ribbon mic in the back of the bass amp, and made his own ribbon out of a piece of audio tape which, he told David Katz, was the key to selectively recording lower frequencies. This emphasis on bass is a hallmark of reggae, where typically the bass guitar is mixed at a higher volume than the other instruments.

Bob Marley's reggae is melodically and harmonically quite complex—there are usually many countermelodies. These might be played by horns, organ, clavinet, piano, or guitar. "Buffalo Soldier" is a good example of this. That said, in reggae, the bass is often the main melodic instrument. By the eighties, many reggae songs reduced the role of these other melodic instruments and broke the music down to a rhythmic backbone of bass and drums, with just the bass playing a melodic line. Organs, horns, and guitars always had a mainly rhythmic role in Jamaican music (with occasional solos), but now they rarely ventured into melodic territory; solos were minimal, if they existed at all. This is similar to how James Brown's funk records were constructed. In Brown's hands, his entire band became a drum kit, each contributing to a complex polyrhythmic sound.

Reggae can be played with all sorts of drum patterns, but Bob Marley's reggae was overwhelmingly dominated by the one drop. During the seventies, very few of his songs veered from this beat, though, as the decade progressed, he was pressured to keep up with reggae's ever-evolving fads back home. Drummers like Sly Dunbar had begun turning away from the one drop and playing the kick drum on all four beats in the bar. Known as *steppers*, this rhythm formed the backbone of a lot of late-seventies reggae, which you can hear in Marley's "Exodus" and "Punky Reggae Party." In fact, Wailers drummer Carlton Barrett refused to play the steppers beat for "Punky Reggae Party," so Bob asked Sly Dunbar to play on the track.

Like ska and rocksteady, reggae still accentuated the afterbeat with the guitar, organ, and piano. In the immediate period after rocksteady, 1968–1970, the feel of the music changed with the guitar, in particular, playing two

The great Studio One keyboardist Jackie Mittoo, pictured here on the back cover of *A Tribute to Reggae's Keyboard King*. Mittoo was one of many studio musicians who supported the Wailers regularly during the 1960s.   *Author's collection*

afterbeat hits: instead of *chank*, it went *ka-chank*. This can be heard prominently in one of the first songs deemed to be reggae, Studio One's 1968 song "Nanny Goat" by Larry and Alvin.

The other major change was that the organ took a prominent role for the first time, with a rhythm reminiscent of mento. Known in reggae as the organ shuffle or *bubble*, the right hand plays the standard eighth-note afterbeat skank on the "and" notes, but now also plays a staccato sixteenth note before and after it. When musicians count sixteenth notes in a four-note bar, they will say, "One-e-and-a, two-e-and-a, three-e-and-a, four-e-and-a." The bubble, then, plays on "*e-and-a.*" This gives a chugging forward momentum that makes reggae more rootsy than rocksteady. One of the earliest songs to feature the organ bubble is the Beltones' "No More Heartaches," while Lester Sterling and Stanger Cole's "Bangarang" put the double-guitar skank and the organ shuffle together. (Interestingly, the latter marked pianist Glen Adams's first time playing an organ.)

In the wake of rocksteady, there were many rhythmic changes to the music in the seventies; they were all still considered reggae, though sometimes they gained subgenre designation. In the period 1969–1971, an up-tempo variation of reggae became popular with skinhead punks in the UK. This was before the term *skinhead* meant racist. Instead, these were British youth that had a thing for Jamaican music. Skinhead reggae, also known simply as early reggae, tends to feature a guitar skank played in a similar rhythm to the organ bubble. Many hits of the period were fun and dance-oriented, sometimes with nonsensical lyrics and often full-blown organ-led instrumentals. Dave and Ansel Collins's "Double Barrel" and Symarip's "Skinhead Moonstomp" are two of the best-known examples.

Early reggae examples by the Wailers include "Wisdom," "Thank You Lord," their cover of "Sugar, Sugar," and much of the track listing on the Beverley's label's 1970 release *The Best of the Wailers*: "Soul Shakedown Party," "Stop the Train," "Caution," "Cheer Up," and "Do It Twice."

This era of quicker, happier reggae was short-lived, and during the Wailers' tenure with Lee Perry they began to work on songs that were thematically weightier, musically heavier, and all-around starker. The music was usually slower, but in the early Perry material (recorded late in 1970 and released on the *Soul Rebels* album), you can hear the reminiscence of the organ-style guitar skank, making this era a nice bridge between the skinhead style and later roots reggae. The drumming is mostly centered on variations of the one drop, and the bass is firmly in the reggae mode: big, broad, and melodic. Check out tracks like "Soul Rebel," "Soul Almighty," "Corner Stone," "400 Years," and "Reaction." The band was progressing quickly at this point, with a definite agenda to shift their sound toward rootsier pastures.

With the release of the tracks that were brought together on *Soul Revolution II* in 1971, we can see progress made again. The musicians were now adapting lots of different kinds of reggae guitar—for instance, single chanks, but this time slower than in the rocksteady era, on "Keep On Moving," and double chanks on "Kaya." One of the standout tracks here is "Sun Is Shining"—not the 1976 version from *Kaya*, but the original Lee Perry–produced version in all its glory, with Peter Tosh playing melodica and the entire song focused on the afterbeat chanks and sparse bass. "Don't Rock My Boat," later recorded as "Satisfy My Soul," also has the stark heaviness of the Perry era, which laid the groundwork for the international roots reggae of the Island Records years.

Dub, Jamaica's Contribution to the Birth of Remix Culture

Along with the progressive emphasis on bass and drums and rhythm over melody, a new subgenre of reggae emerged in the early seventies called dub. Based on the practice of versioning, producers like Lee Perry, Herman Chin-Loy and King Tubby began to manipulate (i.e., remix) songs by adding effects like reverb and echo and deconstructing the songs by selectively silencing tracks. The first full-blown dub album, Herman Chin-Loy's *Aquarius Dub*, came out in 1973, the same year Lee Perry released *Blackboard Jungle Dub*, which consists of remixes of existing backing tracks including some of the Wailers' songs ("Kaya," "Dreamland," "Keep On Moving").

Bob loved all kinds of music, but he felt reggae was the most perfect music, because, as he told Fikisha Cumbo in 1975, "You getting a three-in-one music, you know. You getting a happy rhythm with a sad sound with a good vibration." In other words, its rhythm was danceable and happy, but its sound was mournful and bluesy—which is what is meant by the term *roots music*. And, most importantly for Bob, reggae was Jah music. As he told Patrick Barrat, "Some think reggae will soon run dry, but this music is a Rasta music, and therefore has no end."

17

The Sound System Effect

Competition and Innovation

The youth of America during the fifties and sixties predominantly heard new music live or broadcast over the radio or television—Alan Freed's *Moondog House*, Dick Clark's *American Bandstand*, and *The Ed Sullivan Show*. The idea of the discotheque—going to a club where a deejay spun prerecorded music on records—didn't really take off until the late sixties, and hit its stride with disco in the seventies.

Jamaicans, who lacked the infrastructure and economic resources for widespread radio and television, were way ahead of the curve when it came to dancing to records. Deejays had set up turntables and speakers—called sound systems or sounds—to play records at parties all over the island since the early fifties. These systems were originally quite small, with speakers strung up in trees and between lampposts. Coxsone Dodd's Downbeat started out with a modest 35-watt Bogen amplifier and some 12-inch Celestion speakers with University tweeters. Because of the lack of local radio, by the sixties sound systems were the main way people would hear hits—first imports from America or Trinidad, then local music.

Sound systems did not only provide youths like Bob Marley the chance to keep up with new musical trends, they also had a tremendous impact on the development of the Jamaican music industry, and therefore reggae music. First, they institutionalized competition as one of the driving factors behind Jamaican music, meaning that producers and artists continually sought to create something new that their competitors lacked. This led to rapid evolution in not only the kinds of music produced in Jamaica but also the kinds of technology used and the ways musicians interacted with it. Second, sound systems were important testing grounds for new records and new artists, providing almost immediate feedback on songs recorded, in some cases, that same day.

The Competitive Edge

The first sound-system clash occurred in 1952, and was between Tom the Great Sebastian and Count Nick. Today, sound-system clashes still routinely provide

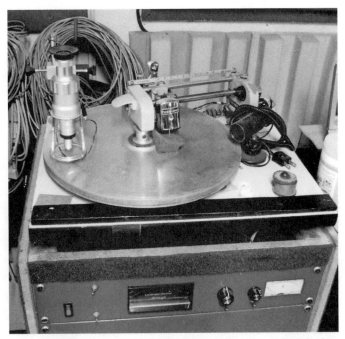

An old dub plate–cutting machine (no longer in use) at Tel's dub plate studio in Kingston. *Brent Hagerman*

entertainment events that seek to win over an audience from a rival sound with sheer volume and also exclusive songs. Whereas in Tom the Great Sebastian's days an exclusive track was one bought in from America (with the disc's label scratched off to keep its title secret), today's sound systems pay top entertainers to record one-off dub plates of their hit songs, to be played exclusively on their system. Bob Marley and the Wailers were part of this industry, producing exclusive dub plates throughout their career. For instance, "Rainbow Country" was originally released only as a dub plate to Jack Ruby's sound system, and the still-unreleased "Babylon Feel This One" was commissioned by the Twelve Tribes Sound.

As well as leading to the production of dub plates, the competitive nature of sound-system culture became one of the hallmarks of the Jamaican recording industry. Sound-system rivalries were often violent, with Duke Reid even hiring henchmen to sabotage his competitor's dances and equipment, resulting in his set—the Trojan—superseding Tom the Great Sebastian's as the island's top sound by 1956. By the time sound operators like Duke Reid and Coxsone Dodd had added recording studios and record labels to their sonic empires, this culture of heated rivalries was firmly entrenched.

Sometimes, this might result in mimicry: when songs about a new dance craze like the Jerk became popular, for example, the Wailers responded with

Duke Reid spinning records at his early sound system, taken from the CD tray insert of Justin Hinds and the Dominoes' *Corner Stone.*

Author's collection

Vinyl plants like this one at Sonic Sounds in Kingston still kick out records.

Brent Hagerman

"The Jerk," "Ska Jerk," and "Jerk All Night," all in 1965, and then "Jerking Time" in 1966. Similarly, the craze for songs about "rude boys" resulted in the following from the Wailers: "Good Good Rudie," "Rude Boy Ska," "Rudie Part Two," and "Rudie's Medley."

Mostly, though, these musical rivalries meant that Jamaican artists sought to stand out from their peers by providing something original. When producer Bunny "Striker" Lee unveiled the "flying cymbal" technique on songs like Johnny Clarke's "None Shall Escape the Judgement," everyone wanted to copy it. But drummer Sly Dunbar, working over at Channel One studios, wanted to one-up it. He started playing a beat known as *rockers*.

In 2006, he explained to me what drove this innovation:

> I could sense that if everybody's going to play this fly cymbal, then after a while everything is going to sound the same. So I was trying to cut something else to try and create something else. "When the Right Time Come" [by the Mighty Diamonds with Sly on drums] was successful, and Joe Joe [Hookum] at Channel One studio started to give me the go-ahead to be free, to create anything I wanted to on the drums. This is when I really started going for it. I would go home in the evening, and I would just work out patterns in my head, and I would listen to things like Lloyd Knibb [drummer for the Skatalites] would play, and I would take ideas from that and develop on that.

Sly changed the beat of reggae again in the late seventies when he was on tour with Peter Tosh, in an attempt to make reggae sound bigger and heavier. He shifted away from the sparse one drop, where the kick and snare only hit on the "three," toward playing the kick drum on the one and three (what he calls "playing it forward"). This evolved into what ended up becoming known as a *steppers* beat or a *straight four*, wherein the kick plays on all four beats of the bar. He also moved away from rim shots in favor of a full snare hit, which he calls "open." He explained how this came about to me:

> When I did the Peter Tosh tour with the Rolling Stones, the energy for reggae wasn't there. We noticed with the one drop that there was no energy from the drum section. We start touring and we get up to the rock festivals and we realize with the one drop, not every engineer could really mic it in a live situation to really make it come more powerful. But the rock 'n' roll drummers' drums were powerful. I said, "Wow," you know? I wanted to get more energy from the drums so I realized you had to start creating the open snare and putting the kick forward so you could really slam it, especially when you play at these festivals. So that is where the idea came from. So when I come back from tour I start recording the open snare and putting the kick forward.

Channel One, once a powerhouse of reggae in the 1970s, is now vacant. Sly Dunbar formed
part of the house band here in the 1970s.   *Brent Hagerman*

It was this drum sound that defined the rhythm of Sly's eighties band, Black
Uhuru. "If you listen to most of the Black Uhuru songs, I don't think there is any
one drop in the Black Uhuru stuff," he says.

Similar innovations occurred through technological advances. Studio
One's use of tape echo made it unique—until other studios figured out how
that repeated guitar sound was made. The entire genre of dub was created by
groundbreaking producers like Herman Chin-Loy, Lee Perry, and King Tubby,
who used existing studio technologies like reverb, tape echo, and even faders
in ingenious ways.

This need to innovate on the part of the producers, studio musicians, and
vocalists is what drove the rapid changes to the music in the sixties and seventies and saw it pass through the ska stage into rocksteady, then multiply quickly
into various forms of reggae. Bob Marley released examples of each of these,
even though he is best remembered as a proponent of roots reggae.

Bob Marley, like other innovative Jamaican musicians, always balanced
paying respect to the music's roots with adding something new. He drew from
existing songs and created new ones; he borrowed from tradition yet broke new
ground. The Wailers were also exceptional in their business practices. When
they established their own record label, few artists on the island had done this
before them. When they broke from the established practice of vocalists being
accompanied by professional studio bands in 1970—when they stole Lee Perry's

studio band, the Upsetters, and made them Wailers—again they were unique in doing so. When they signed to Island Records and released a fusion of Jamaican and American rock styles on *Catch a Fire*, they again pushed the envelope.

While on the surface these innovations might not seem directly influenced by sound system culture, the intensely competitive nature of that culture imprinted itself on the reggae consciousness. Sure, there were followers—artists and producers that simply produced whatever was popular at the time—but Jamaican music history is exceptional in its wealth of sonic explorers. These producers, musicians, and vocalists took existing traditions and refashioned them into new sounds, new genres, new ideas, and new traditions. Bob Marley was

Peter Tosh, performing in 1978 with bassist Robbie Shakespeare.
Photo by Tim Duncan, Creative Commons license

certainly one of them, but he is one among many inventive pioneers in the Jamaican musical pantheon.

The Testing Ground

In their first recording session at Studio One, the Wailers recorded "Simmer Down," a song Bob thought so incidental that he hadn't even considered recording it until his bandmates urged him to do so. After the song was recorded, Coxsone played it on his Downbeat Sound System that night to gauge the crowd's reaction. Legend has it that they loved it so much, he had to repeat the song seventeen times. (This is a pretty standard trope in Jamaican music history, and if all these stories are true, those dances must have had a lot of repeat songs.) When Coxsone saw that the song was a hit in the dance, he had a pretty good idea that he could sell copies of it if he pressed it. When "Simmer Down" was released, it topped the charts in Jamaica. The testing-ground method worked like a charm.

What this meant for reggae history—and Bob's music in particular—is that Jamaican music was first and foremost produced for the local audience and the sound systems. With very little hope of radio play, most Jamaicans would have first heard Bob either at one of his live shows (which were comparatively rare at this time) or during his more frequent spins at the sound systems. So, the sound systems helped popularize the Wailers. But they also determined the kind of material they recorded, as the group was tailoring its sound to the tastes of the sound-system audience. This meant that there was a certain amount of trend-following (recording ska versions of American R&B hits, like "Ten Commandments of Love," for instance), content about local happenings that went down well with the crowd ("Mr. Brown" was based on a newspaper story of a crow riding through town on a coffin), and material designed to appeal to local subcultures like rudies and Rastas.

Sound-system culture, then, was integral to the development of Bob Marley's music, and to the evolution of Jamaican music. And while there are parallels to scenes in America and Britain, where independently programed radio shows and competitive live-music scenes promoted and honed the skills of amateur musicians, the sound-system process is quintessentially Jamaican.

18

Rebel Music

A Guide to the Albums of Bob Marley

I f you ask a casual Bob Marley fan if they own any of his albums and they say yes, that album will most likely be *Legend*. This is not an album *per se*, but a greatest-hits compilation. It is, however, Marley's best-selling record. It's also the best-selling reggae record of all time, and the second best-selling greatest-hits album of all time after the Eagles' *Their Greatest Hits (1971–1975)*, having moved thirty-three million units worldwide since its release in 1984. *Rolling Stone* named it #46 in its list of the five hundred greatest albums of all time. In the last week of 2017, it became only the second record to spend five hundred weeks on the *Billboard* 200. (The other record? Pink Floyd's *Dark Side of the Moon*.) Not bad for an album that Island Records was apprehensive about releasing, for fear that no one would remember who Bob was three years after he died!

This chapter isn't about *Legend*, however: it's about digging a bit deeper into the Marley catalogue. For anyone attempting to listen to Bob Marley's material in the original album release format, the plethora of CD reissues—many of them compilations with the same or similar material—on the market might seem overwhelming. From 1962 to 1973, Bob's music was most commonly released as singles, often under different record labels in different regions. Tracking these singles is not the point of this chapter either, but if you are interested in doing so, I recommend these two excellent discographies of Bob Marley's releases: *Bob Marley and the Wailers: The Definitive Discography* (Steffens and Pierson, 2005) and *Bob Marley: His Musical Legacy* (Collingwood, 2005). These authors provide meticulous session and release details for vinyl collectors.

Here, though, I simply want to provide a helpful guide to the albums Bob Marley released during his lifetime. Of course, CDs had not been invented yet, so these were originally released on vinyl, and later cassette. The only record listed here that falls outside of that time period is *Confrontation*, which is the only full album of new material released after Bob died that was put together by his band and family. As you will see below, because of the nature of the reggae industry, some of these are not albums in the conventional sense, but really compilations.

The Wailing Wailers (October 15, 1965)

Track listing: "Put It On," "I Need You," "Lonesome Feelings," "What's New Pussycat?," "One Love," "When the Well Runs Dry," "Ten Commandments of Love," "Rude Boy," "It Hurts to Be Alone," "Love and Affection," "I'm Still Waiting," "Simmer Down."

Released in late 1965, this is the first full-length album of Wailers material. It is not, however, an album in the traditional sense. Instead, it is a collection of singles released between 1964 and 1965 through Studio One. All the songs were recorded at Studio One and produced by Coxsone Dodd. In this sense, then, it is an early best-of. Two of these songs would show up on later Wailers albums in new versions: "Put It On" was re-recorded for Lee Perry's *Soul Revolution II* and *Burnin'*, in a slower, roots reggae style; and "One Love" changed dramatically into a world-renowned anthem on *Exodus*.

Soul Rebels (December 1, 1970)

Track listing: "Soul Rebel," "Try Me," "It's Alright," "No Sympathy," "My Cup," "Soul Almighty," "Rebel's Hop," "Corner Stone," "400 Years," "No Water," "Reaction," "My Sympathy."

This is the first of two albums produced by Lee "Scratch" Perry, and was attributed to Bob Marley and the Wailers. Perry's infamous Black Ark studio wouldn't be built until 1973, so these songs were recorded at Randy's Studio 17 by Vincent "Randy" Chin at 17 North Parade in Kingston in the summer of 1970. Again, this is a compilation of already released singles, and the band didn't even realize Perry had licensed the songs for release in the UK before it appeared on Trojan. This ultimately led to the demise of their relationship.

This era is typically described as a time when the Wailers were moving away from the more commercially minded material they recorded with Coxsone Dodd and Danny Sims (of JAD) and beginning to focus on more serious material. You can hear the subgenre that came to be known as roots reggae starting to take shape. Some of the musicians here—most notably the Barrett brothers' rhythm section—would remain with Marley for the rest of his career. "400 Years" was redone for *Catch a Fire*, and Peter Tosh went on to issue a scorching version of "No Sympathy" on his solo debut, *Legalize It*, in 1976.

Soul Revolution II (c. mid-1971)

Track listing: "Keep On Moving," "Don't Rock My Boat," "Put It On," "Fussing and Fighting," "Duppy Conqueror," "Memphis," "Riding High," "Kaya," "African Herbsman," "Stand Alone," "Sun Is Shining," "Brain Washing."

Released in 1971, this is the second (and last) album of Wailers material produced by Lee "Scratch" Perry. Like its predecessor, it too was attributed to Bob Marley and the Wailers. Some releases had *Soul Revolution* on the label and *Soul Revolution II* on the cover, but it is typically known as *Soul Revolution II*. The idea here is that *Soul Rebels* was a sort of *Soul Revolution I*. This was a fertile period for the Wailers; several of these songs would be re-recorded later ("Keep On Moving," "Duppy Conqueror," "Kaya," "Sun Is Shining," and "Don't Rock My Boat," the latter renamed "Satisfy My Soul"). Perry released a companion album to this called *Upsetter Revolution Rhythm*, comprised of the backing tracks with no vocals.

The Best of the Wailers (August 1, 1971)

Track listing: "Soul Shakedown Party," "Stop That Train," "Caution," "Soul Captives," "Go Tell It on the Mountain," "Can't You See," "Soon Come," "Cheer Up," "Back Out," "Do It Twice."

The 1970 Beverley's release that wasn't a "best of" compilation at all.   *Author's collection*

Recorded between 1969 and 1970, before the band became involved with Lee Perry, this album was not released until 1971. Despite its misleading title, it is not a best-of compilation. Instead, its title was probably a sly marketing trick on the part of producer Leslie Kong. Kong recorded the ten tracks, and some refer to this as the first work the band conceived of as an album, instead of a collection of singles. Peter Tosh's "Stop That Train" would show up a few years later on *Catch a Fire*, and his "Soon Come" is also on his solo album *Bush Doctor*. Marley experimented with a new version of "Soul Shakedown Party" (called "Soul Shakeup Party") for the *Survival* album, too, but it never made it past the demo stage.

Catch a Fire (April 13, 1973)

Track listing: "Concrete Jungle," "Slave Driver," "400 Years," "Stop That Train," "Baby We've Got a Date (Rock It Baby)," "Stir It Up," "Kinky Reggae," "No More Trouble," "Midnight Ravers."

The Wailers signed to Chris Blackwell's Island Records in 1972, and this was their first release for the label. It was attributed to the Wailers and originally packaged to look like a Zippo lighter, complete with hinged lid. The group recorded the album on an 8-track recorder at Dynamic Sounds in Jamaica themselves, but Chris Blackwell remixed it in London and added some studio musicians to help give it a reggae-rock crossover appeal. Blackwell also wanted a shorter record, so he omitted "High Tide or Low Tide" and "All Day All Night," which can be found on subsequent reissues of the album.

Catch a Fire peaked at #171 on *Billboard*'s 200 and #51 on its Black Albums chart, but initial sales were weak, with the album moving less than fifteen thousand copies of the original pressing. It was a slow burner, however, and is now revered among fans and critics, with *Rolling Stone* tagging it as the 126th greatest album of all time.

The album produced two singles for the international market (the Wailers' own Tuff Gong label continued to release different singles locally): the light and fluffy "Baby We've Got a Date" (which confusingly appears on the album as "Rock It Baby"), and the much darker "Concrete Jungle." It also contains one of Marley's best-loved songs, "Stir It Up." "Concrete Jungle," "Stir It Up" and "Rock It Baby" are new versions of songs the Wailers had recorded and released before, as were Tosh's contributions "400 Years" and "Stop That Train."

The much sought-after original "Zippo lighter" album cover.
Photo by Brent Hagerman, courtesy of Mark Logan

Trojan issued this compilation after *Catch a Fire* was released in an attempt to cash in on the Wailers' newfound international exposure.
Author's collection

African Herbsman (July 1, 1973)

Track listing: "Lively Up Yourself," "Small Axe," "Duppy Conqueror," "Trenchtown Rock," "African Herbsman," "Keep On Moving," "Fussing and Fighting," "Stand Alone," "All in One" (a medley of "Bend Down Low," "Nice Time," "One Love," "Simmer Down," "It Hurts to Be Alone," "Lonesome Feelings," "Love and Affection," "Put It On," and "Duppy Conqueror"), "Don't Rock My Boat," "Put It On," "Sun Is Shining," "Kaya," "Riding High," "Brain Washing," "400 Years."

Released by Trojan in the UK, this album includes songs from *Soul Rebels* and *Soul Revolution II*, as well as some Tuff Gong singles that had not been released on LP before. As such, it is a mix of Lee Perry productions and the group's self-productions. It contains some of the group's local hits of the period that would become set list standards and featured on *Live!* and *Babylon by Bus*: "Trenchtown Rock" and "Lively Up Yourself," the latter of which was redone for *Natty Dread*. It also has an excellent original version of "Small Axe," which later showed up on *Burnin'*. Trojan issued this compilation after *Catch a Fire* was released in an attempt to cash in on the Wailers' newfound international exposure.

Burnin' (October 19, 1973)

Track listing: "Get Up, Stand Up," "Hallelujah Time," "I Shot the Sheriff," "Burnin' and Lootin'," "Put It On," "Small Axe," "Pass It On," "Duppy Conqueror," "One Foundation," "Rasta Man Chant."

A prolific year for the Wailers, 1973 saw two Island releases, both attributed to a group (the Wailers), not Bob Marley plus backing band. This time, the group recorded at Harry J's Studio on Roosevelt Avenue in Kingston, but, as with *Catch a Fire*, did the mixing and overdubs at Island Records in London. It reached #151 on *Billboard*'s Pop Albums chart and #41 on the Black Albums chart, though again it sold poorly. It is the last album to feature the original vocal trio, as Peter Tosh and Bunny Livingston had left the group by the end of the year. The album boasts one of the only true writing collaborations between Marley and Tosh, the fiery "Get Up, Stand Up." This was also the record's only single, which seems strange in retrospect, considering that it also contains classics like "Burnin' and Lootin'" and perennial favorite "I Shot the Sheriff." This last song would play a key role in Bob's rise to fame when Eric Clapton's cover of it reached #1 on *Billboard* in 1974.

   Like most of Marley's other Island records, there are a few recycled songs here: "Put It On" was previously recorded for Studio One and Lee Perry, and

The last album with the original trio of Bob, Peter, and Bunny.
Author's collection

This album marks the transition between the Wailers as a vocal trio,
and Bob Marley and the Wailers as an artist with a backing band.
Author's collection

both "Small Axe" and "Duppy Conqueror" were new versions of Perry-era songs. "Pass It On" was eleven years in the making. It was actually supposed to be recorded by Bunny Livingston in 1962—at the same session Bob cut "One Cup of Coffee" for Beverley's—but Bunny was stuck in school and arrived late.

Bunny Wailer has indicated that the album was supposed to be titled after his song "Reincarnated Souls," but that this was changed and the song was relegated to a B-side after he left the group.

Natty Dread (October 25, 1974)

Track listing: "Lively Up Yourself," "No Woman, No Cry," "Them Belly Full (but We Hungry)," "Rebel Music (3 O' Clock Roadblock)," "So Jah Seh," "Natty Dread," "Bend Down Low," "Revolution."

This album marks the transition between the Wailers as a vocal trio and the Wailers as Bob Marley's backing band. Attributed to Bob Marley and The Wailers, *Natty Dread* has many of the same core musicians as the previous two records, but backing vocals are now supplied by the I-Threes—who include Bob's wife, Rita Marley, alongside Marcia Griffiths and Judy Mowatt—instead of Peter and Bunny. Only one international single was issued from the album, "Natty Dread," but several did come out in Jamaica.

Natty Dread reached #92 on the *Billboard* Pop Albums chart and #44 on the Black Albums chart. Only two of the nine Island Records releases did not contribute a track to the later popular compilation *Legend*, and *Natty Dread* is one of them. *Rolling Stone* likes it, though, calling it the 196th greatest album of all time. Again, a few of these songs can be found in earlier incarnations in the Marley catalogue. "Lively Up Yourself" was a Jamaican favorite released as a single on Tuff Gong in 1971, and "Bend Down Low" had already been recorded numerous times as far back as 1966.

Live! (December 5, 1975)

Track listing: "Trenchtown Rock," "Burnin' and Lootin'," "Them Belly Full (but We Hungry)," "Lively Up Yourself," "No Woman, No Cry," "I Shot the Sheriff," "Get Up, Stand Up."

Recorded on the *Natty Dread* tour at the Lyceum in London on July 19, 1975, the only song here not previously released by Island is a remarkable version of "Trenchtown Rock." One of the highlights on *Live!* is the slow gospel version of "No Woman, No Cry," which, because of its inclusion on *Legend*, has become the

This is the sound of Bob Marley capturing the hearts and ears of British audiences.   *Author's collection*

definitive version. The original release of *Legend* faded the song out during the guitar solo, however, so that it was only four minutes and five seconds long. *Live!* has the full seven minutes and eight seconds in all its glory. "No Woman" was released as a single and reached #22 in the UK charts, staying there for seven weeks. *Live!* captures the moment when Bob Marley was just breaking, and its popularity introduced him to a new white middle-class fan base.

Rastaman Vibration (April 30, 1976)

Track listing: "Positive Vibration," "Roots, Rock, Reggae," "Johnny Was," "Cry to Me," "Want More," "Crazy Baldhead," "Who the Cap Fit," "Night Shift," "War," "Rat Race."

Here, on his second album without Peter and Bunny, Bob really hits his stride thanks in part to the addition of two American blues guitarists (Al Anderson and Donald Kinsey), who help continue his crossover sound. Peter and Bunny also released debut solo albums this year, *Legalize It* and *Blackheart Man*, respectively.

Bob's only Top 10 album, thanks to the singles "Johnny Was" and
"Roots Rock Reggae."   *Author's collection*

Rastaman Vibration reached #15 in the UK and #8 in the US, where it was
Bob's only Top 10 album. It spawned two singles: "Johnny Was," and Bob's highest charting single in the US, "Roots Rock Reggae," which peaked at #51. The
material again revisits earlier songs like Studio One's "Cry to Me" and the Lee
Perry–era "Man to Man," which shows up here as "Who the Cap Fit." (Though the
original version of the latter was credited to Marley and Perry, this one is credited to the Barrett brothers.) He also recycles older lyrics (from "Rainbow
Country" and "Freedom Time") into "Roots, Rock, Reggae" and "Crazy
Baldheads," respectively. "Night Shift" was supposedly written about his stint as
a forklift driver in a Delaware Chrysler factory, and "War" has become his
definitive treatise on racism. It was also Bob Marley's favorite Bob Marley song.
The lyric is taken almost verbatim from Haile Selassie's speech to the United
Nations General Assembly in 1963. Just as with *Natty Dread*, no tracks from this
album show up on *Legend*.

Exodus (June 3, 1977)

Track listing: "Natural Mystic," "So Much Things to Say," "Guiltiness," "The
Heathen," "Exodus," "Jamming," "Waiting in Vain," "Turn Your Lights Down
Low," "Three Little Birds," "One Love / People Get Ready."

The *tour de force* album that produced many of Bob's most popular songs.   *Author's collection*

Most of the tracks on *Exodus* (ranked #196 in *Rolling Stone*'s greatest-albums list) and *Kaya* were recorded together in London, after Bob left Jamaica in the wake of the attempt on his life. The brilliance of this era of Marley material is that it marks the point when he truly combines militant Rastafarian reggae with radio-friendly pop sensibilities, and the music doesn't suffer one iota. Perhaps this is why, in 1999, *Exodus* was named the best album of the twentieth century by *Time* magazine, which recognized both its "message of love" and "anthem of revolution."

This point wasn't lost on Island, which heavily weighted *Legend* with *Exodus* material: five of its fourteen songs are drawn from this album. Bob revisits a few songs here: a different version of "Natural Mystic" was previously recorded at Black Ark in 1975, and "One Love" is a radical departure from its Studio One ska origins. Its soothing universalism was slogan-ready, and to Bob's credit he packs a hefty Rasta-theological message into a song that most of the world sees as a simple (though not puerile) anthem of universal peace and love.

Exodus is rich with singles and not just 45s, with Island now releasing 12-inch singles that allowed for bigger bass and longer tracks, helping get Bob's music into the disco clubs. Both "Exodus" and "Jamming" (with non-album track "Punky Reggae Party" on the B-side) received this treatment. "Waiting in Vain" was also released as a single, and longtime fans of Bob Marley might have noticed that the song bears similarities to his old Studio One single "I'm Still

Waiting." The album did very well in the UK, where it charted for fifty-eight weeks, peaking at #8 in November 1977. And the "Jamming" single cracked the Top 10, reaching #9. In the US, radio programmers categorized it as R&B instead of rock, resulting in both "Exodus" and "Waiting in Vain" reaching the R&B Top 20 and Top 40, respectively, but not registering on the pop charts.

Kaya (March 23, 1978)

Track listing: "Easy Skanking," "Kaya," "Is This Love," "Sun Is Shining," "Satisfy My Soul," "She's Gone," "Misty Morning," "Crisis," "Running Away," "Time Will Tell."

Recorded together with *Exodus* and then divided into two albums, this material has often been considered more romantic and introspective, which caused concern that Bob was drifting away from political engagement and Rastafari testaments. Reviewers wondered if he was selling out. It definitely did better on the charts in the UK, though, peaking at #4, but was a modest seller in the US, reaching only #50. It produced two singles, "Is This Love" and "Satisfy My Soul." The former reached #9 on the UK charts, and the latter reached #21.

"Satisfy My Soul" was first recorded as a rocksteady song called "Don't Rock My Boat" in 1968. Other recycled songs here include "Sun Is Shining" and

Recorded at the same time as *Exodus*, *Kaya* is an often-overlooked gem.   *Author's collection*

"Kaya," originally recorded for Lee Perry in 1970 and 1971, respectively. Also included are two songs said to speak directly to his assassination attempt in December 1976: "Time Will Tell" is supposedly a message to his would-be assassins, while "Running Away" is a response to criticism that he turned tail and ran from Jamaica in the wake of the shooting.

Babylon by Bus (November 10, 1978)

Track listing: "Positive Vibration," "Punky Reggae Party," "Exodus," "Stir It Up," "Rat Race," "Concrete Jungle," "Kinky Reggae," "Lively Up Yourself," "Rebel Music (3 O' Clock Roadblock)," "War / No More Trouble."

This is Bob's second live album, recorded at the Pavillon de Paris, June 25–27, 1978, during the tour for *Kaya*. It reached #40 in the UK charts but was not well received by critics. Its double-album format seemed a bit bloated, and the performances are not as powerful as those on *Live!* Three singles were released from it: the much loved "Stir It Up," which is quicker and far more intense than the album version; the medley of "War" and "No More Trouble"; and "Exodus," which like the medley came out on a 12-inch. The B-side to this included "Jamming," and, somewhat tellingly, a song from the better-selling *Live!*, "No Woman, No

Received tepidly by critics at the time, *Babylon by Bus* is still essential listening for reggae fans.   *Author's collection*

Cry." The album's poor initial reception hasn't stopped contemporary fans from loving it, with Allmusic.com calling it "arguably the most influential live reggae album ever." Of course, everything is arguable.

Survival (October 2, 1979)

Track listing: "So Much Trouble in the World," "Zimbabwe," "Top Rankin'," "Babylon System," "Survival," "Africa Unite," "One Drop," "Ride Natty Ride," "Ambush in the Night," "Wake Up and Live."

Probably in response to criticisms of *Kaya's* lighter material dedicated to the love of women and herb, this album is a fiery return to militant form, with songs about the politics of blackness, pan-Africanism, decolonization, and Rastafari. It marks the first in a planned trilogy of albums carrying similar themes. Bob died before the final installment was finished, but *Confrontation* certainly has many thematic links with *Survival* and *Uprising*.

Survival was the first album to be recorded at 56 Hope Road, where Bob had recently built his new Tuff Gong Studio. For the first time on an Island studio release, none of these songs revisit older material, though "Ride Natty Ride"

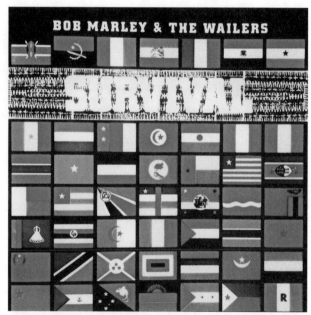

Originally titled *Black Survival*, this is Bob's no-holds-barred, politically charged magnum opus.   *Author's collection*

borrows a few lines from "Soul Rebel" and "Corner Stone." It produced three singles: "So Much Trouble in the World," "Survival," and "Zimbabwe." *Survival* again did well in the UK, reaching #20, though its singles fared worse, with only "So Much Trouble in the World" reaching #56. Still, for such a hard-hitting, stellar album, it is criminal that none of its tracks made it onto *Legend*.

Uprising (June 10, 1980)

Track listing: "Coming in from the Cold," "Real Situation," "Bad Card," "We and Dem," "Work," "Zion Train," "Pimper's Paradise," "Could You Be Loved," "Forever Loving Jah," "Redemption Song."

The last album released during Bob's lifetime, *Uprising* finds him in high spiritual gear. In America it reached #45 on the Pop Albums chart and did slightly better on the Black Albums chart, peaking at #41. In the UK, the album ascended to the Top 10, reaching #6 and staying on the charts for seventeen weeks.

"Could You Be Loved" was a strong single in the UK, reaching #6 on the Club Play Singles and #56 on the Black Singles charts. It was a deliberate fusion of American R&B/disco that paid off even though it left many reggae purists

The last LP released in his lifetime, *Uprising* included the reggae/R&B crossover hit "Could You Be Loved" and the acoustic "Redemption Song."
Author's collection

shaking their heads. In its wake, Island actually released "Three Little Birds" from *Exodus* as the next single, probably because it had become popular via a television ad. It reached #17 in the UK. The only other single from *Uprising* was "Redemption Song." One of Bob's all-time most recognizable songs, it actually did quite poorly at first. The Bob Dylan–esque, acoustic folk nature of the song was unexpected for his audience. A full band version was paired with it on the 12-inch single, which also included "I Shot the Sheriff." (You can really see Island's marketing wheels spinning with some of these choices.)

Confrontation (May 23, 1983)

Track listing: "Chant Down Babylon," "Buffalo Soldier," "Jump Nyabinghi," "Mix Up, Mix Up," "Give Thanks and Praises," "Blackman Redemption," "Trench Town," "Stiff Necked Fools," "I Know," "Rastaman Live Up"

This album was released two years after Bob died. The tracks were recorded at various points in his career, with some being outtakes from other albums and

A posthumous release, with new songs drawn from outtakes and demos.
Author's collection

others half-finished songs reconstructed from demo recordings. "I Know" dates back to 1975 and was first released as a single (at Bob's request) just after he died. "Rastaman Live Up" and "Blackman Redemption" were recorded in late 1978 or early 1979; they were probably originally conceived as part of the *Survival* album, but didn't make the cut. Different recordings of both of these songs, with the Meditations singing backup, were co-produced by Lee Perry later in 1979 and released as Jamaican singles.

"Mix Up, Mix Up" may have been an outtake from *Survival* as well, given its origins in a mid-1979 session at Tuff Gong Studio, while "Give Thanks and Praises" seems to have been an outtake from *Uprising*. "Trench Town," "Stiff-Necked Fools," "Chant Down Babylon," "Buffalo Soldier," and "Jump Nyabinghi" were all recorded in mid-1980, and were probably intended by Bob for inclusion on *Confrontation*. "Jump Nyabinghi" was originally released as a dub plate in Jamaica, but tracks were added to it for its inclusion here. "Stiff-Necked Fools" updates 1970's "Wisdom" with similar lyrics but a different melody.

"Buffalo Soldier" became Bob's first posthumous hit, and Island Records accompanied it with his first music video. *Confrontation*, like his other albums, was a better seller in the UK than in the US: the album reached #5, and "Buffalo Soldier" reached #4.

19

Redemption Songs

Bob's Earliest Musical Influences

When Nesta Robert Marley was born in the hamlet of Nine Mile in February 1945, Jamaican music wasn't on the radar of British and American music lovers, and reggae music wasn't even invented yet. In fact, Jamaica didn't even get a proper recording studio until 1951, so if you wanted to hear Jamaican music, you pretty much had to travel to Jamaica. The most popular singer in America was the Tin Pan Alley crooner Bing Crosby, who, along with the Andrews Sisters, had the #1 hit with "Don't Fence Me In" the week Marley was born. In Jamaica, audiences flocked to hear hometown entertainers with names like "Black Bing Crosby" or the "Jamaican Sinatra." And in the UK, music lovers were swept away by Welsh songbird Dorothy Squires' "The Gypsy," backed up by the Billy Reid Orchestra.

But there were hints of a Caribbean music invasion coming—one that would ultimately see the music of Bob Marley and the Wailers played around the world, with Marley being dubbed the third world's first superstar. That hint can be found on the US *Billboard* charts for the week of February 10, 1945—a few days after Marley's birth. The Andrews Sisters scored a #1 hit with a straight-laced version of Lord Invader's coy calypso "Rum and Coca-Cola." The Trinidadian song dominated the top position of the American charts for eight weeks, even though it was a thinly veiled critique of American imperialism. That calypso spirit—an infectiously rhythmic dance tune that packed a politically-charged sucker punch—would live on in the rebellious reggae that Bob Marley would come to symbolize three decades later.

Taking reggae music to the world obviously wasn't on young Nesta's mind when he was running barefoot over the green mountains of Nine Mile. But music did play a role in his early life. As was typical among rural Jamaican boys, he had a guitar made out of a sardine can given to him by his cousin. He also blew out tunes on a homemade cane fife. And, once he arrived back from his foray with his father to Kingston around age six, he began to sing regularly.

There were four main sources of music in the child's life, and each of them provided an influence on the music he later wrote and played around the world: church, live folk music, music broadcast over radio, and sound systems.

Church Music

Many of Bob Marley's most famous songs are blatantly religious. Take a listen to "One Love," with its lyric about Armageddon, or his many songs praising Jah Rastafari, and you'll hear a man with deep religious convictions. Bob famously sang that all he had was "redemption songs." And while his religious affiliations changed over the years, from Pentecostal to Rastafari to finally a mix of Rastafari and Ethiopian Orthodox, he began and ended his life/career singing redemption songs.

On the homepage of the Shiloh Apostolic Church—the church Bob attended as a child—visitors are introduced to the church with an answer to the question, "What Kind of Church Is This?" The answer includes the following: it is a "Hands Clapping" church, a "Foot Stomping" church, a "Body Rocking" church, a "Devil Chasing" church, and a "Red, Blue Fire Hot" church.

Bob grew up Christian but converted to Rastafari in his early twenties. Much of the music he made was Rastafarian, in so much as it promoted Rastafarian values and worldview. But the music of Bob Marley and the Wailers was also certainly hands-clapping, foot-stomping, body-rocking, devil-chasing, and red, blue fire-hot. Like his American counterparts Elvis Presley, Johnny Cash, and Jerry Lee Lewis, Bob Marley's musical palette and fire-and-brimstone theology were grounded with one foot in Pentecostalism.

Bob's mother was a devout Pentecostal, his grandfather less so, which is somewhat surprising, given the fact that church was—and still is—an important part of the upbringing of a large part of Jamaica's population. Bob's mother, Cedella Malcolm, attended the Shiloh Apostolic Church—both the one in Nine Mile and the mother church in nearby Alva—where she sang in the choir, often with Bob in tow. In 1975, Bob told the *Ann Arbor Sun*, "The first time I hear singing it was my mother singin' gospel." Ciddy remembers that Bob used to hum along with her to gospel songs like "Precious Lord Take My Hand."

Later, when he moved to the US briefly with his mother in the mid-sixties, Bob would again attend church with her sporadically. He loved the communal singing and the music, but by that time he was suspicious of Christianity's dogma, and had started to take a keen interest in Rastafari.

The influence of Pentecostal worship styles can be seen in Bob Marley's performance, the churchy harmonies in the Wailers' own harmonic singing (and, later, in that of Marley's backing singers, the I-Threes), and the Pentecostal hymnal that informed his songwriting. The hymnal that was used in the Shiloh Apostolic Church was and still is called *Redemption Songs: One Thousand Hymns and Choruses*. Bob released his "Redemption Song" in 1980, on the *Uprising* record. It was the last song on the last album released while he was still alive. Symbolically, then, Bob Marley's earliest musical experiences and last musical statement revolve around that book. Many of Bob's earliest recorded songs were thematically Christian, with lyrics and themes drawn from the Bible. (I examine some of these connections later in this book, in the chapter "Let the Lord Be Seen in You: Early Christian Songs.")

Jamaica Folk Music Traditions

Most of the music Bob heard growing up would have been performed live. His grandfather owned a radio, which he listened to on Sundays (presumably instead of going to church), but recorded music was not something that everyday rural Jamaicans encountered in the 1940s. Church music was live and interactive: you sang, clapped, and danced along with the hymns. You also made your own music at home. Omeriah played fiddle, accordion, organ, and four-stringed banjo, though not often, and Cedella had an uncle that played in a katreel band.

Country-dances and socials would often feature quadrille or katreel bands, playing songs derived from European ballroom dance music such as the lancer, mazurka, and quadrille. In the post-emancipation period, the instrumentation of these ensembles would closely resemble their European cousins: fiddles, fifes, and guitars. But by the mid-century, a creolized version was augmented with instruments of partial or whole African ancestry, like banjos, a rhumba-box, and various drums and percussion instruments. At some point, this music became known as *mento*. Jamaican music historian Garth White says that mento could be "heard at village dances, fairs and concerts, and on occasion at the 'tea-meetings' put on by community organizations." In addition, "They provided background music and accompaniment for maypole and quadrille dancing." Before the fifties, mento was Jamaica's only indigenous popular music, and Bob would have heard a lot of it, live and, later, on radio.

Like the music that Bob Marley would become known for outside of Jamaica, mento was also a hybrid. Bob's music combined Jamaican reggae with American soul and rock 'n' roll. Mento itself was a syncretic amalgam of European set-dance music and African rhythms using instrumentation from both cultures: fiddle, flute, clarinet, saxophone, and guitar from the former, plus banjo, drums, and the rhumba box, which is a bass instrument with mbira-style metal keys that are mounted to a wooden box with a sound hole. During the slavery era, music traditions from Africa were refashioned by African-Jamaicans as they came into contact with European music via sailors, soldiers, and planters. Poor whites from Ireland, Scotland, and England worked as bookkeepers and indentured servants in Jamaica and would have influenced the cross-cultural musical pollination. The music traditions they brought with them, such as the Morris and Merry-Andrew dances, or Celtic and British folk music, would have been seen and heard by enslaved Africans. The former musical director of Jamaica's National Dance Theatre Company, Marjorie Whylie, says that mento was the "product of what had started in the seventeenth century, with the dynamic collision of the cultures of Europe and Africa," and the first dance in Jamaica to enjoy national popularity.

In the forties, mento bands sprang up in Kingston due to the increased migration from countryside to city. This new, urbanized mento tended to use modern instruments (saxophone, clarinet, piano) and often accompanied eroticized dance routines. In the wake of World War II, mento was seen as rural folk music next to the hipper American swing. Many of Kingston's nightclubs featured American-style big-band jazz acts. While these bands would mostly play American swing standards, they would occasionally include rhumbas, calypso, and mento.

The first Jamaican singer to record mento was Louise Bennett, or "Miss Lou," who cut songs for Melodisc in 1950, but that was in London. When Stanley Motta established Jamaica's first record studio and record label in 1951 (MRS), it was to record this new urban mento by acts like Lord Fly, the Ticklers, Lord Composer, and Baba Motta. By the time Jamaicans started recording mento in Jamaica, the calypso craze had already swept the United States. As early as 1912, Trinidadian calypsonians were being recorded by American record labels; by 1945, the Andrews Sisters' single "Rum and Coca-Cola" was selling upward of seven million copies, and when Harry Belafonte—born in New York to Jamaican parents—released an LP titled *Calypso* in 1956, it became the first album to sell more than one million copies.

The widespread popularity of calypso put pressure on Jamaican mento bands to adopt the title *calypsonian* if they wanted to sell records outside Jamaica, and mento was often dubbed *kalypso*, to cash in on Trinidadian calypso's popularity. International record companies were busy promoting "island music," and calypso became the *de facto* term for all music from the British Caribbean. Motta's records subsequently carried the name *calypso* for many songs and artists. Mento is often considered a Jamaican variant of calypso, however, and while the terms were interchangeable in Jamaica in the fifties, and the words *calypso* or *calypsonian* were used extensively in the band names of mento acts as well as their song titles, its origins are mainly Jamaican folk music. Mento shared with calypso the trend of documenting current events in song, and as early as the thirties, itinerant singers on Kingston's streets, such as Slim and Sam, would sell their lyrics in tract form for a penny each.

Many mento musicians found work in tourist venues by advertising their music as calypso, even though it was really mento. Lord Flea, for instance was quoted in 1957 as saying, "If the tourist want calypso, that's what we sell them."

Mento's popularity waned as young Jamaicans came under the sway of American big-band music in the years after World War II, American R&B in the fifties, and ska in the sixties. Eventually, mento was relegated to the tourist resorts on the north coast, where it was enjoyed as authentic Jamaican folk culture. Today, the most visible mento bands are found in hotels, at airports, and on cruise ships.

Mento had a tremendous impact on Jamaican popular music. Deadly Headley, who played saxophone on Marley's "Nice Time" in 1967 and "Ride Natty Ride" in 1978, traces modern Jamaican music to mento. He told Kenneth Bilby, "As Bob Marley say, 'Feel it in de one drop'—we have to go back to mento. Even de youth dem today, wide dis present dancehall music—is mento! Everything coming from mento, man."

While the instrumentation was very different, ska, rocksteady, and reggae continued to use many of the same rhythms and themes, and even periodically the same melodies, tunes, and lyrics. Jamaican music evolved by building on the music that came before. Licks, themes, lyrics, rhythms, and bass lines are routinely recycled or reinvented into new songs.

Jamaican Radio

When Bob Marley was a small child in Nine Mile, the concept of homegrown radio stations playing local music had not yet developed in Jamaica. In 1940, there was only one national radio station, ZQI, which acted as a sort of part-time broadcaster throughout the forties, airing news and a bit of American or Latin pop for as little as four hours a day. In 1950, it was bought by the English company Rediffusion Limited and became RJR (Radio Jamaica and Rediffusion), which largely just rebroadcast foreign programs featuring bland easy-listening artists popular in mainstream America, such as Frank Sinatra, Bing Crosby, Patti Page, and the Andrew Sisters.

Older Jamaicans often talk about listening to Rediffusion, a synonym for radio at the time. Small, affordable transistor radios weren't available until the mid-fifties, so at the time Bob was born, most Jamaicans were not able to afford either a gramophone or radio. Those who could, like his grandfather Omeriah, would tune into sermons from Kingston on Sundays and be able to pick up radio from further away—most likely Cuba, or the occasional R&B song from WINZ in Miami.

In Kingston, reception was better for offshore signals. When Bob moved there in the mid-fifties, there were several more options for hearing recorded music. US R&B was the most popular form of music for Jamaicans, but gospel, jazz, and even country were heavily influential to Jamaican musicians. Bob liked dance music in the fifties; he told the *Melody Maker* in 1973, "I listened to Ricky Nelson. Elvis, Fats Domino." He listened to this early R&B and rock 'n' roll alongside rhythms from nearby nations like Cuba, Trinidad, Panama, Haiti, and the Dominican Republic.

Rita Marley remembers tuning in to Miami stations in the sixties to listen to Otis Redding, Sam Cooke, Wilson Pickett, Tina Turner, the Impressions, the Drifters, the Supremes and the Temptations. On a clear night, Kingston's residents might also pick up stations from New Orleans and even Tennessee.

Jamaica received a second radio station in 1959: the Jamaican Broadcasting Corporation (JBC). Neither station catered to ghetto-dwellers, however; rather, they played music that the island's elites would enjoy. That meant very little American R&B and a constant diet of classical music, US pop ballads, and jazz.

Jamaica's youth wanted more of the new American styles, and since the radio stations weren't about to cater to them, a new group of entrepreneurs arose to fill a hole in the market: the sound-system men.

Sound Systems

Kingston had its share of live music venues in the forties, fifties, and sixties, where mento bands, jazz bands, and American touring acts would play. After Bob moved to Trench Town, he saw American R&B acts like Brooke Benton, the Impressions, and Dinah Washington. But the main way ghetto-dwellers in Jamaica heard new music in the fifties was not at a live concert or music club but via a sound system.

Sound systems are like itinerant discotheques on steroids. They feature a selector who plays records—initially on a single turntable, then later on the now-ubiquitous double turntable—amplified by towering homemade speaker boxes designed to drown out any rival systems. They might set up a dance in a church hall or school, but most often they could be found at outdoor lawns, which might just mean the backyard of someone's house. Besides R&B, these sound systems also played mento, Latin, and even big-band jazz in order to cater to diverse demographics including the uptown crowd.

The early sound-system operators depended on a few things to draw crowds: the size and quality of their equipment, the rarity of their repertoire, and the charisma of their talent. One of the first operators, Tom the Great Sebastian, started in the early forties, playing R&B sent to him by a friend in New York. Patrons would be able to hear exclusive songs on his sound, and an operator would be wise to keep the names of each record a secret, in order to increase their exclusivity over rival sound systems.

In the late fifties, Chris Blackwell, later of Island Records fame, earned good money by importing records from the States, scratching the labels off, and selling them to sound systems. Sound-system owners like Coxsone Dodd, who ran Sir Coxsone's Downbeat, started to do the same, making it difficult for any would-be rival scout to make out the names and artists, thereby giving them a competitive advantage in an industry that developed sound clashes between rival sounds.

Besides going for the music selection, dancers would also be attracted to the personalities who emceed the proceedings. Starting off as American-styled deejays jive talking over a record's introduction, toasters took this talk-over phenomenon to a new level, eventually paving the way for rap. Early toasters like Count Machuki or King Stitt became celebrities in their own right as they elevated the role of sound-system deejay to musical artist. Stitt even committed the first toasting to record, with songs like "Fire Corner" and "Lee Can Cleef" in 1969.

Not only would Marley have heard and attended sound systems as a youth in Kingston, he would also have heard radio programs sponsored by these sound systems, like Duke Reid's *Treasure Isle Time* or Tom the Sebastian's *Sebastian Time*. Locally recorded music—especially ska and later reggae—was not frequently played on the radio. Some mento artists had radio hits in the mid-sixties (Lord Flea, Lord Fly, Count Lasher) as mento took on the mantle of nationally significant indigenous music. But as Jamaican musicians began creating their own music in the early sixties, one of the only ways to get on the radio was through the same sort of sponsorship relationship found between the sound systems and radio stations. Recording studios like Studio One, for instance, would pay for a program of their locally produced records to receive airplay.

20

Kong and Gong

Bob at Beverley's, 1962 and 1970

Leslie Kong does not have the cultural cachet of world-renowned Jamaican producers like Coxsone Dodd, King Tubby, or Lee Perry. But he played a key role in Bob Marley's career, and in the birth of reggae. Kong recorded Bob during two periods: he was the first producer to take a chance on Bob when he recorded him as a solo artist in 1962, and he then produced a strong set of songs with the Wailers in 1970. Like almost all the other relationships between Jamaican producers and the Wailers, this one would not end amicably. In fact, Bunny Livingston is said to have fatally cursed Kong.

Beverley's: Bob Marley's First Recordings, 1962

Leslie Kong, a Chinese Jamaican, ran Beverley's Record Shop and Ice Cream Parlour at 135A Orange Street in Kingston with his brothers, Cecil and Lloyd. He decided to get into the music business when a teenager named James Chambers wrote a song called "Dearest Beverley." He booked studio time to record Chambers, who changed his name to Jimmy Cliff, and Beverley's was born.

While Jimmy Cliff was storming the local charts, Bob Marley—or Robbie, as he was known to his friends—was sweating it out as a welder's apprentice on South Camp Road, hoping to make it as a singer. He had already auditioned for Kong but failed to make an impression. He needed a way into the music business, and a friend at the welding shop supplied it. Desmond Dekker, fellow welder and songwriter, had already recorded for Leslie Kong and knew Cliff, who was working as a talent scout for the producer. Through Dekker, Bob was able to secure an audition with Cliff. Amazingly, Bob was sixteen at the time, and Cliff only fourteen! This historic meeting led to a recording date at Ken Khouri's Federal Studios, where Bob tracked his first two songs—"Judge Not" and its B-side, "Do You Still Love Me?"—backed by studio band, the Beverley's All Stars.

It is often stated that these songs were issued under the name Robert Morley, but this is untrue; they were credited to Robert Marley. Bob fought hard to keep his own name, however, as Kong didn't like the name Robert. According to the 2012 documentary *Marley*, Kong had insisted it be changed to Adam Marley.

Bob evidently lost the fight for his next release, though. He only had one more recording session with Kong, which produced "One Cup of Coffee," also in 1962. A slightly rewritten cover of an American country song by Claude Gray, it was credited to Bobby Martell, a pseudonym Kong felt might have more commercial potential than Robert Marley. Many sources also insist that a fourth song was recorded for Beverley's called "Terror," but it has not been located.

Bunny Livingston was supposed to record his own composition, "Pass It On," at this second session, but he got held up at school. By the time he got there, Leslie Kong was so mad at having paid for studio time that he refused to let Bunny sing. Judging by the nature of their relationship later in life—particularly the alleged curse mentioned above—this perhaps wasn't such a good decision on Kong's part.

Bob Marley, future King of Reggae, barely made a ripple in the music industry with those first few records. Kong put his energies into other, better-selling artists like Jackie Opel and Derrick Morgan and all but ignored Marley. Bob did play some live shows promoted by Kong in May Pen and Montego Bay in the summer of 1963, but in his account of the Wailers' early years, *Simmer Down*, Masouri reports that this was the end of their business relationship until the end of the decade.

In the meantime, Bob, Bunny, and now Peter Tosh would go on to audition unsuccessfully for Prince Buster and Duke Reid, before finally finding a home at the Motown of Jamaica, Studio One. There, the Wailers would become a household name on the island and eventually go down in history.

Soul Shakedown Party: Bob Returns to Beverley's, 1970

In the years since Marley first recorded with Kong in 1962, Kong's fortunes had risen. In 1964, he recorded Millie Small's "My Boy Lollipop," a ska cover of Barbie Gaye's 1956 hit. Small's infectious song became a worldwide hit—the first Jamaican song to do so. But Kong really hit his stride in 1968, when he recorded a clutch of songs that helped push Jamaican music from the rocksteady era into the reggae era. One of the most significant of these was Toots and The Maytals' "Do the Reggay," the song that gave the new beat its name. He also produced Desmond Dekker's "Israelites" and the Pioneers' "Long Shot Kick the Bucket," both of which became huge hits in England, and was responsible for the Melodians' "Rivers of Babylon." In the late sixties, several of the songs issued by Beverley's would end up on a soundtrack album that would go on to introduce reggae to a whole new generation of English and American kids: *The Harder They Come.*

It made sense, then, for the Wailers to come knocking on Leslie Kong's door early in 1970. Kong, more than any other producer on the island, had experience in breaking Jamaican music internationally. Perhaps this was the man who could finally do the same for the Wailers.

Marley and the Wailers recorded ten songs for Leslie Kong in May 1970, and two of my personal favorite Marley songs are among them: "Soul Shakedown Party" and "Caution." Kong still didn't have his own studio, so the songs were recorded at Dynamic Studios, owned by Byron Lee. Once again, the Beverley's All Stars backed them up, though this time around the band was completely different. Bassist Jackie Jackson, drummer Mikey "Boo" Richards, keyboardists Winston Wright and Gladstone Anderson, and guitarist Hux Brown injected these songs with a driving US Southern soul feel.

Jimmy Cliff, who rose to international fame when he starred in *The Harder They Come*, was a fourteen-year-old talent scout for Beverley's when he successfully auditioned Bob Marley.

Author's collection

The First Reggae Album

This set of songs represents a turning point in the career of the Wailers, and in reggae in general, because they were eventually released as a full album. Jamaican music was still singles-based, and albums were only collections of previously released singles. This was unlike the rock world, where, since seminal records like *Pet Sounds* and *Sgt. Pepper's Lonely Hearts Club Band*, the album format had become the main way fans engaged with music, and also promised an artistic vision spread out over several songs.

Whether or not *The Best of the Wailers* was the first reggae "album" of previously unreleased songs is up for debate. However, the Wailers approached Kong with this idea for a full album. Some sources suggest that a few of the songs were released as singles first; others, like Marley expert Roger Steffens, insist that these were not released until the album came out, because the point was a standalone LP.

Regardless, the band members were not happy with Kong's chosen title: *The Best of the Wailers*. By this time, the Wailers had recorded well over one hundred

Despite its misleading title, a good argument can be made that *The Best of the Wailers* was the first reggae record conceived of as a full album, as opposed to a collection of singles. Reggae lore states that the poor choice of title led to the death of the album's producer, Leslie Kong.

Author's collection

songs with several different producers over a six-year period. To think that their most recent ten songs were the best they had ever done or, as Bunny would point out, the best of what was still to come, was ridiculous. Bunny Wailer was furious when he heard about the impending album, and he threatened Kong indirectly. If you release this album, he reportedly told him, you will die.

Kong ignored Bunny and released the album in Jamaica in August 1971, making *The Best of the Wailers* the first standalone reggae album, whether it was conceived as such by the band or not. The choice of title—while perhaps a good marketing strategy at the time—is unfortunate, as it downplays its album-length artistic-vision and, like Studio One's compilation album from 1965 (*The Wailing Wailers*), simply sounds like another collection of singles.

The details of its inception aside, *The Best of the Wailers* is a solid testament to the band's creativity and maturity, capturing them at the moment when reggae was still young. This era is generally called "early reggae" or skinhead reggae (because of British skinheads that danced to it), and the beat is quicker—closer to rocksteady, rather than the slower one drop rhythm of Marley's Island Records output of a few years later. It failed to attract much attention at home or abroad, though, leaving the band disheartened yet again.

You might be wondering what became of Leslie Kong. He died at his home on April 9, 1971, at the age of thirty-eight. Cause of death? Officially, it was listed as a heart attack. As far as I know, Bunny Wailer had a good alibi.

Cheese Party

Somehow, one of these Beverley's songs got into the hands of JAD (the label owned by Johnny Nash and Danny Sims), which made a mess of it. The vocal track for "Soul Shakedown Party" was used in a remix released in 1985 on an album called *Bob, Peter, Bunny, and Rita*, the original instrumental tracks having been replaced by American studio musicians with a penchant for synthesizers, synthesizers, and more synthesizers, effectively turning the soul party into a cheese party. Perhaps, in 1985, this made sense to someone's ears. Today, it is safest to stay away from these remixes and seek out the real deal.

21

Hooligans

The Wailin' Wailers at Studio One, 1964–1966

In 1963, Jamaican producers Duke Reid (Treasure Isle Records) and Prince Buster made their worst career decisions: they turned down Bob Marley. Bob's first crack at breaking into the music industry with Beverley's in 1962 went nowhere, so he auditioned for these rival producers.

In music history terms, what followed was almost as big of a mistake as what happened a year before, when Decca A&R man Dick Rowe passed on a young group from Liverpool called the Beatles, supposedly telling their manager, Brian Epstein, "Guitar groups are on their way out." Reid and Buster had their fair share of hits, but none of their artists achieved the heights of Bob Marley, and it is no hyperbole to call the Wailers the Beatles of Jamaican music.

Studio One, the once-mighty center of Jamaican music, dubbed the Motown of Jamaica, taken in 2015. *Brent Hagerman*

Rejected by much of the Jamaican musical establishment, Bob decided to abandon hopes of a solo career and looked instead to form a group. He joined forces with long-time collaborator and half-brother Bunny Livingston (who, by 1965, was calling himself Bunny Wailer) and new friend Peter Tosh. They woodshedded their skills in Joe Higgs's backyard on Third Street, which was around the corner from Bob and Bunny's place on Second Street.

It was in Higgs's yard, or one close to it, that the original Wailers formed. At first, the group included fellow Trench Town singers Junior Braithwaite, Beverley Kelso, and Cherry Green. It was unusual to have so many singers together; most groups at the time were duos (Bunny and Scully, Higgs and Wilson). Toots and the Maytals were having success with the vocal-trio format, and eventually the Wailers would as well, but for the time being there were six singers trading leads and harmonies. Together, they set their sights on securing a deal with Jamaica's premier record label, Studio One, run by Clement "Coxsone" Dodd.

By the mid-sixties, Coxsone was Jamaica's Berry Gordy, his studio its Motown. He even copped the Detroit label's motto, turning "The Young Sound of America" into "The Sound of Young Jamaica." But if you're going to borrow, you might as well do it from the best: Motown was the United States' most success-ful black-owned business of the sixties. Studio One, which had been housed at

13 Brentford Road since 1963, became the most important studio of the early sixties, and its house band, the Skatalites, responsible for setting the pace and bar for Jamaican music of the period. Coxsone was a powerful man in the music business: he had his own radio program, sound system, Musik City record shop, and studio, and he released music on several labels, including Studio 1, Coxsone Records, Downbeat, Musik City, No. 1 Studio, Supreme Records, and even a gospel label called Tabernacle.

The Wailers had an "in" at Studio One. Fellow Trench Town resident Alvin "Seeco" Patterson knew Dodd and helped them get an audition in early July 1964. (If you head over to the chapter on all the musicians that played in the Wailers, you'll notice

Seeco Patterson helped the Wailers get an audition at Studio One in 1964.   *Photo by Tomaz Jardim, Creative Commons license* that Seeco was a mainstay in the band throughout the seventies.) It took two auditions—the first was a failure—but eventually the Wailers embarked on a two-year relationship with Dodd that would see them record between eighty-five and one hundred songs and have several domestic hits.

Further in the Motown vein, Studio One provided many of the tools to help its acts succeed. Dodd would at times pay for stage clothing, make his record collection available to his acts so that they could study what made a success-ful song, and pair older musicians with younger in a mentor relationship. The Wailers came under the wing of Skatalite saxophonist Roland Alphonso, who added to Joe Higgs's lessons by instructing them in basic music theory, record-ing technique, and musicianship. Many of the studio musicians had learned their trade while attending Alpha Boys School, a Catholic institution with a vibrant music program. For Bob, Peter, and Bunny, music lessons were out of reach, so these impromptu tutor-student relationships were essential for their development.

Hit-Makers

Studio One launched the Wailers. They regularly placed hits in the local charts, and by 1965 they had five songs in the Top Ten. Not a lot of local music was played on the radio, but producers like Coxsone could sponsor one-hour shows to have their own acts played. Besides this early radio play, any new Wailers song would be introduced to the public at Coxsone's Downbeat Sound System dances, with Dodd either playing the track on its own or having the band mime the vocals over the top. (Later, this practice developed into artists performing over the top of instrumental records, and became the foundation for dancehall.)

Sound systems were a good testing ground for new material and provided an economical and fast way for a producer to judge return on their investment. Throughout the sixties, bands like the Wailers would have their music tested at the various local sounds. Producers like Coxsone and Duke Reid took handfuls of their new songs to the popular sound-system operators each week to gauge the crowd's reaction. Later, when the Wailers were on their own, they would take their dub plates to systems like Merritone, where Dennis Thomas would spin their new material amid existing hits.

If a song was a hit in the dance, producers knew it was worth the expense of pressing and promoting a single. Further, by providing the audience an exclu-sive taste of the song, they created a demand for the product. If the audience didn't like a track, it could be shelved indefinitely.

The group's first hit was "Simmer Down." One source says Bob wrote the song two years before, and had won several competitions singing it, including

The Wailers were not the only successful vocal group at Studio One. This com-
pilation also includes well-known artists like the Gaylads, the Clarendonians,
Carlton and the Shoes, the Viceroys, the Maytals, the Heptones, the
Gladiators, the Royals, and the Ethiopians.   *Author's collection*

the Opportunity Knocks contest at Ward Theatre. Others say the song was
newer. For some reason, though, when the Wailers auditioned for Coxsone, Bob
didn't sing it.

There are various versions of the story of how the song came to be recorded.
Some say Coxsone, not hearing anything he wanted to record, asked the group
if they had any other songs, and that's when they pulled out "Simmer Down."
Or, he sent them away to write their own material, and they first came up with
"It Hurts to Be Alone," only writing and recording "Simmer Down" later. Or, they
failed their original audition, but Seeco took them back to Studio One, insisting
that they play "Simmer Down" for Coxsone, who fell in love with the song.

Legend has it that, right after it was recorded, Coxsone took the song to a
dance in Jones Town to test it out on the audience. The response was enthusiastic, and the crowd demanded that he repeat it several times. The details of its
release are sketchy: some sources say it topped the local charts in either January
or April 1964, but most likely it wasn't recorded until July of that year; Bunny
Wailer himself remembers it being a hit in August, during the Independence
Day celebrations. Beverley Kelso remembers it being played repeatedly on RJR
the week of its release.

Regardless of when it came out, the song made a huge impact and turned the Wailers into local stars overnight, selling around eighty thousand copies and charting as the ninth most popular song of 1964. This was a considerable amount since, for Dodd, sales of more than five thousand were considered a hit. Chang and Chen, in their *Reggae Routes* history of Jamaican music, write that the song "had the unique Marley touch" with its "imaginative use of Jamaican proverbs and dialect" and "burning topicality."

"Simmer Down" helped earn the Wailers a reputation as rude boy sympathizers, or even rude boys themselves. While the song actually called for these self-styled gangsters to control their tempers, it had the added effect of bringing the group credibility. The rude boys themselves liked the group, and the Wailers would go on to address them (sometimes sympathetically, sometimes not) in later songs like "Hooligans," "Rude Boy Ska," and "Good, Good Rudie."

The Wailers recorded for Studio One until the summer of 1966. In that time they placed many songs in the local charts, including "It Hurts to Be Alone" and "Lonesome Feelings" (#3 and #11, respectively, in 1965), and "Rude Boy Ska" and "Put It On" (#6 and #8, respectively, in 1966). Some of these songs were licensed to British labels like Trojan and Ska Beat and released in the UK. In fact, almost sixty Wailers songs had come out in Britain by 1970. (And to think that 1973's *Catch a Fire* is often thought of as the group's "debut" album!)

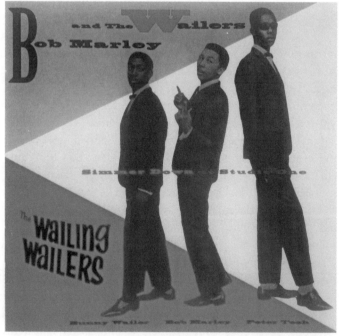

There are several collections of the Wailers' Studio One output on the market, like this one, *Simmer Down at Studio One*.   *Author's collection*

Studio One Technology

It is fascinating to remember how primitive the conditions at Studio One were in 1964 by comparison to modern recording methods, with digital audio workstations and nearly limitless tracks.

Coxsone first started recording on a 1-track machine at Federal Studios, where he produced early-sixties hits by groups like the Maytals. He earned enough capital to build the Jamaican Recording and Publishing Company Ltd. in October 1963—otherwise known as Studio One—at the north edge of Trench Town. His first tape recorder was a 1-track mono Ampex 350. In order to capture each instrument, he used several mics—one for each instrument, three or four for the drums, one for the backing singers, and a Neumann U-67 for the lead vocal. He would send the signals through two six-channel Lang boards and into the Ampex.

Once a song was committed to tape, there was very little you could do to alter it. If an instrument was too loud or quiet, you had to adjust the microphone placement and record the song again. This is the old fashioned way of mixing. This situation was helped out by the fact that Coxsone used seasoned

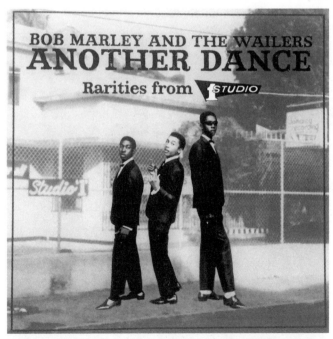

With upward of one hundred Wailers songs having been recorded at Studio One, fans will find them spread across various compilations like *Another Dance: Rarities from Studio One*.

Author's collection

musicians who were used to controlling their own dynamics. They could stay in the background when needed, but would literally step up to the mic when a solo was required.

During this time, the singers and band recorded at the same time, in the same room, just as if they were playing a live gig. If someone messed up, you either lived with it, or, if you had the time, did another take. Vision Walker told Roger Steffens that when he was singing with the Wailers, they generally did three takes of a song, but the first take was always the best. Many people feel that this kind of recording produces more authentic, and therefore better, records. They are in the moment, imperfect but heartfelt.

In the summer of 1965, Coxsone brought back a new recorder from London: an Ampex 252 2-track. This allowed for greater control over the recording process. Now the vocals could be recorded on a separate track asynchronously, at a different time from the instruments. This is how all of the subsequent Wailers tracks were put down. The group sang softly alongside the band as they recorded the rhythm track, and then, after that, recorded their real vocals while listening to the backing track through headphones. If a singer missed a harmony, there was no need to stop the whole band and start again; the singers could re-record just the vocals by punching-in or re-recording just the section that needed it. Though they initially missed the excitement of singing with the

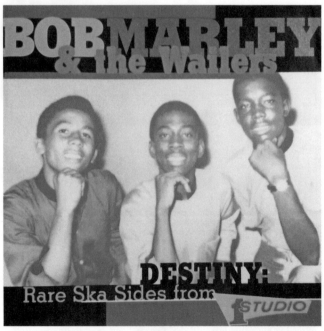

Yet another Studio One compilation, *Destiny: Rare Ska Sides from Studio One*.   *Author's collection*

band, this method allowed them to sing softer and with more nuance, and provided much more clarity to the vocals. "One Love" was the first song recorded by the group by using this method.

The 2-track machine could also be used to add supplementary material to a song. For instance, on "Do It Right," the instrumental backing track and vocals were recorded separately, as usual, but then mixed down to a single track so that Coxsone could add a novelty percussion track consisting of metal can-openers striking beer bottles.

It wasn't until May 1966 that the Wailers had access to a 4-track machine at Studio One. The first song they recorded in this way (really just Peter alone) was "The Toughest."

On the Job at Studio One

Being a hit-maker in Jamaica in the sixties didn't mean you were on easy street. Wailers fans all over the island thought of them as rich and successful, because they were now musical celebrities played at dances and on the radio, but that was far from the case. Beverley Kelso told Roger Steffens that for a time they worked at the studio every day, sometimes for several days in a row without going home. If they weren't recording their own music, they were backing up other artists, adding harmony to their songs.

The Wailers took on other jobs at the label in order to make more money. Peter Tosh started working as a session musician, playing guitar, organ, and melodica. Bob worked as an unofficial A&R man for Coxsone, auditioning groups and choosing American R&B songs for other artists to cover. He also did some arranging for other groups and was assigned to Rita Anderson's group, the Soulettes, as their musical coach and manager. (Bob and Rita became close, of course, and eventually married.) Besides working these extra jobs to make ends meet, artists were also expected to help out with the chores. Those artists that weren't recording would cook for the rest.

Studio One Money

There is a recurring trope in pop music history of record execs cashing in at the expense of their exploited artists. Jamaican artists had it worse than most, and while some of this may have had to do with corrupt or greedy studio owners, it was aided and abetted by the Jamaican industry. "There were no contracts, royalties, residuals or any of the other usual guarantees," writes Stephen Davis, author of *Bob Marley: Conquering Lion of Reggae*.

Bunny Wailer in concert at Reggae Geel, Belgium, 2014.
Photo by Peter Verwimp, Creative Commons license

In the sixties or seventies, a Jamaican artist would be paid a flat fee for recording a song but would rarely see royalties from future sales. That's because the copyright to that song remained with the producer. A singer was free to record that same song elsewhere for another flat fee, but the new producer then owned the copyright for that version.

The Wailers re-recorded several songs during their career in the sixties, and Marley often returned to his earlier catalogue, revisiting songs like "Stir It Up," "One Love," and "Satisfy My Soul." In the later sixties, many of Coxsone's artists were fed up with his tight-fisted ways and went to re-record their hits for other producers like Bunny "Striker" Lee. This allowed them to have some extra compensation for their intellectual property within a system that favored producers over artists.

The Wailers had the enviable position of being paid a weekly stipend, but it was rarely augmented by royalties, and when royalties were paid, the weekly stipend was deducted first. Peter has said that Coxsone paid them three pounds a week (nine pounds a week to share between them), and on top of that they received somewhere between ten and twenty pounds for every track they recorded. Expenses like stage clothes were deducted from their earnings.

Dodd seemed to provide other incidentals as well. He allowed Bob to stay on the premises when he was without a home, purchased his wedding suit for him, and provided him with a ticket to Delaware, where he went to live with his mother in 1966. He also continued paying Bob his stipend while he was in the US, no doubt keen to ensure the return of a lucrative artist.

Eventually, the Wailers came to realize that Coxsone was keeping a lot more of the money than he was sharing. Songs like "Mr. Talkative" were licensed to Island Records and sold in the UK, but that money failed to find its way into their pockets. In fact, they were not even aware that many of these songs made it outside of Jamaica.

In a 2011 blog post, Bunny said that when they first met Island head Chris Blackwell in 1972, Blackwell told them he had given Coxsone "hundreds of thousands of pounds sterling" in royalties for the band, but the Wailers had received nothing. Blackwell says he doesn't recall that conversation, and that from about 1962 to 1964, he paid Coxsone a flat fee (not royalty-based) for material.

Leaving Studio One

The membership of the Wailers was fluid during the Studio One period, with even Bob being replaced for eight months, while he was in Delaware, by Vision Walker. Junior Braithwaite had immigrated to the US in mid-1964, and Cherry Green and Beverley Kelso drifted away gradually, leaving Bob, Peter, and Bunny as the Wailers.

Money woes and the feeling of being exploited would ultimately lead to the demise of the Wailers' first successful professional relationship and record deal. First, Bob got greedy. He took advice from Joe Higgs and Seeco Patterson, who told him to keep a larger share of the band's earnings. This didn't sit well with his "equal" partners, Bunny and Peter, and resulted in Higgs and Seeco being

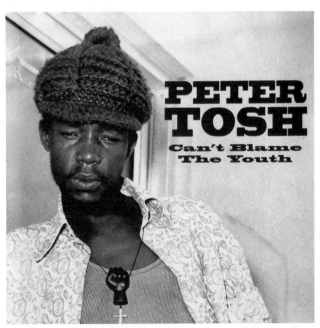

Peter Tosh, from the compilation album *Can't Blame the Youth*.
Author's collection

shunned from the group for a while. Then, Coxsone suggested to Bob that he would be more successful as a solo artist, though he did not comply.

Coxsone was not a man to be trifled with, and several sources indicate that he kept a revolver to intimidate any artist that might ask for money. He sent henchmen to beat up Joe Higgs after he requested money he felt was owed to him. Speaking to *Melody Maker* in 1973, Bob said of the local producers, "If your record sells good, the producer pretends he's gone to Nassau when you come by the office. In Jamaica, you're expected to use your knife, or your machete, or your gun."

Just as Coxsone was a hard man, so too were the Wailers hard men. When they were unjustly spurned, they fought back. When the group asked for more money, Coxsone scoffed. Bunny, whose bitterness is palpable in many interviews, has stated that Coxsone kept them poor so that they couldn't go out on their own. But Bunny held his tongue—at least until Bob left for Delaware. By the time Bob returned in October 1966, Bunny had violently confronted the producer by threatening him with a ratchet knife. That spelled the end of the band's tenure as Studio One artists.

Bob wanted to give Dodd one more chance, so he convinced the others to try a new kind of relationship. They would return once more in the fall of 1966, but this time they rented the studio, hired the musicians, and produced their own songs, arranging for Dodd to distribute the material using his connections. This would allow them more control over the finances, and a bigger cut of the profits. They set up their own label, Wail'n Soul'm, and released "Bend Down Low" and "Freedom Time." The former was a major hit locally. The group sold some copies themselves and did well with that, but they saw very little money from Dodd for the discs he distributed. This led to renewed distrust, and the group cut ties with him for good.

22

Soul Brothers and Spiritual Sisters

Different Band Names

During the sixties and early seventies, most Wailers songs were released under variations of the Wailers name. The core group at that time consisted of Bob, Bunny Livingston, and Peter Tosh, but the credits varied on the original Jamaican singles, and sometimes the same song would be credited to a different band name when it was given an international release.

The Many Versions of the Wailers

Bob was most often the lead vocalist on these tracks and, despite Peter Tosh later claiming that the name Bob Marley and the Wailers was not used until Island Records head Chris Blackwell made Bob the leader of the group in the early seventies, many early Jamaican singles carried this credit. And, in fact, it was Blackwell that initially suggested the group go by the name the Wailers, to sound more like a cohesive rock group. This is how the first two albums on Island—*Catch a Fire* and *Burnin'*—are credited. Island only switched to "Bob Marley and the Wailers" once Peter and Bunny left the group.

Here is a list of the ways Wailers songs have been credited when Bob sang lead up until the group signed with Island Records in 1972: the Wailers, the Wailin' Wailers, the Wailers Group, Original Wailers, Bob Marley and Wailers, Bob and the Wailers, B. Marley and the Wailers, and even Bob Marley and the Wailing Wailers. Before joining with Studio One in 1964, they were sometimes billed at early live shows as the Teenagers or the Wailing Rudeboys. In 1965, they were also presented at one uptown Kingston club as Bob Marley and the Wailing Rude Boy Wailers.

Peter and Bunny left the group in November 1973, and Bob would go on to release almost all of the rest of his music as Bob Marley and the Wailers, though there are a few tracks, such as "Rainbow Country" and "Reggae on Broadway," that are credited simply to Bob Marley. However, both Peter and Bunny often recorded with the same backing band as Bob in the seventies, and at times their own solo work was credited to Peter Tosh and the Wailers, or simply the Wailers. And, to make things more confusing, some songs are credited to the Wailers or the Wailers Band but feature just the backing band. In fact, after Bob's death, the backing band continued touring and recording as the Wailers Band, and then later the Wailers, with a revolving membership.

The following list shows how Wailers songs were credited during Bob's lifetime.

(Someone Else) and the Wailers

When Peter Tosh sang lead, the songs were often attributed to the Wailers, Peter Touch, Peter Touch and the Wailers, Peter Tosh and the Wailers, Peter Touch and the Chorus, and once, mistakenly, to Bop and the Belltones. (Peter's early Jamaican releases used Touch instead of Tosh, but this was often changed back to Tosh for international pressings.) When Bob went to Sweden for a few months in 1971 to work on the soundtrack for *Want So Much to Believe*, Peter recorded some solo material with the Upsetters—soon to be called Wailers—and Soul Syndicate. These were released under names like the 3rd and 4th Generation, Peter Toush (which was no doubt a misspelling), and Peter Touch.

When others sang lead—most notably Bunny Livingston and Junior Braithwaite—top billing did not apply. The only song that may have been credited to Bunny Livingston and the Wailers was "Dreamland," recorded with Lee Perry in 1971, though this probably was originally issued as a Wailers record. Bunny did release a few duets with Rita Marley credited to Bonny and Rita in early 1965, and then Rita and Bunny in spring 1966. In 1974, Bunny released some singles on his own Solomonic label on which he sang lead and Peter sang harmony, and these are credited these simply to Wailers. In 1972, a song called "Searching for Love" had Bunny singing lead and all of the contemporary Wailers (including the I-Threes) backing him except Bob. This track was credited to Heat, Air, and Water, while the B-side version (with no vocals) was credited to Tuff Gong All Stars. It was probably recorded while Bob was out of the country, in either Sweden or London.

When Bunny and Peter left the group and Bob carried on with the Wailers name, Bunny changed his surname to Wailer as a way to keep his connection to the group's legacy. All his subsequent releases starting in 1975 carry the name Bunny Wailer.

Bob Marley in the Sixties

If you find yourself digging through a vintage vinyl bin someday, looking for rare Bob Marley records, you will have to search beyond the names listed above. Some singles carried slight credit variations, often having to do with the different personnel the group recorded with, or because the producer decided to alter the artist credit slightly. The following is a list of all the different artist credits for songs where Bob either sang lead, shared the lead, or the Wailers were included in the billing and Bob sang on the track.

Bobby Martell

Bob's second release for Beverley's in 1962, "One Cup of Coffee," was attributed to the pseudonym Bobby Martell, with the backing band listed as Beverley's All Stars. Perhaps it sounded more American than Marley. There is a persistent myth that his first release for Beverley's, "Judge Not," was credit to Robert Morley, but this is untrue. That song, the first he ever recorded, was credited to Robert Marley.

The Wailers and the Mighty Vikings

Two songs were released in Jamaica under this credit in 1964. The Mighty Vikings were another backing band that Studio One periodically used.

The Wailers and Soul Brothers Orchestra

The only songs to carry this name are "I'm Still Waiting" and "Ska Jerk," recorded at Studio One in 1965. The Soul Brothers were a group led by saxophonist Roland Alphonso that included most of the Skatalites after they broke up. Later, on the Wailers' first independent recordings from 1966—"Bend Down Low" and "Freedom Time"—a similar name was revived: Bob Marley and the Wailers with the Soul Brothers. This version of the Soul Brothers was a stripped down version of the Skatalites with just bass, drums, and piano.

Soul Brothers

When Coxsone Dodd released the near-instrumental song "Guajara Ska," he attributed it to the Soul Brothers. Two of the Wailers—Peter and Bunny—do indeed sing a repeated chorus on it, though, and because of this the later CD reissue was attributed to Bob Marley and the Wailers.

Bob Marley and the Spiritual Sisters

This is my favorite band name, courtesy of Studio One in 1965. The sisters here refer to two sometime female Wailers: Beverley Kelso and Cherry Green, who sing harmony along with Bunny and Peter on the religious "Let the Lord Be Seen in You" and a cover of Irving Berlin's "White Christmas." A similar name (without *the*) was used for "Just in Time," where Rita Anderson and Marlene Gifford sing harmony. This song was also released under the attribution the Soul Harmonizers.

Joanne Dennis and the Wailers

Joanne "Joey" Dennis was a friend from Trench Town, and on the 1965 song "Don't Cry Over Me" she is backed up by Bob, Peter, and Bunny on harmony. This song was never issued by Coxsone and only came to light on Heartbeat Records' *Wailers and Friends* in 1999.

Rita Marley and the Soulettes with the Wailers

Bob and Rita Anderson were married in February 1966, and subsequent singles give Rita's married name. According to Steffens and Pierson, she recorded "That Ain't Right" with all three Wailers in July of that year, though if this studio date is accurate, Bob could not have sung on the song because he was working in Delaware from February to October. It was not released until 1999's *Wailers and Friends*, but was played regularly on Coxsone's sound system.

Bob Marley Plus Two

A few songs were released under this name in spring 1968. They include another version of "Bend Down Low," "Nice Time," and "Mellow Mood," recorded for the American label JAD run by Johnny Nash and Danny Sims. In Canada, these songs were released under the name *Bob, Rita, and Peter*, which tells you who the "plus two" were. Where was Bunny? Unfortunately, the Kingston constabulary did not share the Wailers' views on ganja. He was charged with possession of marijuana and spent just over a year in jail during this time.

Whalers

A group of songs was issued under the Dutch spelling in 1970 and released on Trojan records.

Bob and Rita with Lester Sterling's All Stars

Even though "Hold on to This Feeling" featured harmony vocals from Bunny and Peter, this song is a duet between Bob and his wife, recorded in the summer of 1970. It is a cover of the Junior Walker song.

Bob, Peter, Bunny, and Rita

JAD released the album *Bob, Peter, Bunny, and Rita* in 1985, after Bob's passing. It includes songs he recorded for the label in the late sixties and early seventies, remixed with new instrumentation from studio musicians in New York. Did I mention it's horrible?

Ras Dawkins and the Wailers

Bob, Bunny, and Peter backed up several singers while at Lee Perry's Upsetter label in 1970–1971. At times, the Wailers' name got added to the credit. One song ("Picture on the Wall") was credited to Ras Dawkins and the Wailers, but another two ("True Love" and the Temptations cover "Cloud Nine") were attributed to Carl Dawkins and the Wailers. Ras and Carl were the same person. Dawkins, by the way, had spent some time fronting a band that Wailers bassist Aston "Familyman" Barrett had put together called Youth Professionals. Apparently—says Familyman—he was quite the front man.

Interns

When 1970's "Mr. Chatterbox" was first released in Jamaica, it was credited to Bob Marley and the Wailers, but on its UK release by Trojan it was wrongly credited to the Interns.

Bob and Upsetters Band

When the Wailers recorded with Lee Perry, they used his backing band, the Upsetters. Only one track bears this name, an instrumental version of "Keep On Moving." There is also a pressing of "Keep On Skanking" released as the Upsetters. When the Wailers split with Perry in 1971, they would take the Upsetters with them, and together the new group would go on to be called the Wailers.

U-Roy and Bob Marley

The Wailers sing "Kingston 12 Shuffle," based on the same rhythm track as "Trenchtown Rock," alongside pioneer deejay U-Roy on this 1971 track. Some copies carried the credit Bob Marley and Hugh Roy.

23

The Toughest

Wailers Songs Recorded Without Bob Marley

Bob Marley was in Delaware from February to October 1966. During this time, the Wailers continued to record at Studio One, with Peter Tosh, Bunny Livingston, and Constantine "Vision" Walker forming the main group and Rita Marley often joining them. Other occasional vocalists included Marlene Gifford and the vocal group known as the Gaylads: Horace "Bibby" Seaton, Winston Stewart, and Maurice Roberts. Vision, Marlene, and Rita also had their own vocal group called the Soulettes.

Peter Tosh and Bunny Livingston would go on to have successful careers of their own during and after Bob's life, and this nine-month stretch in 1966 provided a proving period for them. Both Peter and Bunny recorded songs during this period that they would later revisit and become identified with: Bunny's "Dreamland" (written by Al Jolson), and Peter's "The Toughest." Peter would also take his first crack at the Temptations' "Don't Look Back," a song he revisited in 1978 as a duet with Mick Jagger.

While Bob was gone, significant changes occurred in both the Wailers and Jamaican music in general. First, Bob's later material would be rife with political and religious themes, but these were slow to develop. His early songs were more often about romantic relationships, dancing, and rude boys. Left on their own, Bunny and Peter had more freedom to record their own songs, and it is here that the Wailers' music really starts to take on a more political character and begins to point ever so slightly to the Rastafarian path that all three musicians would focus on again and again in song for the rest of their careers.

Second, Bob's absence coincided with the gradual shift away from the jazzy and horn-driven, up-tempo ska that Studio One helped pioneer toward the slower and more romantically themed rocksteady era. This is not to say that there weren't slower love songs before, but the instrumentation and feel of rocksteady set it apart from ska and laid the musical foundation for what would emerge, in a few short years, as reggae.

Here are the songs recorded during that nine months when Bob was away.

As B. Marley and the Wailers, or Bob Marley and the Wailers (Without Bob)

The first song Peter and Bunny recorded after Bob left was a straight-up ska take on the African-American spiritual "Sinner Man" with Skatalites drummer Lloyd Knibb and pianist Jackie Mittoo. Peter recorded this song numerous times throughout his solo career, sometimes as "Oppressor Man" or "Downpressor Man," but here both remaining Wailers share the lead vocal. The song was attributed to B. Marley and the Wailers, but Bob wasn't actually on it.

Peter and Bunny also share the vocals on "Guajara Ska," which for all intents and purposes is an instrumental that merges Cuban guajira with Jamaican ska. In fact, the original track was released as an instrumental under the name the Soul Brothers, even though it had Peter and Bunny repeating the phrase "Guajara ska" throughout the chorus. Later CD reissues attribute it to Bob Marley and the Wailers, no doubt to cash in on Marley's name, even though he's nowhere to be found on the track.

As the Wailers (with Peter Singing Lead)

"Rasta Shook Them Up" was recorded without the rest of the group in April 1966, shortly after Ethiopian Emperor Haile Selassie's historic visit to Jamaica. Selassie was revered as the living God by Rastas, who showed up in droves to see his plane land at Palisadoes Airport in Kingston on April 21. All three Wailers were seriously interested in the African-Caribbean religious movement at this time, but they were not fully committed to it. This is borne out in the song—it does not fervently promote the Rastafarian faith, as Peter's later songs would, but merely provides a journalistic retelling of the Emperor's arrival. Peter introduces the song in the Ethiopian language of Amharic. The "Rasta" in the song refers, of course, to Selassie, whose pre-throne name was Ras Tafari Makonnen, and whom all three Wailers would later refer to as Jah Rastafari.

"Rasta Shook Them Up" is the first statement of Rasta faith in the Wailers' catalogue. According to Masouri, "Rasta Shook Them Up" is the first instance of Rastafari mentioned on record, though the Wailers had actually sung "Rasta, Ras will be there" on the Christmas ska "Sound the Trumpet" back in 1964.

The song is based on a mento by Lord Creator called "Archie Buck Them Up." The backing vocals on "Rasta Shook Them Up" were provided by the Gaylads and, despite Peter being the only Wailer on the song, it was attributed to the group.

"Rasta Shook Them Up" was the only song released under the name the Wailers during this period in which Peter sang lead. However, he did sing lead on another song at a Wailers session that was never released. In August 1966, he covered Bob Dylan's "Blowing in the Wind" during the same session at which Bunny covered Dylan's "Like a Rolling Stone" (see below).

As the Wailers (Bunny Singing Lead)

What is more surprising than Peter taking the lead singing duties is that Bunny did so too. Peter had on occasion sung lead before; Bunny had not, but when you hear some of these songs, you wonder why. Younger than Bob and Peter, less charismatic than Bob, and less outspoken than Peter, Bunny was overshadowed in the group, and his contributions as writer or lead vocalist were few and far between. His turn at taking the lead vocal didn't occur until Bob was in Delaware in 1966, but he didn't waste it.

As noted above, Bunny sang lead alongside Peter in March 1966 on "Sinner Man" and "Guajara Ska." His next session saw the inclusion of Soulettes vocalist Constantine "Vision" Walker to round out the vocal trio. Here they recorded the easygoing soulful love song "Sunday Morning," but the other two songs recorded that day were not easygoing at all. In fact, they are proud, defiant, and self-confident, in true later-Wailers vein. "He Who Feels It Knows It" is a late-era ska track that Bob would later mine for its lyrics ("Every man think that his burden is the heaviest" and "Who feels it knows it Lord") in his 1978 song "Running Away." "Let Him Go" is one of the Wailers' best rude-boy anthems, and was their first rocksteady hit.

What makes these three Bunny songs even more compelling is that Count Ossie plays percussion on them. Ossie was by this time a renowned Rastafarian Nyabinghi drummer whose cultural cachet had risen dramatically a few weeks earlier when he performed for Haile Selassie.

The growing connection to Rastafari would blossom in Bob's absence. This can also be seen in Bunny's composition "I Stand Predominant," a song that seems to praise Selassie as the "one and all" who helps the singer "stand above all." The song subtly points to the new religious worldview adopted by the group and, tellingly, uses the Rasta phrase "I and I," meaning the oneness between humanity and Jah.

Bunny also recorded his first version of "Dreamland" during this period, but it was not released. The song furthers this new spiritual direction, though. A rewrite of the El Tempos' "My Dream Island," it describes a deathless heaven on Earth across the sea. While it never mentions the continent by name, in Bunny's hands this paradise is Africa. The theology of the song, while partially drawn from Ethiopianism (a form of black Christianity that emerged in the British colonies in the eighteenth century, interpreting the Bible and Christian history through an Afro-centric lens), fits with the Rastafarian worldview of Africa as the Promised Land, the home of the living God (Haile Selassie), and therefore a sort of real-time heaven. "Dreamland" wasn't released until years later, but it marks an early engagement with Rasta ideas by Bunny and the Wailers.

The addition of Rastafarian drumming and nascent Rasta-centric lyrics were a telling signpost of the direction the group was heading in. Bob may have emerged as the most recognizable and vocal Rastafarian working in reggae music, but this direction was established by his two bandmates before him.

Other original songs that Bunny sings lead on under the Wailers mantle are "Rock Sweet Rock," "Jerking Time," "What Am I Supposed to Do," and "Dancing Shoes." He also led the group on covers of "I Need You" (a retitled version of the Temptations' "Baby, Baby I Need You," written by Smokey Robinson), and Bob Dylan's "Like a Rolling Stone." The latter keeps most of the original's chorus but overhauls the arrangement, melody, and lyric, revising it as a kind of folk-rock-steady. Also recorded but not released was a cover of the Impressions' "Little Boy Blue," and a version of big-band standard "Sentimental Journey."

As the Wailers (with Peter and Bunny Singing Lead)

The only song where both artists share lead duties that was attributed to the Wailers is a cover of a song by Peter, Paul, and Mary called "Lemon Tree" (originally written by Will Holt). It's a pretty innocuous song with both singers crooning the lyric, and bears none of the newfound confrontational or mystical spirit we see in other songs of the era.

As Peter Touch

Unlike Bunny's solo work, much of Peter's "non-Bob" material was released under his own name, or variations of it. One of his signature songs, "The Toughest," was first recorded while Bob was away in May 1966 and credited to Peter Touch, even though fellow Wailer Constantine "Vision" Walker sings backup on the track. There is no sign of Bunny, however.

The song's lyric not only positions Peter as formidable ("Anything you can do, I can do better"), it also milks a familiar theme in its lyrics: self-righteousness. In other words, Peter is not only tougher than you: he's more morally upstanding, too. According to Peter, the song was written in response to Coxsone Dodd's encouragement of the group to cover sappy American hits. This time, he wanted Peter to sing the submissive "I'm Your Puppet" by James and Bobby Purify. "The Toughest" is Peter in all his angry, defiant glory, stepping out from Coxsone's yolk—the Peter Tosh his diehard fans love to love. It was an early high point in his career, too, as the song gave him his first local big hit.

As Peter Touch and the Chorus

When Peter Tosh first recorded "When the Well Runs Dry" and the Temptations' "Don't Look Back," they were released under the name Peter Touch and the Chorus. Who's the chorus? Bunny, Vision, Rita, and sometimes Marlene Gifford—essentially the Wailers plus the Soulettes, while Bob was out of town. Peter leads this same lineup through the bouncy "Making Love"—a song as salacious as it sounds—and one of the best songs in his catalogue, "Can't You See."

"Can't You See" sounds more like the British Invasion–era blues-rock of the Kinks or Rolling Stones than any Jamaican band, and it foreshadows Tosh's later experimentations in merging rock and reggae (and, indeed, predates Bob's own experimentations with the same). Peter took another crack at this song when the group recorded with Leslie Kong in 1970—it can be found on *The Best of the Wailers*—but the Studio One version from 1966 is way better, and one wonders what Bob thought about this new direction when he returned to Jamaica in the fall!

As Bop and the Belltones

When Peter recorded "Treat Me Good," it should have been released as a Peter Touch and the Chorus single, just as "Can't You See" was. But mistakes happen, and I'll wager he wasn't too pleased when this song was mistakenly credited to Bop and the Belltones (another Studio One group featuring Rudolph "Bop" Simmonds, sometimes listed as Bob and the Beltones).

24

Freedom Time

The Wailers (Try to) Take Control of Their Music

After toiling at Studio One for just over two years, recording somewhere around one hundred songs, reaching the status of national celebrities but still living in poverty, the Wailers were quickly coming to the same conclusions as many black artists in the United States. They were working hard and producing hits, but their producers and record companies were seeing the fruits of their labor.

Feeling exploited and cheated by the underhanded Jamaican music industry, the Wailers followed paths laid out by the likes of Ray Charles, James Brown, and Sam Cooke, and attempted to control their own destinies by controlling every aspect of their product, from composition to recording to pressing to selling. They would have many failures—and would be ripped off—but the group managed to release music on their own record label, and eventually Bob Marley was able to control his music to an extent not seen previously in Jamaica—or in most other countries, for that matter. He told *Melody Maker* in 1973 that Prince Buster was the first artist to break away from the stranglehold that producers had them in. This started a revolution, causing Lee Perry, and then the Wailers, to do the same.

Bob had been working in Delaware for several months in 1966, before coming back to Kingston in the fall. Some sources have said his aim was to emigrate, but others suggest that the trip was specifically designed to help the Wailers become independent. Bob himself seems to have been open to either. In 1973, he recalled moving to Wilmington because of the hardships of living in Kingston, before deciding to return to continue with the band.

The band needed seed money to start their own business—a record label. They initially approached Bunny's father, Thaddeus, but he declined to give them a loan. After all, music seemed like a pretty precarious investment in 1960s Kingston.

Wail'n Soul'm

With no help arriving from their families, Marley's Delaware money was used to allow the Wailers to self-produce their first recording session in November. Despite officially having split with Coxsone Dodd, the group must have been on good enough terms with him to rent out his studio for their own productions. The trio recorded their first version of "Bend Down Low" (which they would later re-record several times) and a track called "Freedom Time," a celebration of their newfound freedom from Coxsone.

These two songs were included on the first 45 released on the band's own Wail'n Soul'm imprint, named for the Wailers and the Soulettes. They struck a short-lived distribution deal with Dodd but complained that he allowed black market pressings as a way to dilute their profits. They had better luck selling records themselves, setting up the Wail'n Soul'm Records shop at 18A Greenwich Park Road in Trench Town, which was where Rita and Bob lived with Aunt Viola. Record distribution took place via bicycle.

The songs released on Wail'n Soul'm between late 1966 and spring 1968 are some of the most gorgeous and infectious Wailers material ever recorded: "Nice Time," "Hypocrites," "Mellow Mood," "Thank You Lord," "Bus Dem Shut," "Stir It Up," "I'm Hurtin' Inside," "Pound Get a Blow," "Mus' Get a Beatin'," "Chances Are," "Fire Fire," and "Don't Rock My Boat." Many were written on a break from

Wail'n Soul'm Singles Selecta collects many of the songs issued on the Wailers' own record label, Wail'n Soul'm, between 1966 and 1968. These represent some of the most gorgeous and infectious Wailers songs ever recorded.   *Author's collection*

The CD cover for *Wail'n Soul'm Singles Selecta.*

Author's collection

Kingston, when Bob, Rita, and the rest of the Wailers spent time in Nine Mile, farming and retreating from the cutthroat Kingston music business. They can be found on a compilation album called *Wail'n Soul'm Singles Selecta*. These tracks are prime rocksteady—deep repetitive bass grooves, chugging single-guitar chanks, and one drop rhythms. The rocksteady era is notable for beginning the recycling of riddims (a.k.a. versioning), and some of these tracks went on to provide foundational bass lines for later reggae songs. The "Hypocrites" riddim can be heard on rockers like Jacob Miller's "Keep On Knockin'" (1979), dancehall hits like Half Pint's "Mr. Landlord" (1983), and Bounty Killer's "Ghetto Dictionary" (2002).

After their last attempt to record at Studio One with former members of the Skatalites on "Bend Down Low" and "Freedom Time," the rest of the material was helmed by a new set of musicians who would come to define the rocksteady era: Jackie Jackson on bass, Hugh Malcolm on drums, Lynn Taitt on guitar, and Winston Wright on piano. Many of these same musicians would return for many of the group's recordings over the next few years and would anchor the excellent *The Best of the Wailers* LP, produced by Leslie Kong in 1970.

Tuff Gong

While the Wailers were betting on a deal they signed with JAD in 1968 to further their fortunes in America, their contracts allowed them to continue releasing their own music in the Caribbean. They did so first under the Wail'n Soul'm imprint, and then, in 1970 or 1971, they changed the name of their label to Tuff Gong. Their record store moved to King Street in Kingston, and was now called the Soul Shack.

They continued to have hits on the domestic front, but these were not as lucrative as they had hoped, even without middlemen. With that said, they issued a few tracks on Tuff Gong in 1971 that captured the attention of the country and became massive hits locally. In the seventies, "Trenchtown Rock" and "Lively Up Yourself" would go on to become favorites among Marley fans who heard the latter on *Natty Dread* and stellar live versions of both on the 1975 album *Live!*

They also tried their hand with a few the local producers, recording with Leslie Kong in early 1970 (resulting in the album *The Best of the Wailers*, as covered in chapter 20) and then with Lee Perry from mid-1970 to early 1971 (see chapter 26). In each instance, the band would be left feeling exploited by their producers, which solidified their resolve to take control of their own music and destiny. But the time with Scratch, especially, was a time of musical growth among the group.

The need to have control over his music and business was inculcated in Bob through the many negative experiences he had with Jamaican producers. When the Wailers later signed with Island Records, they kept this in mind, and they

The modern day location of Tuff Gong, 2015.   *Brent Hagerman*

made sure their contract allowed them to retain control of their product in the Caribbean market. This meant that they often issued singles or records on Tuff Gong after their Island Records releases in the seventies. The reason for this, as Marley explained to Fikisha Cumbo, was to stymie music piracy: "Sometimes you release it in Jamaica, right, but you come to New York, hear the record selling there. Yet nobody have any permission to sell it."

Throughout the decade, Bob worked to build up a recording and distribution empire. By 1978, he had established his own recording studio, called Tuff Gong, at Hope Road; he owned his own pressing plant, too, and planned to use the Tuff Gong label to promote other artists. In fact, when his Island Records deal was up for renewal after *Uprising* in 1980, Bob looked into signing a package deal with Polygram that would include his Tuff Gong artists alongside his own work.

25

Reggae on Broadway

Breaking into America, Almost

An exciting opportunity arose in the winter of 1968, when African-American singer Johnny Nash and his business partner Danny Sims heard Bob Marley and wanted to sign him to their JAD records. They were on vacation in Jamaica, probably in January 1968, when they were introduced to the Wailers at a Rastafari ceremony called a *grounation*. When they heard the Wailers sing, they heard the sound of money. To the Americans, Bob's songs sounded like radio hits.

Nash was interested in breaking Jamaican music in North America, and he thought that Marley was the guy to help him do it. Whereas other Jamaican singers might have trouble in the American market due to their heavy accents, Bob's

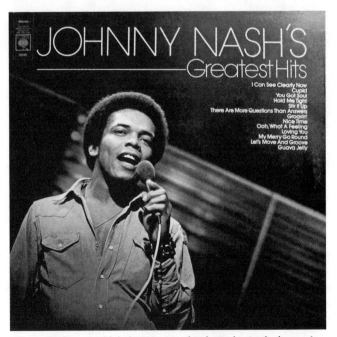

Johnny Nash's record label, JAD, signed Bob Marley in the late 1960s. Nash went on to record several of Bob's compositions, including "Stir It Up."   *Badgreen Records*

words were easy to understand. And, even if Bob's own recordings didn't sell, his songwriting could gel with Nash's slick pop-produced sound.

Nash went on to cover several songs that Bob wrote, like "Guava Jelly," "Comma Comma," and "Stir It Up," and the pair co-wrote "You Poured Sugar on Me" from Nash's 1972 album *I Can See Clearly Now*. Nash's reggae was sterile and soft compared to what was going on in Jamaica—kind of like Bill Haley compared to Elvis, or the Monkees compared to the Beatles—but Bob understood the benefits this exposure could bring. *Melody Maker* quoted him saying of this relationship in 1973, "We appreciated him singing the kind of music he does—he was the first US artist to do reggae—but he isn't really our idol. That's Otis or James Brown or Pickett, the people who work it more hard."

Besides using Bob's writing to further his own career, Nash felt he could turn Marley himself into a chart-topper in the States. To facilitate this, he and Sims signed each member of the Wailers to a publishing and management contract and began demoing dozens of songs on a 1-track tape recorder at Sims's house in Russell Heights, Kingston. They were put on a weekly retainer, earning American dollars for the first time—some sources say as much as $200 each. Their song publishing was through Sims's company, Cayman Music, which was administered by CBS Records. Between 1968 and 1972, Nash and Sims recorded almost a hundred songs by the group, many of which would remain unreleased until after Marley's death.

Nash and Sims wanted to professionalize Marley and his associates. They flew in Jimmy Norman, songwriter with the Coasters, to coach them in singing and writing. They were also not at all enthused with the Jamaican studios or musicians, feeling the equipment to be shoddy and the talent sketchy. They financed the purchase of a new 3-track tape recorder—the first on the island—for Randy's Studio 17 and tracked the Wailers on it. Then they took these tapes to Incredible Sounds Studios in New York, where they overdubbed many songs with top studio musicians from the Atlantic Records stable like Bernie Purdie (drums), Chuck Rainey (bass), Eric Gale (guitar), and Richard Tee (piano). These were the cats who had previously played with luminaries like Aretha Franklin and Quincy Jones, so they were no slouches.

America, Europe, and the First King of Reggae

JAD didn't give the Wailers the breakthrough they had promised, but they did manage to get Bob work outside of Jamaica. In the spring of 1971, they flew him to Stockholm, Sweden, to record the soundtrack to *Want So Much to Believe*. The film, released in September of that year, was panned, and Bob's contribution was slight; he can be heard only in two instrumentals, "Fifteen Minutes" and

"Masquerade Dance." However, they did introduce Bob to Texan keyboardist Johnny "Rabbit" Bundrick, who would go on to provide uncredited keys on *Catch a Fire*'s rock-reggae crossover tracks.

Another opportunity came when CBS, through JAD's connections, released the first Bob Marley track on a major label. "Reggae on Broadway" was recorded with Nash's backing band, the Sons of the Jungle, which included Bundrick, and was credited simply to Bob Marley. The track went nowhere. Marley was angry at CBS's perceived lack of promotion and felt that the company, like JAD, was spending more time promoting Johnny Nash. When the single failed to catch on, a planned album for CBS was scrapped.

Through Johnny Nash, Bob met keyboardist Johnny "Rabbit" Bundrick. Rabbitt would go on to play keys on *Catch a Fire* with the Wailers.

Photo by TimDuncan, Creative Commons license

The Wailers had played their first international show on New Year's Eve 1971 in New York, backed by the Debonaires, in a Caribbean showcase. At the time, the *Gleaner* called the group "Jamaica's most popular staging group." They went on to perform in Pennsylvania and Delaware, but international exposure was still nascent. This was supposed to change with their JAD connections.

It was through JAD, however, that Bob Marley scored his first UK tour in March–May 1972. An acoustic tour of British high schools was booked for Nash and Marley, with Bob opening for Nash and then accompanying him. Each performed a half-hour set during two high-school assemblies each day. The intention of this strategy was to interest record-buying teens in reggae, and, as its popularity grew, the tour branched out to include a full band at concert venues.

The Sons of the Jungle backed up Bob, who initially played without Peter and Bunny. Once the other Wailers joined the tour, they performed alongside members of British reggae band the Cimarons. They were incensed, though, at how Johnny Nash was billed. Since the release of *I Can See Clearly Now* and its subsequent chart success, Nash—a Texan playing easy-listening reggae—was calling himself the King of Reggae, and Bob Marley and the Wailers were relegated to opening his show.

26

Shocks of Mighty

The Upsetter Schools the Wailers

Between August 1970 and April 1971, the Wailers laid down about forty songs for Lee "Scratch" Perry. Many critics see this as Bob's most fertile period, writing and recording songs of a level that were never matched. David Katz sums up the shift in the Wailers' musical thinking during this period this way: "Instead of just aping the soul of black America, Perry had the Wailers totally reconfigured their sound by stripping it back to the basics, encouraging the trio to express themselves in a more raw and distinctly Jamaican way, rather than simply shadowing their American heroes."

Scratch helped Marley change his vocal style, too. Marley's vocals before and after the Lee Perry period are noticeably different: they are more evocative at quieter levels, and more Jamaican/less American soul. If you listen to Perry's own "Dreadlocks in Moonlight"—a song he originally wrote for Bob but decided to record himself—you can hear a lot of the vocal qualities that Marley adopted from him.

Enter the Barretts

Scratch's infamous Black Ark studio in Washington Gardens wouldn't be built until 1973, so for the time being he recorded the group first at Dynamic Sounds Studio and then at Randy's Studio 17. One of the keys to the shift toward a *dreader* sound was that the Wailers used Perry's studio band, the Upsetters. At the core of the Upsetters was the drum-and-bass sibling duo of Carlton and "Familyman" Barrett. The group started as the Hippy Boys with Lloyd Charmers, guitarist Alva "Reggie" Lewis, and organist Glen Adams, recording tracks for producers like Bunny Lee, Sonia Pottinger, and Leslie Kong. In fact, members of the group, including the Barretts, worked on several early reggae hits like Max Romeo's "Wet Dream" and Dave and Ansell Collin's "Liquidator."

The Barretts' contribution to the Wailers' sound cannot be overstated. Up until this point (mid-1970), the Wailers had always recorded using the typical Jamaican formula of singing group plus studio backing band. The band changed depending on the studio, and even depending on which musicians showed up to the studio that day. This meant that the Wailers had never had an exclusive backing band of their own, as professional studio musicians would play with numerous vocal acts. By this time, Peter Tosh and Bob Marley had begun playing rhythm guitar on some of the band's recordings, and Bunny occasionally played percussion, but their songs were always recorded with the musicians present that day, who would learn them on the fly.

Bob was so taken by the work of the Barrett brothers that the relationship between them almost immediately surpassed the normal singer/studio musician level of collaboration. Familyman told his biographer, John Masouri, "When Bob and I first join forces, it wasn't just like any other artist and musician working together on one or two sessions. I wasn't a session musician for the Wailers, because I become part of a thing. We become part of the Wailers band."

The Barretts wouldn't legally become part of the Wailers until later, but his point is valid here—Familyman and Carlton collaborated with the Wailers singers, and, under the eye of the creative and slightly mad genius Lee Perry, fulfilled a vision to develop a sound that was as rebellious and dread as the lyrics the Wailers were beginning to sing.

Long gone were the American teenage bubblegum covers and songs about dance crazes. The Wailers helped take the focus of reggae off of the poppier and quicker reggae of the late sixties and away from Jamaicanized covers of American pop and soul. The material with Perry dealt with existential

Lee "Scratch" Perry performing in 2015. As a friend and producer, Perry had considerable influence over the Wailers' musical direction between 1970 and 1971, resulting in a more mature sound that laid the groundwork for Bob Marley's rootsier direction on his mid/late-1970s material.

Photo by Manfred Werner—Tsui, Creative Commons license

matters ("Duppy Conqueror"), the corrupt local music business ("Small Axe"), mystical mavericks ("Soul Rebel"), and biblical proverbs ("Corner Stone"). The sound of the music was more haunting and melancholy, even on tracks that seem dreamy and euphoric lyrically, like the original "Sun Is Shining" ("Sun is shining, the weather is sweet / Make you wanna move, your dancing feet") and the herb-induced "Kaya."

This was the sound of a group that meant business. And, as the Wailers' lyrics changed more and more to reflect their Rastafarian beliefs, the Barretts pounded out heavier rhythms to accompany them, consciously trying to match dread lyrics with a dread sound. Roots reggae is generally defined as reggae that is musically harder or heavier, usually meaning more prominence is given to the bass and drums over the melody instruments. John Masouri suggests that the Wailers' rhythm section is due credit for matching the weightier lyrics with fitting arrangements: "The Barretts were now seeking ways in which to make the music sound 'dread' and to convey the power of Jah, as described in the Book of Revelation."

As in all reggae, the Wailers' bass lines are the backbone of the song. But unlike much of the reggae coming out of Jamaica, where the bass was restricted to short ostinatos, the lines that Familyman played under Bob's songs began to explore a wider melodic territory. I asked him about his approach to playing bass in the Wailers in 2003. He indicated that his style was derived from his love of singing: "I play a melodic bass, like I'm singing baritone. I always design a bass line to let the vocal swing and sway on top of that with the heartbeat of the drum coming from my brother."

Songwriting

Many sources have indicated that Lee Perry worked closely with Bob on the songs from this period. Initial pressings of tracks like "Duppy Conqueror" and "Small Axe" were credited to both writers, though Perry was removed in reissues or re-recordings. Bunny Wailer, however, has maintained that Scratch had nothing to do with the composition of these songs.

Money Woes Again

Acrimony was how every relationship between the Wailers and a producer had ended so far, and their union with Scratch was no exception. They had hoped that he would be different, and this is why they settled on a verbal agreement for a 50/50 split in all profits. The Lee Perry material was released on two albums, *Soul Rebels* (1970) and *Soul Revolution II* (1971). However, Perry licensed the records to Trojan in the UK, but apparently didn't mention this to the band. Bob found out about this when he saw *Soul Rebels* in a record shop while in London in 1971. The group felt Perry had double-crossed them. His position wasn't strengthened when he also reneged on the profit-splitting deal and instead gave them ten cents on each record. This led not only to arguments but also to a physical altercation, resulting in Bunny knocking him over.

This is reminiscent of the rupture with Coxsone. Reggae mythology states that Lee Perry subsequently brought a bottle of acid to a meeting with Peter, ostensibly to frighten the band into accepting the financial deal. According to Bunny, though, he and Peter chased the producer away. And for his part, Scratch has maintained that there was no acid.

Bob and Scratch

Despite the way the relationship ended, Bob would return to work with Scratch throughout his career. The songs he recorded with Scratch were often very different from the Island Records material he released in the seventies, and they offer snapshots of Bob writing first and foremost for a Jamaican audience.

Soul Rebels was one of two Wailers records released by Lee Perry.
Author's collection

In early 1974, having already released *Catch a Fire* and *Burnin'*, he recorded a vocal track called "Turn Me Loose" over the riddim for "Kaya," a song he had previously laid down with Perry in 1971. The next year, he recorded "Rainbow Country" and the first version of "Natural Mystic" with Perry at Black Ark. These were issued as singles but not released on an Island LP. Most notably, he went to Lee Perry when, after hearing reports of Haile Selassie's death in August 1975, he wanted to immediately record a song of assurance and faith. The result was the poignant "Jah Live," plus a dub version called "Concrete." In the fall of 1976, he returned again to Scratch to record a peace song for the Smile Jamaica concert. They laid down versions of both parts of "Smile Jamaica" at Black Ark and Harry J's.

Bob also got Scratch to record "Keep On Moving" and "Punky Reggae Party" in the summer of 1977. While the former as an update of an Impressions song first covered by the Wailers in 1971 with Perry, the latter was Bob's lyrical response to punk. It is also one of his only songs of the period to feature the steppers drumbeat—the rhythm, fashionable in Jamaica at the time, was seen as more contemporary than the by-now old fashioned one drop his band was used to playing. None of the Wailers played on these tracks, which were recorded in London, Miami, and at Black Ark in Kingston.

Bob's final recording session with Lee Perry was in mid-1978. This time, the Wailers were present at Black Ark as Bob recorded a song about the very Jamaican pastime of playing dominos ("Who Colt the Game") and "I Know a Place."

27

What's New Pussycat?

Strange Songs That Marley Covered

During their tenure at Studio One, the Wailers were making pop records, and this point shouldn't be forgotten. Sure, Bob later became associated with militant roots reggae—a genre that never really crossed over into pop consciousness in the US, though it did, briefly, in the UK—but during this period the band was striving to make music that appealed to record buyers and dance patrons. Many of their early original songs were about teenage romance and dancing. In the liner notes to *Destiny: Rare Ska Sides from Studio One*, Pierson and Steffens remind readers that "few of the fans who came to Jamaican music in the mid-seventies were aware that the Wailers had always performed these songs. The Wailers always felt that they should sing a variety of songs for a variety of people."

Like most successful pop acts, the Wailers were striving for success, so they listened to producer Coxsone Dodd when he suggested songs that they could cover. Coxsone was interested in finding new demographics to which to market his music, and would get the group to record everything from spirituals and mento to doo-wop and Tin Pan Alley pop alongside their ska material.

Given Marley's revolutionary later catalogue, it seems incongruous now to revisit his covers of Tin Pan Alley fare, British Invasion ballads, lovesick teenage schlock, and, wait for it, Christmas carols. Peter Tosh biographer John Masouri assures us that Peter was not happy with what he saw as concessions to the market, wanting instead to focus on rebellious material. Bob, however, seemed to be game to try whatever it took to make his name and get ahead in the music business.

Christmas in Kingston

Coxsone Dodd knew a lucrative trend when he saw one. Why not get his new band to record a Christmas song or two? The Wailers, in fact, recorded two winter chestnuts while at Studio One. "Sound the Trumpet" was released on the Studio One LP

Christmas in Jamaica soon after they joined the label in 1964. Its alternate title is "Christmas Is Here," and it is actually a pretty riotous yuletide romp, thanks to the rambunctious ska beat the Skatalites lay down and a trumpet solo that quotes "Santa Claus Is Coming to Town." It's also more revolutionary than it sounds, since it is the first Wailers tune to mention Rasta: "Rasta, Ras will be there." By comparison, their take on "White Christmas," recorded a year later, is nothing short of laughable, and enough to make it into this book's list of worst Marley songs (see chapter 29).

Teenagers in Love with American Pop

Brill Building writing duo Doc Pomus and Mort Shuman penned "Teenager in Love," which gave Dion and the Belmonts a hit in 1959. Likely due to its popularity, Coxsone had the Wailers try their hand at it in 1964. The song rethinks the chord progression, adds a bridge, overhauls the lyrics, and throws in a Tommy McCook sax solo. It's a good example of how Jamaican musicians deconstructed American hits for their local audience. And while it's certainly incongruent with his later conscious reggae, for a cover of a song the Rock and Roll Hall of Fame has called one of the "greatest songs in rock and roll history," it's a decent remake by a teenage Marley.

Another teen-rocker that the Wailers borrowed was teen idol Jimmy Clanton's "Go Jimmy Go" in 1964. The song was also the title of the 1959 Alan Freed film that starred Clanton alongside rock 'n' roll royalty Chuck Berry. Clanton's no slouch with the R&B/rock 'n' roll, but his song sounds pretty square next to the Wailers' version, and is at about half the tempo. "Go Jimmy Go" is one of the best tracks from the ska-era Wailers.

Blue-Eyed Reggae

By 1970, the Wailers had been done with Coxsone Dodd for four years, but they occasionally still dipped into the American pop well for a cover or two. Coxsone's business plan had obviously had an effect, and JAD Records encouraged this cover. The group's self-produced "Give Me a Ticket," sang by Peter with harmony by Bob, Bunny, and Rita, was a slowed-down, brown-eyed version of the blue-eyed Box Tops' "The Letter." Listen to this song next to Paul Simon's "Mother and Child Reunion" sometime. The backing band is pretty much the same, and the similarities are noticeable.

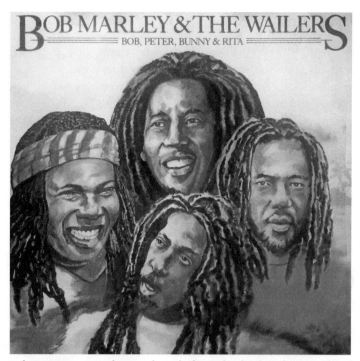

Bob, Peter, Bunny, and Rita, released after Bob's death and consisting of heavy-handed synth overdubs whose shelf life has long passed, has to be the worst Bob Marley record available.   *Author's collection*

Like a Rhinestone Rasta: Bob's Country Covers

Jamaica has had a long but overlooked love affair with American country and western music. Toots and the Maytals offered a convincing cover of "(Take Me Home) Country Roads" in the seventies, and even Bob Marley was no stranger to a little lonesome cowboy crooning. One the very first songs he recorded in 1962 was a reworked country favorite from the year before, Claude Gray's "I'll Just Have a Cup of Coffee (Then I'll Go)." Bob called his version "One Cup of Coffee," and, of course, it has none of the slick, sophisticated Nashville sound of the original.

The other country song in Marley's repertoire was "Sea of Heartbreak," which was reworked in the Wailers' hands as "Where's the Girl for Me." The original reached #2 on the *Billboard* Hot Country Singles and Tracks chart in 1962, as sung by Country Music Hall of Famer Don Gibson. Johnny Cash did a splendid cover on *Unchained*, and he also covered Marley's "Redemption Song," so there are two examples of reggae and country fusion.

The Jamaican Beatles

When the Beatles landed in New York in February 1964, they turned the American music industry on its head. These reverberations were also felt five hundred miles southeast of the US, in Kingston, where numerous versions of Beatles hits would be recorded over the next decade. The Wailers, who some Kingstonians referred to as the Jamaican Beatles, added their voices to this chorus with a take on "And I Love Her" in 1965, one year after the original. Years later, when Island Records put together a posthumous video for "One Love" to promote the *Legend* compilation, it would include footage of Paul McCartney dancing and lip-synching to the tune. The British Invasion had an effect on Peter Tosh, too. His own song "Can't You See," recorded twice during his tenure with the band, has obvious nods to British Invasion rave-ups.

What's with the Slapstick?

A stranger Wailers song never existed than "What's New Pussycat?" Bob Marley covering Tom Jones? The fact that the Woody Allen slapstick film this song is from is about a womanizer, though, makes the subject material not entirely outside of Marley's wheelhouse. Once more mining the gold records written by Brill Building songwriters (in this case Burt Bacharach and Hal David), the Wailers recorded this within a few months of the release of the original. In the competitive Kingston music biz, you had to stay current, although the liner notes to *Destiny: Rare Ska Sides from Studio One* suggest that the Wailers only reluctantly agreed to record it. The backing band is the Skatalites, who never met a square song they couldn't round the corners off of.

Like a Rolling Stoned Wailer

Technically, Bob didn't cover Dylan's "Like a Rolling Stone," but his bandmates took a stab at it and "Blowing in the Wind" while he was working in Delaware in 1966. "Blowing in the Wind" has never been released; "Like a Rolling Stone" is more of an adaptation than a cover, as Bunny Wailer really only borrows Dylan's chorus, composing new verses over what feels like a ska attempt at the Righteous Brothers' "You've Lost That Lovin' Feelin'." It really doesn't sound like it should work, but Bunny totally owns it, and it's a rare gem that deserves to be aired in public. Dylan, for his part, wasn't a complete stranger to reggae either. In the eighties, he recorded with Sly and Robbie on the tasty, reggae-flavored *Infidels*.

Little Green Apples

Written by Nashville songwriter Bobby Russell and previously a chart hit in country and adult-contemporary versions, the Wailers' 1969 version of "Little Green Apples" will make you wonder what the hell they were thinking. Peter Tosh sings lead on this track, which bears some resemblance to the James Brown version that inspired it.

28

Bob Marley's Record Collection

The Influence of American Soul

When trying to pin down the various influences on Bob Marley's music, it is not hard to hear echoes of earlier forms of Jamaican popular music (quadrille, mento), neighboring Caribbean music forms (Trinidadian calypso, Cuban rhumba), British and American folk and rock, and, even more distantly, the vast musical cultures of Africa. But the one influence that Marley consistently wore proudly and clearly in his music was that of American R&B. Two artists in particular stand out: James Brown and Curtis Mayfield. In 1973, Bob told a journalist that the Drifters were his greatest influence, and that songs like "Magic Moment" and "Please Stay" had inspired him to put a singing group together. These three artists probably influenced Bob more than any others.

Bob's love of R&B was certainly not unique in Jamaica. Says historian Garth White of musical taste in fifties Jamaica, "The appeal of rhythm and blues to the Jamaican black masses was almost total." And Jamaicans, he says, preferred grittier R&B—not lightweight romance numbers but the harder-driving music of Fats Domino and Louis Jordan. The Marley fan only familiar with his Island Records releases might miss the R&B connection. These songs were certainly influenced by American music, but less blatantly so than his songwriting from 1962 to 1971. Here is a breakdown of where and how soul music finds its way into Marley's songs.

R&B or Soul?

The term *rhythm and blues*, or R&B, was coined by *Billboard* editor Jerry Wexler (who later became an Atlantic Records music producer and A&R man) and was used by the magazine to replace the term *race music* in its charts in the late forties. Both R&B and race music were umbrella terms for music created by and for African-Americans. In the sixties, the term *soul* was popularized as another umbrella term for black music of the period, but it was more accurately applied as a subgenre of R&B that married secular dance music to the more expressive gospel music of the black church. Given Marley's own repertoire of religious music—both Christian and Rasta—it is no surprise that he was drawn to the gospel/R&B hybrid of American soul.

Not only does *soul* connote a connection to church music, soul by the late sixties was also often message music. Calypso, mento, and to a lesser extent ska and rocksteady, were highly rhythmic forms of music that had been used as carriers of topical and political messages before, but artists like James Brown and Curtis Mayfield took this to a whole new level. Brown's 1968 hit "Say It Loud—I'm Black and I'm Proud" was played regularly on Jamaican radio. This song, according to Masouri in *Wailing Blues*, "proved a revelation to Jamaican musicians like Bob Marley" because of its "format of blending dynamic rhythm, a serious lyrical agenda and pop sensibilities into one crucial package."

Of course, Marley wasn't just interested in the spiritual and political dimensions of music. He also wanted to be a soul star like Otis Redding.

Bob Marley's Record Collection

When Bob joined up with Studio One, Coxsone Dodd allowed him access to his record collection. Dodd's R&B records included Motown acts Stevie Wonder, Marvin Gaye, and the Marvelettes, doo-wop groups the Drifters and the Impressions, gospel groups the Caravans and Highway QCs, and New Orleans R&B like Lee Dorsey. He also had a respectable collection of jazz, country, rock, Latin, and folk—anything that was big at the time or could provide an education in music for his stable of artists. But according to the producer himself, in the liner notes to the 1977 compilation *Early Music*, "Bob liked the Impressions, the Tams, and the Moonglows the most." We can tell which artists Bob was most drawn to by looking at the songs the Wailers covered in the sixties.

Doo-Wop

The Wailers' favorite radio station in the sixties was WINZ from Miami, which played the latest American hits. They had patterned themselves after African-American doo-wop groups, and they loved songs they heard on the radio like "My Prayer" by the Platters; "Under the Boardwalk," "Up on the Roof," and "On Broadway" by the Drifters; "I'm Not a Juvenile Delinquent" by Frankie Lymon and the Teenagers; and "Tears on My Pillow" by Little Anthony and the Imperials.

The Wailers covered "Ten Commandments of Love," previously done by both the Moonglows and Little Anthony and the Imperials. But you can also hear direct links to some of these artists in the group's original compositions like "Dance with Me," recorded at Studio One in 1964. It was written by Marley but borrows heavily from the Drifters' 1963 hit "On Broadway," which was written by Tin Pan Alley R&B royalty Leiber and Stoller and takes its name from another Drifters song. "Dance with Me" is also a precursor to Marley's 1972 flop "Reggae on Broadway," the intro to which has similarities to "Dance with Me" and also invokes another Drifters song in name ("On Broadway"), though it bears no similarities to that 1959 hit.

Bob's love of doo-wop can also be heard in his Rastafari conversion song of 1967, "Selassie Is the Chapel." Suggested to him by spiritual advisor Mortimo Planno, the song is based on American doo-wop group the Orioles' "Crying in the Chapel." The Orioles topped the R&B charts with the song in 1953, and Elvis put it in the Hot 100, and the British charts, in 1965.

Jamaica's Motown

While the doo-wop influence certainly informed the group's work throughout the sixties, there are many more examples of Northern soul (a.k.a. Motown) in their repertoire of covered and original songs. Bob especially loved Stevie Wonder and Marvin Gaye, as well as "You Really Got a Hold on Me" by the Miracles and "Dancing in the Street" by Martha and the Vandellas. Both Trench Town and Studio One have been called Jamaica's Motown, and the Wailers certainly kept the comparison alive. Their 1965 track "Ska Jerk" was based on the melody for Junior Walker and the All-Stars' 1964 hit "Shotgun" but was reworked to capitalize on the jerk, an American dance craze of the time. Junior Walker and the All Stars' "Gotta Hold on to This Feeling" was also given the Wailers treatment as "Hold on to This Feeling" in 1970, with Bob singing lead.

They did their best Temptations impression on 1966's "I Need You," which is a cover of "Baby, Baby I Need You," written by Smokey Robinson and voiced by Bunny while Bob was in Delaware. Peter also tackled one of the Temptations' songs, "Don't Look Back," while Bob was away. The Temptations remained influential on the group in later years. In 1978, Peter revisited "Don't Look Back" as a duet with Mick Jagger called "You Gotta Walk (Don't Look Back)."

Smokey Robinson proved to be a popular songwriter with the Studio One crowd. When Rita and the Soulettes covered his Miracles song "Choosey Beggar" as the Jamaicanized "A Deh Pon Dem," the Wailers, sans Bob, helped out. In fact, Rita has said that, by the end of the sixties, the Soulettes were being billed as the "Supremes of the Caribbean" on their tours around the islands.

The Wailers borrowed from two separate Motown groups for their 1965 song "Playboy," a rewrite of the Contours' "Do You Love Me" that also stole its title from the Marvelettes' hit of the same name.

The Impressionable Wailers

Of all the American R&B groups, the Wailers loved the Impressions the best. They were the most covered group in the Wailers' repertoire. The band's mix of doo-wop harmonies, pop sensibilities, R&B rhythms, and gospel influences appealed to the Wailers and influenced their own treatment of ska, rocksteady, and reggae. By 1965, even the Wailers' publicity photos bore their influence—the one found on the cover of *The Wailing Wailers* was a copy of an Impressions photo. The Impressions' 1964 album *Keep On Pushin'*, with its civil rights consciousness, also appealed to the group, who would go on to write songs of political commentary themselves, calling for social justice.

The Impressions began as the Roosters in 1958, and perhaps it is no coincidence that vocal coach Joe Higgs used to joke with the cocky Wailers by calling them by the same name. When the Impressions performed at the Carib Theatre in Kingston in 1966, the Wailers were in the front row.

The songs either directly covered by the Wailers or highly influential on the band are numerous. They covered "I Made a Mistake" (1965), "Just Another Dance" (1965), and "Long, Long Winter" (1970). They also covered songs that the Impressions had recorded but not written. In these instances, the Wailers' versions were most directly inspired by the Impressions' versions. We can hear this in their take on Peter, Paul, and Mary's "Lemon Tree" (1966) and the traditional gospel song "Amen" (1965).

Many more songs were heavily influenced by specific Impressions songs, either as rewrites or by ripping off a lyric here and there. "It Hurts to Be Alone" (1964) borrows lines from the Impressions' "I'm So Proud," and "Where Is My Mother" (1965) co-opts a verse from "Little Boy Blue." "Riding High," recorded in 1970, borrows elements from the Impressions song of the same name. "Talking 'Bout My Baby" was rewritten as "Diamond Baby" in 1965. "One Love" (1965) is a rewrite of the Impressions' "People Get Ready," and when Bob re-recorded the song for *Exodus*, he titled it "One Love / People Get Ready." The Impressions' "I Gotta Keep On Movin'" inspired aspects of the Wailers' "Rude Boy (Gone a Jail)," and was also covered almost faithfully by the band in 1971, the Wailers' "Keep On Moving" exchanging the Impressions' 6/8 swing feel for a standard reggae 4/4 one drop. Marley would revisit this song again in 1977, making Curtis Mayfield of the Impressions the only songwriter he covered during the Island Records years.

James Brown

The Wailers weren't only inspired musically and visually by American soul. By 1965, their stage show had the makings of a Jamaican James Brown experience, wherein Bob would feign exhaustion, drop to the floor only to be caught by the band, and then bounce back to the microphone to finish the song. They loved the Godfather of Soul's music, too, and many of their own songs demonstrate this. Lee Perry says that Bob wanted to sound like James Brown, and he came close to doing so on the Perry-produced "Black Progress." It starts out with a Sam and Dave "Soul Man" soundalike intro, but the majority of the song is a thinly veiled rewrite of Brown's 1968 hit "Say It Loud—I'm Black and I'm Proud."

The Wailers' first Perry-produced track, "My Cup," was a rewrite of Brown's "I Guess I've Got to Cry, Cry, Cry." Brown's "There Was a Time" became "Feel Alright," with Bob changing the lyric "Augusta, GA" to "Augustus, JA." You can also hear the Brown influence on other tracks such as the Jamaicanized funk of "Soul Almighty," the James Brown–like exultations in "Caution" ("Hit me from the top, you crazy mother-funky!"), and the vocal interjections on "Soul Captives."

Southern Soul

Southern soul also held sway on the early Wailers. The group loved Otis Redding, and his influence can be heard on "When the Well Runs Dry" (1965), which borrows lyrics, though not the feel, of "You Don't Miss Your Water (Till Your Well Runs Dry)." Bob also let loose some of his funkiness on "Soul Shakedown Party," which includes the American slang line, "Hit it brother, y'all."

29

Milkshake and Potato Chips

Marley's Worst Songs

Having a Bob Marley poster in your college dorm room is a sure sign that your musical taste is hipper than that of your peers. Since the seventies, this poster has been used to indicate that you have no time for the flavor-of-the-month, mind-numbing offerings of the pop charts; your musical palette is pure. You, sir or ma'am, are a rebel, and your revolution will have a kick-ass soundtrack. That is until you hear the songs listed below. Then your revolution might shrivel up like a balloon in a freezer. Bob Marley may have made some of the world's coolest grooves, but even the King of Reggae clicked on the shit switch sometimes.

Having a favorite Marley song is something all of his fans can be proud of (mine changes, but it currently revolves between "Nice Time" from the Wail'n Soul'm era and the 12-inch version of Lee Perry–produced "Punky Reggae Party"), but a least favorite? Mine used to be "Waiting in Vain," because of my sheer exhaustion at hearing it played and covered by literally everyone. But as I dug deeper into his catalogue, I realized there are several songs that actually make me wince, and a few that make me embarrassed for him. (But seriously, with hundreds of songs to his name, I think we can forgive him a few ear-turds.)

For many fans and critics, Bob Marley's music is uncompromising, and the songs that critics have tended to complain about are the ones where he appears to be trying too hard to reach pop-crossover success. To be fair, the notion of artistic authenticity from which this music-journalist standard is derived began during the rock discourse of the sixties, when experimentation was rewarded and anything derivative was knocked. Black music in America and Jamaica had different ideas of what was authentic, and covering a few popular songs probably didn't pollute those ideals. And some of these songs probably sounded at least okay at the time, even though as modern listeners we are left shaking our heads.

With those caveats in mind, here are the Bob Marley songs that no one needs to hear again.

The Covers

The Wailers took many foreign covers and reworked them into simply stellar Jamaicanized adaptations, demonstrating their ability to pay homage to their influences while remaining true to their own artistic vision. However, a few of those covers have not stood the test of time, and are best left to history.

"White Christmas"

While working with Coxsone Dodd at Studio One, the Wailers recorded many songs that they probably were embarrassed about later, a few Christmas songs among them. They really delivered coal with their 1965 attempt at Irving Berlin's "White Christmas." Inspired by the Drifters' 1954 doo-wop version, the band at least made the song somewhat relevant to the Jamaican experience by changing the lyric "just like the ones I used to know" to "not like the ones I knew before." That's not enough, however, to save it. This is not to say there's anything inherently wrong with Caribbean Christmas songs. It's just that the Wailers are straining to force a fairly staid, Tin Pan Alley ballad into a Jamaican idiom, and the result falls far short of later reggae-Christmas experimentations such as Jacob Miller's excellent dubby LP *Natty Christmas* (1978).

"Sugar, Sugar"

Imagine if Bob Marley covered a bubblegum pop song by a fictional group of teenagers in a television sitcom based on a comic book. Guess what? He did. Not exactly rebel music. "Sugar, Sugar" was a 1969 hit from the US cartoon *The Archie Show*, originally sung by the Archies. They were sort of like the Monkees, except they were, well, not real people. Truth be told, Marley's version doesn't actually suck, and it is far cooler than the source material. Wilson Pickett added some credibility to the song with his soul cover in 1970. To the Wailers' credit, their version, recorded at Randy's Studio in 1970, steers clear of both versions, and the saccharine lyrics are helped immensely by the members of the Supersonics, who guide the song into more groovy territory. Still, this is unabashedly reggae-pop, and many critics have slammed it because of its conspicuous bid for crossover success. Masouri, in his *Wailin' Blues*, calls it "blatantly commercial" and "out of sync" with the contemporary reggae scene, marking a "definite low point" of their career.

"Milkshake and Potato Chips"

During a talk called "Unearthing Marley's Oral History" at the 2015 International Reggae Conference in Kingston, Marley historian Roger Steffens made it clear what his least favorite Marley song was. Referring to the downright embarrassing "Milkshake and Potato Chips," Steffens told the audience that nobody ever needs to hear the song again. He's right: it's atrocious. Biographer Timothy White calls it a "freakish" song, "a puerile novelty song about a girl who pays more attention to junk food than to her fiancé."

The track was one of a number of songs written by Jimmy Norman (of the Coasters) and Al Pyfrom. In 1968, at the request of JAD Records, Bob traveled to Norman's apartment in the Bronx to hear songs Norman had penned for him. Frustrated with his lack of success in the Jamaican music business, he was trying out American pop styles. As Steffens told the *New York Times* in 2002, Marley "was trying everything in the first years of his career he could to have a major hit. He saw this as a way to put himself in somebody else's hands who could guide him to American chart success." To make matters worse, the track was remixed by JAD for inclusion on the ill-advised 1985 album *Bob, Peter, Bunny, and Rita.* The keyboards and programmed-drum overdubs are heavy-handed, and they make an already weak song unbearable.

Original Songs

It might be blasphemous to say it, but the reggae gods didn't always smile on Bob's creations. In context, most of these songs make sense—often, he was bidding to further his career with attempts at widening his fan base—but that doesn't mean they have aesthetic appeal today.

"Reggae on Broadway"

Bob Marley's relationship with Johnny Nash and Danny Sims of JAD Records was supposed to break him into the American market. Many of the songs he wrote for them reflect his attempts at appealing to black Americans, and "Reggae on Broadway" is no different. Recorded with Sons of the Jungle in London in April 1972, "Reggae on Broadway" is notable because it was Bob's major label debut, released on May 26, 1972, by CBS. Like his other reggae-pop work, it tends to be slammed by modern critics for its lack of rebelliousness; the overproduction reflects the commerciality of the music business, and Bob's attempt to appeal to a black pop demographic is generally seen as a temporary lapse of his values. David Katz once called it "heavily commercialized dross."

The main problem is that the song is conflicted musically, and simply doesn't know whether it is reggae, rock, or funk. Instead of forming a convincing pastiche, its piecemeal arrangement leaves bits and pieces sticking out all over the place—a heavy electric guitar here (rock?), a tremolo guitar there (country?), an attempt at funk with a baritone sax on the chorus. It's a hybrid, to be sure, but of what, exactly, it's hard to tell.

"Dance Do the Reggae"

Produced at the same ill-fated JAD sessions as "Reggae on Broadway," "Dance Do the Reggae" is, confusingly, not really a reggae song at all. Instead, it is an example of trying to throw several musical styles at a wall (or a music chart, in this case) to see what sticks. Unfortunately, nothing does. The mawkish flute trills and tenor sax solo suggest a love ballad that fits awkwardly next to a modestly good, up-tempo chorus. This song didn't get anyone dancing, to reggae or otherwise.

"No Woman, No Cry"

No, I'm not talking about the stately and epic live version that graces the 1975 album *Live!*. That version is among the best way to spend seven minutes and eight seconds of your life. The original, though, is a different story. Released on the *Natty Dread* album a year earlier, it sounded like a demo recording that, once a producer heard it, would then be cut from the final track listing. First, the tempo clocks in around 200bpm (compared to the live version's 155bmp), if you count it in half time—which is the standard way to think of reggae—making the song sound rushed and voiding the whole reassuring but sexy vibe of *Live!*. But that's not the worst of it. Somebody had obviously just bought an early drum machine (perhaps a Hammond Auto-Vari?) and thought it would be a good idea to send the drummer out for a smoke while the tape was rolling. This is the squarest Bob Marley song in existence, and it bears almost no resemblance to the barnburner live version.

"Disco Nights"

Bob Marley was asked to produce American disco singer Martha Velez's *Escape from Babylon*. In doing so, he wrote "Disco Nights" with her and oversaw the Wailers as they recorded versions of their songs like "Bend Down Low," "Get Up, Stand Up," and "I'm Hurting Inside" (renamed "Happiness"). Reviewer Scott Blackerby described "Disco Nights" as "hideous," admitting, "I can honestly say I've seldom heard someone handle reggae rhythms with less success." I disagree, in that the backing is as organic as you would expect from the Wailers. What feels more incompatible is the overwrought vocal performance, which belongs in Philadelphia, not Kingston, though I guess that was the point of a disco-reggae crossover.

"I Know"

Recorded in 1975, "I Know" was not released until after Bob died. In fact, it was the first single issued after his passing in 1981. This song has Marley's lyrical prowess, but the production tries too hard to traverse into pop R&B territory. It's dominated by a synthesizer that, while probably cutting edge in 1981, now sounds schmaltzy. It was included on the posthumous LP *Confrontation* with another crossover attempt, "Could You Be Loved." This latter song successfully marries R&B and roots reggae, though, and its heavy radio play helped keep Marley's legacy alive in the years between his death and the release of *Legend*.

"Buffalo Soldier" (King Sporty Mix)

"Buffalo Soldier" is credited to Bob Marley and Noel Williams, a.k.a. King Sporty. Williams, who died in 2015, was a Miami-based Jamaican who worked as a deejay at Studio One in the sixties before emigrating. He helped out the Wailers in 1975 when he bailed out Marley's art director, Neville Garrick, who had been jailed for trying to smuggle ganja into Miami. It was also Sporty who connected Marley with Alex Sadkin, who engineered *Rastaman Vibration* at Criteria Studios.

The song we all know and love was recorded in 1980, but it didn't come out until after Marley passed, first issued by Island Records in 1982 and then appearing on *Confrontation* in 1983. But then a remix of this song—about African-American army units during the US Civil War, dubbed Buffalo Soldiers by indigenous Americans—was released immediately after, and it has not stood the test of time at all. Known as the King Sporty Mix, it is a strangely roots-less, electro-pop version of a Marley song. Gone are the organic vibes of the Wailers, replaced by the rather soulless, fast-paced playing of Miami session musicians. Even Bob's vocals are unconvincing, and have little of the impact of the better-known version.

The song also had a rather dubious release history, not in character with Marley's anti-corporate persona. A few weeks after Island released the original single, the label reissued it for a limited time with a free copy of the King Sporty Mix included on a separate disc in an attempt to get fans to buy the single twice.

The last thing I'll say about this song to support its inclusion on a list of worst Bob Marley songs is that the chorus (the scat-sang "woe yoe yoe" part) is clearly lifted from a sixties children's TV program called *The Banana Splits Adventure Hour*. Once you Google its theme song—"The Tra La La Song (One Banana, Two Banana)"—you will have that stuck in your head every time you hear "Buffalo Soldier." In Marley's defense, he may have lifted the melody from the Dickies' 1979 punk version, which was a Top 10 single in the UK.

The Worst Albums

The streaming generation doesn't do albums—I get it. But once upon a time, you worked hard to save up money to buy an LP, and then had to listen to the entire thing, even the filler—it was too much bother to skip tracks. Well, there are a couple of Marley albums that make it worth your while to walk across the room and lift the needle. Or, in this case, put on a new record altogether.

Bob, Bunny, Peter, and Rita

There are some dubious Bob Marley compilations out there, and most of them seem to have some connection to JAD. Bob recorded a lot of demos for the company that only began to see the light of day after his death. Generally, the songwriting is very good, though some of the recordings are of demo quality. *Bob, Peter, Bunny, and Rita* was released in 1985, and while it features songs that were originally recorded in Jamaica, the backing tracks were replaced by US session musicians, under the heavy-handed production of Joe Venneri (who had a Top 10 hit with "The Lion Sleeps Tonight" with his band, the Tokens).

This is the album "Milkshake and Potato Chips" can be found on (if you want to actually find it, otherwise this is good advice to stay away). Not only is the album poorly produced to present the King of Reggae, the songwriting is not up to Bob's usual standards, because he only wrote a few of the tracks. Here are the songs, with their authors listed, in order: "Oh Lord" (Johnny Nash/Bob Marley), "It Hurts to Be Alone" (Bob Marley/Bunny Livingston/Peter Tosh), "Lonesome Feelings" (Bob Marley), "Milkshake and Potato Chips" (Jimmy Norman/Al Pyfrom), "Touch Me" (Bob Marley), "Lonely Girl" (Jimmy Norman/Al Pyfrom/ Dorothy Hughes), "The World Is Changing" (Jimmy Norman/Al Pyfrom), "Treat You Right" (Jimmy Norman/Al Pyfrom), and "Soul Shakedown Party" (Bob Marley). This isn't even the rocking "Soul Shakedown Party" from *The Best of the Wailers*, but a pale imitation.

Never Ending Wailers

This is a set of re-recorded songs from the original Wailers era of 1964–1966, first released in 1993. It is notable because it includes vocals by original members Junior Braithwaite and Constantine Walker, who sing alongside Bunny Wailer, Peter Tosh, Peter's son Andrew, and, through the use of old studio tapes, Bob Marley himself. The project is weakened from a mishmash of material that was revisited numerous times. Some tracks are updated versions of songs originally recorded in 1971 by Bob, Bunny, Peter, and Rita. They were overdubbed in 1984 by Jamaican session musicians, and then reworked again in 1989. In 1993, they were again remixed and placed with some newly recorded songs to finally see the light of day on an album that suffers from taking a group of fairly weak songs (when compared with Bob's entire output) and trying to update them to fit the ever-changing Jamaican trends of 1984, 1989, and 1993. The finished product is sonically incongruent with the older material, and the entire project today sounds tacky and ill-conceived. No wonder it was poorly received.

Honorable Mentions

The Beatles original of "And I Love Her" is timeless. The Wailers' 1965 cover is a waste of your time. Wailers biographer John Masouri ranks this Beatles cover "among the group's worst ever recordings." Bob takes the lead vocal, and by the bridge sounds like he's fallen out of love, and it's a chore just to make it the end of the track.

Nineteen sixty-five was a bumper year for terrible Wailers covers, with "What's New Pussycat?" also seeing the light of day that year. Pierson says the group was reluctant to record it, and it's easy to see why. Masouri calls this novelty cover an "assault on their integrity," and "demeaning" for a group that was trying to be taken seriously. They were also trying to put food on the table, so recording songs that their producer suggested probably made sense at the time. The ska backing track would actually be fine as an instrumental, but Bob's performance can't out Tom Jones Tom Jones, and it never finds its own milieu.

30

Babylon Feel This One

The Best Marley Songs You've Probably Never Heard

With the Bob Marley canon containing hundreds of officially released songs, none but the most hardcore fan has heard everything with Bob's name on it. And, thanks to the Internet, there are also many more discoverable gems taken from rehearsals, songwriting demos, concerts, and alternate studio takes.

Needless to say, the standard Bob Marley fan would be familiar with the man's most popular-selling records internationally (the Island years, 1973–1983) and most of his Upsetter and JAD era (circa 1968–1972), since these have been mined relentlessly on compilations that entice us with different names but often offer the same songs. Given this, the criteria used for the following list is that they avoid the above releases and cannot be found on the Island and Tuff Gong career-retrospective albums *Legend* (1984), *Natural Mystic* (1984), *Rebel Music* (1986), *Songs of Freedom* (1992), *One Love: The Very Best of Bob Marley and the Wailers* (2001), *Gold* (2005), or *Africa Unite: The Singles Collection* (2005), the latter of which included the previously unreleased track "Slogans."

"Lonesome Feelings"

This is an excellent example of sixties ska featuring the Mighty Vikings backing band and a good primer in what the Wailers did best in 1964. Bob's lead vocal is supported by a chorus of Wailers, featuring Bunny and Peter as well as Joe Higgs, Cherry Green, Beverley Kelso, and Sylvia Richards. The singing is ragged and passionate, making it much more exciting than the later, more polished Wailers. The song is simply made for loving and dancing. It was released on the group's first Studio One LP, *The Wailing Wailers*.

"Go Jimmy Go"

A cover of an American early rock 'n' roller that beats the original hands down, "Go Jimmy Go" is a church'd-up ska driven by the Skatalites horn section. It didn't make the band's first LP, but Studio One did issue it on a compilation called *This Is Jamaican Ska.* As on "Lonesome Feelings," the band sounds young and unrefined, but that's its allure. This is the sound of pure optimism in Jamaica in 1964.

"Love and Affection"

Also included on *The Wailing Wailers*, this song perfectly marries Jamaican ska with American doo-wop thanks to the Skatalites' jumpy backing and the Wailers' harmonies. Peter's scat, "Dip dip dip dip da dip da dip," makes the link complete. This is also an example of Bob's recycling of lyrics, as he quotes from "Lonesome Feelings" and "It Hurts to Be Alone." He knew a good line when he wrote one, and he milked it for all it was worth.

"Hooligans"

Written in response to rudies rioting at a show they put on at the Palace Theatre in late 1964, "Hooligans" has the same theme as the better-known "Simmer Down." But while the ska backing is just as furious, Bob's voice is deeper and richer here. This song is also notable for the lyric, "Can a woman tender care cease towards a child she bears," which would later show up in "Johnny Was." Like most of the Studio One–era ska tracks, it's also deeply infectious. Bob certainly knew how to write a pop song.

"Rocking Steady"

On this truly great song that is underappreciated simply because it hasn't had a wider release, Bob reminisces about the romancing effect of dancing to rocksteady music with his baby. The song is closely based on Count Lasher's "Calypso Cha Cha Cha." His vocal is light and airy, and sits perfectly on top of the bass-heavy mix. The song's provenance is murky, but it was probably cut for both Studio One and JAD, though not released until after Marley died. There are several remixed versions of this song, some atrocious (I'm looking at you, JAD) and some excellent. The best, in my opinion, is the one listed as the "Rocking Steady Alt. Take" from Studio One.

"Cheer Up"

Recorded in 1970 and released on the ridiculously titled *The Best of the Wailers*, this track shares similarities to two of Bob's other great songs from the same period, "Soul Shakedown Party" and "Caution." An excellent example of the transition of Jamaican music from rocksteady to roots reggae, it is closer to the former than the latter, mainly because of its energetic tempo. It has the signature three-note guitar chank of the period, derived first from mento and then the reggae organ bubble, and gives guitarist Hux Brown the room to pick out a countermelody throughout. This is the sound that attracted Paul Simon to Beverley's, where in 1971 he laid down "Mother and Child Reunion" with most of the same musicians. We also hear some of Bob's themes of decolonization coming into clearer focus in this song: "We've been down in captivity so long / If we unite then we will be free."

"Rainbow Country"

One of Bob's greatest unheralded songs. I have always felt that "Rainbow Country" would fit in perfectly with the moody, organic feel of *Kaya*. It has the same mournful horns as "Misty Morning," and the serene vocals of "Sun Is Shining," though with a much spookier sound more characteristic of Black Ark, where it was recorded. Familyman's thudding bass underneath the repeated minor two-chord sequence gives it a hypnotic pulse that's further accentuated on Perry's gorgeous dub version. Lyrically, Bob is mining familiar territory—tranquil geography, the emancipatory power of dance and music, and faraway promised lands.

"Music Lesson"

This is truly one of the gems that Bob left us with. Tuff Gong issued it on a 12-inch in 1985, based on a demo recording from 1971, but with updated production. The lyrics are from the anticolonial well also visited by Peter Tosh's "Can't Blame the Youth" and Burning Spear's "Christopher Columbus," where reggae music can teach the youth about the crimes of so-called colonial heroes (Columbus, Marco Polo).

"Soul Shake Up Party"

The 1979 LP *Survival* was a powerhouse of militant Rasta roots reggae, a no-holds-barred song cycle about dismantling Babylon, uniting Africa and calling out Bob's attackers. So it would have been strange if "Soul Shake Up Party" was included on it, but that seems to have been the intention, as it is an outtake from the same sessions. The song remains unreleased, though it can be easily found on YouTube. It's a remake of the 1970 track "Soul Shakedown Party," but with a slower heavier roots feel. The song is full of possibility, and it could have become a live barnburner, had the band developed it.

"Babylon Feel This One"

Another unreleased song that can also be found on the Internet, this was included on a dub plate commissioned by the 12 Tribes sound system, and boasts a bass line big enough for its own zip code. Bob is warning Babylon, as he likes to do, that it is fighting a losing battle against Jah.

Honorable Mentions

If you haven't dipped very deeply into the vast Marley catalogue, chances are these songs will be new to you. They are easily available on a few well-known compilations:

- The original versions, produced by Lee Perry, of "Sun Is Shining," "Small Axe," and "Duppy Conqueror."
- The original, self-produced versions, released by Tuff Gong, of "Trenchtown Rock," and "Lively Up Yourself."
- The Wail'n Soul'm releases of "Nice Time," "Hypocrites," "Bend Down Low," "Bus Dem Shut," "Mellow Mood," and "Hurtin' Inside," available on the *Wail'n Soul'm Singles Selecta*.
- The Lesley Kong–produced "Soul Shakedown Party" and "Caution," available on the *Songs of Freedom* boxed set and *The Best of the Wailers*.
- The *Catch a Fire* outtake "High Tide or Low Tide," available on reissues of that album.
- "Jah Live," available on *Gold*.
- The 1977 Perry-produced "Who Colt the Game," which can be found on *One Love: The Very Best of Bob Marley and the Wailers*.

31

Mix Up, Mix Up

Songwriting Credits, Miscredits, Uncredits, and Lawsuits

I f, like me, you perused the songwriting credits on Bob Marley's albums when you first bought them, you will have been surprised to find out that many of his greatest songs—"No Woman, No Cry," among them—were not written by him. Six out of nine songs on *Natty Dread* list other composers, and eight of the ten on *Rastaman Vibration* do, too.

But then it gets confusing. While "No Woman, No Cry" is attributed to Vincent Ford on the studio release, the live release is credited to "Bob Marley/Vincent Ford." The original 1975 single release of "Natural Mystic" credits Lee Perry, who produced the song, but the later 1977 version on *Exodus* is credited solely to Bob Marley. The original versions of "Duppy Conqueror" and "Small Axe" bear the name of Lee Perry as co-writer, and he's told interviewers that he wrote or had a hand in writing many songs recorded by Bob. Yet subsequent pressings and recordings omit his name. Meanwhile, the single version of "Knotty Dread" was attributed to Bob Marley, but the album version, "Natty Dread," is credited to Rita Marley and Alan Cole. So who actually wrote these songs, and why the obfuscation?

Bob was not at all happy with the standard way the music industry worked. You know: the artist writes, records, and performs the music, and the suits make the most money. Jamaican producers not only took the lion's share of profits, they also held the copyright to songs they produced. This is why Coxsone Dodd is still listed in the music rights organization BMI's database as partial composer for Bob Marley songs recorded at Studio One. Dodd probably never wrote a song in his life—nor was he a producer in the proper sense. He, like most Jamaican producers, merely financed the business, but they did not partake in the creative work.

Marley was tired of this game, and he sought ways to keep more of his own money. He had signed a publishing deal with Cayman Music, owned by Danny Sims, around 1968, and it had served him relatively well, but by 1974 he was looking for ways to hide his royalties and keep more of his hard-earned money himself. To do this, a little sleight of hand was in order. On his two subsequent albums,

Natty Dread and *Rastaman Vibration*, he put the copyright in various friends' names. Legally, many of the songs were attributed to R. Marley, which could have been Rita or Robert (Bob). All the royalties for songs under this scheme were shunted off to an account in the British Virgin Islands, set up by Don Taylor under the name Bob Marley Music. The money, however, went directly to Bob, not to those credited with writing the songs, although some sources suggest that during his lifetime he looked after those whose names he used.

Here are the songs and writers from *Natty Dread* that fall under this scheme:

- "Rebel Music (3 O'Clock Roadblock)"—Aston Barrett and Hugh Peart. Barrett was the Wailers' bassist, and Hugh Peart was Bob's cousin, driver, and herb supplier, a.k.a. Sledger.
- "Talkin' Blues"—Carlton Barrett and Cogil Leghorn (later written as "Legon Cogill" or "Lecon Cogill.") Carlton was the Wailers' drummer, and Leghorn was a friend from Trench Town who helped out with record distribution through Tuff Gong.
- "Them Belly Full (but We Hungry)"—Carlton Barrett and Cogil Leghorn.
- "So Jah Se"—Rita Marley and Willy Francisco. The latter was a pseudonym for Alvin "Seeco" Patterson.
- "Natty Dread"—Rita Marley and Alan Cole. (The original single, called "Knotty Dread," was solely attributed to Bob Marley.)
- "No Woman, No Cry"—Vincent "Tata" Ford. Ford was a Trench Town friend who let Bob sleep on his kitchen floor when he had nowhere else to go.

Here are the songs and writers from *Rastaman Vibration* that fall under this scheme:

- "Positive Vibration" and "Roots, Rock, Reggae"—Vincent "Tata" Ford.
- "Crazy Baldhead"—Rita Marley and Vincent Ford.
- "Johnny Was" and "Rat Race"—Rita Marley.
- "Who the Cap Fit"—Aston and Carlton Barrett. This was an update of Bob's song "Man to Man," originally credited to Bob Marley and Lee Perry.
- "Want More"—Aston Barrett.
- "War"—Alan Cole and Carlton Barrett. This was credited to Bob Marley on the Tuff Gong single, while the words are based closely on a speech by Haile Selassie.

Cayman Music Inc. v. the Bob Marley Estate

Danny Sims, the owner of Cayman Music, would later claim that he didn't realize what was going on with Bob's songwriting subterfuge until he read about it in two Marley biographies in the eighties. Timothy White's 1983 biography *Catch a Fire* had stated, "In order to protect some of his publishing interests in later years, [Marley] reportedly made cunning arrangements to credit many of his songs to hangers-on and ghetto chums." Sims sought retribution for the concealed songs of 1973–1976 and, in 1984, filed a lawsuit against the Marley estate. In the 1987 verdict, Judge Wilk ruled against Cayman Music, allowing the Marley Estate to maintain control over the disputed songs.

Credits, Uncredits, and Court Cases

Whether or not the people listed as writers on these songs actually had a hand in their creation is a matter of debate. Don Taylor's point of view is Bob wrote all the songs and used these names as a loophole to escape paying Cayman Music publishing royalties. Dermot Hussey told Roger Steffens that when Cogil Leghorn bragged about writing "Talkin' Blues," Bob tore a strip off him. This would seem to corroborate his lack of involvement.

Rita Marley says that Bob credited Tata Ford with songs like "No Woman, No Cry" in order to honor a friend, but others have suggested Ford actually wrote some of the lyrics. She and Alan Cole are credited on "Natty Dread," but as Wailers biographer Masouri piercingly states, "It seems doubtful they possessed the poetic genius needed to pen such a remarkable song."

Conversely, there are several cases of Marley collaborators not getting recognition. Bob wrote "Disco Nights" with Martha Velez, but it was credited to Rita Marley. "Zimbabwe" may have been written by someone Bob met in Ethiopia, if rumors are to be believed. Tuff Gong producer Sangie Davis was given a co-writing credit for "Wake Up and Live" on its original release, but there's no sign of his name on subsequent releases, and he only received a small initial payment for his work on the song. Trench Town friend Dessie Smith told Roger Steffens that he'd written many of the songs on *Survival* and *Uprising*. He didn't ask for any credit, though, and he didn't receive any.

Familyman told John Masouri that he co-wrote "Crazy Baldheads," adding that he hurt when he wasn't credited on the album. Wailers keyboardist Tyrone Downie asserts that the Wailers were co-creators of the songs they recorded, and he himself claims credit for writing "Positive Vibration," the verses of "Jamming," and half of "Waiting in Vain," though he is not listed as a co-writer on any of them.

Wailers harmonica player Lee Jaffe insists that he and Esther Anderson helped write "I Shot the Sheriff," though the song is attributed to Bob alone. Anderson claims it is about their relationship—specifically Bob's objection to birth control. He wanted to "plant a seed" in Anderson, as he had done with so many of his girlfriends, but the seed was killed by the contraceptive pill prescribed by the "doctor"/ sheriff.

Anderson told Steffens that she also wrote "Get Up, Stand Up" with Bob in little more time than it takes to sing the song on a flight from Haiti to Jamaica. She has also claimed a co-writing credit for "Burnin' and Lootin'," though officially she is credited for neither.

Musicians, too, were often left uncredited on Marley's albums. Jaffe can be heard on "Rebel Music," but his name is nowhere to be found in the liner notes to *Natty Dread* (reissues included). The names of the studio musicians used on *Catch a Fire*, Wayne Perkins and Rabbit Bundrick, were omitted on the original release, though they are credited on reissues.

In Familyman's telling, many songs, like "Talkin' Blues," were written collaboratively while the musicians were jamming. He remembers Leghorn being present for creative jam sessions, so he may have contributed to the song. Leghorn later took credit for "Them Belly Full" as well. Familyman insists that his brother penned the lyrics to "Talkin' Blues" and was responsible for "Them Belly Full" and "Revolution," and that he wrote the majority of the lyrics to "Rebel Music" and "Want More." Lee Jaffe, though, remembered Bob starting "Talkin' Blues" one morning in Bull Bay and working on it for weeks after, and recalled him writing the verses to "Rebel Music" on a journey from Negril to Kingston.

Aston Barrett v. Universal-Island Records Ltd.

In the spring of 2006, Aston "Familyman" Barrett unsuccessfully sued Universal-Island Records Ltd. and the Bob Marley estate over unpaid royalties for the songs they were credited on (and some they weren't) on *Natty Dread* and *Rastaman Vibration*. As the Wailers' acknowledged bandleader and arranger, the significance of his role in the band was not questioned, but his authorship was. In the months leading up to the case, he told me, "I am the bandleader, musical arranger, and producer. Between my brother and myself, we've co-written eleven tracks with Bob and we register six, but they still refuse to pay." Familyman felt he was the victim of "fraud and forgery" and "one-sided deals" orchestrated by Chris Blackwell and Rita Marley, who he said "refuse to pay royalties, publishing, and merchandising to me and my brother, and that's what I used to use to take care of my band."

The animosity between Familyman and Rita got so bad that she sent US Marshalls to raid his tour after discovering that he was selling T-shirts and posters with a picture of him and Bob on them. Disgusted, Familyman said, "They raid me because I'm selling Bob Marley face. They say they own Bob

Wailers bassist Aston "Familyman" Barrett performing in 2010.   *Photo by Martin Raggio, Creative Commons license*

Marley face but they don't own my face!"

Before the case went to court, he was confident of victory: "I'm sure I'm on the right track. I'm the good guy. We will smoke them out of the cave, get them on the run, catch them and bring them to justice." In court, however, both Chris Blackwell and Rita Marley expressed doubts that Familyman had the songwriting abilities to help Marley pen these timeless songs. Masouri quotes Rita as saying that Bob wrote his songs "whenever he got the feeling, or felt the vibration," not through collaborative jamming with the band.

The judge, Justice Lewison, taking into account testimony from members of the Wailers, Diane Jobson, Chris Blackwell, Rita Marley, Lee Jaffe and Alan Cole, ruled that the disputed songs on *Natty Dread* and *Rastaman Vibration* were the sole creations of Bob Marley. Barrett, who had spent over $1.2 million in bringing the case to trial, was deemed not to be due any royalties.

32

Charlatan or Kingmaker?

The Role of Island Records' Founder Chris Blackwell

There's a good argument to be made that the world would never have heard of Bob Marley if it weren't for a rich white Jamaican named Chris Blackwell. Blackwell provided the money to make *Catch a Fire*, signed the Wailers to Island Records, and had the unique vision and marketing muscle to present Jamaican reggae to the world. After all, Bob Marley had been in the game ten years and had hardly made a dent internationally when he teamed up with Blackwell in 1972. His only release on a foreign label, "Reggae on Broadway," had tanked, and his association with JAD, the American company that was supposed to help him break into the States, was all but over.

There's an equally compelling argument that Blackwell was just another *samfi man*—or con artist—ripping off musicians for his own benefit, and that Bob's genius would have become globally recognized eventually, with or without Blackwell. This is certainly how original Wailers Peter Tosh—who refers to Blackwell as Chris Whiteworst—and Bunny Wailer—who has likened their Island tenure to slavery—felt. Which is true? It depends, of course, on your perspective.

Who is Chris Blackwell? Here's an overview of his rise in the music business and role in Bob Marley's success.

Twenty-One Families

It is often said that there are twenty-one families that control Jamaica, and they all gained wealth as part of the "plantocracy"—the planter class—that made money literally off the backs of enslaved Africans. Chris Blackwell's mother, Blanche Lindo, came from one of these families, and their fortune was made in sugar and its distillate, rum. This familial association with the liquor business apparently worked in his favor. Blackwell's entrepreneurial spirit was discovered while he was attending a prestigious boarding school in England, where he passed the time selling contraband spirits and smokes to his peers.

Blackwell, Chris Blackwell

What do James Bond and Bob Marley have in common (besides both being ladies' men)? Chris Blackwell. Being a well-heeled white Jamaican, he had some pretty serious connections. His mother was a friend of Bond creator Ian Fleming, who owned the Goldeneye estate on the island. If you've seen *Dr. No*, the first Bond movie from 1962, you may remember that it was filmed in Jamaica. Do you know who scouted the locations for the shoot? A young Chris Blackwell. And guess who now owns Goldeneye? A much older Chris Blackwell.

Making It in the Music Biz

Born in 1937, Blackwell started Island Records in 1962, but he had been dabbling in the music business for four years already, finding ways to fit into, and make money off, the fledging Jamaican music industry. He was interested in both film and music, and in order to decide which of them to pursue full-time, he visited a psychic, who told him he'd have success in music. With the stars aligned, he scored a hit with his first label, R&B Records, in 1959, Laurel Aitken's "Boogie in My Bones."

Blackwell also had a lucrative side business selling American records to sound systems, providing soundmen like Duke Reid and Coxsone Dodd the opportunity to purchase songs their competitors lacked. But with Island Records he was able to form a profitable link between music producers in Kingston and music consumers in England, as he licensed distribution rights to the songs from Jamaican labels. This made him a key player in the dissemination of reggae music in the UK, even though he wasn't really a producer in the proper sense. One of these records was "Judge Not" by a seventeen-year-old Robert Marley, notable not because of its popularly (it had none) but because of the future success of its singer.

Island Records was a very small player in the Jamaican and London music industries in the early sixties, but it pulled off a coup when it launched a cover by "My Boy Lollipop" by Kingston's Millie Small into charts around the world through a distribution deal with local producer Leslie Kong. The record would go on to sell seven million copies in 1964, and was the first Jamaican single to become a hit outside of the tiny island. Blackwell had proven his prowess for getting Jamaican music on the world stage.

Though he continued to license reggae for the UK audience, most notably through a company he co-founded called Trojan Records, Blackwell turned most of his attention to the rock album market in the late sixties, working with groups like the Spencer Davis Group, Jethro Tull, Free, Cat Stevens, Fairport Convention, Traffic, Emerson, Lake, and Palmer, King Crimson, and Uriah Heap. Island became the most successful indie label in the UK and gained a reputation for a diverse roster of artists, some of whom pushed the limits of musical convention.

Meeting Bob Marley

The sole reggae artist on Island in the early seventies was Jimmy Cliff. Blackwell managed to secure him the lead role in Jamaican reggae/Robin Hood film *The Harder They Come*. The film had an impressive all-reggae soundtrack—including Cliff, Toots and the Maytals, and Desmond Dekker, but no Wailers—and Blackwell hoped it would be the bellwether for reggae music internationally, causing a demand for Jamaican music. He even invested in the film, and was poised to reap the rewards, with Cliff in the starring role.

Alas, Cliff had other ideas. Unhappy with Island, he departed for EMI Records in 1972, feeling that Blackwell was too enamored with his rock catalogue to do reggae any justice.

So here was Chris Blackwell, a successful rock impresario, laying the groundwork for a reggae explosion, and his only reggae artist had absconded. What's a rich white Jamaican to do? Apparently, sit in his London office and wait for the hand of fate to present him with a golden opportunity. Some guys have all the luck.

Literally a week after Jimmy Cliff left Island, Bob Marley strolled into Blackwell's office. The Wailers were stuck in London; their JAD-organized tour had dissolved, leaving the band high and dry with no money to get home. Through Brent Clarke, the publicist for JAD, Marley had connected with Blackwell, hoping the Jamaican businessman might be interested in investing in a single by the Wailers. Reggae was a singles market—there really had been no complete reggae album, *per se*, outside of the Leslie Kong–produced *The Best of the Wailers*. All of their other releases were collections of previously released singles. So Bob assumed that Blackwell would only be interested in a song or two.

Blackwell had other ideas. He wanted to make reggae palpable for a rock audience, and rock audiences bought albums, not singles. Rock audiences also loved rebels, kind of like the one Cliff portrayed in *The Harder They Come*. He advanced the group eight thousand pounds to go back to Jamaica and record a full album of material to be released on Island Records.

After struggling for a decade and getting nowhere, within a year and a half of teaming up with Chris Blackwell the Wailers had two critically acclaimed and internationally distributed albums, *Catch a Fire* and *Burnin'*—a first for any Jamaican band—supported by appearances on British television (*Old Grey Whistle Test*) and radio (*Top Gear*), and a solid tour schedule, including five shows opening for Sly and the Family Stone.

But all was not rosy. By the end of 1973, both Peter Tosh and Bunny Wailer had left the band. They vehemently disliked Blackwell and saw him as the latest in a long line of charlatans who had gotten rich off their music while failing to compensate them fairly. They also took issue with Blackwell's obvious grooming of Marley as the marketable (and more manageable) front man. When Peter wanted Island to release a solo album for him, Blackwell refused, telling him it would provide unwelcome competition for the Wailers.

Bunny, who today has nothing good to say about Blackwell, did sign a solo deal with him for his 1976 debut, *Blackheart Man*. Legend has it—probably fanned by Timothy White's account in *Catch a Fire*—that Bunny, already attuned to Blackwell's wily ways with contracts, had the record exec include a clause stating that the artist would be released from the contract in the event of Blackwell's death. Once the ink was dry, he quipped, "That means I can get out of my contract at any time."

Bob Marley performing at Dalymount Park, Dublin, Ireland, July 6, 1980.
Photos by Eddie Mallin, Creative Commons license

Blackwell has other critics, too: writing in *Race Today* in 1975, dub poet Linton Kwesi Johnson thought the "rebel Marley" marketing

campaign was a farce, and felt that the whole enterprise smacked of the com-
mercialization of reggae at the hands of a "descendant of slave masters." Bunny
shared these sentiments, feeling that the reggae Bob went on to produce with
Blackwell was a sellout. Wailers bassist Aston "Familyman" Barrett has also
taken aim at Blackwell over unpaid royalties. The Island deal supposedly
included him and his brother Carly, but Familyman insists that royalty pay-
ments stopped once Marley died.

With Peter and Bunny gone, Bob continued to work as Bob Marley and
the Wailers, releasing *Natty Dread* in 1974 and renegotiating a ten-record deal
with Island. For this he received a million-dollar advance, minus $125,000 as
payment for his new home at 56 Hope Road, which Blackwell deeded to Bob as
part of the deal.

Some sources have suggested that Blackwell's musical role in Bob's career
was nonexistent—that he would show up at the studio but not add anything
creatively. Others, like engineer Errol Brown, point out that Blackwell had a
hand in mixing and often had good ideas. One of those was to ditch the band
when they were trying to record "Redemption Song" for *Uprising*, and to have
Bob sing the song alone with an acoustic guitar. This was a daring move—reggae
wasn't solo acoustic music—but it was the right move, and it resulted in one of
Bob's best-loved songs.

Natty Dread was the first album to give Bob a chart position. The ensuing
tour would be recorded and released the following year as *Live!*, which produced
the band's first charting single, a #22 hit on the UK charts. This is the period
commonly thought of as the time when Marley became an international star.
Blackwell's management of Marley's career and legacy after his death went a
long way to ensuring that Bob was and still is a globally recognized superstar.
Would Bob have reached those heights anyway? We'll never know.

33

Reggae, Rock, and Zippo Lighters

Marketing Bob Marley to the World

I n Chris Blackwell's mind, the traditional look, sound, and business practices of reggae weren't going to get it much notice past a few hits. He correctly sensed in the Wailers artists with a harsher, rebellious, edge. For one thing, they had dreadlocks—not afros, like Jimmy Cliff, Desmond Dekker, and Toots Hibbert—and in 1972, long hair put you firmly in the rocker camp. Bob was also an intelligent songwriter. And he had sex appeal. And with those constant spliffs in their mouths, they were bona fide outlaws. These attributes went a long way to convincing Blackwell that Bob could be the key to marketing reggae to long-haired white kids intent on flouting authority.

Blackwell signed the Wailers to a three-record deal and set out to market them like a rock band to a rock audience. Then, after Peter and Bunny left, he re-signed Bob and the rest of the band in a ten-album deal.

Blackwell gave the band three main tweaks. First, the name. It has sometimes been erroneously reported that Blackwell changed the name from the Wailers to Bob Marley and the Wailers, thereby sidelining (and angering) Peter and Bunny. But this is wrong. The Wailers had routinely released singles back home under all sorts of variations, including Bob Marley and the Wailers.

When *Catch a Fire* came out, it was attributed to the Wailers, not Bob Marley and the Wailers. This was on purpose. Up until this point, the name Wailers referred to a vocal trio with music provided by backing musicians. But this isn't how rock worked. Rock music was made by rock bands. Blackwell wanted to market the group as a band, not a trio of singers. He kept the Wailers name, then, but also included some of the backing musicians—brothers Aston and Carly Barrett—in the band photo on the back cover, to make it look like "the Wailers" referred to a full band. Clever.

Second, rock bands released albums, not singles. In fact, Led Zeppelin, one of the biggest rock bands of the era, were so far entrenched in album-oriented rock that they outright refused to release singles (in the UK, anyway). So what did

Blackwell do? He told the Wailers he wanted an entire album. When they delivered it, he remixed it and packaged it in the coolest album sleeve of 1973, sure to drum up attention. It resembled a Zippo lighter, and when you opened the top cover a cardboard flame rose up. Designed by Rod Dyer and Bob Weiner, the cover reflected the rebellious attitude Blackwell hoped to capitalize on. It symbolized both lighting a spliff and the torching of the old social order. This was punk rock before there was punk rock.

Third, together, Blackwell and the band altered the sound of reggae. The Wailers desperately wanted to break internationally, and they didn't mind making some concessions to do it. At the same time, Bob felt that Jamaican records suffered from having a raw, less-produced sound than American records, and he wanted to change that.

Island Records spared no expense in trying to break the Wailers to a rock audience. Rock fans were used to full albums as artistic statements, not collections of singles, and appreciated clever album art. The first pressing of *Catch a Fire* didn't disappoint, with its hinged "Zippo lighter" package and flame. It is difficult to find now, but luckily Busted Flat Records owner Mark Logan had one in his record collection.
Photo by Brent Hagerman, courtesy of Mark Logan

In his essay on "Marketing Marley," Roy Shuker pinpoints the following changes instigated by Island and the band to help make a more rock-friendly record:

- It was the first Wailers record recorded in stereo.
- American session musicians playing keyboards and electric guitar were added to three songs (and their pay rates were doubled).
- Time restrictions in the studio were removed, to allow time for creativity and perfection.
- The tracks were run through cutting-edge audio equipment at Island's studio in London, to clean up the mix and help give it that professionally produced sound.
- The tracks were remixed to accentuate the treble (which rock audiences were used to) and lower the bass. This and the addition of keyboards and guitar

helped to shift the drum-and-bass feel of reggae toward the melodic instrument–centered style of rock.

- Some songs were extended through studio editing. Blackwell wanted longer songs with more going on in them, especially instrumental solos.
- Tempos were increased by speeding up the tapes to make the songs fit more closely within the speed range associated with rock.

The 2001 double-CD re-release of *Catch a Fire* makes clear how these alterations changed the music. One disc is the original album, as released by Island, but the other contains the Jamaican record, as recorded by the Wailers, before Blackwell's remixing and overdubs. Whether these are *improvements* is up to the listener. The Island disc is certainly more produced, and with Perkins' slide guitar and Rabbit's keys there is a lot more melodic and sonic diversity. "Stir It Up" is extended from 3:39 to 5:35, and reverb bathes the guitar chanks before Rabbit's MiniMoog takes it into the realm of psychedelic reggae.

Two songs were also cut from the original album. The Wailers gave Blackwell eleven songs, but he thought that was too "pop" a number. Rock records, he

By including the rhythm section of Familyman and Carlton Barrett in their back cover photo, the Wailers came to represent a full band, instead of the original vocal trio, to many record buyers who were being introduced to the band for the first time. This also effectively erased the contribution of the white American session players on the album, who remained uncredited.   *Photo by Brent Hagerman, courtesy of Mark Logan*

The second pressing of *Catch a Fire* changed from the "Zippo lighter" style and included this band photo on the back cover. Familyman and Carlton Barrett are shown standing behind the three original Wailers.
Author's collection

reasoned, only had nine songs. So he cut "High Tide or Low Tide," thinking it was too close to vocal R&B, and "All Day All Night." That's too bad, though, because "High Tide" is a pretty killer track.

Suffice it to say, these tweaks were all designed to make Jamaican music accessible to white rockers. Blackwell wanted to keep the hypnotic feel of Jamaican reggae but expand it to include rock influences in order to put reggae into the mainstream. He was thinking of radio play in the UK, and in order to get this he needed to appeal to a demographic that thought reggae was a novelty genre. Bringing in Johnny Nash keyboardist John "Rabbit" Bundrick and Muscle Shoals guitarist Wayne Perkins went a long way to making the Wailers convincing to a rock audience.

Catch a Fire was not a runaway success, initially moving only fourteen thousand units, but it garnered critical attention and went on to continue registering steady sales. Blackwell put the band on the road through Britain and the States and released a second record in the same year, *Burnin'*, which included "I Shot the Sheriff." When Eric Clapton covered this song a year later, it cemented Marley's rebel appeal.

Further Changes

There are other considerations as to how Marley changed reggae in the seventies. As noted elsewhere, it became normal reggae practice in the seventies to write new songs over existing backing riddims (known as versioning).

By the time Marley was signed to Island Records in 1972, he was exhausted with the Jamaican music industry practice whereby it was nearly impossible to have control over your songs, since they were recorded by musicians in the employ of a studio boss who was then free to recycle those backing tracks. The Wailers had already moved from a vocal group to a full-fledged band, and now they were writing and recording their own material. By moving away from the versioning template, the Wailers fundamentally shifted away from one of the standard ways of making reggae in Jamaica. This is why you will rarely hear the riddim of a Bob Marley song recycled, even as most other well-known reggae tracks from the same era were or are versioned extensively. So Bob Marley and the Wailers altered reggae by writing their own songs that didn't depend on existing riddims.

Bob Marley grew as a songwriter, too. Compare his songs from this period to other Jamaican releases and you'll see that his writing reflects lessons learned from American rock and soul groups. Jamaican reggae was typically arranged in a simple verse/chorus format, wherein the musical accompaniment remains the same regardless of whether the singer is singing a verse or chorus melody, or a contrasting verse/chorus format, where there are two sections of music: one that accompanies the verse and another that accompanies the chorus. Bridges were rare, as was the typically American Tin Pan Alley AABA arrangement. Many of Bob's songs are more complex, though, and include bridges, pre-choruses, codas, and other elements more typical of American music than Jamaican.

34

Punky Reggae Party

Crossing Over and Back Again

Lloyd Bradley, in his overview of Marley's musical output, feels that while *Catch a Fire* brought in session musicians as a means of "lightening the tunes" for rock ears, *Burnin'* and *Natty Dread* returned to a more conventional Jamaican aesthetic. With 1975's *Live!*, though, Bob Marley settled into an "arena-friendly internationally accessible rock-tinged hybrid" that would remain throughout his career."

By the time Marley released *Exodus* in 1977, his music was firmly able to reach a wide demographic. He spent much of 1977 living in London, and this helped him further amalgamate Jamaican and international styles. "Waiting in Vain," for instance, is overt in its bid for wider ears. As recounted in *The Book of Exodus*, Bob told Vivien Goldman, "It's for people who never dig the Wailers, 'cos dem just couldn't relate. So what I do now is a tune like 'Waiting in Vain,' so dem might like it and wonder what a go on."

On the surface, Bob's most direct crossover might be "Punky Reggae Party." He was introduced to the punk scene while in London, and Don Taylor has said that Bob was a fan of bands like the Clash and Sex Pistols. Like the Clash, he saw a kinship between punk and reggae. Both were protest music from the dregs of society, and both were busy tearing down the empires that tried to keep them marginalized.

To celebrate these combined values, Bob wrote "Punky Reggae Party." The song name checks British punk bands (the Damned, the Jam, the Clash) and employs the arena-rock-reggae feel he'd come to perfect. However, there are a few aspects of this song that suggest that, having successfully crossed over into the rock world, he wanted Jamaicans to know he was still capable of making *Jamaican* music.

First, it was recorded with Lee Perry, the producer Marley returned to when he wanted a homegrown sound on "Jah Live" and "Smile Jamaica." Second, it indicates that he had realized that the one drop music he had been making was starting to sound old fashioned to Jamaican ears. He was committed to it—as 1979's "One Drop" will attest—but he wanted to experiment with the drumbeat that was all the rage back home. This was Sly Dunbar's steppers rhythm, wherein the kick drum hits on all four beats of the bar.

Robbie Shakespeare and Sly Dunbar, as shown on the back cover of the Black Uhuru *Liberation* anthology. Not only were they the most in-demand reggae rhythm section of the 1970s, they also worked with the Wailers on occasion. Sly Dunbar's steppers beat can be heard on "Punky Reggae Party."

Author's collection

As one of main session drummers on the island, Sly's beats drove what was in fashion. Bob wanted that feel, and he wanted to stay in touch with the music going on at home. When I interviewed him in 2006, Sly told me about the first time Bob asked him to play this beat:

> I remember I did a session for him in Jamaica, after he was shot and he came back. I saw Lee Perry and he ask me to come and play the session—not "Punky Reggae," not yet. And I played the session. Lee Perry says, "I want a one drop," and Bob says, "No, I don't want a one drop from Sly. I want your kind of beat because I want to sing on your beat." So I start playing straight four, and he said that's what he wanted. I don't remember what song came from that session. We did three songs that night but I don't know what became of those songs. If it is released I don't know.

According to *The Definitive Discography*, the first Jamaican session recorded after Bob Marley got shot was "Punky Reggae Party." So, if Sly's memory is correct, there must have been another session. Or perhaps this was the "Smile

Jamaica" session, which was just before the shooting. This would make sense, since the earliest use of the straight four in a Marley song is probably "Smile Jamaica," which revolves between a steppers beat and a one drop.

After that session, the Wailers recorded the tracks for *Exodus*, on which the title track has Carlton playing a straight four. Yet when it came time to record "Punky Reggae Party," Marley went outside of the Wailers stable, perhaps trying to get a more current sound. Don Taylor thought that Bob felt the Barrett brothers were stuck in the one drop mode, so he looked elsewhere when he came to record this song. He first enlisted Aswad drummer Drummie Zeb in London, but then Lee Perry called in Sly Dunbar to Black Ark to redo the part in the steppers style.

Here is Sly talking about that session: "[I went] up to Joe Gibbs studio to hang out there. So one time he say to me, 'Sly, Lee Perry look for you.' I say, 'Why?' He say, 'It's a song that he get a drummer to play but it can't feel right.' I say, 'What do you mean it can't feel right? So I go see him."

After hooking up with Perry, Sly ended up playing the entire song in one take, and remembers having to wrestle with the fact that there was no count-in. "There was no count-in on the record, like 'one-two-three-four.' So I say to him, 'Go right into record.' In the beginning, if you listen to 'Punky Reggae Party,' there is a snare thing like *tsht tsht*. I was feeling for the tempo, and then I made a fill and went right into playing it. It was like seven minutes long but it was in one take. Sometimes you just catch it."

Master drummer Sly Dunbar with the author.   *Josh Chamberlain*

35

Who Were the Wailers?

The Singers

The Teenage Wailin' Wailers

Almost a decade before the world knew of Bob Marley and the Wailers as an
international recording act, the Wailers were a Jamaican vocal trio made up
of Bob Marley, Peter "Tosh" McIntosh, and Neville "Bunny" Livingston. Jamaican
music is typically recorded by a vocalist or vocal group paired with a professional
studio band, and the early Wailers tracks are no different. As such, the name the
Wailers really only refers to a vocal group up until Island Records label head Chris
Blackwell included some of the backing musicians in press photos for the band in
1973, thereby making the Wailers Bob Marley's backing band for the first time in
history.

When they first joined together in Kingston's Trench Town ghetto, their mentor
and vocal coach, Joe Higgs, referred to them as the Teenagers, after American doo-
wop group Frankie Lymon and the Teenagers, although this was more of an ad hoc
name, and was never used on record. They sometimes referred to themselves as
the Roosters as well. In 1964, when they were getting ready to audition for Studio
One, they felt they needed a band name with more heft—something that, instead of
suggesting dreamy American doo-wop and Tin Pan Alley, spoke of maturity, even
spirituality, and reflected their ghetto credibility. They decided on the Wailers.

The name is often said to have biblical connotations, as in Jeremiah 9:19: "For
a voice of wailing is heard out of Zion." Coming from the ghetto, the name also
symbolizes past hardships. Sort of along this line, Timothy White writes that
Bob once accounted for the band name by stating, "We started out crying." Roger
Steffens points out that, in the Jamaican context, wailing also connotes crying out
for justice, something that became the group's *modus operandi*.

The group's name was anything but consistent. Though they referred to themselves as the Wailers, when Studio One issued the group's first album—really a
collection of previously released singles—it was attributed to the Wailing Wailers.

Membership in the group was also quite fluid. Though Bob, Peter, and Bunny formed the core of the Wailers from 1964 to 1973, many other singers and musicians recorded and performed with them. This chapter looks at all the singers who recorded alongside the core group. The following chapter looks at the various musicians who did the same.

Studio One–Era Wailers

While the name the Wailers generally applies to the vocal trio of Bunny, Peter, and Bob, they were often augmented by other singers during their earliest recordings at Studio One. The original ensemble was really a six-piece vocal harmony group that included a young Junior Braithwaite along with Bob, Peter, and Bunny, plus two female backing vocalists named Beverley Kelso and Cherry Green.

On their first ever release, "Simmer Down," Braithwaite and Kelso harmonize alongside the core group. Like Bob, Bunny, and Peter, they were part of the crowd of budding musicians who hung around Joe Higgs's yard. Other singers joined in from time to time, too. Membership seems to have been quite loose at this time, with various people being drafted in for recording sessions at different times. Bob later explained why the group at one point went from five down to the core of three by saying that the music business in Jamaica wasn't lucrative enough to support a group of five.

Peter Touch

Older Jamaicans still refer to Peter Tosh as "Peter Touch." That's because he was billed as Peter Touch on his early Jamaican singles. The pseudonym was apparently derived from his habit of uninvited touching or pinching of women as they passed him on the street. He took the lead on a few early Studio One sides with the Wailers, and when he did these were attributed to Peter Touch and the Wailers. His first turn at singing lead was on 1964's "Maga Dog," a song he would revisit in his solo career, first in 1971 and then on the 1983 album *Mama Africa*.

When Bob left to work in Delaware in 1966, Peter and Bunny proved that they were more than just supporting singers and each matured. Tosh took this opportunity to write and record the group's first song mentioning Rastafari in the title. "Rasta Shook Them Up" was a response to the state visit of Haile Selassie, the Ethiopian Emperor whom Rastas worshipped as the messiah. Tosh's spiritual turn toward Rastafari blazed a path that both Bunny and Bob would follow for the rest of their careers. Peter also had a rocksteady hit with a tune called "The Toughest" during this time. As with "Maga Dog," Peter would revisit it in his solo career, this time on the 1978 album *Bush Doctor*.

When Bob returned from the US in the fall of 1966, he resumed his place as lead vocalist, though Tosh continued to contribute occasional leads up until his departure from the group in 1973. Some of his best-known songs include "Downpressor Man," "No Sympathy," "Get Up, Stand Up," "400 Years," "Stop That Train," and "Soon Come." All of these, recorded during the Wailers era, would be revisited in his solo career.

Bunny "Wailer" Livingston

As was the case with Peter Tosh, Bob's absence in 1966 allowed Bunny room to shine. He had a storehouse of songs already written, but his first lead vocal on a Wailers track didn't occur until June 1966, when Bob was out of the country. Bunny had previously sung lead on only one recording, a duet with Rita Anderson called "The Vow," released under the name Bonny and Rita. Now, over a year later, he led the Wailers through twelve songs in Bob's absence, including classics such as "He Who Feels It Knows It," "Sunday Morning," and "Let Him Go." Like Peter, Bunny beat Bob to making an overt connection to Rastafari in song with his use of the dread phrase "I and I" in "I Stand Predominant."

With Bob's return in the fall of 1966, Bunny only occasionally sang lead on Wailers tracks up until he left the group in 1973. Some of his standouts are "This Train," "Pass It On," "Reincarnated Souls," and "Hallelujah Time." Like Peter, he would revisit many of his Wailers-era songs in his solo career.

Junior Braithwaite

Bob was always the most prolific, and arguably the best, songwriter of the group, though both Braithwaite and Kelso remember the songwriting at the time as collaborative. Bob didn't always sing his own compositions, and, to make things more confusing, sometimes a song that Bob did not write was attributed to him.

Some of Bob's songs were sung by fifteen-year-old Junior Braithwaite, an important member of the early group. In fact, some historians suggest that Braithwaite was the lead singer of the early Wailers. This is not really borne out statistically, though. From their first recordings together until the time Braithwaite left the band in September 1964, Bob sang lead on nineteen songs, Braithwaite on four ("Habits," "Straight and Narrow Way," "Don't Ever Leave Me," "It Hurts to Be Alone"), and Peter on three ("Hoot Nanny Hoot," "Maga Dog," and "Amen"). All the Wailers' big hits at this time were sung by Bob, except Braithwaite's "It Hurts to Be Alone."

Braithwaite had the most conventionally pleasant voice in the group, and has been compared to Anthony Gourdine of Little Anthony and the Imperials. He could sing higher than the others, and Bob later likened his singing to Michael Jackson's in the Jackson 5. Just listen to him soar on "Don't Ever Leave Me"—he sounds like a Jamaican Michael Jackson for sure.

The band's producer, Coxsone Dodd, felt Braithwaite had the best voice of the bunch. "It was Junior Braithwaite who had the voice and the drive," he would later say, while fellow Trench Town singer Segree Wesley told Roger Steffens, "In my opinion, Bob had the worst voice of all." Even Joe Higgs, their vocal coach, shared this opinion. He always felt that Braithwaite had a better voice than Bob, though he accepted Bob was the group's leader. It has also been said that Bob sang lead more often because he struggled with harmony.

Braithwaite's tenure with the band was short-lived. He departed for the US with his parents in September 1964 with (unfulfilled) hopes of attending medical school. According to Masouri's *Simmer Down*, Coxsone later pondered, "If he hadn't left for Chicago to join his parents, maybe he would have still been the lead singer of the Wailers." He insisted that he "appointed Bob as leader when he left," but other sources strongly suggest that Bob was the group's leader all along. Braithwaite's departure meant that the group could no longer do certain kinds of material: "When he left we had to look for a sound that Bunny, Peter and me could manage," said Bob.

Braithwaite settled in Wisconsin, but he did get one more crack at fame with the Wailers. In 1986, he reunited with surviving original members Peter Tosh, Bunny Wailer, and Beverley Kelso to record tracks for *Never Ending Wailers* (eventually released in 1993), and he performed one song alongside Bunny Wailer and Constantine "Vision" Walker at Madison Square Garden in 1986. Sadly, he was shot and killed in Kingston in 1999.

Beverley Kelso

Kelso was just sixteen years old when she first recorded with the Wailers, and she went on to add her vocals to twenty-five of their tracks. The only female in the original group, Kelso was another Trench Town friend who came to the attention of Bob because of her singing at a political rally at Chocomo Lawn. Her high-pitched voice can be heard harmonizing on several early Wailers sides like "Simmer Down," "It Hurts to Be Alone," and "Lonesome Feelings." Her eventual departure from the group may have had something to do with Bob's later comment that "she was kinda slow-like. She didn't have good timing."

Kelso was the one who brought Rita Anderson to Studio One, where she began her singing career with the Soulettes and fell in love with Bob Marley. In fact, Kelso was the only member of the group who knew that Bob and Rita got married in 1966, as Bob kept it a secret from Bunny and Peter. And, at the time of writing, Kelso and Bunny Wailer are the only surviving members of the original Wailers.

Ermine "Cherry Green" Bramwell

Nicknamed for her reddish complexion (Cherry) and her brother's surname (Green), Cherry rehearsed with the group for the two years leading up to their audition for Studio One. At twenty years of age in 1964, she was older than the others, and it must have seemed strange to be in a group with fifteen-year-old Braithwaite. She was present at the audition, but with a three-year-old child to support she could not attend the inaugural recording session in July 1964.

Cherry later made occasional appearance on Wailers tracks and briefly replaced Junior Braithwaite when he left for the States in September 1964. She can be heard on tracks like "Amen," "Lonesome Feelings," and "What's New Pussycat?" Her last session with the group was in October 1965, when she sang alongside Bob, Peter, Bunny, and Beverley on the churchy "Let the Lord Be Seen in You," a song she once sang in Sunday School. When it was released, the track was credited to Bob Marley and the Spiritual Sisters. In 1969, Cherry immigrated to the US, where she found work as a nurse. She passed away in 2008.

Joe Higgs

Higgs was more than a vocal coach and matchmaker for the Wailers. He was present at most of the early Studio One recording sessions, and he shows up on several Wailers sides, including as baritone harmony vocalist on "Your Love." Two of Higgs's girlfriends occasionally sang with the Wailers, too: Blossom Johnson sings harmony on "Destiny" and "Tell Them Lord," and Sylvia Richards, the mother of Higgs's first child, sings on "Lonesome Feelings."

Higgs made a brief return to the Wailers in 1973. When Bunny departed after the recording of *Burnin'*, Higgs replaced him on the road, and he even made it into some of the publicity photos for the album. He also sang harmony on "Coming in from the Cold," from Bob's final album, *Uprising* (1980).

The Soulettes

Thanks to Beverley Kelso, Rita and her group, the Soulettes, scored an audition at Studio One. The trio, consisting of Rita Anderson, Constantine "Vision" Walker, and Marlene "Precious" Gifford, would go on to be paired with the Wailers on many tracks, with each group assisting the other on harmonies.

Vision (originally nicknamed "Dream") was Rita's cousin, and he and Rita would play an important role in the Wailers while Bob was working in Delaware during mid-1966, adding their voices to many songs behind Peter or Bunny's lead vocal. Vision recorded with all three original Wailers periodically, singing on tracks like "Let Him Go" and "I Stand Predominant," and even adding harmony to Bob Marley's Rastafarian conversion song, "Selassie Is the Chapel," in 1968—his last contribution during Bob's lifetime. He later played percussion and guitar with Peter and Bunny during their solo careers in the eighties and nineties, and added guitar and harmony to some Melody Makers albums as well.

In the mid-eighties, Vision was also part of the *Never Ending Wailers* project, which brought together some previously recorded Bob Marley tracks from 1971 and added overdubs. The project was almost aborted for legal reasons but finally issued in 1993. He currently lives in California and has his own band, Kibah.

Marlene immigrated to New York in 1966, and Vision departed a few years later, probably in 1968. Rita then re-formed the group with Hortense Lewis and Cecile Campbell. They can be found harmonizing on Wailers tracks between 1969 and 1971, and Bob is credited with writing some of the Soulettes' songs. The Soulettes found some international success during this period, as well as opening for touring acts in Kingston, and when they toured abroad, Bob would sometimes tag along to watch over Rita.

Rita Anderson began appearing on sessions with the Wailers in September 1964, when she added her voice to "Oh My Darling" behind Bob and Marcia Griffiths. She also released a duet with Bunny called "The Vow," attributed to Bonny and Rita. While Peter sings on that track, Bob does not. The Soulettes' own career took a back seat to the more popular Wailers, but Rita continued to write, record, and perform with Bob for the rest of his life. During Bunny's incarceration for ganja possession (1967–1968), Rita took over his vocal duties in the group.

Rita and Bob married in 1966 and, when Peter and Bunny left the group in 1973, Bob asked Rita if her then singing partners, the I-Threes, would provide vocal support for the Wailers. According to Rita, anyone who worked with Bob was considered a Wailer. Rita, then, was active with the Wailers longer than any other person except Bob. Her tenure lasted from 1964 until his death in 1981, and she has continued to work to keep his legacy alive in the years since his passing.

The I-Threes

As mentioned above, the I-Threes were Bob Marley's backing singers from *Natty Dread* (1974) onward. Their genesis lies with Rita Marley, who, along with Judy

Marcia Griffiths stands beside Yellowman at Tel's Studio, where they were both recording dub plates, Kingston, 2009.   *Brent Hagerman*

Mowatt, got up onstage at the House of Chen in Kingston one night to sing with their friend Marcia Griffiths. Griffiths first sang alongside the Wailers in September 1964, when she duetted with Bob Marley on "Oh My Darling." She went on to have several hits, most notably "I Shall Sing," "Feel Like Jumping," and a duet with Bob Andy called "Young, Gifted, and Black." The three singers had known each other from their Studio One days (Mowatt had a group called the Gaylettes) and formed a sort of reggae super-group of well-known female performers. Starting in 1971, Mowatt and Griffiths began to show up alongside Rita (sometimes all three, but not always) on Wailers recordings. They are on "Iron Lion Zion," a song originally cut for the 1973 album *Burnin'* but not released until the *Songs of Freedom* boxed set in 1992.

Once Peter and Bunny left, Bob brought in the I-Threes to add backing vocals on the *Natty Dread* record, and they remained his support in the studio and in concert after that. Even though he was married to Rita, he still paid her as another musician.

Other Singers

The singers listed above were the main vocal contributors to the Wailers, but several other people provided backing vocals here and there. Here is a list of some of the more notable ones:

- The Meditations sing harmony on "Blackman Redemption" and "Rastaman, Live Up," both recorded in 1979 and released as Tuff Gong singles in Jamaica. The versions of these songs that later showed up on *Confrontation* (1983) were recorded a few months earlier and feature the I-Threes. The Meditations also provide backup for "Punky Reggae Party," which was recorded by Lee Perry in 1977, first in London and then overdubbed in Jamaica and Miami. The original harmony singers were Aura Lewis and Candy McKenzie; Perry added the Meditations in Jamaica, along with the Congos' baritone singer, Watty Burnett.

- Stevie Wonder sang "I Shot the Sheriff" and "Superstition" onstage with Bob Marley at a show in Kingston on October 4, 1975. You can find a bootleg recording of this performance on YouTube, but it has never been released officially.

- Johnny Nash sang harmony on some of Bob's 1972 songs, including his attempt to break into the American market with "Reggae on Broadway."

- The Wailing Souls (a.k.a. Pipe and the Pipers) sang backup on some tracks in 1971, most notably "Trenchtown Rock."

- Dave Barker (originally of the Techniques, and later of Dave and Ansell Collins "Double Barrel" fame) added harmonies on a few Wailers tracks in 1970, during the group's tenure with producer Lee Perry.

- The Dakota McLeod Backup Singers were used by JAD on several Marley tracks that were overdubbed in the US and released on JAD compilations. These included "Touch Me" and "Lonesome Feelings."

36

Players of Instruments

The Musicians Who Backed Up Bob Marley

In the beginning, the Wailers were not a band *per se*: they were a vocal group. Peter Tosh played acoustic guitar, and Bunny and Bob were learning too, but all the early recordings or live concerts up until the early seventies featured a professional band supporting their vocal group. Sometimes these bands had their own name and identity, and sometimes they were just collections of professional musicians. Many of Jamaica's top musicians would play at different studios under different band names. This was the normal method of recording in Jamaica, and it continued to be until the digital revolution, when producers became able to create their own backing tracks without studio bands. It isn't unique to Jamaica, either: Motown, Stax, and Atlantic had very similar setups in the sixties.

While they rarely get credit, it was these professional backing musicians that created ska, rocksteady, and reggae. Singers might come in with lyrics, melodies, and even chord progressions, but a lot of the songwriting and arranging fell to these bands. Needless to say, they rarely (if ever) received remuneration outside of their standard studio fee.

Because Bob Marley's backing band, the Wailers, had a fairly stable membership in the seventies, it is often assumed that the same players recorded as part of the band in the sixties, but this is not so.

Backing Bands for the Vocal Group the Wailers

Here is an overview of all the bands that backed up the Wailers during their pre-Island recordings. It would probably be inaccurate to consider them "Wailers" in the true sense, because, at the time, the name referred only to the vocal group.

Beverley's All Stars

Each studio in Jamaica had its own stable of musicians, though in reality there was a lot of cross-fertilization. Bob's first few singles were recorded for Beverley's—an ice cream and liquor shop cum record label—and many of this period's iteration of Beverley's All Stars would go on to start the most famous ska band of all time: the Skatalites including Lloyd Brevett (bass), Jerome "Jah Jerry" Haines (guitar), Don Drummond (trombone), and Roland Alphonso (tenor sax).

Bob made his first recordings with this band in 1962, and he, Bunny, and Peter again recorded for Beverley's in 1970. The resulting tracks were credited to the Wailers, but they were backed once again by the Beverley's All Stars (also referred to as Gladdy's All-Stars), though the entire band had changed. This time around, the lineup included: Mikey "Boo" Richards (drums), Jackie Jackson (bass), Hux Brown and Alva "Reggie" Lewis (guitars), Gladdy Anderson (piano), and Winston Wright (organ).

The Skatalites

Studio One's ace in the hole was its studio band, the Skatalites. The most famous ska band in history, the Skatalites formed in June 1964, a month before they first backed the Wailers. The lineup consisted of musicians who had been trained in jazz, cut their teeth on hotel gigs, and helped create Jamaica's first truly original form of music. An all-acoustic band at a time when others were adding electric bass and organ, they would cut twelve songs a day at Studio One, reading charts. The core lineup of the original Skatalites was: Don Drummond (trombone), Tommy McCook (tenor saxophone), Roland Alphonso (alto saxophone), Dennis "Ska" Campbell (baritone saxophone), Johnny "Dizzy" Moore (trumpet), Jerome "Jah Jerry" Haines (guitar), Jackie Mittoo (piano/ organ), Lloyd Brevette (stand-up bass), and Lloyd Knibb (drums). For backing sessions, the Skatalites would typically be augmented by various other musicians who might be in the studio on any given day, most notably guitarist Ernest

The Skatalites backed up the Wailers at Studio One, and many of their musicians would work with Bob Marley throughout his career.   *Author's collection*

Ranglin, trombonist Rico Rodriquez, bassist Cluett Johnson, and drummer Arkland "Drumbago" Parks.

Ernest Ranglin

Though not an official Skatalite, guitarist Ranglin was one of the architects of the Studio One ska sound. He is credited with helping develop the genre, and the word ska, which is an onomatopoeic reference to the sound of his quick guitar *chanks* or chucks. Ranglin played on many Studio One sessions, including several Wailers sides, and helped to arrange early songs like "Simmer Down," "It Hurts to Be Alone," and "I'm Still Waiting."

The Mighty Vikings

A few songs—including "Lonesome Feelings" and "There She Goes"— were recorded in the fall of 1964 with a band called the Mighty Vikings at Studio One. They had fewer horns, so they provided a leaner sound than the Skatalites. This band consisted of: Esmond Jarrett (drums), Desi Miles (bass), Hux Brown (guitar), Lloyd Delpratt (piano), Bobby Ellis (trumpet), Tony Wilson (tenor sax), and Seymour Walker (alto sax).

The Soul Brothers

When the Skatalites broke up in August 1965, saxophonist Roland Alphonso stayed at Studio One with Lloyd Brevett and Jackie Mittoo under the name the Soul Brothers, while Tommy McCook went to Treasure Isle Studios to join the Supersonics alongside Johnny Moore and Lloyd Knibb. Many of the Skatalites would continue to play in both these bands. Many Wailers tracks feature the Soul Brothers, and in fact their only LP for Studio One—*Wailing Wailers*, released in 1966—has the phrase "accompanied by the Soul Brothers" on the cover.

The Sharks

In the post-Skatalites era, other bands would fill in at Studio One at times for the former Skatalites crew, most of whom still worked there regularly. One 1965 track, "I'm Gonna Put It On," was recorded with the Sharks and included ex-Skatalite Roland Alphonso on tenor saxophone. The song was very popular, reaching #4 in Jamaica in February 1966.

The Soul Vendors

The Soul Vendors was yet another name for the group of Studio One musicians that included Jackie Mittoo, Hux Brown, and others. Davis suggests that the Soul Brothers became the Soul Vendors in 1967 after Roland Alphonso quit the band. Their instrumental albums contain many of the foundational rhythms that would be re-recorded for decades to come, such as "Full Up," "Real Rock," "Drum Song," and "Swing Easy."

Lynn Taitt and the Jets

The Wailers last session at Studio One was in the fall of 1966. By the summer of 1967, the Wailers were producing their own songs, and paying for their backing band and studio time at West Indies Studio. The backing band they used for their inaugural Wail'n Soul'm releases was led by Trinidadian guitarist Lynn Taitt, the main architect of the new rocksteady sound. Taitt played in several studio bands, including the Supersonics over at Treasure Isle Studios, but his own band was the Jets, formed in 1966. The Jets' lineup included other ubiquitous players like Hux Brown, Headley Bennett, Hopeton Lewis, Gladstone

As an in-demand studio musician, Jackie Mittoo played keys on many of the Wailers' early tracks. Here he is pictured on his first Canadian solo release, 1971's *Wishbone*.   *Author's collection*

Anderson, and Winston Wright. They played on rocksteady hits like Alton Ellis's "Girl I've Got a Date," Hopeton Lewis's "Take It Easy," and Derrick Morgan's "Tougher the Tough." For the Wailers, they laid down some of the hippest grooves, including "Hypocrites," "Bus Dem Shut," and "Nice Time."

Soul Syndicate

Forming in 1969 and calling themselves first the Rhythm Raiders, then the Soul Mates, Soul Syndicate had many notable musicians pass through their ranks, including drummer Leroy "Horsemouth" Wallace and vocalists Dennis Brown and Freddie McGregor. Many members of Soul Syndicate played with Marley at various points of his career. Guitarist Earl "Chinna" Smith, drummer Carlton "Santa" Davis, and keyboardist Bernard "Touter" Harvey in particular went on to accompany Marley several times in the seventies. Other members included guitarist Tony Chin, who can be heard on "Small Axe," and founder and bassist George "Fully" Fullwood, who can be heard on the original "Sun Is Shining." They were called the Aggrovators when they recorded for producer Bunny Lee. As a band, they supported the vocal group the Wailers in the studio and live at different times between 1969 and 1971. They can be heard on the Lee Perry productions "Who Is Mister Brown" and "Dracula," the former an early but ultimately rejected rhythm track for "Duppy Conqueror." The Upsetters would recut the rhythm for the released version.

The Hippy Boys / The Upsetters

The Upsetters were Lee Perry's studio band, and the core of the group between 1969 and 1970 was the brothers Barrett: Carlton (a.k.a. "Carly") on drums and Aston (a.k.a. "Familyman") on bass. They started as the Hippy Boys with Lloyd Charmers, guitarist Alva "Reggie" Lewis, and organist Glen Adams, recording tracks for producers like Bunny Lee, Sonia Pottinger, and Leslie Kong; then, as Lee's studio band, they became the Upsetters.

The group started to give serious competition to the more established studio bands when tracks they played on—like Max Romeo's "Wet Dream," Harry J. Allstars' "The Liquidator," and the Upsetters' "Return of Django"—became big hits in Jamaica and in the UK. The Wailers began recording with them in late 1969 or early 1970, when they used the Hippy Boys to back up self-produced tracks at Randy's Studio like "Black Progress," "Trouble on the Road Again," and "Comma Comma." They continued recording with the group, now known as the Upsetters, as they crafted a new sound alongside Lee Perry between August 1970 and March 1971. They liked what they heard, and when they left Perry in 1971, they took the Barretts with them, self-producing runaway local hits like

"Trenchtown Rock" and "Lively Up Yourself" in the summer of 1971 for their own label, Tuff Gong.

Once the Wailers signed to Island Records in 1972, this rhythm section would become official band members. Like Marley, Familyman was a Rastafarian, and, according to him, he and his brother played an important role in working with Marley to move reggae from a focus on dancing, romance, and Hollywood outlaws into roots reggae territory, with its connections to social justice and Rastafari.

Sons of the Jungle

While in London in March 1972, Bob recorded a group of songs with Sons of the Jungle, a band led by keyboardist John "Rabbit" Bundrick that had also backed up Johnny Nash. Bundrick would show up later on overdubs on *Catch a Fire*, brought in by Chris Blackwell to give the album more rock orientation. Only one of these songs was released in Bob's lifetime, "Reggae on Broadway," which came out on CBS in May 1972 and flopped. In March–May 1972, Bob toured the UK with Johnny Nash, with both acts backed up by Sons of the Jungle.

Cimarons

Some shows that the Wailers played while on tour of the UK in 1972 featured members of British reggae band the Cimarons, and some members of the band played on a few of the London demos for *Catch a Fire*. According to Wailers bassist Familyman, they wanted a bigger sound at these shows, and they brought in Locksley Gichie on guitar so that they could have three guitarists (with Bob playing rhythm and Peter lead). They also used the Cimarons' drummer, so they could be more like James Brown's band with two drummers, and used their keyboardist as well. This lineup played at the Commonwealth Social Club in Croydon, Surrey.

Other Notable Musicians

Many of the JAD sessions also included uncredited session musicians, while some were overdubbed on the tracks in later years. South African trumpeter Hugh Masekela overdubbed tracks on "Love" and "Rock to the Rock." Famed American session drummer Bernie Purdie played on some JAD sessions in 1968–1969. He can be heard on "What Goes Around Comes Around," "Fallin' In and Out of Love," "Nice Time," "Soul Almighty," "Splish for My Splash," "You Say I Have No Feelings," "Stranger on the Shore," "Bend Down Low," "Rock to the Rock," "Love," and possibly "Rocking Steady." Other musicians include bassist

Chuck Rainey, guitarist Eric Gale, and pianist Richard Tee, all of whom had previously played with luminaries like Aretha Franklin and Quincy Jones.

Bob Marley and the Wailers, the Island Records Years (1972–1981)

When the Wailers (the vocal group) signed to Chris Blackwell's Island Records in 1972, Blackwell wanted to market them as a band in the rock 'n' roll sense, instead of the traditional Jamaican arrangement of vocal group plus backing band. On their first two Island albums, they were simply called the Wailers, and this was assumed to include anyone on the album and in the photos. On *Catch a Fire* this chiefly meant the Barrett brothers, the band's rhythm section—a position they would continue to hold throughout Marley's life—and on *Burnin'* it meant the addition of keyboardist Earl "Wya" Lindo (both in album credits and photos) and percussionist Alvin "Seeco" Patterson (listed in the credits but not included in photos).

Familyman and Carlton Barrett were the only musicians to play nonstop with Bob for the rest of his life as part of the Wailers, and there are only a few tracks recorded between 1972 and 1981 that they are not featured on. After Marley's death, Familyman continued touring and recording with the Wailers Band, a changing assortment of musicians that at times included many of the musicians that had recorded and toured with Bob during his life.

Here is a breakdown, album by album, of the changing members of the Wailers.

Catch a Fire (1973)

Listed contributors: Bob Marley, Peter Tosh, Bunny Livingston, Aston "Familyman" Barrett, Carlton Barrett, Rita Marley, and Marcia Griffiths.

For Island's first Wailers record, released in April 1973, the core group included the Barretts, but there are a lot of other musicians on this album. Rita and Marcia Griffiths are credited as backing vocalists. At Dynamic Studios in Kingston, the band used a variety of keyboard players; they seemed to be sure that they needed a keyboardist, but unsure of which one they wanted. Earl "Wya" Lindo plays on several tracks, but strangely is not included in the album credits.

Besides this core group, there is a host of other Jamaican musicians on the album: Alvin "Seeco" Patterson and Chris Karen (percussion); Tyrone Downie, Winston Wright, and Bernard "Touter" Harvey (keyboards); Robbie Shakespeare (bass on "Concrete Jungle," and possibly "Stir It Up"); Roger Lewis and Cat Coore (guitars on "Stir It Up"); and Sparrow Martin (drums on "Stir It Up"). Many of these musicians would periodically record and perform as Wailers. Cat Coore went on to found Jamaican group Third World and backed up Marley at the Smile Jamaica concert, and Robbie Shakespeare would emerge as reggae's most famous bassist and one half of the world-renowned rhythm section Sly and Robbie.

Once the Wailers had recorded the tracks for this album in Jamaica, they took them to Chris Blackwell, who added overdubs in London by the studio musicians Wayne Perkins (lead guitar on "Rock It Baby," "Concrete Jungle," and "Stir It Up") and John "Rabbit" Bundrick (keyboards on "Concrete Jungle," "Stir it Up," and "Midnight Ravers"). Perkins had been part of the famed Muscle Shoals studio band in Alabama in the late sixties, while Bundrick had previously worked with Bob on some of his JAD sessions.

Burnin' (1973)

Listed contributors: Bob Marley, Peter Tosh, Bunny Livingston, Aston "Familyman" Barrett, Carlton Barrett, Earl "Wya" Lindo, and Alvin "Seeco" Patterson.

The Wailers' second Island album features a stripped-down band. While more people are listed on the album's credits as band members, there are actually fewer musicians on the album than on *Catch a Fire*. In fact, only those listed on the credits played on the album; there were no overdubs by foreign studio musicians in an attempt to help its crossover appeal.

The subsequent tours promoting the record would see the band make only a few personnel changes: Seeco did not go out on the road with them, and Bunny dropped out of the tour in England before it headed to the US. According to Steffens and Pierson, this was because Chris Blackwell told him they'd have to play "freak clubs" there. The band's old Trench Town vocal coach, Joe Higgs, replaced Bunny on tour between July and November 1973, and he even made it into some of the publicity photos alongside Bob, Peter, Wya, and the Barretts. Apparently he had trouble getting paid, though.

Natty Dread (1974)

Listed contributors: Bob Marley, Aston "Familyman" Barrett, Carlton Barrett, Bernard "Touter" Harvey, Al Anderson, the I-Threes.

By the end of 1973, both Bunny and Peter had left the Wailers. Bob and Chris Blackwell decided to keep the Wailers name, but now the billing reverted to

"Bob Marley and the Wailers," which had already been used often on the group's early releases, dating back to the Studio One days. With the original vocal group gone, Bob brought in the I-Threes as regular band members. He also added an African-American blues guitarist, Al Anderson, to give the music more crossover appeal. Familyman told me that he met Anderson while they were in London: "I asked him to tell us where we could get some good smoke." He also said that the backing vocals weren't done by the I-Threes but were instead overdubbed by British singers.

Bernard "Touter" Harvey, who plays on *Catch a Fire*, took over Wya Lindo's keyboard role, though Wya would return on later albums. The recording sessions were bigger than those for the previous album, and also included Seeco once again on percussion; a horn section made up of Tommy McCook, Glen DaCosta, David Madden, and Vin Gordon; and white American harmonica player Lee Jaffe. Jaffe was annoyed that he didn't get credit on the album, and further incensed that the label changed the name from *Knotty Dread* to *Natty Dread*. According to two interviews Jaffe did with Roger Steffens—first for their book *One Love*, and later for *So Much Things to Say*—"knotty" referred to the dreadlocked hairstyle at the time, whereas "natty" meant an "English twit with a top hat." What they don't say is that "natty" is derived from eighteenth-century British slang, meaning tidy and fashionably dressed. In the wake of this record, several other reggae lyrics have used "natty," suggesting either that the two terms were already interchangeable, or that Island's alteration found acceptance in the reggae community.

"No Woman, No Cry" was the only song on the record not recorded in Jamaica, and includes unknown harmony vocalists.

Live! (1975)

Listed contributors: Bob Marley, Aston "Familyman" Barrett, Carlton Barrett, Tyrone Downie, Alvin "Seeco" Patterson, Al Anderson, the I-Threes.

With this album recorded on the *Natty Dread* tour, the only difference to the lineup was that Seeco and the I-Threes had made it onto their first tour (minus Griffiths, who was pregnant at the time), and, notably, Tyrone Downie had taken over keyboard duties, suggesting that once again the keyboard position was fluid in the band. Downie was thought to be a more "rootsy" player than Touter, and a better fit for the band. Bob wanted to have two keyboardists live, just as on the albums, and eventually he would achieve this, but for the time being Downie had to hold down all the keyboard parts, playing Clavinet, organ, and piano. Downie and Earl "Wya" Lindo would go on to form the dominant organ/piano combination in the Wailers.

Rastaman Vibration (1976)

Listed contributors: Bob Marley, Aston "Familyman" Barrett, Carlton Barrett, Tyrone Downie, Earl "Chinna" Smith, Al Anderson, Donald Kinsey, Alvin "Seeco" Patterson, the I-Threes.

For this album, the band expanded once again, notably adding more guitarists and keyboardists. Soul Syndicate guitarist Chinna returned, and another African-American blues guitarist, Donald Kinsey, entered the fold. The son of American blues musician Big Daddy Kinsey, Donald cut his teeth playing with Muddy Waters and Albert King. Al Anderson is credited on "Crazy Baldhead," though he probably also plays on "Rat Race." According to manager Don Taylor, Marley paid his

Earl "Chinna" Smith with the Inna de Yard Allstars at the Uppsala Reggae Festival, 2009. Soul Syndicate guitarist "Chinna" was a recurring supporting musician in the Bob Marley band lineups of the 1970s.
Photo by Joakim Westerlund, Creative Commons license

musicians top dollar, but some still wanted more, which accounts for the switch from Anderson to Kinsey. Some of the usual suspects return, such as Bernard "Touter" Harvey on keys and Tommy McCook on tenor sax. There's also a new keyboardist: Ian Winter, a Rasta and sometime touring chef who can be heard on "War."

Local shows around the time of recording (fall 1975) included most of the above musicians, with the exception of Winter and Anderson. The international touring band was a slightly stripped-down version of the studio band (no horns), though there were two guitarists (Chinna and Kinsley) and two keyboardists (Downie and Wya). They can be heard on the posthumously released *Live at the Roxy*, recorded May 26, 1976.

Exodus (1977)

Listed contributors: Bob Marley, Aston "Familyman" Barrett, Carlton Barrett, Tyrone Downie, Alvin "Seeco" Patterson, Julian (Junior) Marvin, the I-Threes.

Most of the tracks for *Exodus* and *Kaya* were recorded during the same sessions at Island Studios in London, after Bob went into exile following the assassination attempt. As such, the personnel on these records is basically the same. This period saw the addition of another new lead guitarist, Jamaican-born, British-raised Junior Marvin. Marvin had played previously on two non-album tracks, "Rainbow Country" and an early version of "Natural Mystic," which Marley recorded at Black Ark earlier in 1975. At the time, he had his own rock band, Hanson (which was his surname), and had played with Steve Winwood and Toots and the Maytals.

Like most of Marley's other albums, *Exodus* also includes musicians who are not officially credited, including Donald Kinsey and Chinna (guitar), and Bernie "Touter" Harvey and Earl "Wya" Lindo (keyboards). The Zap Pow horns play on songs like "Exodus," but are not credited, which is strange because they *are* given credit for their work on *Kaya*, recorded at the same time. The touring band for *Exodus* was smaller than before, its lineup identical to the official album credits.

Kaya (1978)

Listed contributors: Bob Marley, Aston "Familyman" Barrett, Carlton Barrett, Tyrone Downie, Alvin "Seeco" Patterson, Julian (Junior) Marvin, the I-Threes. The horn section of Vin Gordon, Glen Da Costa, and David Madden are also officially credited on the album.

The extra musicians on *Kaya* are the same as those listed for *Exodus*. The live album *Babylon by Bus* was recorded during the tour in support of *Kaya*. For band details, see next entry.

Babylon by Bus (1978)

Listed contributors: Bob Marley, Aston "Familyman" Barrett, Carlton Barrett, Tyrone Downie, Earl "Wya" Lindo, Alvin "Seeco" Patterson, Julian (Junior) Marvin, Al Anderson, the I-Threes.

This touring band—to promote *Kaya*—was bigger than its previous incarnation. Though the personnel was slightly different, the instrumentation was the same as for the *Rastaman Vibration* touring band.

Survival (1979)

Listed contributors: Bob Marley, Aston "Familyman" Barrett, Carlton Barrett, Tyrone Downie, Earl "Wya" Lindo, Julian (Junior) Marvin, Al Anderson, the I-Threes.

Central to the sound of Bob Marley's 1970s output, Aston "Familyman" Barrett led the Wailers Band after Marley's death and released a solo album on Heartbeat Records in 1999 called *Cobra Style*. *Familyman in Dub* is that album's dub companion.
Author's collection

Unlike the last two records, *Survival* includes more uncredited studio musicians. Seeco's name is missing from the credits for the first time in a long time, though he plays on most of the songs. There was a much larger horn section present, too: Dean Fraser, "Deadly" Headley Bennett, Ronald "Nambo" Robinson, Melba Liston, Luther Francois, Junior "Chico" Chin, Jackie Willacy, and Micky Hanson. Carlton Barrett handed the drumming duties over to Carlton "Santa" Davis and Mikey "Boo" Richards on a few songs, Val Douglas played bass on "Wake Up and Live," and Lee Jaffe returned to add harmonica to "Ride Natty Ride."

The touring band for *Survival* consisted of all the musicians credited on the album except Al Anderson for the first leg of the tour (April–October), but later shows featured both Anderson and percussionist Devon Evans. It was also the first tour to feature horns, in this case Glen DaCosta and David Madden from Zap Pow. This lineup can be seen and heard on the posthumously released DVD *The Legend Live: Santa Barbara County Bowl*.

Uprising (1980)

Listed contributors: Bob Marley, Aston "Familyman" Barrett, Carlton Barrett, Tyrone Downie, Earl "Wya" Lindo, Julian (Junior) Marvin, Al Anderson, Alvin "Seeco" Patterson, the I-Threes.

New Yorker Al Anderson joined as the Wailers' lead guitarist for *Natty Dread* and continued to work with them intermittently until Bob's death. He brought a powerful bluesy edge to the songs that helped them appeal to a rock crowd more used to overdriven electric guitar solos. He later toured with the Wailers Band and the Original Wailers.

Photo by TimDuncan, Creative Commons license

Little changed with this lineup. As always, there were a few uncredited people behind the scenes, though for the most part, the lineup listed above is what you hear on the record. Joe Higgs returned to sing harmony on "Coming in from the Cold," with "Santa" Davis playing drums on the same song.

The *Uprising* tour was to be Bob's last. He collapsed while jogging in New York in September 1980, and played his last live show on September 23, at Pittsburgh's Stanley Theatre. The touring band at the time consisted of the musicians credited on the album, along with Zap Pow's Glen DaCosta and David Madden on horns.

Confrontation (1983)

Listed contributors: Bob Marley, Aston "Familyman" Barrett, Carlton Barrett, Tyrone Downie, Earl "Wya" Lindo, Julian (Junior) Marvin, Al Anderson, the I-Threes, Seeco, Glen DaCosta, Ronald "Nambo" Robinson, David Madden, Devon Evans.

This album was released two years after Bob died and brings together some of the tracks he recorded shortly before his death alongside earlier outtakes and demos. As such, they include musicians from throughout his seventies career, with very few exceptions. Devon Evans shows up on percussion for a group of songs recorded in 1980, and Bunny Wailer plays the repeater drum on "Trench Town"—a rare occurrence of the two original Wailers collaborating in the studio. Soul Syndicate drummer Carlton "Santa" Davis plays on "Chant Down Babylon." A version of "Buffalo Soldier" (known as the "King Sporty Mix") was recorded with King Sporty's band in Miami around the same time as the album track and released as a single in the UK, but the one included on *Confrontation* features the usual suspects, and is much better for it.

Other Notable Musicians

Bob occasionally returned to work with Lee Perry during the later seventies, and when he did so the musicians backing him often differed. When he recorded "Rainbow Country" and "Natural Mystic" in the summer of 1975, and "Smile Jamaica Part 2" in 1976, most of the regular Wailers were present, but so too were the Zap Pow Horns: Glen DaCosta (tenor saxophone), Dave Madden (trumpet), and Vin Gordon (trombone).

Members of Third World backed up Marley at the Smile Jamaica concert. They had played before him on the bill, and since no one was quite sure if Bob was going to perform or not, some of his own band didn't show up until part-way through the show. As such, the Third World guys filled in for some of the Wailers, with Cat Coore first playing bass before handing the instrument over to Tyrone Downie (Familyman was nowhere to be seen) and switching to lead guitar until Donald Kinsey showed up.

When Bob once again teamed up with Lee Perry to record "Keep On Moving" and "Punky Reggae Party" in July and August of 1977, he used an assortment of session musicians. Recording started in London, with Aswad drummer Angus "Drummie Zed" Gaye and Third World's Cat Coore (guitar), Ibo Cooper (keys), and Richard Daley (bass). "Punky Reggae Party" was further overdubbed in Jamaica, and, according to the liner notes to the *Exodus* double CD reissue, bass duties were fulfilled by Boris Gardiner and Val Douglas, drums by both Mikey "Boo" and Sly Dunbar, and horns by Zap Pow.

The Wailers After Bob

Since Bob passed away, Aston "Familyman" Barrett has been at the helm of continuing the Wailers' legacy by touring the world under the names the Wailers Band and simply the Wailers. They first performed post-Bob at the 1983 Reggae Sunsplash as part of a tribute to Marley that included Stevie Wonder. On February 6, 1984, the anniversary of Bob's birthday, they came together again in Nine Mile, and this really marked the start of the Wailers Band as a discrete unit, with guitarist Julian "Junior" Marvin taking on vocal duties. In the fall of 1984, following the release of *Legend*, the Wailers went out on tour with the I-Threes, Ziggy Marley, and Bob's mother, Cedella, who started her own music career in the wake of her son's death. This iteration of the band included the Barretts, Earl "Wya" Lindo, Tyrone Downie, Julian "Junior" Marvin, and Al Anderson. Marvin and Downie shared lead vocals.

Membership was fluid over the years; the band took a hiatus when Carlton was murdered in 1987, then returned in 1989 with Mikey "Boo" Richards on

Jamaica-born but London-raised, Junior Marvin continued the crossover work of American guitarists Al Anderson and Donald Kinsley when he joined the Wailers for *Exodus*. After Marley's death, he toured alongside Al Anderson in the Wailers Band and the Original Wailers.
Photo by Eva Rinaldi, Creative Commons license

drums and released an album of original material, *I.D.* Two more albums followed—1991's *Majestic Warriors* and 1994's *JAH Message*—but each failed to establish the band's own identity. Some musicians who had been part of the Island-era Wailers (Downie, Wya, Seeco, Anderson, Marvin, Marcia Griffiths, Zap Pow) came and went, to be replaced by others who had never played with Bob, such as singers Elan Atlas and Gary Pines. Then, as now, the Wailers live sets were basically a greatest-hits tribute to the work of Bob Marley.

By 2015, Familyman was the only remaining original member of the group. Based on his residency, I went to see the group in February 2016, and I was shocked to find out that while he was featured in the promotional material (the concert program even included an interview with him!), he wasn't onstage. His son, Aston Barrett Jr., played bass admirably, but this was essentially an over-priced cover band, with no members of the original Wailers. My attempts at soliciting an explanation from the band manager, venue manager, and T-shirt salesman (I tried all angles) went nowhere. The venue didn't even realize the band it had booked was essentially a sham. Later that year, it came out that Familyman had parted ways with this iteration of the Wailers and brought legal proceedings against them for their illegal use of the band's name. As of 2018, there is no sign of the Wailers band that toured two years previously without any original members, but www.thewailers.net is the new home of Familyman's re-established band, with whom he once again tours simply as the Wailers. His son has taken over drum duties, and Judy Mowatt's daughter, Shema McGregor, is the backing vocalist.

37

Kinky Reggae

Songs of Love, Sex, and Seduction

In his own estimation, Bob Marley's only vice was "plenty women," but to hear some writers tell it, you'd think all his love songs were innocent romantic crooners, with not a whine-and-grinder in sight. Track for track, he wrote far more revolutionary and spiritual songs than sensual serenades, but this is the guy who supposedly wrote "Midnight Ravers" after a night of lovemaking, and seduced Miss World 1976 with "Is This Love," "Turn Your Lights Down Low," and "Waiting in Vain." It may also have been Miss World who put him in a loving mood on many of *Kaya*'s tracks and then left him forlorn in "She's Gone."

Love was certainly on the brain, but it wasn't always so chivalrous. Reggae historians love to carve a gulf between Bob Marley's spiritually uplifting music and the lusty, fast-talking, slack dancehall that shot to popularity soon after he was gone. For instance, London's *Sunday Times* presented Marley as a singer of "lilting love songs" in juxtaposition to dancehall artists who spout violent and misogynistic lyrics. *Time* magazine said that, after Marley, "Dancehall lyrics were charged with angry diatribes glorifying guns, drugs and sex, and sang often in a fast, talky style called 'toasting.'" Jamaica's *Daily Gleaner* was even more specific, singling out dancehall sensation Yellowman as emblematic of how the music digressed into obscene and pornographic tales in the wake of Bob's consciousness: "Yellowman's canon concerns itself with a celebration of the female anatomy [which is] some way from the spirituality and social concern of Bob Marley." I could go on and on listing journalists who assume that the man who, according to Maureen Sheridan, once said, "Sexual intercourse is a lovely thing," and had a virtually nonstop series of affairs, did not sing about sex. He did.

To call Bob Marley a slack artist is a stretch. *Slackness* refers mostly to raunchy lyrics and performances. Yes, Yellowman had lots of those, and, no, Marley did not. But Bob did sing about getting it on, and this isn't something that should be thought of as somehow haughty next to eighties dancehall, as the sixties and seventies had their fair share of ribald reggae, often by roots singers. Ever hear of Max Romeo's "Wet Dream" or "Play With Your Pussy?" Those were by the same guy who sang "When Jah Speak," "War Inna Babylon," and "Selassie I Forever." Or Glen

King Yellowman shook up the reggae industry just as Bob Marley passed in 1981 with his crude slackness, causing many critics to position him as Bob Marley's polar opposite and condemn him for the demise of reggae. Of course, Bob Marley was no stranger to singing about sex himself.   *Author's collection*

Adams and the Hippy Boys' "I Want a Grine"? (Incidentally, Fams and Carly of the Hippy Boys went on to become the mightiest Rasta roots rhythm section better known as the Wailers.)

Bob's kinky songs are less blatant, to be sure, but he still had them. In this, he's part of a rich cultural tradition that imbues Caribbean music forms. Unlike the relative prudery of British and American music, where Elvis's vulgar swinging hips caused a moral panic and the Rolling Stones were banned from singing "Let's Spend the Night Together" on *The Ed Sullivan Show*, songs about sex are part of everyday life because, after all, sex is part of everyday life. And, really, people have probably been singing about sex as long as they've been having it. American hokum blues and naughty Irish sea shanties have got nothing on Shakespeare, whose plays were filled with vulgar puns on all manner of sexual topics such as genitalia, sodomy, venereal disease, masturbation, semen, same-sex copulation, and prostitution.

Bob would have been familiar with the long tradition of lewd Trinidadian calypsos, which tended to employ double-entendres in a wink-wink, nudge-nudge way so that everyone knew what they were talking about. Mighty

Sparrow's "The Big Bamboo" wasn't a tree, and "Saltfish" didn't refer to a culinary delicacy. Euphemisms for the male phallus abound in calypso: golden sword, wood, coil, ram, banana, water hose, stick, pogo stick, rod of correction, drum stick, key, or blade. Female genitalia might be referred to as a garden, pum-pum, or gearbox.

Like its Trinidadian cousin, the Jamaican mento played in Kingston's clubs in the fifties had a decidedly lascivious side. For mento, the sexiness was more in the dancing than the lyrics, with popular dances like the Rent-a-Tile, named after the fact that partners were locked together in intimate thrusts on one tile of floor. The *Dictionary of Folklore* says of this erotic dance, "The woman tantalizes her partner into a frenzy with seductive rolling of the haunches and belly and works herself into a state of autointoxication."

Marley would have also been familiar with a few mento singers' risqué lyrics, like Mary Bryant's "Tomato," Tony Johnson's "Give Her Banana," Lord Power's "Let's Do It," Lord Lebby's "Dr. Kinsey Report," and the Starlights' "Soldering," which was even banned by Jamaican radio. The point is that slackness wasn't miraculously invented by dancehall reggae, and that Marley came out of a musical tradition that saw nothing wrong with celebrating a little sex.

The Wailers' Sexy Songs

Despite Bunny Wailer telling Roger Steffens, "Wailers didn't have to sing no dirty things," they did. During their tenure at Studio One, the Wailers recorded a few songs about lovemaking and backed up other artists doing the same. Their later gifted producer, Lee "Scratch" Perry, was, at the time, an employee of Studio One, and he released his share of naughty songs with help from the Wailers.

The Wailers' "Rude Boy Ska" would live on in a naughty version recorded by Lee Perry under the name King Perry called "Pussy Galore." Named after the James Bond character, the song was obviously not-too-veiled slackness. Peter and Bunny even sang back up on this, repeating the lyrics "sweet sweet pussy galore."

Lee Perry and the Soulettes also released the salacious "Doctor Dick," and, yes, that's Bob's soon to be wife, Rita Anderson singing, "Stick a me up, doctor, let me feel it." "Rub and Squeeze" is another Lee Perry tune with backups courtesy of the Soulettes. How else is this affiliated with Bob? It uses the same backing track as the Wailers' "I'm Gonna Put It On," a song that is marginally religious ("Lord, I thank you") and therefore exemplifies a very Jamaican pairing of the sacred and profane.

This mixing of the sacred and secular was common for soul music. Ray Charles's "This Little Girl of Mine" was a take on "This Little Light of Mine."

Sam Cooke's "Lovable" was simply a secular version of "Wonderful," recorded earlier with gospel group the Soul Stirrers. This influence can be seen in Bob's songs like "Satisfy My Soul Jah Jah," a religious song, whose secular counterpart, "Satisfy My Soul Babe," swaps the comforting role of God with a woman. Incidentally, in the latter Bob sings of the "strange desires I have for your love."

While Bob was away working in Delaware, the other Wailers recorded their raciest song yet, "Making Love," sung by Peter and harmonized by the other early Wailers, including Rita. Paul McCartney must have been paying attention, because his bass line from "Ob-La-Di, Ob-La-Da" could have been lifted from this.

As "Satisfy My Soul Babe" attests, Bob's songs generally left a little more to the imagination than Lee Perry's did. His love songs for Rita included "Chances Are," "Nice Time," "Stir It Up," and "No Woman, No Cry." Out of these, the only really horny song is "Stir It Up," and you can hear Scratch's influence. Though it is thought to be an innocuous song of love, Yellowman pointed out to me several times (in defending his own use of slackness) that Marley's line "I'll push the wood, I'll blaze your fire / Then I will satisfy your heart's desire" uses the Jamaican euphemism for penis—wood. In his estimation, the song is pure slackness, and I tend to agree. It's not a cooking pot Bob wants to be stirring. By the same token, "Nice Time's" use of "rock" ("I wanna rock with you, rockin' / Won't you rock with me?") could also connote sex in the same way rock 'n' roll originally did.

Another song that is often cited as risqué is "Bend Down Low," though with lyrics like "Bend down low, let me tell you what I know," that might be a far-fetched interpretation. "Guava Jelly," like "Stir It Up," might be just about hugging and kissing, but the line "Come rub 'pon me belly like a guava jelly" suggests something a bit more carnal. Again, Yellowman cites this song as an example of Bob's slackness, and he ought to know. He's penned a few lyrics about "rubbing" himself, and these aren't about adolescent petting: "Mek we rub and go down, mek we whine and go in," and "Let me rub up up up on a big fat ting" are prime examples of the King of Slack's sex-lyrics. In Bob Marley's hands, this interpretation works. Now go and listen to Barbara Streisand's 1974 cover and see if she gets the deeper meaning.

According to the liner notes to the *Songs of Freedom* boxed set, Bob's "Back Out," from the 1970 Beverley's sessions, is about the cramped and public living conditions in Trench Town's tenement housing. But biographer Stephen Davis gets closer to the truth when he calls the song a "classic Wailers sex chant." In a series of corrections to the boxed set's liner notes, *The Beat* said the following about the song: "It is, according to Bunny, who co-wrote it, actually a bawdy takeoff on a children's song sung by students about their teacher, 'Mistress

Martin'" and alluding to her private parts." So, in other words, prime naughty, natty dread.

"Do It Twice," another Beverley's song, is also oblique. It could be a song of heartache, or it could be an invitation into the bedroom—twice. Biographer Timothy White says of the song, "After making love, he confesses to his partner that he has found her so delightful that he would like to start all over again."

"Am a Do," an outtake from *Natty Dread*, channels James Brown with Marley's use of the term *badself*. He also revisits the theme of "Do It Twice" in this ribald track: "I've got to do it with you again . . . Do it with your badself, let me feel rude."

Again, using clever wordplay characteristic of Caribbean songwriting. Bob's "Lick Samba" is a homophonic of "lick some back," or to have sex. "Lick" here means to strike or hit—both common actions used to describe the male role in coitus. In the song, Bob tells his lover that he's ready—morning, noon, and night. Again, he might just be in a dancing mood, but he's probably more interested in dirty dancing.

The most thorough treatment of sex in a Bob Marley song is "Kinky Reggae" from *Catch a Fire*, but it's not exactly straightforward. Interpretations range from the song being about trying to score ganja in Piccadilly Circus to Bob visiting a prostitute by the name of Miss Brown, to a narrative about a sugar-cane cutter with brown cane stalk on her shoes (boogas is slang for sneakers), to a homoerotic episode in which Bob contemplates fellating a man named Marcus, to Marcus offering the singer a loose woman. There's a lot of racy innuendo here that suggests the song is more about sex than sugar.

For Carolyn Cooper, the song's meaning is clear: a temptress named Miss Brown offers kinky sex, and Bob, the typical uptown playboy, wants to hit and run. It's a bit reminiscent of the Stones' "Brown Sugar," which came out a year earlier, though in Mick Jagger's hands, the use of the title phrase is highly problematic, as the song manages to be both racist and sexist. It's a white male fantasy wherein black women are whipped by a "scarred old slaver," and are reduced to wanton dancing harlots.

Soft Porn Soul Rebel

The Wailers' album art generally evokes a scrappy band of natty rebels, close-ups of Bob, or Rastafarian iconography. But the album cover for the Lee Perry–produced *Soul Rebels* (1970) is none of these, and it would fit better alongside the soft porn of the Trojan *Tighten Up* series, many of which sought to entice male reggae aficionados with pictures of topless, brown-skinned women.

The Wailers had no input in, and were apparently not happy with, the soft porn cover art for *Soul Rebels*.   *Author's collection*

Soul Rebels was licensed to Trojan for UK release, and the same graphic designer who put together the *Tight Up* records must have been assigned to it, because the cover shows a near-bare-breasted black girl wielding a machine gun and wearing army fatigues. Sexy? You bet. In keeping with the band or song cycle? Not even close. The label obviously never listened, or paid attention, to the militant material ("400 Years") or the Rasta mediations held within ("Soul Rebel"). The band members weren't consulted, and nor were they happy with the finished product.

38

Midnight Ravers

Bob's Views on Cross-Dressing and Homosexuality

It's no secret that Jamaican culture is deeply homophobic, and many reggae artists pen openly violent lyrics towards gay men, for whom patois speakers have innumerable derogatory terms such as *batty bwoys* (*batty* being a term for buttocks], *chi chi men*, and *maama men*. Anti-gay lyrics have become something of a show of Jamaican values for artists like Buju Banton, who famously sang about shooting gay men in "Boom Bye Bye." For Banton, singing these songs is akin to giving the middle finger to the liberal critics he thinks are trying to corrupt Jamaican values through a new sort of cultural imperialism (you see, he believes that being gay is anti-Jamaican, and something that is imported from Western liberalism). So much for "let's get together and feel all right."

The trend toward these toxic lyrics gained momentum in the nineties (examples include Papa San's "Sorry," Shabba Ranks's "Dem Bow," Bounty Killer's "Can't Believe Mi Eyes," TOK's "Chi Chi Man," and Beenie Man's "Bomb and Dynamite"), and has more recently sparked outrage internationally, as homophobic Jamaican artists have had their concerts canceled in the US, Britain, and Canada. But did Bob ever sing about homosexuality? The short answer is no, but the more interesting one is . . . maybe.

Midnight Ravers

"Midnight Ravers," from *Catch a Fire*, is the closest Marley comes to expressing views on non-heteronormative performances of gender and sexuality. First demoed in London in February 1972, the track was recorded in Jamaica in October of that year and released as the album's final track the following April. This is to say, then, that it was among the first Marley songs to be heard by an international audience.

Musically, it follows a mesmerizing minor-key two-chord sequence—slow, dread, and heavy—not unlike other songs of this period ("No More Trouble," "Burnin' and Lootin'"), though not quite as anthemic as other minor-key jams of the period, like "Get Up, Stand Up" and "I Shot the Sheriff." Thematically, it is one of Marley's many songs of social commentary, particularly the kind where he's calling out society's sinful behavior. Other songs of this ilk are "Hypocrites," "Stiff Necked Fools," "The Heathen," and "Guiltiness." But whereas he usually positions himself as the (self-)righteous Rastaman in these songs, "Midnight Ravers" finds him in danger of getting lost among the sinners. And what, exactly, is the aberrant behavior here? As Bob Marley never spoke about the song in interviews, we can only guess.

Was Bob Homophobic?

For some, the sin in the song is homosexuality, while others think it is about cross-dressing. The song begins by stating that a man and a woman cannot be told apart because "they're dressed in the same pollution." This could be referring to many things. A few commentators have speculated that it is about sexual confusion in the form of homosexuality. One of them posted to the online reggae blog 18 Karat Reggae.

In one post, the site calls "Midnight Ravers" Jamaica's first anti-homosexual song, adding that it can "be easily interpreted by anyone with a high school education." According to the post, the song's lyrics, which speak about horseless chariots—ten thousand of them—allegorically refer to unnatural phenomena, because chariots can't move without horses. (Unless Bob was talking about the horseless carriage, which, by the way, used to refer to the automobile). The site then connects this with homosexuality by somehow assuming metaphors about horseless chariots obviously refer to "unnatural" same-sex relationships. This blog, which claims to promote tolerance and respect, continues with an astonishing analysis of the song that says more about its author than Marley.

First, Marley apparently used the word "coming" in the song (to say that chariots are coming, as opposed to arriving, or driving, or moving) "as a sexual undertone . . . as if to say men and women were cumming in an unnatural way not intended by nature, such as men with men and women with women." These unnatural people, the blogger tells us, feel shame for their sexual sins, and this is borne out in the song when Marley tells us that the riders of the chariots have their faces covered. "No one hides when they are proud of what they are doing. So the covering up of their faces actually show that they were closet gays."

I can think of several other interpretations for the above lyrics, each more likely than this "righteous," "truthful," and "clean" polemic. However, homophobia would fit in with Jamaican and Rastafari culture of the time (and, unfortunately, today as well). So whereas I think this blogger is reading too much in the lyrics of the song, the sentiment that there is something sinful about sex and/or gender fluidity probably isn't far off.

Others have also understood the song to be about homosexuality, but, interestingly, in an opposite way. A blog posting on gay-positive reggae site www.soulrebels.org suggests that the song is about Marley coming to terms with the fact that homosexuality is a natural part of creation. It arrives at this conclusion by pointing to verse two, where Marley sings that there is no solution to his problem. The author reads this as confirmation that there is no solution to the phenomenon of homosexuality, "but to accept that it's part of creation." The post reads the song through the mantra of "One Love," suggesting open-mindedness, universal love, and respect, and surmising that it came on the heels of Bob's first sojourns into the comparatively more gay-friendly cities of Europe.

This reading of the song is hopeful at best, but probably not what Bob was thinking. Two sources in particular give us a clue to Bob's attitude toward homosexuality, and they are not gay-positive. According to his manager, Don Taylor, Bob, like many of his compatriots, believed homosexuality was a sin. Taylor said that Bob abhorred gays and bisexuals, whom he came in contact with through Chris Blackwell, who had many gay friends. And, when asked by the Caribbean *Times* in 1975 for his views on homosexuality, he scoffed, "Sodomy? Me nuh wan' deal wid." In Jamaican parlance, not dealing with something doesn't mean ignoring it; it more closely connotes condemning it.

Androgynous Fashion Statements?

"Midnight Ravers" does appear to be about clubbing in the UK and/or Europe, where Bob spent several months prior to recording this song. However, it might just be an innocent commentary on androgynous fashion choices. Wailers bassist Familyman has indicated that the song was inspired by walking through Portobello Road, Harlesden, and Piccadilly Circus in London, telling Masouri, "It was different for us, seeing how people moved and how they were dressed." Marley archivist and author of *Bob Marley: The Complete Annotated Bibliography*, Joe Jurgensen, agrees, writing on www.soulrebels.org, "I just think it has to do with the crazy London nightlife scene.... Everybody is dressed wild and acting wild."

These midnight ravers could also refer to celebrity cross-dressers like glitter-rock star David Bowie, who had unveiled his androgynous "Ziggy Stardust" persona earlier that year, having previously worn a dress on the cover of his 1970 LP *The Man who Sold the World*.

The song certainly appears to have a clear connection to Rastafarian thinking around cross-dressing, according to Jamaican activist and intellectual Cecil Gutzmore. As a Rasta, Marley would have had strong objections to a man in female clothing. This kind of boundary-crossing would be understood as an act against the natural order of life, wherein people are born as one of two genders and adhere to strict gender coding, particularly around dress.

Other reggae songs police these gender discrepancies, too. Michigan and Smiley's 1981 hit "Diseases" tell us that when "girls dress up inna trousers," Jah—the Rastafarian name for god—is displeased. The *Daily Gleaner* reported that Papa Michigan wrote the lyrics after being shocked at seeing women wearing man's clothing—i.e., pants—in clubs. He explained that, as a Rasta, "Wi a look towards the Empress in dem dress and dem skirt," proffering Empress Menen Asfaw, Haile Selassie's wife, as the role model Rastafarian women should follow in choosing their attire. In other words, from a Rasta point of view, men wear pants, women wear dresses. This interpretation could easily work with "Midnight Ravers."

Poet, actor, and academic Kwame Dawes has offered the most complete commentary of the song, suggesting that it is a "surreal walk into the nightmare of the last days—as if the singer has walked into a world of debauchery and strange ways." Ah, the last days. That's not a phrase you hear often when talking about rock icons. But this is the kind of thinker Marley was—Rastafarians are Book of Revelation, fire-and-brimstone believers, and the second verse of "Midnight Ravers" sounds like it's right out of John the Revelator's vision.

Dawes suggests this refers to motorcycle riders showing up to a club (a little more believable than the 8 Karat blogger). The nightmare refers to unnatural clandestine activities that are afoot: cross-dressing and swinging, which the singer judges to be filled with "confusion" and "pollution." Marley fears being led astray by the midnight ravers, and then he becomes one, too, at the end of the song. This is Marley's vision of Babylon: a world overtaken by sexual sin, where people are confused about their true identities, and where the righteous can slip down the slippery path of debauchery.

So was Bob Marley anti-gay? It's hard to say, but we can't draw a clear conclusion from this song, which is probably about the Rastafarian aversion to cross-dressing. Nor should we project our contemporary values (whether they be gay-positive or gay-negative) on historical figures.

Or Maybe the Song's Not About Gender at All

Despite commentators looking for profound gendered meanings in "Midnight Ravers," Sheridan, in *The Story Behind Every Bob Marley Song*, suggests that it was about Bob's own love of nightlife and his sex drive. Bob, she says, was moved to write the song after an evening of making love to Pat Williams, mother of his son Robbie. He woke in the morning and scribbled the lyrics on a nearby Kingston phone book.

Part 3

The Mystic

39

Let the Lord Be Seen in You

Early Christian Songs

The Wailers always had a religious streak. Bob Marley's favorite book was a King James Bible personalized with pictures of Jah Rastafari himself, Haile Selassie. As a member of the Twelve Tribes of Israel, he would strive to read "a chapter a day," and numerous sources speak of the Bible as his companion. Vivien Goldman, a journalist who covered the *Exodus* tour, writes that it "would live open beside him, a ribbon marking the place, as he played his guitar by candlelight in whichever city he found himself. He had a way of isolating himself with the book, withdrawing from the other laughing musicians on the tour bus to ponder a particular passage, then challenge his bred'ren to debate it as vigorously as if they were playing soccer."

This is to say that Bob was intimately familiar with scripture, and any fan with an inkling of the contents of the Bible realizes he drew from it regularly in his songwriting. In *The Bible and Bob Marley*, author Dean MacNeil finds 137 biblical references in Bob's Island Records material alone. To be clear, that's 137 references across 83 songs—or about 1.7 references per song. The biblical books that were most important to Bob, based on this usage, are drawn from the Old Testament: Psalms (26 percent) and Proverbs (18 percent). This is somewhat fitting, as the first is a book of songs and the second a book of wisdom.

This does not mean, however, that Bob Marley read or used the Bible in the same way as Christians do. As a Rastafarian, he engaged with the Bible outside of Christian tradition. His interest in Rastafari began in the mid-sixties, and it really only started to present itself articulately in his songwriting in the early seventies. But his use of the Bible and Christian themes dates back to the first song he recorded in 1962, "Judge Not," which is based on Matthew 7:1: "Judge not, that ye be not judged."

Bob attended a Pentecostal church in Nine Mile while growing up with his mother, who sang in the choir. Among his early musical influences were the songs based on biblical themes as laid out in his church's hymnbook, *Redemption Songs: One Thousand Hymns and Choruses*. He would draw on this Jamaican Pentecostal musical heritage throughout his career as he translated the inspiration and wisdom found in biblical messages into his own songs.

Marley's connection to Christianity was reignited at the end of his life when he was baptized into the Ethiopian Orthodox Church, becoming a Christian Rasta. This relationship came full circle—symbolically, at least—when the Anglican Church of Jamaica decided to include two Wailers songs in their hymnal in 2007. Marley's "One Love" and Peter Tosh's "Psalm 27" can now be found in pew books.

Given the two songwriters' personalities, we might expect Bob to laugh at this usage; the vehemently anti-Christian Peter Tosh is probably turning over in his grave. But Church spokesman Reverend Ernle Gordon dismissed any incongruences with the songs of two well-known Rastamen showing up in Christian worship, telling the *New York Times*, "They may have been anti-church, but they were not anti-God or anti-religion." Well said. As the songs below show, Bob was very pro-church—for a while, at least.

Original Lyrics with Biblical Themes

As previously mentioned, Bob's first song, "Judge Not," is based on Jesus's moral teachings, as laid out in the Sermon on the Mount. Bob takes the chorus directly from the Gospel of Matthew when he sings, "Judge not before you judge yourself," while the verses make it clear that he wants to live without others passing judgment on him. In this way, the song comes off less like a Christian admonishment and more like a statement of personal freedom. That's a pretty smart way to universalize a biblical message.

The Wailers' original 1965 recording of "One Love" was a thorough rewrite of the Impressions' "People Get Ready." "People Get Ready" was itself a response to Martin Luther King Jr.'s 1963 March on Washington and "I Have a Dream" speech, and, according to a 1993 NPR interview with songwriter Curtis Mayfield, the lyrics were inspired by the "preachings of my grandmothers and most ministers when they reflect from the Bible."

The train theme found in "People Get Ready" was common in American soul and gospel at the time, and signified movement forward toward civil rights and the commonality of all humanity. "One Love" keeps a few lyrics, alters others, and adds much of the band's own religious language about praying, fighting holy battles, and the return, presumably, of Jesus to Earth. Marley's additional call for "One love, one heart / Let's get together and a-feel all right" is in keeping with the universal theme of the civil rights movement and the belief that he shared with his daughter, Cedella, that "nobody is beyond redemption. Nobody." It is little wonder that this entreatment for universal respect, community, and happiness—both with and without its religious context—has come to summarize Bob's philosophy for many fans.

Another early song that contains a scriptural reference is "Cry to Me," originally recorded in 1965 and then redone for *Rastaman Vibration* in 1975. While the song does not really demonstrate a strong Christian thematic lyric, when Bob sang, "Lord that leadeth me, yeah, And now I'm by the still water," he was obviously thinking of Psalm 23:2.

When the Wailers went into Kingston's Federal Studios in the early days of 1970, they must have been in a spiritual mood. They recorded four songs that day, each with biblical references. Alongside their third crack at "This Train," they also taped "Adam and Eve," which was a cover of a song by another Jamaican band, the Bleechers. The lyric draws on the Genesis creation story, providing a pretty standard sexist Christian/Rasta reading that a) the serpent in the Garden of Eden is Satan (it's not in the original Jewish text), b) "woman is the root of all evil," and c) this is the reason there is sin in the world today.

With "Wisdom," Bob turned up the biblical references considerably, repeating lines from Proverbs word-for-word in stanza after stanza: "The lips of the righteous teach many / But fools die for want of wisdom" (Proverbs 10:21), "The rich man's wealth is in his city / Destruction of the poor is poverty" (Proverbs 10:15). Bob revisited the song in 1980, in the renamed and much rearranged "Stiff Necked Fools," which Peter Tosh re-recorded as "Fools Die" in 1981.

The final song from this session, "Thank You Lord," was first recorded by the group in 1967, in a rocksteady style, but updated for the 1970 session with the faster early reggae feel and rich choral backing vocals. The lyrics differ slightly, and the first song finds Bob feeling thankful for his blessings but also steadfast in his confidence of his own righteousness, because he won't succumb to temptation. He then cites the biblical book that perhaps most shaped his worldview: "I have learned my lesson in Revelation."

Both the self-righteousness and the Book of Revelation would become standard tropes in Bob's religious material as his engagement with Rastafari deepened into the seventies. Interestingly, though, the later take does not include these lyrics. It's possible they were removed after the fact, because there is a noticeably heavy-handed studio edit just before they are due to come in. Here, Bob alters the last verse, removing the mention of Revelation, and humbly submitting to the Lord through prayer.

Gospel, Hymns, and Spirituals

American gospel groups like the Highway QCs, Caravans, Swan Silvertones, and Sam Cooke's Soul Stirrers were favorites of the Wailers, and some of their Studio

One material found them voicing gospel songs in a similar vein. Coxsone Dodd even released some of their more overtly religious material on his spiritual label, Tabernacle. They turned Alex Bradford's "Let the Lord Be Seen in You" into "Let the Lord Be Seen in Me," and "I Left My Sins Behind Me" into "I Left My Sins." Those and Bradford's "Just in Time" were all released under the moniker Bob Marley and the Spiritual Sisters in 1965. They also gave the Highway QCs the ska treatment with "Somewhere to Lay My Head" in 1964, and would cover traditional African-American spirituals, often with a nod to existing American versions. Their "Amen" (1965) closely follows the Impressions' version. "Sinner Man" had been previously recorded by the Swan Silvertones and Nina Simone when the Wailers did it in 1966, recording it several times with Peter Tosh singing. The song evolved in his hands into "Downpressor Man" (1970, 1977) and "Oppressor Man" (1971). Peter also sang lead on "Go Tell It on the Mountain," using the book of Exodus/civil rights–inspired lyric "let my people go" instead of the Christmas carol version, "Jesus Christ is born."

Other spirituals to make their set list include "This Train," a re-cut of the traditional American song "This Train Is Bound for Glory" that includes the lyric, "Oh my little Jesus, my lord." The original trio sang it in 1965, 1967, and 1970, and Bob recorded a new demo of it in Sweden in 1971. "I Am Going Home" is a country-church-ska version of "Swing Low Sweet Chariot" from 1964. That year they also recorded a version of "Nobody Knows the Trouble I've Seen" as "Nobody Knows."

In 1964, the Wailers recorded the mento staple "Wings of a Dove," a song was that popular with ska bands because the Blues Busters and Prince Buster also recorded versions of it. The song is based on Psalm 55:6, containing the lyric, "If I had wings like a dove then I would fly away and be at rest," and is also an adaption of the Albert E. Brumley hymn "I'll Fly Away." This hymn was later used as the basis for "Rastaman Chant," as found on *Burnin'* in 1973, and was also sung by the I-Threes at Bob's funeral.

Bob recorded his last gospel song in 1968. The Wailers tapped the father of gospel music, Tommy Dorsey, for his "The Lord Will Make a Way Somehow." Sounding like an American soul band, Marley and crew turn this gospel standard into a funky, medium-tempo ballad. It is somewhat fitting that his last gospel recording would be a Dorsey composition, as his mother remembers him humming along to Dorsey's "Precious Lord Take My Hand" while living as a boy in Nine Mile.

40

Rastaman Chant

Reggae and Rastafari

To feel the reggae beat is to think Rasta," declares Nathaniel Samuel Murrell, in the introduction to *Chanting Down Babylon: The Rastafari Reader*. In *Reggae, Rastas, and Rudies*, media theorist Dick Hebdige calls reggae "the Rasta hymnal."

Reggae and Rastafari have a long symbiotic relationship such that many reggae artists adopt Rastafarian style, names, dress, speech patterns, themes, and ideological bents in their lyrics (often without actually becoming Rasta), and, in turn, the once-small Jamaican sect has enjoyed global popularity. Reggae culture has been so imbued with Rastafari—everything from the ubiquitous red, gold, and green colors to pictures of Haile Selassie—that it is often difficult to discern which artist or which song would be considered authentically Rastafarian by either the artist or other Rastas.

We have Bob Marley, mostly, to thank for this symbolic union of everything Rasta with everything reggae. By the mid-sixties, Bob was increasingly influenced by the still-nascent Rastafarian sect. He would go on to become the chief proponent of the religion internationally, and its tenets and worldview would be laid out in his songs, which speak of the living black god, Jah Rastafari, and an end-times battle between good and evil. In fact, Bob and his early spiritual advisor, Mortimo Planno, saw his musical and spiritual missions entwined: as he took reggae to the world, he also planned the global expansion of the religion.

Now it is commonplace to see a smiling dread on a tourism ad for Jamaica, and for many foreigners, this is the (stereo)typical image of what Jamaicans look like. In the sixties, however, Rastafarians had a bad reputation in Jamaica, where they were called "blackheart" men and thought to be thieves and crooks. The police would harass them for their ganja use, and in some instances would perform the humiliating ritual of shaving their heads. Jacob Miller's "Big Stripe" took up this theme in song, arguing that the police were granted promotions for jailing Rastas. Dancehall deejay Yellowman told me that when he was attending school in the sixties and seventies, teachers "would scare children and tell them Rastas would kill them."

Polite, upper-class society distained Rastas and reggae, both of which were considered vulgar expressions of the black ghettos. Any foothold either gained that allowed them to scramble out of the ghetto—such as Bob's move uptown to 56 Hope Road, or the fawning of the international press—was feared as a threat to the established order.

Today, it is almost expected of reggae musicians to don dreadlocks and sing incantations to the "Most High," but Garry Lowe, the Jamaican bassist for Canadian rock-reggae band Big Sugar, told me that walking down the street with dreadlocks would once bring you scorn. In his book on Bob's early life, *Before the Legend*, Chris Farley notes that Bob shocked his audience at the Regal Theatre in Kingston during an Independence Day concert in 1968 when he "strode out in Rastaman garb and sandals and was booed and mocked by some in the audience." Farley likens this cultural shift away from pop acts wearing suits and singing love songs to Dylan doing electric.

Dread Rhythms

Bob's songwriting in the seventies was the vehicle that enabled Rastafari to flow across borders, both cultural and geographic, to reach a global audience, but he was by no means the first—or only—Jamaican singer to marry Rastafarian consciousness and Jamaican music.

The first instances of Rastafari in Jamaican popular music could be found through drummers, not singers. Early Rastas adopted many songs and rhythms from the African-Jamaican religious tradition known as Kumina. These were transformed into the liturgical music of Rastafari at Pinnacle, a Rasta commune near Spanish Town. Pinnacle was destroyed by a police raid in late 1953, and the inhabitants filtered down into Kingston's ghettos, where they continued playing kumina music in neighborhoods like Trench Town. Bob Marley would encounter this music from the time he moved to Trench Town in the late fifties.

Kumina evolved in the hands of master Rastafarian drummer Count Ossie, a member of the Rastafarian Repatriation Association of Adastra Road in eastern Kingston. Ossie was instrumental in drawing on these rural rhythms and fashioning a new, urban kumina rhythm that influenced both reggae and Rastafarian Nyabinghi drumming, as heard on his albums with Mystic Revelation of Rastafari.

Count Ossie is an archetypal figure of the reggae/Rasta connection. At this time, there were Rasta camps around Kingston's ghettos, and Ossie's camp was frequented by many of the city's musicians—notably several Skatalites, like Don Drummond, Rico Rodriquez, and Tommy McCook. The Wailers, of course, spent two years singing with the Skatalites at Studio One.

The stature of these Rasta camps among Kingston's music industry grew. When Prince Buster left Coxsone Dodd's Downbeat sound system and established his own Voice of the People sound system, his first order of business was to play for Ossie and the camps. He told Lloyd Bradley, in his book *Bass Culture*, "A new sound have to be passed by them, a kind of respect thing, then you know they're going to be on your side."

When Prince Buster moved into record production not long after that, he tapped his Rasta camp connections and enlisted the Count Ossie Group to provide kumina drumming on the Folkes Brothers' "Oh Carolina" (1959). "Oh Carolina" became an international hit record—one of the earliest recorded on home soil, too. It is strongly symbolic in that it represents the merging of liturgical Rastafarian drumming and popular song. It also provides clues to the development of reggae, as you can hear the strong afterbeat played by the drummers, which became a hallmark of later reggae.

The influence of Count Ossie and the Rasta camps seeped into Kingston's music scene gradually from this point on. The Skatalites began to compose instrumentals with names clearly inspired by the Afro-centric orientation preached by their Rastafarian brethren, such as "Farther East" and "Addis Ababa," and then even more conspicuously citing the *de facto* Rastafarian prophet in "Tribute to Marcus Garvey," or their Rasta beliefs in "Reincarnation."

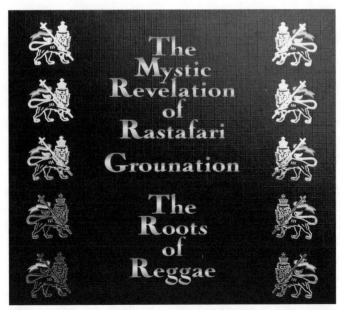

Count Ossie and the Mystic Revelation of Rastafari was a Nyabinghi drumming group that proved influential rhythmically and philosophically on many Jamaican musicians in the 1960s.

Author's collection

Bob's First Statements of Faith

The Wailers' first statement of Rastafarian faith came when Peter Tosh penned "Rasta Shook Them Up" after Selassie's visit in 1966. A few months later, Bunny Wailer brought Count Ossie to the studio to add drums to "Sunday Morning," "He Who Feels It Knows It," and "Let Him Go." Peter Tosh would also utilize Count Ossie on his collaboration with U-Roy, "Earth's Rightful Ruler," in 1969.

Bob was a little behind the other two in adding Rastafarian elements to his music. His first clear statement was 1968's "Selassie Is the Chapel." The same session produced "A Little Prayer," with Mortimo Planno preaching over Rasta drumming. Neither song had a wide release; Planno believes only twenty-six copies were pressed, with almost half of those being sent to Ethiopia.

Bob would continue recording songs that could easily be mistaken for Christian, such as "Adam and Eve" and "Thank You Lord," but gradually his lyrics turned more toward Rastafarian ideas, notably starting with 1970's "Jah Is Mighty." This song is a version of "Corner Stone," which is based on Psalm 118:22: "The stone which the builders refused is become the head stone of the corner." But whereas "Corner Stone" could be mistaken for an expression of a Christian biblical proverb, "Jah Is Mighty" could hardly be mistaken for anything but a Rastafarian declaration of faith.

The Rasta Influence on Reggae

Marley's avid Rastafarian stance was, by now, no anomaly in reggae music. Reggae became increasingly politicized in the sixties and seventies as Rastafari had a growing effect on the music. This era marks a transition not only in Marley's music but also in reggae in general. With more and more reggae artists sympathizing with Rastafari, and a growing number of producers willing to let them do it on record, the Jamaican music industry zealously embraced Rastafari.

With the Rastafarian-led cultural awakening of the seventies, reggae music wholeheartedly adopted Rastafarian chanting and the drumming so integral to this early connection. A nyabinghi drum known as a repeater was regularly featured in reggae tracks. Indeed, Bunny Wailer used to play one on Wailers songs. When Rasta drums weren't actually on reggae tracks, these nyabinghi rhythms would often be taken up by other instruments.

The internalization of Rastafari into reggae in the seventies influenced other aspects of the music as well. The vocalized rhythmic patterns of later dancehall deejays in the eighties, for instance, are based on repeater drum patterns.

Roots reggae in general is characteristically subversive, matching the revolutionary outlook of Rastafari. Stylistically, it eschews mainstream pop sensibilities of melody in favor of a prominent repetitive bass and emphasizes the rhythm section (bass, drums, organ, guitar) over solo instruments. Whereas in Western popular music melody is dominant, in some styles of roots reggae, such as dub, it is not uncommon to reduce the music to just bass and drums, or at times even dissolve it into sonic washes of reverb and echo. Musically, reggae emphasizes the opposite beat to Western pop. Common beat patterns for rock music stress the downbeat, but reggae often omits the downbeat (as in the one drop) and stresses the upbeat. It also uses vernacular speech—patois—instead of "proper" colonial English, was disseminated largely through private sound system parties or blues dances, and was often recorded by independent producers like Lee Perry or Augustus Pablo, who rented studio time from established, non-Rasta studio owners. In addition, roots reggae was played by followers of the Rasta counterculture, whose choice of fashion revolved around their connection with Africa (dreadlocks; the red, gold, and green of the Ethiopian flag; African military regalia; pictures of Haile Selassie), itself an affront to the colonial (and postcolonial) powers of the day.

Suffice it to say that, by the mid-seventies, roots reggae and pop reggae were two separate genres, the former being represented by Rastas such as Burning Spear, Big Youth, the Abyssinians, the Wailing Souls, Culture, Israel Vibration, the Gladiators, Jacob Miller, U-Roy, Junior Murvin, Max Romeo, Gregory Isaacs, Dennis Brown, and, first and foremost, Bob Marley.

41

Forever Loving Jah

Bob "Sights Up" Rastafari

Though Bob was raised a Pentecostal, his mother realized his spiritual beliefs had changed when he began to argue with her that God is black. He was intrigued by the teachings of the Rastas he met in Trench Town, among them Joe Higgs, and, particularly, Mortimo Planno. Central to their faith was the understanding that Haile Selassie (1892–1975), Ethiopia's black Emperor, was God. Cedella later joined the faith as well, and she believed that God, manifested as Jesus and come again as Selassie, had sent Bob to spread the world of Rastafari.

Who Is Jah Rastafari?

Rastafari derives its name from Selassie's pre-throne name, Ras, meaning duke or prince, and Tafari Makonen. Selassie had been given the title Ras when he became regent of Ethiopia in 1916, but upon Empress Zaudita's passing in 1930, he became emperor. As emperor, he adopted the name Haile Selassie, which means "Might of the Trinity," and the titles King of Kings, Lord of Lords, Conquering Lion of the Tribe of Judah, King of Kings of Ethiopia, and Elect of God.

Some advocates of Marcus Garvey in Jamaica in the early thirties began proclaiming Selassie's divinity for a few basic reasons. First, they believed that Garvey professed the coming of a black king who would lead dispersed Africans home and restore Africa to her former glory. Second, Selassie's throne name indicated that he was the one. "Might of the Trinity" inferred the Christian godhead, and his titles invoked passages in the Book of Revelation generally thought by Christians to refer to the returned Christ. Revelation 19:16 says he will have the name "king of kings and lord of lords." Revelation 5:5 speaks of "the Lion of the tribe of Judah, the Root of David," again regarded by Christians as Jesus. Selassie was not only called the Lion of Judah; using the genealogy found in the *Kebra Negast*, he traced his lineage back to King David through Menelek, the son of David's son Solomon and the Queen of Sheba.

Ethiopian Emperor Haile Selassie I, the man many
Rastafarians, including Bob Marley, believed to be the
living God.   *Public domain*

Once this connection was made, Jamaicans looked further into their Bibles
and discovered, in Isaiah 11:10–12, that the root of Jesse (David's father) would
unite the lost tribes of Israel "from Assyria and Egypt, from Pathros and Cush,
from Elam and Shinar, from Hamath and the islands of the sea." And where is
Jamaica? An island in the sea. So, Selassie was Jesus, and he had returned to
Earth to lead believers in Jamaica and beyond back to Africa.

Eventually, some Jamaicans began preaching that Selassie was "Jah" (short
for Jehovah). Initially, they called him Rastafari, and gradually they became
known as Rastafarians, or Rastafari. They look unfavorably on the term
Rastafarianism, however, because "ism" smacks of Babylonian trickery, as in
Marxism or capitalism.

Jah in Jamaica

Selassie visited Jamaica in April 1966. So many jubilant Rastas lined the runway
at Palisadoes Airport in Kingston, waiting to see him, that he refused to get

off the plane. He eventually emerged once Rasta elder Mortimo Planno was allowed on to the royal plane to ensure the emperor that this unexpected welcome was indeed completely respectful and safe.

Bob missed Selassie's visit to Jamaica. He was working at a car factory in Delaware at the time, trying to earn enough money to allow the Wailers to set up their own record label. But his wife, Rita, was in Kingston, and she has written that as Selassie's motorcade passed her on the streets, he waved, and she and her cousin Vision saw on his palm the stigmata—the mark that symbolizes the nails that were driven through Christ's hands. Rita, a former Sunday school teacher, believed she was in the presence of the living God, and she soon converted to the new religion. Bunny and Peter witnessed Selassie's procession as well, and all the Wailers were changed through the recognition that he was Christ returned.

Rita immediately wrote to Bob, encouraging him to do the same—to "sight up" Rastafari, or recognize Haile Selassie's divinity. Soon, the newlyweds both "locksed up"—started to grow dreadlocks—as an outward symbol of their budding interest in Rastafari and their faith in Selassie as the messiah. Bob initially had to cut off his dreadlocks because his Christian mother disapproved of them, but by 1968 he had started again to grow the mane that would adorn his head for the rest of his life.

Bob's Spiritual Advisor

One of the early influential Rastas in Bob's life was Mortimo Planno, who ran the Divine Theocratic Temple of Rastafari and lived on Fifth Street in Trench Town. His yard was popular with youths because of the good herb he provided, but also because he possessed a library of books on Ethiopian history and the black power movement. When Bob got back from Delaware in late 1966, he found that Peter and Bunny had been hanging out in Planno's yard, soaking up the herb and the teachings. Bob and Rita began to join them.

Planno provided the introduction to Rastafari for Marley, but eventually they parted ways. While Planno was affiliated with Nyabinghi Rastas, Bob also had lots of friends who were becoming associated with a more moderate house known as the Twelve Tribes of Israel.

The Twelve Tribes of Israel

Marley, like most of Rastafarian reggae stars of the seventies (such as Freddie McGregor, Dennis Brown, and Judy Mowatt), belonged to a Rasta organization called the Twelve Tribes of Israel. The most organized house of Rastafari, the Twelve Tribes of Israel had been started in Trench Town by Vernon Carrington, a former juice vendor, in 1968. In Hebrew teachings, the biblical patriarch Jacob had twelve sons, each of whom represented one of the twelve tribes of Israel. For Carrington, these tribes were aligned with months, and members of his Twelve Tribes of Israel took on the corresponding tribal name. November was the Tribe of Gad. Carrington, having been born in November, became Prophet Gad. Marley was born in February, so he was known as Joseph.

When Bob Marley became the carrier of the Rasta message to the world, he really only carried one variety of that message. The open-minded, multicultural universal love that is often thought to be Marley's central message may represent one aspect or denomination of Rastafari, but it by no means represents all Rastas. The group was more open-minded than the Emmanualites or the Nyabinghis, in that they had a vision of a racially integrated world and did not follow as many strict liturgical rules. They did, however, take repatriation literally, promoted reading one chapter of the Bible a day, and believed that ancient scripture held the answer to modern problems.

Bob's View on Selassie

The Twelve Tribes of Israel accepted that Jesus Christ revealed himself in His Imperial Majesty Emperor Haile Selassie I. For Marley, Selassie was clearly God, the Second Coming of Christ, whom he often called "His Imperial Majesty" or Selassie I, pronouncing the Roman numeral as the pronoun *I*. Several of Marley's songs mention him, either directly or indirectly. For instance, in "Zion Train" he says "Praise Fari," whereas in "Duppy Conqueror" he alludes to Selassie by saying "through the powers of the Most High."

Bob proclaimed his faith in Selassie several times. In a 1979 interview for Australian television, he traced the person of Selassie to his biblical prediction:

> Christ say he will return within two thousand years. Now check out the time. This time is 1979 years gone. Say when he returns he will return with a new name, which shall be dreadful and terrible among the heathens. And when he comes he shall be King of Kings, the Lord of Lords, and the conquering lion of the tribe of Judah. In our lifetime, when we look out on the earth, we see who comes with these names, one man is found, is Imperial Majesty Emperor Haile Selassie I . . . so His Majesty is a reality of the Revelation in the Bible.

In interviews, Marley was often more interested in talking about "His Majesty" than his music, because he believed that Rastafari was a worldview that could liberate black people from oppression. It can be quite funny to listen to a discourse between an American journalist who has no idea what Rastafari is and Bob Marley, who patiently explains that Haile Selassie is the living black God. This gets a bit confusing when you factor in that Selassie was not a Rastafarian, never publicly claimed to be Jah, and officially denounced the movement.

In the documentary *Prophecies and Messages*, Marley is asked by an interviewer what Selassie means to him. He first answers that Christ is the "King of Kings, Lord of Lords, Conquering Lion of the Tribe of Judah," and then states, "I and I see Selassie as the Christ the Bible talk about." He told Jamaican radio deejay Neville Willoughby in 1973, "His Imperial Majesty Haile Selassie I is Earth's rightful ruler, and I am a citizen of the Earth and Zion is Ethiopia."

Not all Rastas agree on the divinity—or even what kind of divinity—Selassie possesses. Essentially, Selassie means different things to different Rastas, and many in the movement de-emphasized Selassie's divinity after his passing in 1975. For those who do believe in his divinity, there are several kinds of Rastafarian Christologies (meaning understandings of the Christ). Some of the different beliefs include: Selassie is a reincarnated Jesus; he is a new manifestation of Jesus; he and Jesus are of the same line, but somehow more deeply connected than by mere genealogical descent; Selassie is a manifestation of God, though not Jesus.

Bringing Rastas Together

Even though Bob was aligned with one house of Rastafari, he had dreams of bringing all Rastas together. As with politics, he believed divisions weakened society, whereas unity strengthened social bonds. Babylon, for Bob, was the true enemy, and anyone seriously wanting to chant it down should not be fussing and fighting among themselves. He even went so far as to hold a meeting at his Hope Road residence for all the various Rasta houses, hoping to facilitate the overcoming of their differences.

42

Chanting Down Babylon

Decoding Bob's Mystical Musical Mission

Casual listeners to Bob Marley's music tend to describe it as happy, positive party music that is essentially about peace and love. Certainly there is an element of this, particularly when thinking of the titles of much-loved songs such as "Three Little Birds," "One Love," "Positive Vibration," "Easy Skanking," and "Jamming." But as much as Bob Marley liked to romance, dance, sing, and sip from the ganja chalice, a whole new level of understanding starts to be revealed once you begin to decode his mission.

Understanding this mission starts with the recognition that, for Bob Marley, reggae and Rastafari are intricately linked, and that he used reggae to promote his religious worldview. Speaking to a group of journalists in Philadelphia, including Randall Grass, after the release of *Survival*, he said, "In Jamaica, the more reggae you play, the more Rasta you have. But the more disco you play, then you'll have more eyebrow pencils and lipstick. . . . They want you to think of that glass of wine . . . and that pretty girl, and that car in the car park. You listen to that, you just dead, you'll never get it. You listen to reggae and live the ras-claat life!"

Bob Marley's mission was twofold: musical and religious. He set out to spread reggae music around the world, but as a vehicle for the African-Jamaican religion of Rastafari. Don't get me wrong, I'm pretty sure Bob wanted fame and fortune—he made several career moves to suggest as much—but back in 1967, he and his spiritual advisor, Mortimo Planno, sat down and mapped out a mission to conquer the world. This mission can be decoded by paying close attention to his lyrics, the iconography of his albums and concerts, and his interviews. It has to do with what Marley was ultimately concerned about, to borrow a term from theologian Paul Tillich, and Marley's ultimate concern had to do with an end-of-time battle between good (Jah Rastafari) and evil (framed as the forces of Babylon in the Rastafari worldview). Let me explain.

The *Stations of the Cross* and *Spiritual Journey* DVDs contain the same material, and both are packaged to draw attention to Bob Marley's religious worldview. The choice of title for the former is particularly confusing, as Bob had converted from Christianity to Rastafari.   *Author's collection*

What Is Babylon?

If you listen to enough reggae, you'll have an idea that Babylon means something bad, and that reggae singers always want to "chant it down," whatever that means. Rastas have taken the biblical story of the exile of the ancient Judeans, who were held captive in Babylon during the sixth century BCE, and reinterpreted it for the present era. Black Rastafarians are descended from enslaved Africans who, like the biblical Jews, were also held in captivity. As such, the West is the land of captivity—their "Babylon." More than this, though, Babylon has come to connote all systems of oppression that keep the black population down. In essence, Babylon is evil. So, when Bob Marley talks about Babylon, he's drawing on the weight and authority of a long tradition of resisting oppression.

Bob's Mission

Mortimo Planno was not only Bob Marley's early spiritual advisor. He also had a guiding hand in Marley's music career. Planno interpreted a dream Bob had about a man giving him a ring, telling Bob that it meant he was to be a messenger of Rastafari, with a mission to take this religion to the world. It was in this relationship between Bob and Planno that the mission was hatched: Planno encouraged Bob to write songs with a Rastafarian message and introduced him to the bosses of the American record label JAD. Planno felt that Bob needed a black American company behind him in order to help him break into the US market and share his message with African-Americans. But black America proved to be an elusive audience for Bob initially, as his next record label focused on getting his music in the hands of white rock fans.

As part of his advisory role, Planno even changed the words of the Orioles (and Elvis) hit "Crying in the Chapel" to "Selassie Is the Chapel," adding lyrics that position the Ethiopian Emperor as the returned living God prophesied in the Book of Revelation.

Bob's Early Mission

Bob Marley's mission can be detected in its infancy in early songs that touch on biblical themes interpreted through a Rastafarian framework, such as "Jah Is Mighty" (1970) and "Satisfy My Soul Jah Jah" (1971). But these do not present fully fledged theological statements, nor do they offer listeners much knowledge as to what this religion is about or how it could appeal to them.

The Mission Matures

Marley's religious thinking deepened as his songwriting matured, and by the time the Wailers released *Burnin'* in 1973, his religious mission had come sharply into focus. "Get Up, Stand Up," written with Peter Tosh, is a fiery testament to Selassie's divinity that mocks the Christian view of a far-off god living in the sky, favoring instead a belief in an "Almighty God" who "is a living man." It also rejects the idea that heaven is only attainable after death, presenting instead the Rasta notion that heaven can be found in this world.

But it is "Rastaman Chant," adapted from the gospel song "I'll Fly Away," that offers Bob's first real volley fired against Babylon: "I hear the words of the Rastaman say / Babylon your throne gone down." As a Rasta, Marley saw himself as a primary agent in Babylon's destruction—a battle that would be won by wielding reggae as a weapon. Here, we start to see Marley's mission come to fruition: Babylon will fall because Marley is spreading the message of Jah to the world and crushing evil with reggae music.

Chanting Down Babylon

This is where the chanting comes in. One could read a lot of violence in the songs of Bob Marley. After all, this is the guy who sang, "I feel like bombing a church now that I know the preacher is lying" in "Talkin' Blues." But when it comes to defeating Babylon, physical violence is not enough; spiritual warfare is the preferred method, and for Bob Marley that is chanting down Babylon. To chant here means to verbally and musically call out the sins of Babylon and symbolically destroy it. Chanting, for Bob Marley, was rooted in the Rastafarian belief of Word Sound Power—meaning, in short, that the sound of words have power apart from their meaning. In Rastafarian grounation rituals, chanting is often accompanied by ritual smoking of the herb, drumming, discussions called *reasonings*, speechifying, ritual stomping, and wildly tossing dreadlocks around. A Bob Marley concert would have obvious connections with herb, drumming, speechifying, stomping, dancing, and animated dreadlocks.

Through music—specifically reggae songs and rhythms—Babylon can be crushed. When Marley sang, "A reggae music, mek we chant down Babylon," in the song "Chant Down Babylon," he was bringing the power of Rastafarian ritual into popular music to fight oppression and assist Jah in his battle against evil.

Decoding the Mission

Marley's songwriting was never singular in its thematic breadth, but overwhelmingly the tracks he penned from this time onward further clarified this mission to raise awareness in Rastafari and destroy Babylon.

He does this in several ways. Some songs offer praises to Jah ("So Jah Seh," "Give Thanks and Praise"), while others testify to the protective power of Jah ("Positive Vibration," "Who the Cap Fit," "So Much Things to Say," "I Know"). Marley fetishized the dreadlocked Rasta into a potent symbol of African culture, rebellion against oppression, and black pride ("Natty Dread," "Rastaman Vibration"). A recurring topic is analyzing the role of Babylon in systemic violence ("Crazy Baldheads," "Guiltiness," "Babylon System," "Ride Natty Ride," "Stiff Necked Fools"). Some songs offer a vague sense of foreboding in the face of an uncertain future, with faint biblical overtones ("Natural Mystic"), whereas others promise the fall of Babylon if a righteous course is trod ("Jump Nyabinghi," "The Heathen," "Rastaman, Live Up"). Some call for repatriation to Africa and/or allegiance to Jah ("Exodus") and reignite Garvey's dream of pan-Africanism ("Jamming," "Zimbabwe," "Top Rankin'," "Survival," "Africa Unite").

Importantly, Bob also began to lay out an eschatological vision of how Jah would wipe out evil in the end times. In "Revolution," Jah does this with thunder, lightning, brimstone, and fire, in order to cover the Earth with righteousness—an image taken from Habakkuk 2:14.

In "War," Marley quotes a speech given by Haile Selassie to the United Nations about racism, but in his usage the symbolism can be read either literally or figuratively: either there will be war until racism is abolished, or Selassie will topple Babylon in a final battle of good over evil.

In "One Love"—the song everyone thinks is about good vibes and togetherness—Marley presents a theocratic solution to the world's problems, speaking of the end times and foretelling Selassie's pending victory in the battle of Armageddon.

Marley concert backdrops like the one shown in the *Live in Santa Barbara* footage showed pictures of Marcus Garvey and Haile Selassie, making the political and religious dimensions of Bob Marley's music visually clear.
Author's collection

So far, we've seen that Bob Marley's songs and concerts went far beyond pop music's standard desire to entertain and please fans. Marley entertained, all right, but he had an ulterior motive: the world was locked in a battle between good and evil, and it was his job to fight for the righteous side.

Mission Iconography

These themes are extended by the iconography that adorned Marley's stage and albums of the period. Marcus Garvey, a Jamaican national hero and *de facto* prophet of Rastafari, was often pictured onstage alongside Haile Selassie. They can be seen, for instance, in the concert video *Live in Santa Barbara* in 1979. Marley opens the concert by reciting Psalms 87 but alters the text to exchange "Lord" for "Jah." In Marley's hands, the verse is about Selassie's Ethiopian home and his divine role in the world.

Before Marley died in 1981, he and artist Neville Garrick drafted the cover to what would become the posthumously released album *Confrontation*. The resulting image, of Marley dressed as an Ethiopian-ized Saint George, fighting a dragon, is rich with the symbolism that the King of Reggae is on the verge of defeating Babylon, even after he's passed on from this world.

Freeing the People with Music

Marley's musical mission was not just about using reggae as a vehicle for the dissemination of a religious message. He also had a much more immediate and practical agenda. Jamaica's black population was overwhelmingly poor and relegated to ghetto life with little chance of upward mobility. Bob saw reggae as a way to escape the suffering of the ghetto—for himself, certainly, but also for his fellow Jamaicans. Reggae was a relief mechanism in the ghetto, with the ability for "upliftment," psychologically but also financially. When Marley wants to liberate people with music in "Trench Town," we hear this mission at work. Listeners and dancers could "feel it in the one drop" drumbeat of his music, a rhythm that could fight oppression and resist the madness of the colonial system ("One Drop").

Marley believed reggae could have transformative powers, and judging by the effect his music had around the world to make people happy, perhaps he was right.

43

Black Progress

Race and Identity in Bob's Life and Music

J amaican musicians were keenly aware of the changes in racial discourse in American in the sixties. The influence of the civil rights movement and key personalities like Malcolm X, Martin Luther King Jr., Elijah Muhammad, and Muhammad Ali, influenced both American soul and Jamaican reggae. By the late sixties and early seventies, there was a blooming of black consciousness in the music industry, with James Brown's "Say It Loud—I'm Black and I'm Proud," the Staple Singers' "Respect Yourself," Billy Paul's "Am I Black Enough for You?," Gil Scott Heron's "The Revolution Will Not Be Televised," Stevie Wonder's "Living for the City," Marvin Gaye's "Inner City Blues (Make Me Wanna Holler)," the Isley Brothers' "Fight the Power," George Clinton's "Chocolate City," and the Last Poets' eponymous debut.

Jamaican musicians emulated their American heroes. In the sixties, the Wailers picked up on the revolutionary ideologies of thinkers like Eldridge Cleaver and Huey Newton of the Black Panthers, and combined these with Marcus Garvey's pan-Africanism and Rastafari's sense of racial redemption, centered on Haile Selassie. They were part of a cultural shift in America and the Caribbean that sought to revalorize African history and culture by rejecting material trappings associated with the West and adopting African styles. Rita Marley stopped using makeup. Black American musicians grew out their afros, and many Jamaicans started growing dreadlocks. African-print clothing was common. The Wailers started carving black fists to sell at their record store, inspired by the Panthers' black power symbol. They adopted the red, gold, and green colors of the Rastafarian movement, which are, of course, derived from the Ethiopian flag. Peter also began carving red, gold, and green hair picks for the store.

It was this turn toward racial activism, social justice, and religious rhetoric in the hands of groups like the Wailers that helped change the rocksteady and early-reggae focus on rudies, relationships, dances, and novelty songs about Hollywood heroes and outlaws into conscious roots reggae—music with a social conscience. This is not to say that Jamaican music was devoid of such before— Desmond Dekker's infectious 1967 hit "Israelites" was about the daily struggles of the ghetto, couched in the biblical metaphor of the people of the African diaspora as Israelites in exile. But thanks to the work of artists like Peter Tosh, Culture, Burning Spear, Big Youth, and, most directly, Bob Marley in the seventies, politically charged songs about racial discrimination and the exploitation of the lower classes came to typify and define reggae, particularly for those abroad. Black consciousness permeated Jamaican music in the seventies, its weighty themes seeking to right historical inequities matching its increasingly hard-hitting, heavy roots sound.

Getting on the Train

Marley's racial activism is palpable in many songs. He calls out historical racial oppression and systemic violence in songs like "Slave Driver," preaches that the world will not know peace until racial equality is reached in "War," and tackles the long-lasting effects of the transatlantic slave trade on modern minds in "Redemption Song." His concern for the plight of the black population in the face of systemic discrimination informs a lot of his work. For example, "Survival," originally named "Black Survival," provides assurance to the "black survivors" who have suffered "in every way, in everywhere."

Bob's entire project was about black culture, as it was the self-representation of a man of African descent. But he sang specifically about race very little, at least in his early years. The examples above are all drawn from his later catalogue, when his militant Rastafarian pride was in full view, and other black musicians—both American and Jamaican—were making powerful statements about inequality and discrimination. His treatment of race in the sixties, though, was more in keeping with the tenor of the times. Bob was heavily influenced by American soul music, and his handling of racial themes starts there.

While not overtly about race, "One Love / People Get Ready" is a rewrite of an Impressions song that was written at a time when soul musicians were utilizing the train theme to signify interracial unity. Gladys Knight and the Pips gave us "Friendship Train" in 1969, and the O' Jays cut "Love Train" in 1972. The train accepts everyone, regardless of color, and they all are in pursuit of the same goals, the same destination. In other words, we are all one people. Bob's use of "one" and the theme of togetherness is a meditation on this same theme. His "Zion Train" draws from the same well, particularly with lyrics that mention tickets, but is more specifically geared toward the salvation of blacks. He appealed to the soul/disco audience of the era by throwing in a reference to *Soul Train*, while speaking to the history of slavery when he sings, "Two thousand years of history (black history) / Could not be wiped away so easily (so easily)."

Like "One Love," a number of other songs of his are nuanced reflections of struggle with racial contexts. The themes of equality and freedom in songs like "Soul Captives" work in a universal sense, with open-ended lyrics that rejoice in a future "freedom day" after toiling in the sun. But it doesn't take much imagination to apply this to the history of enslavement on plantations across the Americas, where freedom equals emancipation. In "Freedom Time," a precursor to "Crazy Baldheads," he reminds his listeners of enslavement and argues that freedom is a person's God-given right. The underlying meaning of the song, then, is derived from Bob's own position as an African-Jamaican and his understanding of himself as a member of a community whose present hardships are rooted in the crimes of colonialism.

The Wailers' "Black Progress," from 1970, offers a much more conspicuous treatment of race, but it still stays closely to the racial discourse established by American soul singers. This song in particular was a rewrite of James Brown's chart-topping theme of empowerment, "Say It Loud—I'm Black and I'm Proud." According to funk historian Rickey Vincent, Brown's song "was a turning point in black music. Never before had black popular music explicitly reflected the bitterness of blacks towards the white man." Marley downplays Brown's anger but keeps his appeal to the humanity of his detractors by reminding them that blacks are people too, and his proud insistence that backing down in the face of racial adversity is not an option: "We can't quit until we get our share."

Marley brings his own fire to the song, too, with the theme of fighting a righteous battle that he will so often revisit later. In lyrics not found in the original, he tells his brothers and sisters to fight for their rights. Both Marley and Brown demand the chance "to do things for ourselves," echoing twentieth-century thinkers like Marcus Garvey, who advocated black self-sufficiency, but only Marley speaks of "black dignity," though this is implied by Brown's rap of self-respect.

The Subaltern Sings

If Bob's early songs closely followed the racial themes and musical styles of his American cousins, by the mid-seventies his thinking was seasoned with the racial discourse of Rastafari, whose primary goal was overthrowing Babylon. His sweet music packed a dread punch in its bid to counteract the effects of colonization and racial discrimination. This, in essence, is decolonization through reggae music. His songs were designed to tell history from below, giving voice to the stories and people that colonization had silenced—the black, poor subalterns.

In the eighties, this kind of self-representation became *de rigueur* for hip-hop artists, who addressed crime, unemployment, police brutality, high incarceration rates, and political apathy toward black populations. Hip-hop was about more than social commentary, though; it was about self-expression. It was inner-city black youth expressing their reality using their own means—turntables, microphones, lyrics.

Racial activism in Marley's songs during this period takes three main themes—self-representation of his people, calling out systemic racial discrimination at the hands of Babylon, and offering hope in the form of black redemption through the power of the Most High, Jah Rastafari.

In rejecting the upper-class-sanctioned, postcard-ready version of Jamaica, Bob Marley does not sing about palm trees, beaches, rum cocktails, and all-inclusive holidays in the sun. Instead, he sings about food shortages ("Them Belly Full"), police curfews ("Burnin' and Lootin'"), police harassment ("Rebel Music (3 O'clock Roadblock)"), unequal power distribution ("Crazy Baldheads"), and the deception of Babylon's institutions of power in the form of churches, universities, and governments ("Babylon System"). These are the things that ghetto dwellers put up with.

But his songs of the ghetto don't just detail deficiencies, they also celebrate the vibrant culture of the Jamaican underclasses, chief among them the power and beauty of Bob's chosen medium of expression, reggae, which he calls "the music of ghetto" in "Burnin' and Lootin'."

He reveals the scars of colonialism's grip on modern black people by reminding his listeners of the horrors of slavery ("Didn't my people before me slave for this country?" in both "Freedom Time" and "Crazy Baldheads," and then refuses to believe that the past can remain in the past in "Slave Driver" ("Today they say that we are free / Only to be chained in poverty"). "Redemption Song" clarifies the connection between historical slavery and modern oppression in its bid to decolonize the mind: "Emancipate yourselves from mental slavery / None but ourselves can free our minds."

In the song "Blackman Redemption," Bob doesn't offer much, lyrically, to explain what this redemption is from, or what it entails. The idea is derived from nineteenth- and early twentieth-century black theologians, and the Jamaican father of the back to Africa movement, Marcus Garvey. Garvey and his enormous influence on Marley are dealt with in a separate chapter, but for now, the concept of African redemption is part of a larger way of viewing history that assumes God has a special plan for the black race. In this plan, the oppression of the African peoples is over, and a new era has begun—one in which Africa and her people will be redeemed. It is this concept that Marley draws on in "Blackman Redemption." For him, the road to redemption starts with recovering the lost African self—African music, culture, religion, and pride in blackness.

But it is truly found in faith in His Imperial Majesty, who, as the song states, "is the power of authority"—an Ethiopian God-man who can overthrow Babylon and redeem the black race.

The antidote for European colonization then, is black religion: Rastafari. And for Marley, the perfect way to instigate this is through reggae. He told a journalist during the tour for *Survival* in 1979, "Reggae is a vehicle, is a vehicle that is used to translate a message of redemption to the people upon earth today."

Red Pickney: Bob Marley's Racial Identity

In hindsight, it seems natural that Bob Marley, a lower-class black Jamaican, espoused black activist ideologies. But blackness was something that, in Jamaica, Bob didn't necessarily possess. During the 2008 US presidential campaign, an op-ed piece ran in a Kingston newspaper dismissing the fact that Barack Obama might become the first black president because, well, he's not black. With a black father and white mother, Obama, by Jamaican standards, was of mixed racial heritage, and therefore not strictly black. Historically, he would have been referred to as mulatto, but might now be called light-skinned or brown—both terms signifying his lack of full blackness (and, historically, his lack of full whiteness).

Whereas for many non-Jamaican fans Bob Marley is considered black—and this racial identity seems to be at the heart of much of his music and lyrics—his racial identity is more nuanced. This quote from Don Taylor's memoir helps sum up this complexity: "Bob had the right tint to fit in with the plantocracy, but he lacked the right upbringing." Despite being born light-skinned and possessing facial features of his European ancestry in a country where this complexion and phenotype were historically privileged, Bob Marley was raised by black peasants, moved to a black ghetto, and had no contact with or assistance from his white family.

And he wasn't always treated as black. Roger Steffens neatly sums it up this way: "Whites thought of him as a black child; blacks, critical of mixed-race children, taunted him as 'the little yellow boy.'" When Bunny Wailer first met Bob Marley in Nine Mile, he said he was the only "red pickney" in the place, *pickney* being a term for a child based on the old English term *pickaninny*. Bob's grandmother Yaya called him "German Boy." In Trench Town, he was taunted as "little red boy," "little white boy," or "little yellow boy," leading to youthful skirmishes. Vocal coach Joe Higgs remembers these taunts leading to beatings. Here, being "red," "yellow," or "German" suggests a person lacks blackness and Jamaicanness. In Jamaican usage, "red" refers to a light or yellowish skin complexion in combination with African-derived features like crinkly hair, and is used in a derogatory sense. "Yellow" simply refers to a light complexion. To be German, red, or yellow, then, is to remind the child that he is not black, and put his nationhood in question. This is because, in the national imagined identity, blackness is equated with Jamaicaness, despite the fact that the national motto is "Out of many, one." The one here is reimagined as black, as opposed to strength in diversity, which was the original intent of the motto.

Marley was at times referred to as white as well. According to Davis in *Bob Marley: Conquering Lion of Reggae*, the parents of a black girlfriend during his teenage years resisted the match, telling him they "don't want no white man in our breed." Again, in many circumstances, whiteness was the privileged complexion in Jamaica historically, but here it was used to remind the mixed-race individual that they don't belong. Rita Marley made a similar differentiation when she referred to Bob's light-skinned lovers as white, thereby reinforcing the fact that they were of a different community—uptown instead of downtown.

Bob's take on his mixed parentage shows how he attempted to stand above questions of racial division. In *Marley*, Bob says, "My father is a white, my mother black. Them call me half-caste, or whatever. Well. Me don't deh pon nobody's side. Me don't deh pon the black man's side nor the white man's side. Me deh pon God's side, the man who create me, who cause me to come from black and white."

The teasing and discrimination he felt growing up made Bob question his identity, but it also helped him think critically about race. In her memoir, his wife writes, "His black consciousness covered his light skin." Taken together, though, these experiences probably had a lot to do with his ability to heal racial division and speak to racial unity. Far from just speaking to one community, Marley's global appeal is based in his universality. He extended this racial unity to his understanding of Rastafari, which some at the time felt to be an exclusively black religion, telling British journalist Ros Raines, "A Rastaman can be any nation. Even any race. Just so him heart is pure."

44

Emancipate Yourselves from Mental Slavery

The Influence of Marcus Garvey

I n his concerts, Bob Marley typically had the images of two black men superimposed behind the stage: Haile Selassie and Marcus Garvey. Selassie, of course, was the man Bob worshipped as the returned Christ, the living God. But ideologically, as a Rastafarian and racial activist, Bob was far more influenced by Garvey, a Jamaican national hero whose ideas permeate his songs.

Garvey was at the center of the shift in black thinking in the early days of the twentieth century that resulted in widespread black nationalism, a concern for the history and future of the African continent, pride in black/African heritage, and black self-reliance in all things, including religion. Garvey opened a worldwide debate on race and religion, and in doing so he articulated what was on the mind of many blacks. He was the first person whose mission was to instill pride of race and pride of self in all blacks, turning the word *negro* into a symbol of power at a time when many people of color wanted nothing to do with the idea of blackness. He offered a religiously charged view of ultimate reality, using the existing framework of Christianity that allowed blacks to make Christianity their own, removing at the same time the shackles of colonialist religion. He gave black Christians a new tool to bring them together under one banner and ideology.

It was Garvey, filtered through Rastafari theology, who directly influenced Bob's thinking about a black god, repatriation to Africa, black destiny, African redemption, and black-positive imagery in the Bible. But while he drew on Garvey's ideas often, he only mentioned him by name in song once. In "So Much Things to Say," he reminds his listeners of Garvey's betrayal on his return from the US to Jamaica, when upper-class lawyers—including Michael Manley's father, Norman— ultimately scuttled his political career: "They sold Marcus Garvey for rice." Even so, the imprint of Garvey's ideas permeated Marley's life and works.

Who Was Marcus Garvey?

Garvey was a Jamaican newspaper publisher, labor activist, political organizer, and black nationalist. He established the United Negro Improvement Association (UNIA) with the aim of bringing together the black diaspora and the African people under one flag, one nation, one program, one doctrine. The organization's motto, "One God, One Aim, One Destiny," is echoed in Bob's own "One Love."

Garvey was born in 1887 in the rural coastal town of Saint Ann's Bay, in northern Jamaica, not far from where Marley himself was raised. He was a descendant of the defiant Maroons—runaway slaves who, after a series of wars against their colonial slave owners, lived autonomously in the wilderness.

Marcus Garvey, National Hero of Jamaica, and the man Rastafarians saw as the prophet who foretold the coming of a black God, whom they recognized as Haile Selassie I.
Public domain

By Garvey's own account, his childhood years were unmarred by racism, and he played freely with white children in his neighborhood, not hearing the words *negro* or *nigger* until he was about fourteen, when the white daughter of a Methodist minister informed him she was no longer allowed to play with him because of his color.

Garvey apprenticed at a local printing factory, eventually starting his own publication, *The Watchman*. He spent 1909–1914 traveling throughout Central and South American, the West Indies, and Europe, where he became acquainted with the plight of black workers. While in Central America, he published two newspapers focusing on black labor issues, *La Nacionale* and *La Prensa*.

In London, Garvey came in contact with blacks from around the world whose stories of racial injustice and labor woes matched what he had already witnessed. In addition, he read Booker T. Washington's autobiography, *Up from Slavery*, and it had a profound effect. Of this book, Garvey wrote in 1923, "I asked, 'Where is the black man's government? Where is his king and his kingdom? Where is his president, his country, and his ambassador, his army, his navy, his men of big affairs?' I could not find them, and then I declared, 'I will help to make them.'"

Upon his return to Jamaica in 1914, Garvey immediately set about building a new organization, with the aim of "uniting all the Negro peoples of the world into one great body to establish a country and government absolutely their own." He envisioned "a new world of black men . . . causing a new light to dawn upon the human race." The eventual result was the UNIA, the headquarters of which he had moved to Harlem by 1916.

Garvey successfully captured the attention of blacks worldwide through the publication of UNIA organs like the daily *Negro Times* and weekly *Negro World*, which had a readership of two hundred thousand each week, making it the most popular black paper of the day. By 1919, he estimated the total membership of the UNIA to be over two million, and, in the wake of Booker T. Washington's death a few years before, Garvey was now, along with W. E. B. Du Bois, one of the world's most influential black leaders. During its heyday, the UNIA boasted 996 branches in forty-three countries and claimed over five million members, making it the largest black organization of the twentieth century.

Undesirable Alien Under White Surveillance

Like Marley fifty years later, Garvey was a person of interest to the American intelligence community because of his radical views on things like racial equality. His agitating for black rights in Jim Crow's American did not go unnoticed. J. Edgar Hoover, then under the employ of the FBI's predecessor, the Bureau of Investigation, had his eye on Garvey as early as 1919 and lamented that they couldn't deport this "undesirable alien" because he hadn't committed any crimes. Hoover actually hired the first black agent in the bureau's history to go under cover and dig up dirt on Garvey. He was eventually tried on charges of mail fraud, stemming from a fairly minor marketing mistake in the sale of stocks in his shipping company, Black Star Line. Found guilty, he was sentenced to five years in prison.

Garvey's supporters felt the trial was fraudulent, and Garvey himself, in an anti-Semitic rant, was quoted as saying, "When they wanted to get me they had a Jewish judge try me, and a Jewish prosecutor. I would have been freed but two Jews on the jury held out against me ten hours and succeeded in convicting me, whereupon the Jewish judge gave me the maximum penalty."

Garvey never recovered his stature in the US, but in Jamaica his followers, Garveyites, made sure that his ideas around race and religion lived on in a new religion known as Rastafari.

Garvey's Influence on Bob Marley

We can see Garvey's views on race and religion clearly in Bob Marley's understanding of Rastafari, the blackness of god, the blackness of biblical characters, the positive African presence in the Bible, black pride, self-reliance, repatriation, African redemption, and the notion that blacks are god's chosen race. Here is a breakdown of these connections.

Garvey's Link to Rastafari

When Garvey is mentioned in connection with Rastafari and Bob Marley, it is usually to explain that he prophesied the rise of a black king who would lead the diaspora back home with the words, "Look to Africa when a King is crowned, for your redemption is at hand." The king in question, according to Rastas, was Haile Selassie, who ascended the throne in 1930. With Selassie playing the role of the messiah, Garvey becomes the John the Baptist of the Rastafari movement—the evangelist in the New Testament who harkens the coming of the Christ.

There is actually no historical evidence that Garvey spoke these words, but he did dramatize the values of the UNIA in plays, one of which is called *The Coronation of the King and Queen of Africa*. Regardless of the historical accuracy, Garvey remains a *de facto* prophet for Rastafari, even though at no point in his life did he convert to, or even advocate, Rastafari. In fact, he was a lifelong Wesleyan Methodist Christian. But in the wake of Selassie's coronation, a few Garveyites started preaching the divinity of the African king, and slowly a movement known as Rastafari developed around Garvey's pan-Africanist ideas and Selassie's divinity.

New Black Religion

So, Rastafari traces its roots to Garvey's teachings, but he was never a Rasta. He did, however, advocate the establishment of a new, black-centric religion. Garvey's program of racial unity owed much to his belief that religion was the only thing that had so far provided any sort of commonality among blacks, and, as such, it called for a new black church so that blacks would not have to adopt a foreign faith. But whereas his idea of reforming religion meant the establishment of a black Christian denomination (the African Orthodox Church), his ideas were transplanted in the minds of a few Jamaicans that founded a completely new religion: Rastafari.

God Is Black

One of the central aspects of Garvey's new religion was the idea that black people should worship a black god. But Garvey didn't preach that God was black, rather that God was without race. In *Philosophy and Opinions*, he states, "We, as Negroes, have found a new ideal. Whilst our God has no color, yet it is human to see everything through one's own spectacles, and since the white people have seen their God through white spectacles, we have only now started out (late though it be) to see our God through our own spectacles . . . this is the God in whom we believe, but we shall worship Him through the spectacles of Ethiopia."

He wasn't even the first to espouse this. In the nineteenth century, Ethiopianist preachers like African Methodist Episcopal bishop Henry McNeal beat him to it, declaring that Jesus was a "negro messiah" and that blacks have a right to believe that God is black.

Rastafarians took these proclamations to heart and saw in the person of Haile Selassie I a living, breathing, black Ethiopian god. In 1980, Bob told Saint Maarten deejay Dave Douglas, "Rastafari is God almighty with no apology . . . .we proud to know dat God black."

Black Moses

For Garvey and others, using the spectacles of Ethiopia to interpret Christianity included refashioning of biblical heroes as black people, or black Israelites. The idea of a black Moses, for instance, was a common theme of antebellum literature and sermons. Similarly, Rastafarians see themselves as reincarnated Israelites in a similar state of exile, searching for the Promised Land. Biblical Jews were exiled twice: once in Babylon and once in Egypt. Moses led them out of Egypt to the land of Canaan. For Rastas, the land of exile is the Americas—the new Babylon—and their Promised Land is Africa.

In "Exodus," Bob conflates the biblical story of Moses with the modern day need to flee exile in the West and repatriate to Africa. "Send us another brother Moses," he sings. He traces the lineage of Selassie back to biblical kings David and Solomon in "Blackman Redemption." In "Jump Nyabinghi," he connects modern-day Rastas and the Israelites at the time of the Battle of Jericho. He uses the pronoun we instead of they, signifying either that we as a Rastafarian people are in Jericho, or that we as modern Rastas relive this era of history. "These are the days when we'll trod through Babylon / Gonna trod until Babylon falls."

Positive African Presence in the Bible

Whereas white Christianity taught blacks that they were a subservient race, Garvey used the Bible first as evidence for the equality of humanity, regardless of color, and second to prove the exalted status of Africa and the black race in the eyes of God. By showing a positive black presence in the Bible and rejecting the notion of blacks as a cursed race—often based on the curse of Noah's son, Ham—Garvey convinced his followers that being black was neither a punishment nor an evil thing.

Positive black images in the Bible include Song of Solomon 1:5–6: "I am black, but comely," and Jeremiah 8:21: "For the hurt of the daughter of my people am I hurt; I am black; astonishment hath taken hold on me." Mentions of Africa were also used to show the inclusion of the black population in God's plan. One of the key passages for Garvey was Psalm 68:31: "Princes shall come out of Egypt; Ethiopia shall soon stretch out her hands unto God."

Garvey sought to invert the white Christian concept that to be black was to be cursed by God and to be white was to be blessed by God. In an article called "Marcus Garvey as Theologian," Schluter quotes him as saying that Christianity "teaches us that all that is good is white and all that is bad is black, and without question we accept it as being true. So we think the Devil is like us and God is like the other fellow. Now if this is not propaganda, I do not know what is."

As we see from the examples above, Marley's use of the Bible fell within this framework.

Black Pride

Another area where Garvey was influential on Marley was black pride. Garvey's theology was not passive and subservient; it was, like Rastafari after it, radical and subversive. Garvey found the Christian virtue of meekness baffling, and he rejected the idea that God wanted blacks to be meek. In his 1925 manifesto of racial pride and unity, *African Fundamentalism*, he makes it clear that turning the other cheek is not the way for blacks to succeed. "If they mimic you, return the compliment with equal force. They have no more right to dishonor, disrespect and disregard your feeling and manhood than you have in dealing with them."

In this respect, Garvey shook the firmament for the black upper classes who had just lived through the era where Booker T. Washington called for them to be "happy, docile blacks." Being docile was not part of the Garvey agenda. Black

Marcus Garvey delivering the Constitution for Negro Rights at the
UNIA's Liberty Hall, New York, 1920.   *Public domain*

dignity and the recognition of Africa's (and the African race's) great history,
culture, and potential didn't allow room for humility, and the challenge he
offered to the Christian status quo in this regard is one of the fundamental
nerve-endings of Garveyism: the foundation of black pride. If slavery brought
about the era of black subservience, Garvey was determined that his era would
be that of black autonomy.

Garvey was the first person to succeed in giving the widespread black population a sense of pride in their African heritage and the color of their skin. In
Marcus Garvey and the Vision of Africa, he is quoted as saying, "I am the equal of
any white man. I want you to feel the same way." These sentiments are echoed in
Wailers songs like "I Stand Predominant" (Bunny Wailer), "The Toughest" (Peter
Tosh), and "Get Up, Stand Up" (Peter and Bob), and in Marley's "Survival," among
others. Bob took great pride in his African heritage. In the 1980 Saint Maarten
interview, he connected this with Garvey: "Marcus Garvey seh Africa fi Africans

a home and abroad. Di Ethiopian cya change him skin, neither di leopard cya change his spots you nuh. So once you black you represent Africa."

Self-Reliance

Garvey's belief in the equality of humanity and his emphasis on self-reliance as the key to success went a long way to securing his movement's mass appeal. Taking the theme of Washington's *Up from Slavery*, Garvey taught his people that industry was the road to a better life. In *More Philosophy and Opinions*, he states, "The Negro must be up and doing if he will break down the prejudice of the rest of the world. Prayer alone is not going to improve our condition, nor the policy of watchful waiting. We must strike out for ourselves in the course of material achievement, and by our own effort and energy present to the world those forces by which the progress of man is judged."

His own industry was manifest in the Black Star Line, the first African-American-owned shipping line, and the subject of many reggae songs. In Marley's music we see this most clearly in his cover of James Brown's "Black Progress," when he insists on self-sufficiency, instead of toiling for an employer. In his career, as well, Bob was interested in self-reliance, setting up record labels and stores, buying his own studio, and, where possible, working with black companies and managers.

Repatriation and African Redemption

Garvey's sense of the place of blacks in society was very unique for his time. Unlike Booker T. Washington's accommodationalism or W. E. B. Du Bois's inte-grationalism—two of the main proposed social solutions for race during in this era—Garvey opted for segregation. Other black leaders were attempting to get for their community some modicum of power or respect within the circle of white society—in effect to get them as close to the center of that circle as possible—while still maintaining the status quo. Garvey, however, preached that blacks should, instead, start their own circle, since they would never realistically be allowed into the center of the white circle. In this way, Garvey transformed the Christian message for blacks into a sort of liberation theology intent on offering redemption from physical suffering and systemic racism.

Garvey's popular Back to Africa movement gave his followers an immediate sense of dignity through a connection to Africa and other blacks, plus it gave them a stake in Africa's future by working toward ridding the African continent of European colonizers. For Garvey, liberation was contingent on throwing off the message that blackness and African-ness were worthless and recognizing the possibility of black autonomy. He called this "mental slavery," and he put it this way in October 1937, in a speech in Sydney, Nova Scotia: "We are going to emancipate ourselves from mental slavery because whilst others might free the body, none but ourselves can free the mind."

This line is the template for one of Bob's greatest songs, "Redemption Song," in which he alters the lyric to, "Emancipate yourselves from mental slavery / None but ourselves can free our minds." Redemption, then, comes in the knowledge of the African past that the colonizers tried to wipe away, and in breaking free from the colonial mindset—mental slavery—that remains after political colonization has ended.

God's Chosen Race

Garvey's reading of the Bible not only presented blacks with the possibility of a Promised Land (repatriation to Africa), it also brought Canaan to them by teaching them to become a nation at home. Unlike Du Bois's nation within a nation, Garvey used religion to help draw the lines around his version of black nationalism, enabling the black diaspora for the first time to see itself as a united body and to understand its history as providential and its future as that of a "redeemer race."

The belief that Africans are God's chosen race and have a divinely appointed destiny is known as black destiny, and is part and parcel of Garvey's—and Marley's—understanding of black redemption. For Garvey, this would occur

Marley's now-famous lyrics, taken from a 1937 speech by Marcus Garvey.   *Author's collection*

through the establishment of a black theology within a Christian framework that stressed self-reliance and pan-Africanism. For Rastafarians, however, the black race becomes not only a chosen people but, in fact, a divine people. To be black, in other words, is to possess divinity.

Garvey's Broader Influence

Marcus Garvey had the means and ability to reach millions of blacks with his message through the UNIA, thereby inspiring millions of people with his ideas on race, theology, social justice and African Zionism. His influence on black religion and politics can be seen in major black movements of the twentieth century. Malcolm X's father, a Baptist preacher, was a Garveyite, and black Muslims cited him as the father of pan-Africanism. In 1965, in a speech he gave in Jamaica, Martin Luther King Jr. honored Garvey's influence on the civil rights movement by saying, "Marcus Garvey was the first man of color in the history of the United States to lead and develop on a mass scale and level to give millions of Negroes a sense of dignity and destiny, and make the Negro feel he is somebody." (Garvey's son, by the way, quoted this speech in an editorial posted on www.CNN.com entitled "Pardon my father, Mr. President.")

The black power movement of the sixties was also part of Garvey's legacy, with its renewed emphasis on black nationalism and black pride. Even the first prime minister in decolonized black Africa, Ghanaian leader Kwame Nkrumah, wrote in his autobiography that Garvey was his inspiration.

But perhaps nowhere is Garvey's influence more evident than in Jamaica's Rastafarians, for Rastas see Garvey as their founding father and prophet. The first Rastas were Garveyites, and Rastas base their belief in the divinity of Haile Selassie in Garvey's teachings of that black king from Ethiopia. As well, Rastafarian reggae musicians have created a large canon of songs about Garvey, and in 1964, Jamaica named Garvey its first national hero.

45

African Herbsman

Bob's Religious Love of Ganja

O ne of Bob Marley's most enduring representations in popular culture is as a "herbsman"—a ganja connoisseur and activist—or even as "the Marijuana Marlboro Man," as *Vice* dubbed him in 2014. Countless photographs and posters capture the singer smoking a spliff. The journalists who interviewed him almost always commented on his love for, and routine use of, marijuana. When American session guitarist Wayne Perkins finished a take on "Concrete Jungle," Bob's highest praise was to offer him a puff from his own spliff. He sang often about his love of the holy herb, most notably on the album *Kaya*.

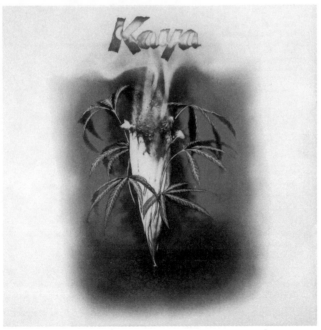

The back cover of *Kaya* is a visual depiction of the album's title.
Author's collection

Those who knew Bob also speak to the regularity with which he indulged. His day at 56 Hope Road began and ended with a sip of the chalice. Waking just before sunrise, he typically shared a bong with whichever guests were around. After some exercise, he'd head to Trench Town to purchase more ganja—a constant supply was required—maybe check in at his record store, play some soccer, visit with his kids, and then head back to Island House for band business and rehearsal, where the chalwa was continually passed around until midnight or later.

Bob's open use and outspoken support of ganja certainly helped cement his rebel appeal among fans. *Catch a Fire*'s original album cover was designed to look like a Zippo lighter, which easily inferred lighting up. When the record was re-released in 1974, the inference was replaced by the real thing: the only album front cover to feature a picture of Bob taking a drag on a spliff. Filmmaker Perry Henzell (*The Harder They Come*) has said that Marley's best career move was embracing a faith that treated marijuana as a sacrament.

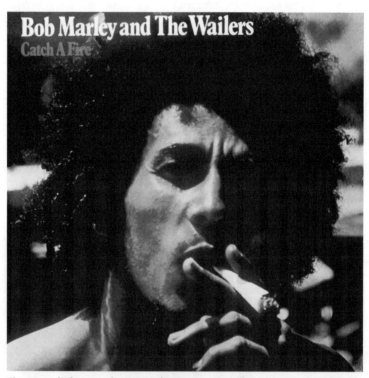

The Zippo lighter on the original 1973 pressing of *Catch a Fire* could easily symbolize lighting up a spliff, but the second pressing in 1974 leaves little to the imagination, as it depicts Bob smoking ganja.   *Author's collection*

Lamb's Bread and Sensimilla

When Lee Jaffe hung out with Bob from 1973 to 1976, he got to sample the best ganja Jamaica had to offer, most of it sourced by Bob's cousin from Nine Mile, Sledger. Sledger was Bob's constant companion when he was on the island, acting not only as procurer of the green leaf but also driver. He's now a ganja farmer in Nine Mile, growing varieties like Purple Skunk and African Ites.

The strain of weed most commonly associated with Bob is called Lamb's Bread, and he went through about a pound of it a week. According to cannabis info site www.leafly.com, "Lamb's Bread is a bright green and sticky sativa strain. The effects have been known to give mass amounts of energy and positive introspection. Stress subsides quickly from the Lamb's Bread buzz, which can help ease depression."

Bob liked to smoke the stronger sensimilla (or sensi) herb, according to Breezy, a pot farmer in Nine Mile. From the Spanish *sin* (without) and *similla* (seed), sensimilla is taken from a female cannabis plant that has not been pollinated. It produces no seeds—so cleaning the herb isn't necessary—and, according to the Colorado Pot Guide, results in a flower with a higher THC content. The King of Reggae and America's first president, George Washington, may have had the love of sensi in common, as Washington wrote about isolating female hemp plants way back in 1765. Bob definitely had better hair, though.

Bob was often photographed with a spliff in his hand, but he smoked it other ways as well. He used an innovative bamboo pipe invented by Winston Anderson—brother of Bob's girlfriend at the time, Esther Anderson—to steam the herb. "You just kind of sip it, you don't really inhale it, and we'd get really high," Jaffee recalls in his book, calling it a "very beautiful way of smoking."

Bob started smoking during the time he was recording at Studio One. In fact, some historians reason that Studio One attracted the best musicians (or at least the ones who were Rasta sympathizers) because Coxsone Dodd allowed them to smoke ganja in the yard outside the studio, whereas other producers wouldn't tolerate it. Original Wailer Beverley Kelso told Roger Steffens that nobody smoked ganja in the initial Studio One days, but a year or so later, Bob, Peter, and Bunny all smoked hard. In her recollection, this had to do with the growing Rasta consciousness of the group—the herb would flow as they began to discuss Rastafari.

The love of herb also greased the wheels of a career move for Marley. When he met American JAD label owners Johnny Nash and Danny Sims, they were ganja neophytes, but once they were introduced to Rasta elder and ganja supplier Mortimo Planno, they developed an affinity for it. Sims even hired a Rastafarian cook who liberally used fresh ganja in his cuisine. JAD soon signed the Wailers to a songwriting contract.

Herb in Jamaica's Legal System

Bob Marley would have cause to celebrate if he were alive today. As of mid-2015, cannabis has been decriminalized in Jamaica—102 years after it was outlawed—perhaps as a sign that the war he waged against Babylon is being won. The ubiquity of marijuana and reggae probably suggested to most people that it was already legal on the island—and that all Jamaicans condone it—but this is not so. Now, however, possession of up to two ounces has been knocked down to a petty offence and will only result in a small fine. You can grow a few plants in your backyard, too, and Rastafari's sacramental usage of the plant is officially recognized and sanctioned.

Predictably, in 2016 the Marley family released its own brand of ganja, hemp products, and smoking accessories called Marley Natural (www.marleynatural. com). Its tagline is "a cannabis brand based on the life and legacy of Bob Marley." Daughter Cedella released a statement to mark the occasion, ensuring fans, "My dad would be so happy to see so many people appreciating the natural, healing power of the herb."

The decriminalization of marijuana has been a long time in coming in Jamaica, and for Rastafarians and reggae musicians in particular. A government report in 1894 saw no reason to criminalize its use and pointed out that, among the Indian population in Jamaica that cultivated it, "the consumption of ganja goes far to prove that these drugs do not tend to evince crimes of violence." Yet in 1913 it was outlawed anyway, and throughout the twentieth century Jamaican authorities compared it to opium, claiming it drove people "half-crazy" and that it could cause injury to self and others. Not until 1972 did a report commissioned by the Manley government revisit the earlier prognosis and recommend decriminalization. In response, Wailers bassist Familyman released the instrumental tribute "Herb Tree," but he'd have to wait another thirty-four years for the government to follow through.

Many a Rasta and reggae man was imprisoned for possession over the years. In the sixties, prosecution for possession got you an automatic eighteen-month sentence. Toots Hibbert of Toots and the Maytals served his time behind bars in 1967. He scored gold when he was released, though. His song "54-46"—his prison number—has gone on to become one of the most loved reggae songs of all time. That same year, Bunny Wailer was sent to Richmond Prison Farm in Saint Mary from July 1967 to September 1968. He wrote his classic "Battering Down Sentence" about the experience. Friend and sometime Wailer Lee Jaffe was busted in late 1974, and had to depend on Rita Marley to bring him food in jail and Bob to bail him out.

Bob did not like to be without his herb. When he visited the Trinidad Carnival in 1973, he was disgruntled because he couldn't find anything to smoke. The Trinidadians back then could party, all right, but they were drinkers, and Bob didn't like that scene.

Traveling from country to country in a reggae band that loves its weed has its hazards. Bob actually had the "provision and supply of marijuana" built into his contract, so manager Don Taylor risked his own freedom at times to smuggle it through customs in countries where they had no herb connections, like Japan. Wailers art director Neville Garrick was busted in Miami for trying to smuggle in pot. Later, after Bob died, the Wailers continued traveling the world, led by Familyman; one former soundman says that in every country they landed, herb would mysteriously be provided: "Usually during sound check someone would come in and hand a big bag of pot to Familyman and that would sustain them for that tour stop."

Did Bob ever get arrested? A few sources claim that he spent time in jail, but this seems unlikely. He was often harassed by the police, and he and Familyman were even busted in England while recording *Exodus*. His defense in court was that he used the herb sacramentally, as a Rastafarian. The judge told him he'd have to suspend this practice while in England. The *New York Times* report on the incident, under the headline "Jamaican Bandleader Bob Marley Pleads Guilty to Possession of Marijuana," added that Marley was fined $85 and Familyman $42.50.

Ganja Music

Affection for marijuana transcends musical genres. Muddy Waters smoked reefers. Hippies toked pot and grass. Willie Nelson rolled a doobie on the roof of the White House. John Prine wore an "Illegal Smile." Rick James loved his "Mary Jane." Toby Keith sang about "Wacky Tobacky." Heavy metal stoners Black Sabbath loved the "Sweet Leaf." Cypress Hill took "Hits from the Bong." The guys in Sublime wanted to "Smoke Two Joints," and Redman taught us "How to Roll a Blunt." But reggae has cornered the market for weed euphemisms: ganja, kaya, tampee, kiki, cran, herb, collie or kali weed, I-lley, goatshit, Ishen, lamb's bread, sensimilla, sensi, draw, Hi grade, I-grade, sleng teng, tu-sheng peng, and kushung peng—all of which can be blazed, smoked, drawn, licked, or sipped in a spliff (rolled in paper or corn trash), pipe, koutchie, chalwa, or chalice.

Reggae artists have waxed liberally about the bud in countless songs, praising its delightful effects, complaining they've been victims of an unjust system that wrongly criminalizes the plant, flouting it in the face of authority, lionizing brave herb vendors, espousing its health benefits, or preaching its divine origin. See: U-Roy's "Chalice in the Palace," Black Uhuru's "Sinsimilla," Sugar Minott's "Herbman Smugglin'," Jacob Miller's "Tired Fe Lick Weed in a Bush,"

John Holt's "Police in Helicopter," Barrington Levy's "Under Mi Sensi," Culture's "International Herb," Cornell Campbell's "A Hundred Pounds of Collie," and the Itals' "Herbs Pirate." Many of Bob's family members and associates rolled up smoking tunes about, well, smoking, too: Rita Marley's "One Draw" and Peter Tosh's "Legalize It" are two of the most popular examples from the Wailers stable.

Bob's Herbal Hymns

There is a lot of herb symbolism on Bob's records. *Catch a Fire* was packaged to look like a Zippo lighter, and the back cover of *Burnin'* features a relief cut of the singer taking a toke. There is a burning joint adorning the back of *Kaya*, whose name itself means "ganja." *Rastaman Vibration* even has a note written on it to say, "This album jacket is great for cleaning herb." But while it may seem that Marley's discography would be full of hemp hymns, there is actually only a handful of lyrics dedicated to the holy herb.

The back cover of *Burnin'*, showing a relief cut of Bob drawing hard on his spliff.   *Author's collection*

"Kaya" (1971, 1978)

Originally recorded in 1971 with Lee Perry, this was the first herb song of Bob's career, arriving almost a full decade after he entered the music business. Not a bold statement to legalize ganja or a statement of Rastafarian faith, it is instead a song about the enjoyment of getting high and the escape it offers from the hustle and bustle of ghetto life. "I've got to have Kaya now," Bob sings, with an immediacy only sated once the herb takes effect, causing him to feel "irie" and ascend high enough (metaphysically) to reach above the rain clouds.

"African Herbsman" (1971)

This is a cool rewrite of Ritchie Havens's "Indian Ropeman." Bob doesn't overtly mention marijuana in this song, but given the fact that his preferred nomenclature for the plant was herb, his "herbsman" would likely be a "ganjaman," though it could also be a bush doctor. Either way, the connotation is clear, and made clearer by the fact that Peter Tosh's later song, "Bush Doctor," is all about prescribing herb.

"Rebel Music (3 O'Clock Roadblock)" (1974)

This song recounts a normal ritual for many Jamaicans in the seventies—trying to dispose of a little "herb stalk" before the police search your car. This particular song was written about a night when Bob, girlfriend Esther, and friend Lee Jaffe were being driven from Negril to Kingston by Bob's cousin and dealer, Sledger. The singer uses the roadblock metaphor to contest the second-class citizenship of, variously, blacks, Rastas, and herb smokers, and to defend the rights of Jamaicans to roam free in their own country and smoke what they wish: "Why can't we be what we want to be? / We want to be free." It resonated with Jamaicans, who appreciated a song about the state of fear they were forced to live in.

"Easy Skankin'" (1978)

Bob starts off the *Kaya* album with this blatant advertisement for herb and its ability to relax him, help him escape, take a break, and ponder deeper things: "Excuse me while I light my spliff / Good god, I got to take a lift." He also tells us of his preference for kaya over alcohol. This is Bob's most forward statement on herb, which—considering his contemporaries had titles like "The Great Collie Herb," "I Love Marijuana" and "Pass the Pipe"—was pretty reserved.

"Jump Nyabinghi" (1983)

A song about the power of music, dance, and the ritual of smoking to bring the community together: "We've got the herb / So hand I the suru board." The suru board is used to cut up ganja buds for smoking.

More Pot Poems

Those are the only conspicuous herb songs in Bob's repertoire, though there are a few other songs that could refer to pot. "I Shot the Sheriff" contains the lyric, "Every time I plant a seed / He said kill it before it grow." This is perhaps metaphorical and meant to apply to any independent plan hatched by the pro-tagonist, although knowing Marley it is probably also a double-entendre refer-ring to herb. He was no stranger to farming it, and he once showed a friend an eight-foot plant he was nurturing in his mother's Delaware backyard.

"Mellow Mood" does not contain any lyrics that obviously indicate it is about smoking, though it's not a stretch to think his mood came courtesy of his chalice: "Mellow mood has got me / So let the music rock me." "Burnin' and Lootin'" contains the lyric, "All them drugs gonna make you slow," which could be interpreted as a tongue-in-cheek reference to the elites' criticism of Rastas regarding ganja. Dawes, in his book *Bob Marley: Musical Genius*, thinks not, though. He suggests that, since Marley did not consider marijuana a drug, the song instead is about the evils of other drugs (specifically cocaine, but also prescription medication, which Rastafari would proscribe), to which marijuana can provide a healthy and revolutionary alternative.

Marley's Herbal Evangelism

Though Marley rarely sang about herb, he talked about it a lot, in part because so many journalists were keen to ask this dreadlocked singer about his chain-smoked spliffs. By the seventies, music fans were no strangers to rock stars that used, sang, spoke about, and got busted for drugs. But Bob's conversations in the press about marijuana were somehow different, filled with evangelism and conviction that this plant was the key to fixing so many of the world's problems.

He took pains to highlight the idea that marijuana was not some danger-ous narcotic that should cause a moral panic. He told the *Ann Arbor Sun* in 1975, "God created herb for man, mon. Let [them] tell me 'don't sniff cocaine' or 'don't take hashish,' great. But when they tell me don't smoke herb, it comes like crazy, mad!"

He took issue, too, with its illegality, telling a New Zealand reporter in 1979, "Why these people who want to do so much good for everyone, who call themselves governments and this and that, why them say you must not use the herb?"

Far from being a danger to society, he said in the same interview, herb provided wisdom and guidance, allowing users to see the world for what it really was: "We just feel them say you mus'nt use it because it make you rebel. Against what? Against men who are craven [greedy] cause them have some material things and them want to captivate your mind and them say 'you have to work and put you on pension and them keep it all.' So herb make you look pon yourself and instead [of wanting] to work for the man, you want to be one of the man too. Not in the sense of how him is but in the sense of why should you have to bow to these things."

Herb also aided in self-reflection, he added, allowing you to become a better person. He told a journalist in Boston in 1975, "When you let the herb inside of you, the spirit of the herb becomes part of you. Good herb manifests a good spirit."

It was a powerful natural substance that deconditioned you by making you look within, at your own life's path. He told the *Village Voice* in 1980, "It's better if you start to smoke herb when you're young. But you got plenty of people who only come upon herb when they're thirty, forty, so when they check it for the first time, it mash-up their head! Because it looks back too far in your life. It makes you check out from your beginning to today before you can go any further. And if you're wrong down the line, then you have to go down and straighten it out."

Smoking Biblically: Herb in the Rastafari Worldview

Bob often connected his usage of pot to his religious worldview. In 1979, he told New Zealand television program *Good Day*, "The more you accept herb, the more you accept Rastafari."

While treated by Rastas as sacrament, herb is not a requirement, so not all Rastas smoke. Those who do smoke do so socially, therapeutically, and ritually, believing herb to be a divine gift.

Ganja functions in several ways in the Rasta community. Communal smoking binds adherents together, creating community—one of religion's most important social functions. It aids spiritual meditation and facilitates philosophical discussions and reflections on faith (or reasonings) that can occur one on one or in ritual gatherings (known as *grounations*).

As with their adherence to the Ital diet, Rastafari base their sacramental use of weed on scriptural justification. Genesis 1:29 is used as evidence of the divine provenance of herb: "God said behold I have given you every herb bearing seed, which is upon the face of the earth." So too Psalms 104:14: "He causeth the grass to grow for the cattle, and herb for the service of man, that he may bring forth food out of the Earth." And its therapeutic properties and ability to resolve global conflict are defended by Revelation 22:2, which states, "In the midst of the street of it, and on either side of the river, was there the tree of life, which bare twelve manner of fruits, and yielded her fruit every month: and the leaves of the tree were for the healing of the nations."

Bob, then, was quoting the Book of Revelation when he told interviewers, "Herb is the healing of the nation." This was often followed by condemnations of alcohol, cigarettes, or drugs, such as when he told Mumia Abu-Jamal in 1979, "Alcohol kill ya, and herb build ya!" This was herbal healing on a macro scale—smoking for the greater good, to bring disparate parties together by heightening feelings of togetherness, leading to peace and understanding.

Herb is also considered a source of inner knowledge and greater wisdom by Rastas, who claim it grew on King Solomon's grave, giving him his wisdom (as Solomon the Wise), hence it becoming known as the "wisdom weed" that allows adherents to commune with the divine. The burning bush in which Moses saw God (Exodus 3) is a symbol for herb, too, wherein "burning the bush" allows believers to see God.

For Rastas, every living thing is organically connected, and there is a positive divine energy in the world. This energy is expressed in the use of I words, derived from the Roman numeral I, signifying the first, after Haile Selassie I. Rastas reconfigure this as the first-person singular I and the first-person plural I and I, in a sort of recognition that all is connected to the divine Selassie. This becomes manifested in a series of I words that make up dread-talk: I-man (the divine in me), I and I (to signify the recognition of the divine present in humans), I-nity (unity), I-rator (creator), I-ration (creation), and I-wa (era). Ganja can induce an altered state of mind called the I and I consciousness, which allows smokers to see the truth of the interconnectedness of all life, including humans and god.

Apart from the metaphysical benefits, pot also offers many physical benefits for Rastas. They adhere to Ital Livity, meaning natural living, which guides their dietary and combustible decisions. As with food, herb should be "Ital," meaning grown without chemical fertilizers, as he explained to *High Times* magazine in 1976. They see herb as healthy—regular smoking ensures perpetual health—but also healthful. Herb is used as a therapeutic medicine, ingested as smoke and in teas, food, and even rum.

The First Ganja Farmers

So how did ganja get to be a sacrament? Well, it started out as a cash crop. From 1940 to 1954, there was a Rasta commune in the hills north of Spanish Town called Pinnacle. This was led by Leonard Howell, one of the early evangelists for Haile Selassie's divinity. With up to forty-five hundred residents, Pinnacle needed a means to sustain itself, and it developed numerous cash crops and staples like yams, gungo peas, coco, sweet potatoes, and, well, marijuana. Ganja was cultivated in small plots around the island before this, but at Pinnacle it seems to have flourished into the first fully fledged ganja farm, designed to meet the growing needs of smokers in nearby Kingston.

With ganja being illegal and authorities believing it led to violent and anti-social behavior, this made Pinnacle (and Rastafarians in general) susceptible to police harassment. The commune was raided several times and finally broken up after the police seized close to one million ganja plants and arrested 138 people in 1954.

Pinnacle residents had smoked the herb and utilized it for its healing properties, but at this point it wasn't considered a religious sacrament. With the destruction of their homes, many headed for the ghettos of Kingston. In the Rasta camps of Kingston, ganja smoking became ritualized, with codes of conduct derived from ritual patterns of other African-Jamaican religions (and some designed to keep attention away from the authorities). Some of these codes included passing the kouchie to the left (as in the song by Mighty Diamonds), blessing it before smoking, not being able to leave until all the ganja was consumed, and emptying the cup only when all the herb was burned.

It was in one of these Trench Town camps overseen by Brother Watson or Wato that ganja became elevated further among Rastas. In the face of government oppression over their recreational (but pretty constant) use of ganja, his group, called the Youth Black Faith, institutionalized ganja, making its consumption part of their religious rituals and beliefs. Reasoning that the government's real aim was to suppress the movement, but secure in the knowledge that biblical evidence proved their usage righteous, it became a religious sacrament. The group even stopped carrying ganja on their persons—only handling it for ritual purposes—in order to minimize police harassment. So it was actually the criminalization and demonization of ganja on the part of the authorities that led to its use formal adoption by Rastas.

The Hindu-Jamaican Connection

There are a few theories about how marijuana made it to Jamaica. Industrial hemp has been used as a fiber for at least ten thousand years, but its usage as an intoxicant in Jamaica probably dates from the mid-1800s, when it could have traveled with indentured servants from India or Central Africa. With the full abolition of slavery in the British West Indies in 1838, plantation owners needed a cheap source of labor. This was secured from May 10, 1845, when the first shipload of indentured servants from India arrived.

The Indian connection makes a lot of sense, as one of the common terms Jamaicans use is ganja, which is the Sanskrit word for hemp. The term may have entered Jamaican parlance from the Indian laborers, or maybe because the British colonial administration used the word when it drafted anti-cannabis legislation. Further, the Jamaican slang *collie* or *kali* is derived from the Hindu goddess Kali, as is the term *chillum*, which is Hindi for a clay pipe. Some Indian laborers took part in Kali pujas that involved drinking bhang or smoking ganja and worshipping the goddess with shouts of "Jai Kali Mai." Jamaicans have long consumed ganja tea for medicinal purposes, and some historians think that the first Rastafarian commune at Pinnacle adapted the use of cannabis as a sacred herb from the Hindus, as well as the chant of "Jah Rastafari," which could be derived from the goddess ritual.

Dreadlocks and ganja may be associated in popular culture with Rastafarians and reggae musicians, but travel to India and you can purchase postcards with dreadlocked Hindu holy men, known as *sadhus*, smoking ganja out of chillums. Sadhus are religious ascetics who have dropped out of society to focus on spiritual enlightenment. Not really interested in things like personal hygiene and clothing, they generally dress in loincloths and wear their hair in long unkempt dreads.

It is possible, then, that these outer manifestations of Bob Marley's Rastafarian identity—dreads and ganja—are actually Hindu in origin. That being said, the origins of both are murky, and both could also have come to Rastafarians from Africa. Ganja was used in the Congo for narcotic purposes, where it was called *dyamba*, so enslaved Africans arriving in the Americas from the Congo may have already been familiar with its effects, though it is doubtful they would have been able to transport any material culture in the ghastly and perilous conditions of slave ships.

The Role of Herb in Decolonization

Herb was a central defense for Marley against the machinations of Babylon. Like wearing dreadlocks and speaking in dread-talk, smoking herb separates Rastas from the status quo, which was designed by Babylon to maintain social control. They see themselves as outcasts from Babylon, but they are fine with this because they have no desire to be part of Babylon. Hence they deliberately cultivate oppositional status through symbolic breaks with the norm. Like the countercultural hippies of the sixties who followed Timothy Leary's advice to turn on, tune in, and drop out, Rastas are turned on and tuned in to deeper reality through ganja, but drop out of social expectations set up by their colonial forebears.

As such, the use of herb played a role in decolonization. Carolyn Yawney's groundbreaking study into Rastafarian rituals states, "The proper use of herbs has a central role in freeing the mind from the fuckery of colonialism. It provides the inspiration necessary to transcend alienating structures of thought. Herbs, they say, are the key to the lock of understanding; God chooses to reveal himself though herbs."

In other respects a law-abiding citizen, Marley would smoke ganja openly in front of anyone, including prime ministers and church leaders. His attitude was that herb was completely normal—simply a plant, yet one with divine provenance. And by the time he became a superstar, his normalizing attitude toward weed was widely accepted even by the authorities in Jamaica.

Herb Good, Drugs and Alcohol Bad

Marijuana is typically regulated by drug laws, but according to Rastas ganja is not a drug. Rastas are against hard drugs like cocaine. There are rumors that Marley may have used cocaine, although there is only anecdotal evidence to support this. His manager, while aware of the allegations, has said he never saw Bob indulge. In her book, Rita insinuates that Bob might have done something harder than ganja on his final tour, for which some New York hustlers were added to the entourage. She heard that he was offered "something," but was unsure if he took it. Biographer Timothy White says Bob was offered cocaine on this tour but does not speculate whether he indulged. Biographer Stephen Davis says that the rumors centered on Marley freebasing coke to maintain his energy in the wake of his deteriorating health.

There have also been suggestions from other artists, such as Lee Perry and Big Youth, that Bob took cocaine. In an interview with *I Know TV*, Big Youth stated, "Marley used to play the ball," referring to cocaine. Lee Perry has even suggested that cocaine use was the reason Marley died: "Bob Marley want to be god but god don't take cocaine . . . if he did not take cocaine he would not lose his immortality."

However, former girlfriend Esther Anderson points to the song "Burnin' and Lootin'" to give us an idea of Bob's feelings on cocaine. In an interview with Roger Steffens, she explained that the lyric "all them drugs gonna make you slow" was a direct response to cocaine use—something he did not condone.

46

Honey for My Strong Drink

The Ital Diet

Bob was a health nut and sports fanatic who would jog and play football daily. At home, he consumed large amounts of freshly squeezed fruit juice, vegetable stews with coconut milk, herbal teas, and fish. Today, if you visit 56 Hope Road, now the Bob Marley Museum, you can see the kitchen where he prepared his tasty juices and roots wine, a nonalcoholic beverage made from herbs and roots. He loved typical Jamaican fare such as rice and peas, stew peas, and Irish moss to drink, though as a vegetarian he shunned Jamaica's national dish; he abstained from alcohol and thought cigarettes were evil (even though he smoked a pound of ganja per week). This may seem contradictory, but his dietary and smoking choices stemmed not just from health concerns but also from Rastafarian beliefs.

Eating Biblically

Rastafarians are not required to follow any dietary guidelines, as each member of the religion is free to live as they see fit. However, many, like Bob, adhere to principles based partially on a literal reading of the Bible and on resistance to Babylon. They strive to be *Ital* (from *vital*), meaning natural, from the earth, and organic, and this guides their eating, drinking, and smoking choices.

From the New Testament, they adopt the notion that the body is a temple and should not be defiled: "Know ye not that ye are the temple of God, and that the Spirit of God dwelleth in you? If any man defile the temple of God, him shall God destroy; for the temple of God is holy, which temple ye are" (1 Corinthians 3:16–17).

But what foods pollute this temple? For the answer to that, Rastas look to the Hebrew Bible or Old Testament, using two scriptures for dietary guidelines. The first is Genesis 1:29: "Then God said, 'I give you every seed-bearing plant on the face of the whole earth and every tree that has fruit with seed in it. They will be yours for food.'" Plant-based foods, then—including ganja—are approved by the divine.

The Bob Marley Museum at 56 Hope Road, Kingston, Jamaica.
Photo by Dubdem sound system, Creative Commons license

Strict Rastafarians also follow a second set of dietary injunctions laid out in Leviticus 11, which contains directives from God to the ancient Hebrews outlining which foods are clean and unclean. There are some pretty obscure gastronomic delicacies that the Most High put off limits—the rock badger and the hoopoe bird, for instance—as well as some more conventional dishes such as pork, fish without scales, and many crustaceans. Other Bible-derived taboos practiced by some Rastas include the idea that menstruating women are unclean (Leviticus 15:19–20) and as such are not allowed to prepare food, while the divine also had a few specific instructions for hair stylists: "Do not cut the hair at the sides of your head or clip off the edges of your beard" (Leviticus 19:27).

Bob Marley's mother was surprised when he first visited her in Delaware in February 1966 and admonished her for cooking breakfast bacon, a meal he enjoyed before converting to Rastafari. "Is a dangerous something dat, you know, Mamma," she recounts him telling her in her book. "It come from de swine where Jesus cast de devil. Is a unclean animal." He then refused to eat anything that had been cooked in that pan. He wouldn't eat eggs because he was allergic to them, so he contented himself with cornmeal, oatmeal, or banana porridge, toast, and fruit when he breakfasted with her. He was also a fan of teas made from Jamaican herbs, called bush teas, like mint and fever grass.

Back home in Jamaica, Bob's wife Rita had a similar reaction when he told her that Rastas don't eat pork. Pork was a staple for poor people in Jamaica because cheap cuts, like pig's tail and trotters, were easily available. It was also a key ingredient in one of her and Bob's favorite dishes: stew peas and rice. At the time, Rita was living with her aunt and had little say over her diet. When she finally announced that she wouldn't eat callaloo and codfish because it had pork in it, her aunt blamed Bob's influence.

Interviewers often asked Bob about his dietary restrictions. As with repetitive questions about his dreadlocks and beliefs in a black living god, he would patiently explain to them that his diet, like the rest of his life, adhered to scriptural dictates. He told the *Ann Arbor Sun*, for instance, that there were "certain meats that can be eaten at times, but many that ya mustn't eat. We don't eat things like pig, lobster, crab, shrimps. Dem things feel nice but can kill ya, because they're made to clean the place where what they eat and live." He told the *L.A. Free Press* that while he ate fish, he didn't eat meat "that have cloven foot and don't chew cud, or chew the cud but don't have cloven foot," and that pigs "have seven devils inside." He relaxed his avoidance of meat in later years for health reasons, when his doctor instructed him to increase his protein intake following the cancer surgery on his toe.

Some Rastas extend the Hebrew proscriptions to include any meat (which they term *dedders*), but many will eat small fish under one foot long. This size restriction is based on the assumption that longer fish are predatory, and this is seen as a hallmark of the ruthless man-eat-man Babylon worldview that Rastafari condemns. Bob himself enjoyed fish tea—a Jamaican soup made out of fish broth—and, while he ate a largely vegetarian diet, he did, according to manager Don Taylor and Cindy Breakspeare, eat meat occasionally, but never pork. Later in life, after the discovery of his brain cancer, he was put on a high protein diet by his doctor (the ironically named Dr. Bacon) that included an eight-ounce daily helping of liver.

(Scotch Bonnet) Pepper, but No Salt

Ackee and salt fish is Jamaica's national dish, but strict Rastafarians won't touch it because they have eliminated salt from their diet. This restriction is not based on the Bible's teachings but has an antecedent in the modern history of the transatlantic slave trade. Many enslaved African-Jamaicans believed that if they maintained a salt-free diet, they would possess the spiritual force to fly back to Africa.

The taboo against salt among the Rastafari is probably derived from this history, which symbolically associates salt with enslavement and Babylon, as salted meat was a staple among the enslaved population, and a body of salt water separates the Americas from Africa. In *A Social History of Indentured African Immigration in Jamaica*, Schuler writes, "In Jamaica, to resist eating salt may have been a metaphor for resistance to foreign ways." Contemporary Rastas probably don't think in these terms when they avoid salt, but resisting Babylon and embracing African culture is a priority.

Honey for My Strong Drink

Rastafarians see themselves as living in Babylon but not obeying Babylon's rules. Anything processed, chemically treated, or artificial is a Babylonian creation, and so Rastas shun most manufactured food products such as canned goods and even refined sugars and flours. Tobacco and alcohol are processed, too, so are also to be avoided, and, like other drugs, are seen as Babylonian creations meant to harm black people. The proscription against alcohol also has a biblical basis in the Nazirite vow described in Numbers 6:1–4, which states, "If a man or woman wants to make a special vow, a vow of dedication to the Lord as a Nazirite, they must abstain from wine and other fermented drink and must not drink vinegar made from wine or other fermented drink. They must not drink grape juice or eat grapes or raisins. As long as they remain under their Nazirite vow, they must not eat anything that comes from the grapevine, not even the seeds or skins."

Bob drank alcohol in his twenties, but by the time Wailers harmonica player Lee Jaffe met him in 1973, he was abstaining from alcohol, though his manager suggest that Bob did drink champagne in London later. He told an interviewer in New Zealand in 1979, "Alcohol make you drunk man . . . when you drink alcohol you don't meditate—you're more giddy-headed. Herb is a consciousness."

His preferred drink, according to "Easy Skankin'," was honey. Keyboardist Rabbit Bundrick later recounted how Bob would make a drink out of honey while they roomed together in Sweden in 1972. Irish moss was a favorite and he'd always keep a big pot of it brewing over the fire at Hope Road. Bob once gave Jaffe a mix of Irish moss and soursop juice sweetened with honey, extolling its Ital virtues of no processed sugar, or "condemned" (i.e., condensed) milk.

Eating While on Tour

It is often said that one of the reasons Bunny Wailer left the Wailers was because he hated touring, especially the lack of healthy Ital food on offer. When Bob and his Rastafarian band went on tour, they had to plan ahead for sources of herb and food. On their first sojourn to the US, when there was no money for personal chefs or attendants, they checked into New York's Chelsea Hotel, a place where a band of dreadlocked Rastas smoking spliffs all day would not cause a stir, even though this scene would have been novel elsewhere in New York at the time. Many of the Chelsea's rooms had kitchens, allowing them to prepare their own meals. Purchasing staple ingredients of rice, beans, fruit, and vegetables from nearby markets, the band would blend the fruit into juice, and Carly, the drummer, would cook the vegetables into an Ital stew.

As the Wailers tours grew bigger, they gained a large entourage including, importantly, a Rastafarian Ital chef. Two such cooks were Mikey Dan, who joined the band on the *Natty Dread* tour in 1975, and Gilly Gilbert, who became Bob's personal chef at Hope Road. Gilly made sure to stock Jamaican spices, like scallions and Scotch-bonnet peppers, and would prepare the musicians fresh fruit juices and Jamaican dishes like the cassava flatbread known as "bammy," and fry fish.

Because of his dietary restrictions, Bob was careful where he ate and who cooked the food. Don Taylor, his manager from 1974 to 1979, said that eating out was an event that had to be planned ahead. On one occasion he was invited to dine at the Beverly Hills home of Pascalene Bongo, Bob's lover and daughter of Gabon's president, Omar Bongo. Bob only agreed to attend after arrangements were made for the meal to be cooked by the owner of Delrose's Jamaican Restaurant—the only place Bob would eat in L.A.

The Queen of Sheba's Fresh Produce

Like Bob, Rita Marley followed an Ital diet. In the mid-sixties the couple lived for a time on Bob's family farm, and they worked the land to grow their own food. Later, when they were living in Kingston, Rita convinced him to buy her a farm in Clarendon Parish, where she could grow fresh organic food for the family. Not wanting to be dependent on and sidelined from her husband's life as he took up residence uptown with his mistresses and bandmates, Rita decided to go into business for herself, selling fruit, vegetables, and Ital meals to dreads in Bob's entourage who were ever-present at Hope Road. She called her venture the Queen of Sheba Restaurant, and it is still functioning today, now catering to the tourists of the Bob Marley Museum. Interestingly, during my first trip to Kingston in 2003, the menu steered clear of alcohol and meat, as you would expect. However, Marley fans visiting today can imbibe in a Red Stripe and chow down on jerk chicken.

The Next Generation of Ital Chefs

Bob and Rita's children internalized the lessons around healthy and Ital food. Both Ziggy and Cedella have recently published cookbooks that focus on health: *Ziggy Marley and Family Cookbook: Delicious Meals Made with Whole, Organic Ingredients from the Marley Kitchen* (2016), and Cedella Marley's *Cooking with Herb: 75 Recipes for the Marley Natural Lifestyle* (2017).

47

Natty Dread

The Significance of Bob's Dreadlocks

Bob Marley's most distinguishing physical feature was his hair. Celebrities typically have hair that either willfully bucks social conventions (the mop-topped Beatles) or epitomizes conventional beauty standards (Marilyn Monroe's platinum blonde waves). Bob Marley falls into the former category. But his dreadlocks represented more than your average unkempt, angsty rock coif—though they functioned as that, too. Bob's chosen hairstyle was, in fact, the outward manifestation of his political alignment with pan-Africanism, and a scripture-based gesture to publicly demonstrate his spiritual alignment with Rastafari.

Young Jamaicans—both men and women—looking to get in touch with their African roots and follow the teachings of Rastafari in the sixties began growing their hair into dreadlocks. Bunny Wailer told Steffens and Pierson that after Haile Selassie visited Kingston in 1966, the three Wailers "stopped the kind of dancehall, whorehouse life. No more drinking beer, no more nightclub vibe," and made "a Nazirite Vow neither to drink nor cut our hair." Perhaps he was speaking figuratively, though, because Bob wasn't on the island when Selassie visited, and, according to his mother, had already started growing his locks. In fact, Bob had started "dreading up" earlier in the sixties, but he revolved between nascent locks and a combed-out afro typical of African-American youth. When he went to live with his mother in Delaware in 1966 (during the time Selassie visited), he allowed his hair to be trimmed to make it easier to find work. Later, when he returned to work, he kept his hair covered by a tam.

The Nazirite Vow

Bob once commented on the Nazirite vow Rastas take when they grow their locks, with Farley quoting him as saying, "Our lawgiver is Moses . . . when you take a vow to be a [Rasta], which is African, then you shall let no comb nor razor come up on your hair and you shall let the locks of your hair grow. Now this is the locks of my hair, so this just going by the Bible. Everything we do is not a self-taught thing, you know. It's both your conscience and the Bible."

So what does this Nazirite vow actually say? In the book of Numbers, a Nazirite is a Hebrew man or woman who has made a vow of dedication to the Lord. This vow includes three restrictions, all of which Rastas follow: avoiding alcohol (Numbers 6:3); never touching a corpse, even if is a parent (Numbers 6:6-7); and not cutting one's hair (Numbers 6:5 states, "During the entire period of their Nazirite vow, no razor may be used on their head. They must be holy until the period of their dedication to the Lord is over; they must let their hair grow long.")

The Nazirite vow signifies separation from the life of the typical community to focus on living a more godly life, usually for a limited time. Some, though, were designated as lifelong Nazirites, like Sampson. That Sampson's unshorn locks were the source of his tremendous strength (Judges 16) was not lost on Rastafarians.

Natty Songs

Bob spoke of dreadlocks in song sparingly. "Trench Town" recounts his daily ritual to wash his dreadlocks at Cane River, after running on the beach at Bull Bay, while "Rastaman, Live Up" encourages all Rastamen to get in touch with their African culture by growing their dreadlocks. He was aware, of course, that locks alone do not make one a Rasta, telling Ros Raines, "There are quite a few false Rastas around . . . not every man who wears locks need be a Rastaman."

Where we see him expounding more metaphorically on dreadlocks is when he uses the terms *natty* or *dread*, which refer to a dreadlocked Rasta. "Ride Natty Ride" uses both terms to refer to the resilient Rastaman treading through Babylon on a mission to defeat it. We also see this in "Roots" ("Roots, natty roots"), "Smile Jamaica" ("Hey, dread, fly, natty dread"), "Zimbabwe" ("Natty dread it inna Zimbabwe"), "Natty Dread" ("Natty dreadlock in a Babylon, a dreadlock Congo Bongo I"), and "Blackman Redemption" ("Natty Congo, a dreadlock Congo"). The use of "Congo," like "Bongo," further emphasizes the African origins of the Rastaman. In "I Know," Bob extends the meaning of natty to refer specifically to Jah Rastafari when he sings, "Natty will be there to see you through" (later switching to Jah).

Shock Factor: The Origin of Dreads

Why exactly do Rastas wear dreadlocks? One of the standard explanations is that the style originated from pictures of Kenyan Mau Mau warriors that were carried in newspapers in the forties and fifties. These African warriors wore their hair in long dreads and were the subject of international news stories due to their rebellion against the British colonial government. There's a lot there that would have appealed to the budding Rasta movement—African warriors resisting the British.

Another theory has to do with the Indian immigrant population on the island. Not only is the term *ganja* and the plant itself thought to come from them (as explained in chapter 45), it is possible that Hindu sadhus inspired dreadlocks. There is evidence that dreadlocked sadhus were on the island in 1910.

The problem with these theories is that, while they both make sense, there is no evidence to back them up. Jamaican anthropologist named Barry Chevannes tracked down the real story when he interviewed several Rastas in the seventies. The natty hairstyle actually originated with a Jamaican Rastafarian organization known as the Youth Black Faith, based in Trench Town in the late forties and run by Brother Watson, or Wato. The interesting thing about this group is that they were reformers unhappy with the way some of the Rasta elders ran things. Wato's group initiated some of the main manifestations of Rastafari we know of today—dread talk, dreadlocks, and the sanctification of ganja. Even the term *dread* comes from them. To be *dreadful* was to be disciplined and dutiful, and this evolved into meaning upright, so that to be dread is to be righteous. Second, wearing the hair in long locks was not in fashion among Rastas at this time. Conversely, Rastamen typically had beards and were known as beardsmen. The beard was in imitation of Selassie and Jesus, who had or were thought to have had beards, but was also a symbol of identity that separated their brethren from the average clean-shaven Jamaican man. This rejection of colonial social norms marked the Rasta brethren apart. Only later did they connect scriptural justification in the Nazirite vow of Samson to the rejection of trimming the hair.

Wato's group extended the Nazirite ordinance on growing hair by adding a ban on combing, so that long hair grew into locks. This was by design, as locks had a shock value, making them look like an outcast or religious fanatic. Again, this was all about contempt for upper-class notions of decency, beauty, religion, and righteousness, and even an open confrontation with these values. Wearing dreadlocks meant taking pride in one's African heritage, assurance of righteousness, and the refusal to bow to colonial power.

This decision led to a split, though, as not all Rastas agreed with the path of the dreadlocks. By the fifties there were two houses—the House of Dreadlocks, and the House of Combsomes—though it is the dreadlocks that have survived, as is demonstrated in Marley's own life.

48

You Want to Smoke One with Bob?

A Trip to the Mausoleum

If you travel to Nine Mile and you're not from Jamaica, chances are you are there to visit the Bob Marley Centre and Mausoleum, which was built on the grounds of his childhood home after his death in 1981. The property, inherited from his grandfather Omeriah, was home to Bob and his family periodically when they wanted to get out of the city. Bob planned to build a mansion in Nine Mile for the family and wanted eventually to stop touring and settle down there. After his passing, it became a fitting final resting place among the Dry Harbour Mountains he played in as a barefoot child.

Like the graves of other dead celebrities (Elvis's Graceland comes to mind), Marley's property has been turned into a gated shrine and gift shop to both commemorate the king of the reggae and sell Marley mementos to tourists. It might strike some as gaudy and commercial, but the compound has a definite Ital charm, having been kept in the family and employing local workers.

Getting There

Most tourists who visit the mausoleum come from the north coast resorts or the cruise ships in Montego Bay and Ocho Rios. You can get tour buses from these places, but you can't do that from Kingston, which is where I arrived from. My trip to Nine Mile was in the back of a Kingston taxi I hired for US $140 for the day. The journey took two and a half hours through traffic and over neglected roads. My esteemed driver, Ted, knew the general direction but not the specifics. He also apparently didn't believe in maps or GPS. He easily got us through traffic in Spanish Town, navigated the narrow passage over the Rio Cobra at Flatbridge, stopped for beef patties in Bog Walk, passed through Linstead, and then climbed up and over Mount Diablo. But when we turned off the main roads at Moneague, Saint Ann, things got slower. By the time we hit the village of Claremont, we were

On the road to Nine Mile.   *Brent Hagerman*

only twelve miles from Nine Mile (I learned this later, with the aid of a map).
But it took us close to an hour to drive them. The roads at times seemed no more
than paved cattle trails that coiled around hill after hill. We routinely stopped to
ask for directions along the way. Ted would hail someone down and they, always
friendly, would say, "Nine Mile, just up ahead." That went on for the whole hour.

We periodically passed official signs to the mausoleum, but we knew we
were getting closer as the houses and tiny restaurants along the way took on
more and more of the Rasta colors and symbols. We finally made it to Nine Mile
(after, of course, traveling through Eight Miles). It's a tiny hamlet with one road
running through it, and plenty of red, gold, and green to remind you where
you are.

Seventeen Varieties of Ganja

Once we were in the village, we were stopped by a friendly dread who told us
to park the taxi along the side of the road, offered us large, cone-shaped spliffs,
and proceeded to try to get us to take a tour with him of a farm with seventeen
different kinds of ganja. We skipped the tour and realized we weren't even
parked at the right place. We had to walk about fifty meters down the hill to get
to the main gate. There, more dreads offered us more herb—I'm not sure which

of the seventeen varieties was up for grabs, though. We went in the gates and the dreads stayed outside, which for the time being puzzled me.

Inside the Compound

The mausoleum is perched on a hill in the middle of a compound surrounded by high walls. An unwelcoming steel door lets you into a gravel parking area at the base of what has now become known as Mount Zion. It was called Sugar Hill in the days when Marley lived here, but according to our tour guide Marley himself altered the name.

It is unclear when you first enter the parking lot exactly where the mausoleum, or the house that Marley grew up in, is situated. After we ascended some steps at the far side of the lot, things became clearer. Marley's grandparents' house is just above road level. We were told that he was born in it. His grandparents, Omeriah and Alberta Malcolm, owned the house, and his mother, Cedella, lived there when she was not at her residence in Miami. She has since passed away, too, and is now buried in the mausoleum on the hill.

The compound houses a restaurant and a large souvenir shop (larger, in fact, than its sister shop in Kingston, at the Bob Marley Museum), which sells Marley memorabilia such as T-shirts, CDs, posters, commemorative rolling papers, and cigarette lighters. We purchased tickets for the tour ($15 US) in the gift shop and met our dreadlocked guide in the restaurant, the balcony of which offers a stellar view of the lush, rolling hills beneath us. Our guide was dressed in Rasta fatigues: a beige military-style button-up shirt and a red, gold, and green tam. He had started as a manual laborer here, he told us, planting grass and building some of the stone columns, but now worked as a guide.

The first stop on the tour was the balcony of the restaurant overlooking Omeriah's and Alberta's house. The guide told us how Bob was born there, and how, six months later, the house on top of the hill was built for him and his mother. As we left the restaurant we stood in front of the large gate to the mausoleum compound itself, which is surrounded by a zinc fence—a wall within a wall—so tall that it is hard to see in from outside; once inside, the tremendous view of the hills is almost always totally blocked.

Once we were inside the gate, the guide pointed to a small clearing to our right where we could see four graves—white stone grave plots. Two were for Marley's grandparents, the other two for an aunt and an uncle. The guide also pointed out that Marley's grandparents are buried six feet below the ground, but that Bob is buried six feet above the ground. The raised height of his grave symbolizes the heights—culturally, socially, spiritually—he achieved in life.

We walked up the stone path to the Marley's childhood house and were shown a small rock garden where the stones spell out "Bob Lives."

Next, we went to the house where Bob and his mother lived. The original two-room house, once a dull wooden shack with a corrugated steel roof, has been rebuilt in stone and trimmed with the ubiquitous red, gold, and green. Over the threshold is a sign that reads, "One Love," and on the door itself another states simply, "Bob Lives"—both sentiments are ubiquitous at the site. It has been maintained but not renovated, giving the sense that it is somehow authentic (in stark contrast to the gift shop, restaurant, and bathrooms). We were asked to remove our shoes before entering, out of respect for Bob.

The house is sparsely furnished—two chairs in the first room, a few small tables and a bed in the back room. There are pictures—mostly drawings of Marley—on the walls, and gifts left for him by fans (a letter, for instance, sat, still readable, on a chair in his room).

At various stops on the tour, the mausoleum's guides would illustrate their stories about Marley's life with short renditions of applicable Marley songs. For instance, after exiting the house we were brought to a stone painted red, gold, and green, called Mount Zion Rock, which we were told was where Marley used to meditate, and where he wrote the song "Talkin' Blues." On cue, the guide

No Marley pilgrimage site would be complete without a gift shop.   *Brent Hagerman*

broke into a verse and chorus about sleeping on the ground, with this rock for a pillow. To the east of the mausoleum is a small area with an outdoor cook stove that provided the basis for a chorus of the anti-rude boy song "Simmer Down." (Just to be clear, the song was about street gangs, not cooking!)

The Mausoleum

We left the house by the side door and stood in front of the mausoleum, a large white cement structure, similar in size to the house but with a tall pointed roof and cathedral windows facing south, making it look like a small chapel. We walked around the exterior of the mausoleum to look at the symbols on the stained-glass windows, which furthered the chapel motif.

The first, on the east side of the building, shows the Star of David. As the sun rises each day, its light passes through the star and rests on Marley's tomb inside. For Rastafarians, the Star of David is a reminder that Haile Selassie traced his lineage back to King David. Selassie himself is signified on the next window, which holds a picture of a lion: Selassie's royal titles included Lion of Judah, his royal seal was a lion, and the Ethiopian flag during his reign carried the symbol of a standard-bearing Lion of Judah against a red, gold, and green backdrop.

The gates to the mausoleum complex.   *Brent Hagerman*

Another window depicts a pastoral scene with four flowers. We were told that these were for the birds in the song "Three Little Birds," but no explanation was offered as to the incongruity between the number of birds and flowers. The next window contains a picture of a tree that the guide said could be likened to the sycamore tree mentioned in Marley's song "Time Will Tell." He then pointed out that growing beside us was an actual sycamore—the only one in Jamaica, brought here from Africa by Marley's mother. The final stained-glass window contains an image of a person standing, which the guide explained depicts Egyptian burial practices. Marley, he added, was laid to rest lying down, with his tomb facing the east and the rising of the sun.

Once we walked the circumference of the building (with shoes still off), we entered the mausoleum through a doorway trimmed in the familiar colors of Rastafari. A "One Love" sticker could be seen over the lintel, but on the brown wooden door was a different sign: "Jah Love." We left our shoes outside, and were instructed that cameras and audio recorders were prohibited.

The first thing you notice once you enter is the smell of ganja, which was when I realized the role of the dreads outside the gate: they were "selling" us the ganja to smoke sacrificially in front of Bob's remains. Ganja vendors outside the compound provide a much-appreciated service for many visitors. Bob, of course, was an avid ganja smoker, and he promoted the spiritual benefits of the holy herb. The museum couldn't do that without fear of legal trouble, so by leaving

Stones arranged in the grass along the path to the mausoleum.   *Brent Hagerman*

Tour guides at the mausoleum periodically break into song to help narrate Bob's life. When showing one stone on the property, my guide began singing, "Cold ground was my bed last night and rock was my pillow too," from the song "Talkin' Blues." This picture is of a cassette of the album of the same name, which features live recordings from San Francisco in October 1973, originally broadcast over KSAN-FM, plus extracts of an interview with Bob and outtakes from *Natty Dread*.
Author's collection

that up to local entrepreneurs—who, no doubt, offer a very valuable service for many of the visiting tourists—the museum is able to enhance the visit of its participants while staying on safe legal ground. As I looked down at the base of the tomb I saw the remains of several partially and fully enjoyed spliffs. That was the cue for the guide to ask, "You want to smoke one with Bob?"

The room is ruled (spatially and symbolically) by the hulking presence of the six-foot marble rectangular block that the tomb was built for. The marble is shrouded by several clothes and flags—most likely left by fans, because many seemed out of place, or at least created symbolic tensions with Bob's Rastafarian beliefs: for instance, Tibetan prayer flags, a Christian country-kitchen kitsch blanket that read "God Loves You," and a pin that said "I'm stylish." Rastafari is typically open to cross-cultural and interreligious interaction, often stressing that all people believe in one God with different names. As such, Tibetan Prayer flags or Christian axioms are not necessarily out of place. But another cloth had the symbol of the skull and crossbones. Blatant symbols of death like this are avoided by Rastafarians, and this reminded me of a story dancehall star Yellowman told me about one of his guitarists, who also had a rock back called Dead Dog. The guitarist had made a demo tape to give to a producer, but upon reading the name the Rastafarian producer threw it out the window, such is the aversion to death among Rastas.

There is a large photo of Cedella and her younger son Anthony, who was killed in a police shootout in 1990, in the room—a solemn reminder that this is a family burial plot, not simply a celebrity pilgrimage site. Both Anthony and Cedella are interred under Bob. Other material objects inside the shrine include a painting of Marley with long dreads and flowing red, gold, and green robes, carrying a lamb and staff (an obvious Jesus-as-shepherd motif); a magnificent brass bust of Marley, donated by Canadian fans, according to the guide; and several small trinkets.

Marley himself is encased in a brass casket and is embalmed to preserve his body, so that he apparently looks the same today as when he was buried. His wife decided to embalm his body the way pharaohs and kings were preserved among Egyptians and tribal Africans, so that, as the *Village Voice* reported in 1982, "generations to come will be able to break the seals, draw Bob out, and gaze upon him." If we could see into his casket, we'd see him dressed in jeans, a red, gold, and green vest, and a denim jacket—his chosen outfit for many stage shows—and underneath his Rastafarian woolen tam is a wig made from his own dreadlocks, as his hair fell out during cancer treatments before his death.

The objects he was buried with reflect his interests in life. He wears the ring Selassie's son gave him—the one that can be seen on his finger in the cover photo for *Legend*. In one hand is placed a guitar, and in the other a Bible. He was also buried with a football—his favorite sport—and a marijuana bud.

Pilgrimage Meets Tourism

As we exited the mausoleum and descended the hill, we were directed to a sign over the exit gate: "One Love, One Heart, Tip Your Tour Guide and Feel Alright." Talk about pilgrimage meets tourism. Strangely, when we got to the gift shop—which of course you exit through—it was closed, but the workers agreed to open it up for us so I could buy an overpriced shirt for my daughter.

Whether you imbue the site with deeper spiritual significance or not, the tour is framed as part pilgrimage to a sacred site. This isn't far removed from

The door to Bob's childhood home.   *Brent Hagerman*

other hallowed pop-culture pilgrimages such as Graceland or the Motown studios. But in Marley's case, the religious symbolism is perhaps more tangible. One thing that separates the Bob Marley Centre and Mausoleum from these other places is that while there are certainly financial considerations, it lacks the meticulous calculated fleecing of Graceland, or the run-down rote history of the Motown Museum. Instead, the Nine Mile compound seems like it is run by people who really care about Marley's life and legacy, many of whom grew up in the same community. There is a similar feel to the Bob Marley Museum at 56 Hope Road in Kingston. Sure, there are gift shops with inflated prices, and lots of commemorative kitsch, but it's nice to see that they are still run by the Marley estate, not an arms-length multinational behemoth.

On the long car ride back to Kingston after dark, Ted found his way without help. It was the first time this lifelong Kingston resident had been to Nine Mile, and like me he was he impressed with its beauty.

49

Leaving Babylon?

The Failed Attempt to Move Bob's Body to Africa

Grave tourism. It's a macabre pilgrimage that fans make to the final resting place of stars they love. Some of the most frequently visited are Elvis Presley's at Graceland, Memphis; Jim Morrison's in Père Lachaise Cemetery, Paris, France; Jimi Hendrix's in Renton, Washington; and Bon Scott's in Freemantle, Australia (which is also a National Historic Site). Would anyone bother visiting these sites if the remains of their celebrities weren't there? It's doubtful. For the tiny village of Nine Mile in Saint Ann, Jamaica, Bob Marley is really the only tourist draw, and the most significant artifact the Bob Marley Centre and Mausoleum has is the reggae singer's mummified body.

Bob Marley's body became the subject of a controversy in 2005 when Rita Marley announced that she intended to move his remains from his mausoleum in Nine Mile to Shashemene, Ethiopia, for his sixtieth birthday. That would have been on February 8, 2005. She wanted to do this because, as a Rastafarian, Africa was Bob's spiritual homeland. She told the *Guardian*, "Bob's whole life is about Africa, it is not about Jamaica. He has a right for his remains to be where he would love them to be. This was his mission. Ethiopia is his spiritual resting place."

Sounds fair, right? The dude often sang about Africa, and he obviously didn't want to remain in Babylon, what with all the talk of chanting it down. Perhaps this is what Rita thought, too. She didn't bargain on the fact that Jamaicans would not take lightly to the removal of their most famous son, though, and her announcement ignited a public dispute over the body of the King of Reggae.

Her critics—a very vocal cadre indeed—included the government, the business community, fans, Rastafarians, and, of course, the tourist industry. When her plan met with resistance, Rita at first denied the claims, then attempted to quell the controversy by suggesting it was a family matter (in other words: stay out of family business, you pesky fans). And then, finally, she decided to leave the man where he lay, though she did hint in the press that she might reconsider this decision at a later date.

Now, Rita wasn't making a spur-of-the-moment decision. A year before the announcement, she had made it clear in her autobiography that Bob's burial in Jamaica was always meant to be temporary: it was "for the time being, because the most fitting would be Africa, the place he dreamed about and saw himself. And we're looking forward to doing that someday. Let his bones be put in the earth of Africa. That was his dream."

There's good evidence to suggest that Bob did really want to live out his life and be buried in Africa. In a 1973 interview with Neville Willoughby, he said, "Now I must pick a place on Earth where I must live, and I know I want to live near my father, and my father lives in Ethiopia. So I must live where my father is." When Willoughby asked for clarification—"In other words, literally you hope to go and live in Ethiopia some day?"—Bob replied, "I don't hope. We are going and near, near. This is 1973 going near to '74 now, and Jah said, 'Before one of my word pass away heaven and earth crash.' Dig. And he said he is gone to prepare a place that where he is I-man, I shall be there also."

After the assassination attempt in 1976, Bob talked of moving to Africa, but was delayed by the Twelve Tribes of Israel, the Rastafarian organization to which he belonged. They were facilitating the repatriation of Rastafarians to Shashemene, an Ethiopian settlement established on land donated by Haile Selassie, and told Marley it wasn't his turn yet. To a Rastafarian like Marley, Africa was a sacred place, home to the living God and ancestral homeland of black people everywhere. Repatriation to Africa has been a significant goal for Rastas since the movement's inception in the thirties, and is a recurring theme in many a reggae song. Bob's songs were no different. Just think of "Exodus," a song about repatriation from Babylon to Selassie's Zion.

There are several sides to this controversy. At its heart is the ownership and control of Bob's body, but it was also about control of his legacy and even identity. Was he first and foremost a Jamaican? An African? A Rastafarian? For those opposed to the move, Marley represents the king of Jamaican music and the best of Jamaica, and his continuing physical presence is required in order to commemorate, perpetuate, and even market that image. For those in favor of the move, moving Bob to Africa is necessary in order to achieve the singer's spiritual goals and honor his religious beliefs.

Jamaica's Hero

Before he gained international recognition and had streets named after him in New York (Bob Marley Boulevard) and London (Bob Marley Way), Bob Marley was considered a dirty hoodlum in Kingston, but by 2005 Jamaicans of all stripes loved him. Surprisingly, he has not yet been made an official National

Hero of Jamaica, but he was and is a cultural hero and global icon of whom Jamaicans have every right to be proud. So it's easy to understand that when Rita wanted to take his remains away from Jamaica, there were detractors. Add to this the fact that Bob Marley is also a big business, and you can begin to understand the anger over the proposed move. There are several cottage industries that cater to tourists interested in his legacy and depend on them for their livelihood—taxi drivers, tour operators, restaurateurs, ganja vendors. Not to mention the government and corporate interests in the tourist industry, which earns more than a third of the country's GDP.

Angry fans responded to the idea by writing letters to local papers: "What about his spiritual ties to Jamaica? Wasn't Bob born and raised in Jamaica and didn't he call Jamaica home?" wrote one to the *Jamaica Observer*. "Has Rita lost her mind? Bob loved Jamaica. He wouldn't have made it his home if it were otherwise," wrote another to the *Gleaner*. Fans from home and away feel it is important to keep Bob where he is. A Vermont university student visiting Nine Mile couldn't understand why Rita would propose such a thing: "Why in the hell would she want to do that? Bob put Jamaica on the map. Now that I'm here, I think I know where he was coming from; same place he ended." For this fan, the place itself helped make sense of who Marley was—a boy raised in those green hills. Removing him from that geography would somehow diminish the connection.

A taxi driver who shuttles tourists to the site stated, "He's *our* legend," suggesting that if Marley's body was moved it would cause a riot. A caller to a local radio show announced that Rita Marley should be stoned if she follows through with the plans. It wasn't just the local papers that carried the story. The *Los Angeles Times* reported that workers at the mausoleum "have vowed physically to block any disinterment, and fans warn such an effort could lead to bloodshed." The *Guardian* quoted one mausoleum tour guide as saying, "If they try to move him there'll be war."

The animosity on the part of those making a living from the Mausoleum as a tourist attraction is understandable. The tourism industry has a lot to lose if Marley's body departs the region. As the country's *de facto* One Love ambassador, Bob's legacy popularizes Jamaica around the world. Fans come to visit significant locations to his life—56 Hope Road, Nine Mile, Tuff Gong Studio. Jamaica's tourist board even adopted his 1976 song "Smile Jamaica" to attract visitors looking to feel irie with a little fun in the sun. Marley wrote the song at the request of Prime Minister Michael Manley as a patriotic celebration of the island, and the title was used for the concert designed to bring an island torn by political strife together. Bob's history is Jamaican history, and he clearly cared deeply for the island and its people.

It is not surprising, then, that the Jamaican government threatened to block efforts to remove his remains. Maxine Henry-Wilson, Jamaica's minister for education and culture at the time, told the *Jamaica Observer*, "The country is clearly of a mind that the remains should stay here." And the government seemed to be of the mind that it had control over his remains—any exhumation would have to go through it and ultimately be settled by the courts, regardless of what the family wanted.

Citizen of the World?

While is it easy to see how Jamaicans might be opposed to the moving of its world renowned superstar, an argument could be made that, as a global icon, Bob Marley transcends one country. Even though Bob had his roots in the West Indies, his branches reach around the world. That is true in life and in death; his grave has visitors from Japan, South Africa, America, Europe, and throughout the Caribbean. In many ways, his international impact made him a citizen of the world: the *New York Times* called him the most influential artist of the second half of the twentieth century; *Time* magazine named *Exodus* the greatest album of the twentieth century; the BBC called "One Love" the anthem of the millennium. This doesn't erase his Jamaicanness, but it does help to put his global legacy in perspective.

Bob Marley's Pan-Africanism

Though he was Jamaican born and bred, Marley's religious and musical mission was intimately tied to Africa. He was keenly interested in African politics of independence, African history, and the role of the African diaspora in the continent's future. Many of his songs take up pan-African themes, such as "Africa Unite" and "Zimbabwe." He also understood former Emperor of Ethiopia Haile Selassie as a god-man, worshipping him as Jah Rastafari. Marley believed there would be a final apocalyptic battle between good and evil in which Selassie would defeat the forces of Babylon and Rastas would then be repatriated home to Africa. The end goal for Marley was indeed Africa, and Africa was the geographic center of Marley's cosmology. It is for these reasons that Rita Marley can legitimately say that her husband's whole life was about Africa.

In order to fully appreciate Bob's thinking around Africa, an overview of his Rastafarian beliefs is in order. A Christian who converted to Rastafari in the late sixties, Marley's religious life was fundamentally Jamaican yet focused absolutely on Africa. His religion was founded in Jamaica in the thirties, but it is identified as African-derived. Marley, following the Afro-centric philosophy of Jamaican national hero Marcus Garvey, self-identified as an African. African-Jamaicans are, of course, of African descent. Their ancestors were forcibly brought to the island where they were enslaved. This forced dispersal—or diaspora—is at the heart of how Rastafarians understand their place in the world. Africa is not only their homeland—it is the Promised Land. And Jamaica, and the rest of the West, is considered Babylon, the land of exile. When you're in exile you want to go home. Rastas interpret the Bible through an Ethiopian lens, so 12,000 people from each of the Twelve Tribes of Israel spoken of Revelation 7—which adds to 144,000—is taken to refer to exiled Africans waiting to go back to the homeland in this Marley quote from 1976, found in Sheridan's *The Story Behind Every Bob Marley Song*: "Today is not the day, but when it happen[s] 144,000 of us go home." So from this point of view it makes sense that Rita Marley would want to take her husband's remains back home.

Bob also spoke of his future as being in Africa when interviewed by Karl Dallas for *Melody Maker* in 1975: "My future is in a green part of the earth. Big enough me can roam freely. I don't feel Jamaica gonna be the right place because Jamaica look a bit small. That mean we put a circle some time round Jamaica, mean my thing will have finish, need somewhere new, Ethiopia, adventure, know what I mean?"

His ultimate dream, he told *Rolling Stone* in 1976, was the dream of every Rastaman—to "fly home to Ethiopia and leave a Babylon."

Marley's Rastafarian Beliefs About Death

As a terminal cancer patient, Bob Marley obviously knew that death lay ahead. He even discussed writing a will and indicated to his manager that he wanted all his children to have his money when he died, though he died intestate (which caused lots of hassles for the family). But he often spoke as though he didn't believe in death. Rita wrote in *Essence* in 1995 that, as a Rasta, you would never hear Bob Marley say, "If I die" or "When I die," because Rastas believe in everlasting life on Earth. He told Goldman in a 1979 *Melody Maker* interview that, sure, a person could die if they stuck their head under an oncoming bus, but he insisted, "You have to avoid [death]! Death does not exist for me. God gave me this life and my estimation is, if he gives me this, why should he take it back? Only the Devil says that everybody has to die."

In the same interview, he said, "I don't believe in death in flesh or in spirit." And according to the documentary *Spiritual Journey*, Bob predicted he would die at the age of thirty-six. These seemingly contradictory ideas are held together with the belief that death is the result of sin. He explained to Goldman that those who do not sin will not die: "Preservation is the gift of God. The gift of God is life. The wages of sin is death. When a man does wickedness, he's gone out there and dead."

This refusal to acknowledge death is common among Rastas, who see themselves as liberated from its power. Theologically, this is a reversal of Christianity, which they see as death-centric: Jesus died to save sins, believers die to get heaven, a sacred Catholic symbol is Christ perishing on an instrument of death. Christianity taught the enslaved Africans that death was their release from slavery: if they were obedient, subservient, and patient, they would achieve their reward in the afterlife. Rastafarians identify as descendants of enslaved Africans and see themselves in a similar scenario of "sufferation" at the hands of Babylon. They saw through this colonial Christian ploy to deceive blacks, instead insisting that Rastas do not have to die to see God but that they can live to see God by visiting Africa, a sort of real-time heaven. Bob reiterated this belief when he told a journalist in Switzerland in 1980, "If de preacher read the Bible and tell you, you have to die to go to heaven, then he is not reading the Bible, because the Bible tell you, you haffi live in a heaven, you don't die and go to heaven. . . . You know, a lot of places on earth could be, but Africa is our heaven, because that is where we come from."

This extreme rejection of death causes Rastas to make leaps of logic. Death, when it does occur, is explained as the wages of sin—a Rasta who holds steadfast in his or her faith in Haile Selassie can't die, so if you do die, you must have sinned. Twelve Tribes Rasta leader Prophet Gad implied this when he told Bob Marley that Rastas can't get cancer. Marley had just been diagnosed with melanoma at the time, so, following this argument, he must not have been a true Rasta, or must otherwise have committed a grievous sin, as death is a punishment from Jah for those that stray from the righteous path.

In addition to this rejection of death, there is a general refusal to touch or even discuss dead things. When the Grateful Dead flew Bob to San Francisco in the hope of signing him to their eponymous record label, he refused to do so because the label had "dead" in its name. When Bob, Rita, and Don Taylor were shot in 1976, the other Rastas present refused to touch Don's motionless body, thinking he was dead. It was actually Bob, having himself sustained two gunshot wounds, who overcame the Rasta aversion to death and tended to his manager. In his book *Rastafari*, Chevannes recounts an instance where a Rastafarian refused to touch or bury his deceased mother, reasoning, "I man don't deal with the dead, only with the living."

This denial of death even relates to funerals, which Rastas see as an example of Christianity's death-cult that is in opposition to their life-affirming philosophy. There is a biblical basis for this in Psalms 6:5, "For in the grave there is no remembrance of thee," and in Jesus's directive in Luke 9:60 to "let the dead bury their dead."

Peter Tosh offers his rationale for why he doesn't attend funerals in the song "Burial": "I ain't got no time to waste on you / I'm a livin' man and I got work to do." Bob sang backup on an earlier version, called "Funeral."

It is no wonder, then, that both Tosh and Bunny Wailer (who later covered this song) refused to attend their friend's funeral. Bunny felt that Bob's death was the "wages of his sin and corruption." As Ras Joe told the *Village Voice* in 1982, "Them man are livers—they do not deal with death." Given this, it is doubtful Marley would have attended their funerals, either.

Reincarnated Souls

So far, the Rastafarian understanding of death is that it doesn't exist, that it is the result of sin, or that it does occur but should be avoided at all costs. The next question is: what happens after death? Prophet Gad—the guy who insinuated that Bob wasn't a pious Rasta—has an idea. In a 1997 interview on IRIE FM's *Running African* show, he said, "When death come, it come. But right now we're trying to avoid that death business. But when that come, you can't run from it. As for us, we don't die. We only sleep, waiting for the resurrection."

Gad's belief in resurrection is similar to the death beliefs of Africans throughout the Caribbean during slavery, who thought that their dead would be resurrected in Africa. This fits quite well with Rastafari, as the afterlife becomes the fulfillment of repatriation.

While this is different from resurrection, there is also some belief among Rastas of reincarnation, wherein a soul exchanges one body for another. Rastas see themselves as reincarnated ancient Israelites. This is actually the theme of the Wailers song "Reincarnated Souls," released as the B-side to "Concrete Jungle" in May 1973. For Rastas, Marcus Garvey is said to be the reincarnated John the Baptist. Haile Selassie, according to some sources, is the seventy-second manifestation of God on Earth, and/or the biblical King David. Marley himself was a reincarnated Joseph (the one with the Technicolor dream coat, not the husband of Mary).

Unlike in Hinduism, this reincarnation is not a circle of life/death/life but rather several bodily manifestations of the same person over generations. Death need not be in the equation for Rastafarians, as they believe that a person can simply disappear, or take many diverse appearances. Early Rastafarian leader Leonard Howell is considered to have disappeared, not died. Rita Marley saw Bob disappear, not die. "Bob didn't die," she writes. "He's somewhere, I'll see him sometime," because he underwent a "reincarnation." She also explained to Malika Lee Whitney, "It was a rest, and I can say that this man is coming again."

All this is to say that Bob was indeed a son of the Jamaican soil, but upon ceasing this life (not dying, remember) he may have already left Babylon and journeyed back to Ethiopia. Is it so strange, then, that his body should follow?

Between Babylon and Zion

Given the Rastafarian beliefs surrounding death, one would think that Rastas would either wholeheartedly advocate for his move to Africa (his spiritual home-land, and all that) or avoid the topic altogether (death, what death?). But as in any area of life, there is a diversity of opinion here, too. Marley's spiritual advi-sor—the man who mentored him in his early Rasta days and met Haile Selassie in person—agreed with Rita's proposal to move Bob's remains. Benjamin Cole, a friend and fellow Rasta from Trench Town, thinks being buried in Ethiopia is Rastafarian destiny. In an editorial for *Rasta Ites*, Exodus 13:19 (where Moses takes the bones of Joseph out of Egypt to the Promised Land—in this case Israel) was cited as a biblical precedent to take Bob's bones to Zion, which in the Rastafarian case means Ethiopia.

Another noted Rastafarian thinker and dub poet, Mutabaruka, agreed with Rita's proposal, reasoning in a *Jamaica Observer* interview, "Bob Marley seh him is a Rastaman and him must goh ah Ethiopia." He wasn't too keen on the gov-ernment's objection, which he saw as "part of a broader conspiracy to separate the King of Reggae from his Rastafarian beliefs." Perhaps Mutabaruka is on to something. Certainly, this debate can be said to have shown that the govern-ment, the tourism industry, many Jamaican citizens, mausoleum custodians, local businesses, and international fans have ignored Marley's religious beliefs.

But not all Rastas or Rasta sympathizers agree with this. Ras John, of www.reggae.com, writes that when Marley knew he was terminally ill, he left Germany and wanted to go home to die in Jamaica, not Africa. The removal of his remains "would be a sad betrayal of Bob, Jamaica and fans of his music and message whose seed grew out of fertile soil in Jamaica."

Roger Steffens, a prominent reggae journalist and broadcaster who has promoted Marley's music in America since the early seventies and written extensively on reggae and Bob Marley throughout his life, also believes that Marley should remain in Jamaica. He makes an interesting argument based on a historical reading of Rastafari and the post-imperial politics of Ethiopia, telling the *Jamaica Observer*, "Bob never expressed any interest to be buried in Ethiopia. They don't believe that Selassie is God in Ethiopia, and that was the prime motivation behind Marley's music. The country that created the faith of Rastafari is Jamaica, not Ethiopia."

Rastafarian author and filmmaker Barbara Blake-Hannah concedes that Marley did say he wanted to live in Ethiopia but counters that he never said he wanted to be buried there. She offers four reasons why Jamaica should remain Marley's home. First, taking into account the political situation in Ethiopia at the time of Marley's death, she argues that Marley would not have wanted to be buried in a country led by Marxist-Leninist dictator Mengistu, who not only dethroned Haile Selassie but also removed the imperial lion from the Ethiopian flag. In an article for the *Jamaica Observer*, she wrote, "This was not the Ethiopia Bob wanted to live in, much less be buried in. If he had expressed such a desire before dying, Bob's close ties with the Ethiopian Orthodox Church and its western hemisphere archbishop would have made this instantly possible." Second, Marley's burial in Nine Mile brought the life of "this son of Jamaican soil" full circle, and the rural locale is in harmony with his naturalist beliefs. Third, she contests the right of Rita Marley to determine exactly what constitutes Bob's family and who gets included and/or left out of the decision making: "Does 'the family' include all of Bob's children and the mothers who gave birth to them?" Finally, in a move that seems to contradict other Rastafarian statements on the matter, she argues, "Rastas—Bob especially—have always considered Jamaica as 'the throne of Jah' and the present center of the spiritual universe." Her argument transforms Jamaica from the land of historical captivity to the land made sacred because it is where Haile Selassie revealed himself to the Rastafari. This is made palpable when Blake-Hannah says that Marley was a son of "JAH-maica." The island, then, once Babylon, can now be viewed as a suitable resting place for a deceased Rastafarian.

From Africa to Jamaica to Africa

Bob Marley's mausoleum is symbolic of his two sides, which are themselves at the heart of the debate over his body: the Jamaican and the African. The physical ground is Jamaican. Bob was born and grew there. Yet the site is adorned with many African symbols: pictures of Haile Selassie, the lion of Judah, the sycamore tree, and Egyptian images on the stained glass windows. Ethiopian flags fly side-by-side with Jamaican flags, and Ethiopia's national colors, adopted by Rastas, are ever-present. Marley's body faces east, toward Africa.

The practice of burying personal objects with the deceased has connections to West African burial traditions, where the deceased is believed to share the same passions and appetites in death as in life. Musically, too, the Marley songs that can be heard at the site are imbued with lyrical and rhythmic references to Africa. For those who understand the African and Rastafarian symbolism at the site, the mausoleum was clearly marked as a Rasta/African space, but it is firmly on Jamaican soil. In life, Bob Marley was many things to many people. The controversy over his body demonstrates that he is as multivalent in death and he was as in life.

Part 4

The Myth

50

One Love

Bob Marley the Icon of Peace

W hen I ask my history of popular music students what they think of when they think of Bob Marley, the phrase I hear most often is "one love." The second most common answer? His love of ganja. Bob Marley, Rasta philosopher—spliff in one hand, guitar in the other—preaching of a brighter tomorrow where discrimination and oppression are a thing of the distant past. Peace, love, and understanding—that's what Marley represents to many of his fans, summed up nicely by one of his enduring choruses, "One love, one heart, let's get together and feel all right."

As an icon of peace, Marley is kind of like a dreadlocked sixties hippy (though bud-powered instead of flower-powered): no war and no squares, just unruly long hair, good weed, free love, and good vibes. Indeed, in her book *The First Rasta*, Hélène Lee links the sixties ideals to the burgeoning Rasta movement that Marley popularized in the seventies: "The youth of the world, raised on 'peace and love' clichés and reefer, were looking for new gurus. The hippies thought the Rastas were everything they wanted to be, and reggae music seemed to express their inchoate ideals." At its root, this portrait is based on the belief that Bob Marley had one central, universal message: peace and love.

Bob Marley, Purveyor of Universal Love, Peace, and Unity

Distilling Marley's message down to "One Love" makes perfect sense for a lot of people, including the BBC, which named the song "One Love" the anthem of the millennium. The Jamaican tourist board has used both "One Love" and "Smile Jamaica" as slogans, while in June 1978, Marley was awarded the United Nations Peace Medal of the Third World for his part in the One Love Peace Concert.

Recently, *One Love: The Bob Marley Musical* launched in the UK. The production focuses on Marley's role in quelling a civil war on Kingston's streets by uniting people with his music and message. The official Bob Marley website (bobmarley.com) asked New Yorkers what Bob's central philosophy, one love, meant. The answers speak to the feeling that Bob's message was about peace and love: "unity," the commonality at the heart of the world-family, "an anthem to the human spirit," "one connects to all," "understanding one another."

Bob's wife, Rita Marley, summed up his message at a press conference in 2007: "Our family is committed to keeping the legacy and teachings of Bob alive to spread 'One Love' worldwide through the power of music." In 2006, the Houston-based Annual Bob Marley Festival Tour was renamed the "Universal Love" Legends of Rasta Reggae Festival Tour. The festival distills reggae's message—most clearly articulated by Bob Marley—down to universal love, peace, and unity.

The idea that Marley had a fundamentally pacifist central message can be broadly found across many stripes of cultural movers and shakers. When the Grammy-winning Soweto Gospel Choir chose to sing "One Love," they did so because it reflects their goal of uniting people. Soloist Zanele Mkhwanazi said that the dream in Bob Marley's music is that "where there's unity there's peace."

For many people, Bob's music and mission can be summed up as "peace-promoting." The designers of the three-CD *Forever Bob Marley* compilation must have thought so, too, judging by the iconography stamped on each CD.   *Author's collection*

The head of Amnesty International has echoed this, saying, "Everywhere I go in the world today, Bob Marley is the symbol of freedom. And I speak of him not only as a musician but as a transcendent champion of human rights and justice." In the essay that accompanies a 1996 interview CD, music critic Chris Welch wrote that the singer "always preached love and non-violence." Toronto's *Now Magazine* listed Marley's "War" as one of its top ten songs about peace, alongside "Give Peace a Chance" by John Lennon and "Masters of War" by Bob Dylan.

Even normally staid academics gush over his pacifism: the *Peace Review: A Journal of Social Justice* calls him an enduring "symbol of peace and freedom," and Paul Gilroy, author of *The Black Atlantic*, hails Marley's "opposition to all war and his stalwart advocacy of peace."

While Marley does have lyrics dealing with violence, his most enduring songs tend to project a positive worldview: helping others is good, quarrelling is bad ("Positive Vibration," "Wake Up and Live"); playing music, especially reggae, and dancing will bring people together, make things better, and even help overcome oppression ("Jamming," "Punky Reggae Party," "Smile Jamaica," "Trenchtown Rock," "Roots, Rock, Reggae," "Chant Down Babylon," "One Drop"); a little love—platonic, erotic, take your pick—is always a good thing ("Is This Love," "Mellow Mood," "Do It Twice," "Rock It Baby," "Stir It Up," "Turn Your Lights Down Low"—okay, he sang a lot about getting it on); your duty is to keep the faith and trod the good road ("Could You Be Loved"); when reality gets you down, spark up a spliff ("Easy Skanking," "Kaya"); sun and rainbows, not storms and clouds ("Soul Rebel," "Sun Is Shining," "Rainbow Country"); the righteous will prevail over the wicked ("Duppy Conqueror," "Ride Natty Ride"); and just general good vibes ("Lively Up Yourself").

And then there's that gospel of Disney sentiment that appeals to the optimist in us all: that things eventually work out for the best ("No Woman, No Cry," "Three Little Birds," "One Love," "Rastaman Live Up," "Coming in from the Cold"). Taken together, these songs make a powerful case that in the Bob Marley worldview, peace will win out—and that's a good thing. Marley's own words can be used to support his representation as an icon of peace: as he told Neville Willoughby, "Rasta don't believe in violence."

You don't have to look very deep into his life and music to see that the peace-minded Marley was the real deal, and that his activism stood him apart from most other entitled chart-toppers of the seventies. While most pop stars in the mid-seventies, for instance, were working on their disco crossovers (I'm looking at you, Mick Jagger) or their lines of blow (hello, Eagles? Fleetwood Mac? Keith Richards?), Marley had the weight of the world on his shoulders. In 1976, he quelled election violence on Kingston's streets by orchestrating a ceasefire between warring gangs. Then he held a free concert, Smile Jamaica, to bring everyone together. The problem was that the gangs were aligned with one of two political parties in town, the JLP and the ruling PNP. Someone got it in their head that Marley was supporting the ruling party by putting on the concert (he wasn't) and shot up his house two nights before the show. Bob, his wife Rita, and their manager Don Taylor were all hit by the bullets.

In the wake of a historic treaty between the gangs, political violence erupted yet again. In 1978, Marley instigated another musical balm in the form of the One Love Peace Concert in Kingston and brought Prime Minister Michael Manley and opposition leader Edward Seaga onstage together, joining their hands in a symbolic show of unity.

In the fan world of reggae, the three original Wailers have been imbued with separate, Beatle-like personalities. Peter Tosh is the militant, Bunny Wailer the mystic, and Bob Marley the pacifist. This image of Bob Marley as a broker of truces and advocate for the downtrodden with a central message of peace and unity is the one that has echoed across the decades and resonated with so many of his fans worldwide.

51

I Shot the Sheriff

Bob Marley the Revolutionary

Outside of Jamaica, reggae music often evokes rum cocktails, palm trees, and all-inclusive beach vacations, not ghettos, gang warfare, and the ongoing struggle for decolonization. As the last chapter shows, Marley is typically presented in popular culture as an icon of peace, and there's certainly truth in the fact that he sang about peace, love, and unity. Many of his actions supported these values, too. But this is only half the story. Whereas he once stated, "Rasta don't believe in violence," he also sang, "It takes a revolution to make a solution" in "Revolution," wanted to bomb a church in "Talkin' Blues," and made an anthem out of murderous self-defense in "I Shot the Sheriff."

So, as much as Bob is remembered as the "One Love" superhero, there is also an enduring representation that positions him first and foremost as a natty rebel, a political protest singer, a shit disturber. In "Bob Marley and the Politics of Subversion," Keisha and Louis Lindsay claim that there is a "uniquely powerful message implicit in Marley's work" that is centered on revolution as "a process of social transformation over time." Writing in the *Socialist Review*, Brian Richardson likens Marley to the revolutionary Che Guevara, calling him a "roots revolutionary," while *Beat Knowledge* calls him a "revolutionary poet." Pictures of Marley defiantly smoking fat spliffs don the walls of college dormitories, and dozens of companies on the Internet can sell you militant-looking Bob Marley apparel to go with your Che Guevara T-shirt and Fidel Castro hat when you want to look your insurgent best.

This longstanding image of Bob Marley as revolutionary is not by accident—Bob Marley was marketed as such by Island Records. The Rastafarian outlaw image was conceived by Island Records owner Chris Blackwell as a way to market reggae. A wealthy white Jamaican with a successful, British-based progressive rock–oriented label, Blackwell had never been able to find a way to break a reggae artist to the mainstream rock audience. British teens, Blackwell's chief demographic, thought of reggae as novelty music; BBC Radio 1 deejay Tony Blackburn thought of reggae songs as "rubbish." Sure, ghetto-seasoned scorchers like Desmond Dekker's "Israelites" had cracked the charts there, and there was a growing dedicated group

Images of Bob Marley and Che Guevara on the back of a delivery truck in Ouagadougou, Burkina Faso: pop culture's ubiquitous revolutionary icons.   *Photo by Adam Jones PhD, Creative Commons license*

of skinhead fans that appreciated Jamaican rudie culture, but many Jamaican songs seemed gimmicky to British rock fans, simply lightweight Carib-pop crossovers that lacked substance. Millie Small's "My Boy Lollipop" or Bobby Bloom's "Montego Bay" for example. Thanks to artists like Bob Dylan and the Beatles, rock, by the late sixties, was treated by its fans as serious music—music that should stand up to repeated listens and experiment with breaking boundaries, not follow mainstream conventions. These listeners weren't looking for Johnny Nash's pop-reggae "I Can See Clearly Now," they wanted Traffic, T. Rex, and Led Zeppelin.

So Blackwell had an epiphany of sorts on how to interest English youth in Jamaican music. What he needed was a Jamaican artist with rock 'n' roll swagger. Rock 'n' rollers weren't polite bow-and-scrape artists, they were troubled malcontents who caused social panic by providing teenagers with an edgier music and worldview than that of their parents. Elvis's hips shook the establishment by making the teenager girls scream. His sneer was a "fuck you" to polite society that enticed teenage boys to pick up guitars and continue the revolution.

Many in England answered his call: John Lennon, Pete Townshend, Keith Richards, Eric Clapton, Jeff Beck, rock heroes who gave voice and confidence to the youth subculture. The rock 'n' roll revolution changed what teenagers expected out of music—it should be first and foremost rebellious in music, lyric, and image. Chris Blackwell knew this, and he understood that reggae was, at its core, subversive music—the music of liberation for black people. He just needed a way to translate Jamaican rebel music for white kids raised on rock 'n' roll.

Blackwell found the template for a reggae rock star in *The Harder They Come*, an independent Jamaican film he helped to fund in hopes that it would break reggae outside Jamaica. Island Records artist and Jamaican hit-maker Jimmy Cliff (the guy who initially discovered Bob Marley in 1962) starred in the film as a convincing outlaw reggae singer named Ivan. The soundtrack—all recorded at Beverley's and released by Island—was infectious beyond belief, and together, the music and film helped introduce a gutsier, more authentic Jamaican music culture abroad.

Blackwell became convinced that he needed a real-life maverick like the one in the film to really take reggae to the rock crowd. As fate would have it, Jimmy Cliff left Island Records the same week Marley walked into Blackwell's London office. The Wailers were stranded in London, and had sought out Blackwell first to help finance plane tickets back home and then to discuss putting out some of their music. They had bounced between different producers and record companies for a decade and hadn't found one that could break them outside of Jamaica. They saw in Blackwell the same possibilities he saw in them—a new chance to promote Jamaican music abroad.

Having been in the business over a decade, Blackwell knew of Marley and the Wailers and had, in fact, distributed some of their material in Britain. He knew the band had a reputation as bad-asses. They had had a string of local hits about Jamaican gangster culture, known as rudies. One of them (Bunny) had been in jail. They dressed like ragamuffins and donned budding dreadlocks—a hairstyle that scared the shit out of the upper classes in Jamaica and was viewed with open distain among white Brits and Americans. Instead of sticking to polite love songs, they wore their Trench Town ghetto roots on their sleeves ("Trenchtown Rock," "Concrete Jungle"), and were beginning to sing songs about colonialism ("400 Years"), resistance ("Downpresser"), black power ("Black Progress"), Rastafari ("Jah Is Mighty," "Screw Face," "Satisfy My Soul Jah Jah"), and ganja ("Kaya," "African Herbsman"). Blackwell was warned that they were difficult to work with, and that if he advanced them money he might as well kiss it goodbye.

The band's relationships with producers generally ended in acrimony amid allegations of exploitation and cheating. Their song "Small Axe" was even a thinly veiled rebuff to the big three (or "big tree," as Marley sings) players in the Jamaican music industry—Studio One, Federal, and Treasure Isle—and a promise to cut them down. They recorded this with producer Lee "Scratch" Perry, but shortly thereafter they left him when he tried to shortchange them. Bunny punched him to the ground and the Wailers stole Scratch's studio band, the Upsetters.

While these traits would have scared away the complacent suits of the pop industry, they helped endear the band to Blackwell, who saw a confluence between these confrontational Rastamen and the countercultural rock heroes both British and American teenagers adored.

"When Bob walked in, he really was that [rebel] image" from *The Harder They Come*, Blackwell told Chris Salewicz in his book *Reggae Explosion*. The label owner deftly used the Wailers' authentic renegade attitude to create a demand for their music and message, even fashioning their first album like a Zippo lighter (to light a spliff). And this is how Marley was marketed as an exotic revolutionary third-world poet until his death in 1981 and even beyond—Island's 1986 compilation was dubbed *Rebel Music*, after the song of the same name.

Rebel Music

Of course, Marley as counterculture icon is more than simply a publicist's invention. Marley wrote his fair share of anti-authoritarian songs, stretching right back to his days at Studio One. Some, like "I Shot the Sheriff," entice us with their romantic Wild West imagery while striking a deeper chord with parables of just violence in the face of police harassment. Suspicion of authority recurs in other songs like "Rat Race," in which he states, "Rasta don't work for no CIA," and in "Revolution," where he cautions against granting politicians favors, as this will give them leverage over you. "I Shot the Sheriff" went a long way to establishing Marley's image as a rebel in pop culture. When Eric Clapton covered it in 1974, Marley received international recognition as a revolutionary, which delighted him.

As a black Jamaican and a Rastafarian, Marley understood the dehumanizing effects of institutional violence caused by the colonial legacies of racism and classism. He saw his music as a weapon against them. His lyrics often refer to acts of violence as a necessary part of the revolutionary struggle, and Marley once told an interviewer that, were he not a musician, he would be a revolutionary. The theme of resistance pervades his songs: he sang about slavery in the present tense ("Slave Driver," "Redemption Song"), advocated leaving the West and returning to Africa ("Africa Unite," "Exodus"), protested against the criminalization of ganja ("Rebel Music"), chastised the church for whitewashing God ("Babylon System," "Get Up, Stand Up"), spoke of war as the wages of racism ("War") and endurance in the face of systemic calamity ("Survival"), validated armed struggle for a righteous cause and supported independence from European colonizers ("Zimbabwe"), turned the tables on Babylon ("Chant Down Babylon," "Them Belly Full (but We Hungry)," "The Heathen," "Crazy Baldhead," "Jump Nyabinghi"), and promoted general resistance of the established order ("One Drop," "Burnin' and Lootin'").

Tuff Gong

Marley's rebelliousness can be found in more than his defiant song lyrics and a clever marketing campaign. He was the real deal. Nicknamed "Tuff Gong" for his capabilities in a fight, according to some sources, Marley and his bandmates were no strangers to running askance of the law and resisting the system. When Jamaican radio stations refused to play reggae music in the sixties, the Wailers coerced deejays with threats of violence. When Marley thought his manager, Don Taylor, was skimming off the top of his earnings, he took him into his mother's bathroom in Miami and pointed a gun at his head—an act of intimidation designed to cancel their management contract. That same manager writes in his memoir, "Bob had one burning desire: to lead a revolutionary assault on the forces of Babylon by giving voice to the downtrodden and the oppressed through his music." He had become the leader of a motley group of outsiders in Jamaica—some pacifistic Rastafarians, but others bona fide political gunmen. (Taylor even alleges that he saw his boss give money to arms dealers.)

Aside from his personal toughness, Marley was also deeply respected for his love and support of African and African-Jamaican culture, and the people of Jamaica's ghettos. Colonial religious and education systems disparaged blackness and Africanness and the stringent race and class system in Jamaica tossed ghetto dwellers to the bottom of the heap of humanity. By celebrating his roots, Marley was standing up for his people. He did this symbolically, with his music, but he recognized the need for tangible assistance as well—his accountant estimated that he financially took care of well over four thousand people.

Peacenik or Revolutionary?

So, if you're paying attention, in the last chapter Bob Marley was a peacenik and now he's a revolutionary. What gives? Obviously, he was human, and humans are complex creatures. Both sides are represented in his life and music, but some of us prefer to see peace as his central message while others prefer the iconoclast, the ghetto kid turned third-world star that subverted the upper classes by overturning their oppressive values. Members of this crowd—the pro-revolutionary fans—tend to get their blood up over what they see as sanitized, even whitewashed depictions of the Tuff Gong.

Here's Ian Boyne, writing in Jamaica's daily *Gleaner* in 2015: "There has been a systematic campaign to de-radicalise Marley, to drain his lyrics of their revolutionary impact and to sanitise him as a good boy serving the interests and values of capitalism." His point? By focusing on peace, love, and unity, we shouldn't be blinded to Marley's more radical messages—the fiery anti-estab-lishment lyrics that are so central to his appeal to oppressed people globally.

Boyne hints at a systematic campaign to sanitize Marley, but sociologist Michelle Stephens has researched it. She has traced the evolution of Marley's image from that of a Rastafarian outlaw in the seventies to a natural family man in the eighties and a natural mystic in the nineties. Whereas the slogan of "One Love" was key to building a multiculturalist image associated with Marley in the eighties, it replaced his defining militant slogans of the seventies such as "Get Up, Stand Up," "Africa Unite," and "Movement of Jah People" (from "Exodus"). Bob Marley's image has gone through a systematic cleansing at the hands of consumer culture and publicity machinery in order to, as Paul Gilroy states, wipe clean "any embarrassing political residues and that might make him into a threatening or frightening figure." This has resulted in Marley being refashioned, variously, as a patron saint of soccer, ganja, and Rasta machismo.

52

Real Reggae

The Construction of Authentic Reggae

Quick test: who is the King of Rock 'n' Roll? I'm hoping you guessed Elvis, because it would be embarrassing (for you) if you didn't know that. Queen of rock 'n' roll? Either Janis Joplin, Stevie Nicks, or Tina Turner, depending on who you read. Queen of Soul? Aretha Franklin. King of Pop? Michael Jackson, of course. Queen of Pop? Madonna. Or Lady Gaga, if you were born after 1990. King of Rap? According to Barrack Obama, it is Jay Z, though I'm sure Kanye West thinks it's him. Queen of Disco? Donna Summer. King of Disco? Apparently one was never crowned. King of Dancehall? Beenie Man wrote a song by that name, but Yellowman had the title long before him, so I'm going with Yellowman. And, finally, King of Reggae? It's universally accepted that this title goes to Bob Marley. After all, his records in the seventies did more to popularize reggae outside of Jamaica than those of any other artist.

Popular music is filled with performers given royal honorific titles to indicate their dominance of their genre. Some it's hard to argue with: Dick Dale is the King of the Surf Guitar because, well, who else would be? Rihanna is the Caribbean Queen. I can buy that. Ozzy Osbourne as Prince of Darkness? Who could argue with that? Nickelback as the Sell-Out Sultans? Seems about right. (Okay, I made that one up.)

Others seem like a stretch: Avril Lavigne as Pop-Punk Queen sounds suspiciously like something her publicist dreamed up over too many iced skinny-vanilla lattes. Adele as Queen of Soul? You're good, Adele, but you're no Aretha Franklin. Neil Diamond as the Jewish Elvis? Is that even a thing? Bill Haley as King of Rock 'n' Roll? I'm pretty sure nobody ever called him that. Or, if they did, they were wrong. King of Schlock 'n' Roll, more like it.

The King of Reggae

But Bob Marley seems legit, right? He has certainly dominated the reggae genre internationally since the early seventies, and his *Legend* compilation has sold upward of thirty million copies—making it the best-selling reggae album of all time—so his title makes sense from a popularity point of view.

I'm not sure anyone actually thinks Bob Marley invented reggae. (Wait, I take that back: a Google search for "Did Bob Marley invent reggae?" actually turns up that very question on answers.com. Really, people?) But his popularity means that he's the world's best-known reggae artist, and he is typically considered the best example of what Jamaican reggae is. You see, for many non-Jamaican journalists and reggae fans, the music Bob Marley released on Island Records between 1972 and 1983 (in other words, his most popular stuff) stands as the most authentic example of reggae music. (Most Jamaican reggae fans, on the other hand, understand the genre as much more diverse.)

This holds true for many other musicians, too. Reggae bands in Europe, North America, Japan, New Zealand, and Africa, for instance, have copied the instrumentation the Wailers used in the seventies (organ, clavinet, rhythm and lead electric guitars, horns, bass, drums, percussion), their musical style (downtempo roots reggae centered around a one drop drum beat), their production method (real musicians in a studio recording an original song, instead of a vocalist or vocal group adding a new "song" to an existing backing track), their lyrical content (overwhelmingly geared toward social justice, positivity, ganja, and Jah), and even their visual aesthetic (dreadlocks, ragamuffin clothing, and the Ethiopian/Rastafarian colors of red, gold, and green). I'm thinking of bands like Steel Pulse (UK), Aswad (UK), Soldiers of Jah Army (US), Big Mountain (US), Midnite (US), Christafari (US), John Brown's Body (US), Kana (France), Danakil (France), Kuie Hond (Netherlands), the Human Rights (Canada), Sawa (Japan), Nasio Fontaine (Dominica), Alpha Blondy (Côte d'Ivoire), Lucky Dube (South Africa), and Mo'kalamity and the Wizards (Cape Verde/France), to name a few.

This is no coincidence, of course. Bob Marley was the leader of the movement to globalize reggae, so it makes sense that he would be heavily influential on aspiring reggae artists who, perhaps, are not as familiar with the hundreds (if not thousands) of other Jamaicans to have recorded reggae since the mid-sixties. And because his music of liberation reached all the corners of the Earth, he became a compelling figure for oppressed peoples everywhere who have articulate diverse grievances and resisted all forms of oppression through the appropriation of sacred Rastafarian symbols such as Haile Selassie, dreadlocks, ganja and the African continent. This is evident in reggae groups such as Sequoia Crosswhite (Lakota Native Americans) and Unity Reggae Band (Maori), and also in Sinéad O'Connor's (Irish Catholic) Rasta-themed reggae album *Throw Down Your Arms*.

But it goes beyond this. It's almost as if Bob Marley = reggae.

Does Bob Marley = Reggae?

Haskins, in his book *One Love, One Heart*, sums up Marley's musical legacy this way: "Although there were numerous other talented reggae musicians, none captured the hearts and minds of people around the world as Bob Marley did. To many, Bob Marley *was* and still *is* reggae." Marley didn't just capture the hearts of minds of fans, he also captured the ears and pens of American music journalists, and they are the ones that had the power to make sure his name became synonymous with reggae.

Legendary *Creem* and *Rolling Stone* critic Lester Bangs was among a flotilla of American journalists and photographers whom Island Records flew to Kingston in 1976 to entice them into writing about Jamaican music, and, of course, heralding Bob Marley as a third-world poet-rebel-prophet. The American press was cool on reggae, but this all-expense-paid week in Jamaica kick-started real interest in it, cementing a love affair with Bob Marley. These journalists fanned the trend that Bob Marley's music is the most genuine expression of Jamaican reggae, and that any reggae that strays from its sound, themes, and look is somehow just plain inferior. Their articles positioned Bob Marley's brand of seventies Rasta-roots reggae as the flagship example of the genre.

The marketing campaign was so successful, however, that it arguably nearly crippled the reggae industry in the States after Marley died in 1981, because many American journalists stopped paying attention to reggae once Marley was gone from the scene. Some went searching for the next Bob Marley, but they found that the most popular stars in Jamaica were dancehall toasters like Yellowman, who made his name rapping vulgar boasts and raunchy bedroom lyrics over vinyl records—not a "real" musician in sight. This sounded (and looked) nothing like Marley's rebellious Rasta-reggae, and it fueled the argument in many critics' minds that Bob Marley's music epitomized the golden age of reggae, whereas dancehall was just a shallow and subpar distant cousin.

Foreign rock critics, who historically praised politically and socially engaged music from the folk revival (Bob Dylan, Joan Boaz) to the civil rights movement (Sam Cooke, Curtis Mayfield), and from psychedelic rock (Jimi Hendrix's "Star Spangled Banner," Jefferson Airplane's "Volunteers") to punk rock (the Clash, the Sex Pistols), but had no time for message-less disco ("Love to Love You Baby," "Stayin' Alive"), clean-cut Philly Soul (*Soul Train*, "Love Train"), or middle-of-the-road adult contemporary pop (David Cassidy, Captain and Tennille), had fallen in love with Marley's songs because they saw in them a mirror of their own countercultural values. Anything that didn't follow the Marley template was treated as rubbish.

Marley Good / Dancehall Bad

Lloyd Bradley's excellent history of reggae, *Bass Culture*, outlines how Marley's enormous crossover appeal into white markets had the effect that he came to represent reggae music for many people globally. So, because reggae was marketed internationally as Rasta music, international audiences associated Rasta-centric roots reggae with authenticity in the genre.

Dancehall photojournalist Beth Lesser saw firsthand how this had a detrimental effect on trying to break dancehall overseas. In her gorgeous coffee table book *Rise of Jamaican Dancehall Culture*, she argues that once this link was established, "It was hard to throw an entirely different model into the mix without getting resistance." In other words, American journalists weren't interested in any reggae that didn't look and sound like Bob Marley.

In *Wake the Town, Tell the People: Dancehall Culture in Jamaica*, Stolzoff remembers how journalists became gatekeepers of authenticity in reggae. "Reggae critics," he writes, "especially foreign-based ones, were nearly unanimous in their condemnation of the dancehall style, because the most popular songs of the new style were not inspired by the 'Rasta consciousness' that so many American and European counterculturalists had come to love and admire."

Burton, writing in *Afro-Creole: Power, Opposition, and Play in the Caribbean*, suggests that the dancehall music after Marley underwent a "de-Rastafarianization" that excised its potency. This went hand in hand with stylistic changes to the music and image shifts from "dreadlocked prophet-singer" to "designer-dressed DJ." For Burton, reggae in the eighties lacked the racial and political consciousness of the Wailers, so was therefore deemed less worthy.

Even in Jamaica, the nostalgic argument is often made that the music Marley played was more authentic than contemporary reggae. Sometimes, this has to do with the music's lyrics. A deputy police commissioner told the *Daily Gleaner* in 1987 that Marley's music "portrays hope and morality," in contrast to some dancehall that promotes drug use. (Perhaps he'd never heard Marley speak about ganja?) Other times, this is more centered on the idea of realness or authenticity. A police sergeant told the same newspaper that whereas contemporary dancehall was full of "stupidity," Marley's music was "real, real, real."

In 1989, the *Daily Gleaner* carried a story entitled, "Can Reggae Music Bounce Back?" It reported, "The consensus is that reggae music has been going through a dry spell. Within the reggae scene the death of Marley in 1981 is widely held to have abruptly halted the music's extraordinary development from an indigenous Jamaican dance form into the profound expression of an international black consciousness . . . With Marley's demise, the music, as a coherent cultural phenomenon seemed to lose momentum."

This is not unlike rock journalists of the same period trumpeting rock as art and disco and rap as manufactured crap. In this case, though, dancehall was the genre that critics positioned in opposition to Marley's roots reggae, even though dancehall has dominated the Jamaican industry since Marley's death.

For these critics, dancehall is understood as a less complex music form than its predecessors. Writing in *Sound Recording Reviews*, musicologist Rick Anderson makes a typical judgment about reggae after Marley: "As electronic percussion and synthesizers pushed guitarists, bass players, and wind players from the studio, reggae's rhythms became more minimalist and more robotic; in some cases, entire songs were built on an aggressive and unchanging three-against-two triplet pattern."

If you're following along, this means that authentic reggae should be roots reggae, not dancehall, socially conscious, not bacchanal, and played by Rastafarian musicians from Jamaica. Who do we know that fits this profile? Mr. Marley.

The Reggae Grammy or the Marley Grammy?

A sheer monopoly of the Marley brand over the reggae Grammy is suggestive that the popular music establishment still sees the Marley brand as "authentic" reggae; it is the yardstick by which to measure all others. The Grammys represent acceptance into the mainstream American pop market—something that has eluded most reggae artists not connected with the Marley brand. As you will see in the Grammy chapter of this book, over half of the reggae Grammys given out have gone to artists associated in some way with Marley (family or musicians that played with him in the Wailers).

This dominance of Marley over all things reggae might seem fine if you're a reggae fan from Bangor, Maine; Lyon, France; or Quito, Ecuador. But what if you're a bona fide reggae star in Jamaica who is routinely ignored by the international community because they stopped paying attention to reggae after Marley died?

Dancehall dominator Buju Banton, who consistently topped the charts in Jamaica during the nineties and 2000s, once complained to a Kingston newspaper that the public's fixation on Marley as authentic reggae has hurt dancehall's growth because all new artists are compared to Marley. He also told a crowd at the University of the West Indies in Kingston, "You know, they say that the greatest musician in Jamaica is Bob Marley. I don't believe that because we have greater musicians to come. Bob was the most promoted, and well promoted, and we have to appreciate that because it's our culture. But don't kill our culture . . . Enough is enough."

While he was subsequently heavily criticized by many Marley fans, including Ziggy Marley, Banton's point was not that Marley was unworthy of the attention, but rather that contemporary and future Jamaican musicians shouldn't have to live in his shadow. So maybe there's a negative side to the global popularity of Bob Marley after all.

But Isn't Bob Marley's Music Actually Authentic Reggae?

This whole discussion, including the title King of Reggae, assumes that what Bob Marley played was, in fact, reggae. Reggae is a genre of popular music invented in Jamaica and derived from earlier forms of Jamaican music such as rocksteady, ska, and mento. It is uniquely Jamaican. But much of Bob Marley's music of the seventies was anything but fully Jamaican. As an innovative musician interested in broadening his appeal and succeeding on the world stage, he was open to foreign musical influences that would make his music more appealing to white rock fans. Working with Island Records' Chris Blackwell, Marley's musical innovations included expanding his songwriting structures and instrumentation to reflect American and British rock and soul, increasing the role of the electric guitar by using American blues guitarists in the Wailers (Wayne Perkins, Al Anderson and Donald Kinsey), and even presenting the Wailers as a sort of rock "band" instead of a vocal group.

This last point may seem insignificant, but in the Jamaican context it is quite important, because it highlights how the composing and recording method of the Wailers differed from traditional Jamaican reggae. By the early seventies, Jamaican hits were virtually all based on the versioning practice, where studio bands recorded backing tracks, or riddims, that were then recycled several times by new vocalists. This enabled producers to create multiple songs with minimal financial investment, as they only paid once for a backing track. Bob Marley, on the other hand, wrote and recorded music with his own band starting in the early seventies, which meant that each song had a completely unique musical backing. Just to reiterate—this is how American rock was written and recorded, but not Jamaican reggae.

It bears noting that Island Records was aware it was constructing an air of authenticity around Bob Marley and the Wailers. Chris Blackwell knowingly left white American musicians off the credits for *Catch a Fire* in order to not diminish the authenticity of an all-black Jamaican band.

This is not to say that reggae traditionally bore no international influences. Jamaican popular music of the sixties and beyond was heavily influenced by black American music in particular, and less so by other genres like country and even British Invasion rock (to the extent that many Jamaican artists covered the Beatles: check out the Harry J. All Stars' "Don't Let Me Down," which will not, in fact, let you down). But the point is that Marley's music was quite different from much of the music played in Jamaica in the seventies because of his rock-reggae hybrid in structure, sound, and recording method.

Was Marley the King of Reggae in Jamaica?

No. While he was an influential and well-loved public figure, there were reggae artists that were more popular than he was back in Jamaica. Bob's international celebrity grew feverishly after his shooting in 1976 and the 1977 release of *Exodus*, but at home he rarely had best-selling records. Jamaicans preferred the homegrown true Jamaican sound to the international reggae now purveyed by Marley.

The year-end Jamaican charts from Marley's last four years—when he was really making waves internationally—are instructive here. In 1978, his only song in the chart was "Blackman Redemption," at #25. The following year he did a little better, getting "Ambush in the Night" to the #24 position. In 1980, "One Drop" reached #4, while "Bad Card" sat at #25, although it showed up again at #15 in 1981. But that's not exactly a powerful showing in his one's backyard.

But Jamaican audiences had hundreds of other artists to choose from. Artists who were consistently more popular than Bob Marley, according to the charts, included Dennis Brown, Culture, Jacob Miller, and Beres Hammond. In fact, Bradley says that Johnny Clarke was the top roots reggae singer for the second half of the decade in Jamaica, not Bob Marley. But I'm betting most of the reggae fans around the world have never heard of him (if this means you, fix this right away and check out his righteous "None Shall Escape the Judgement.")

With bigger markets to contend with, Marley didn't spend much time catering to the quickly evolving musical trends in Jamaica during his international years. For instance, local releases generally had dub mixes on the B-sides of singles—something Marley singles usually omitted in favor of another album track, as was common in the American market.

Marley was somewhat mindful of how the sound of reggae was changing back home, however, and he didn't want to seem out of touch. Whereas the vast majority of his seventies songs use the one drop drum beat, it was starting to sound outmoded next to the new rockers sound that was driven by Sly Dunbar's heavier stepper's rhythm. Marley hired Dunbar to bring this contemporary beat to his "Punky Reggae Party" as a way to let his audience know he was still relevant on his home turf. He also continued to make available exclusive mixes of songs for local sound systems, called dub plates. Collingwood lists the

Wailers' known dub plates, released and unreleased, in *Bob Marley: His Musical Legacy*, and says that the mixes on these tracks were far "rootsier" than the radio releases, probably meaning bass-heavy.

So, the music Bob Marley played in the seventies wasn't exactly Jamaican reggae. Or, perhaps a better way to put it is that his seventies material was a different kind of reggae than the rest of Jamaica was making at the time. It was a hybrid of Jamaican reggae, American soul, blues, and rock. But it was this rebellious sound that became what non-Jamaicans thought of—and loved—when they thought of reggae. Foreign critics fell in love with his rock-reggae hybrid, too, and they didn't appreciate reggae music that strayed from this.

Ain't Nothing Like the Real Thing

So far, I've tried to convince you that Bob Marley isn't authentic reggae. Now I'm going to try and convince you of the opposite. By the late sixties and early seventies, reggae was making in-roads in the British charts. Trojan Records launched its *Tighten Up* series in 1969, and, while this series did well with the skinhead subculture, which helped put the second installment at #2 in the charts, rockers found songs like Val Bennett's "Spanish Harlem," Joya Landis's "Angel of the Morning," Dandy's "Reggae in Your Jeggae," and Max Romeo's "Wet Dream" quaint and kitschy.

In contrast, the material most British audiences first heard from Marley in 1972—"Concrete Jungle," "Slave Driver," "No More Trouble"—was street-smart, gritty, and sounded to them how they imagined the slums of Jamaica sounded. Island Records bargained that there was a hunger for what it called authentic reggae, meaning music that wasn't making concessions to the pop marketplace. Motown was slammed by rock critics in the sixties for this very sin—it was felt that the label had somehow watered down black music to make it appeal to the white mainstream (because, you know, it was polished and well-produced— that's called using professional recording techniques, not whiteness).

Rock historians will tell you that African-Americans invented the major pop genres of the twentieth century—blues, rock 'n' roll, disco, hip-hop—but in each case struggled to cross over to mainstream white audiences because white artists appropriated their styles with greater success. The Rolling Stones and Eric Clapton capitalized on the blues and then sold it back to Americans; Elvis borrowed songs from blues and R&B singers like Arthur Crudup ("That's Alright Mama") and Roy Brown ("Good Rockin' Tonight"), and was the first rock 'n' roll singer to score a major label contract, eclipsing black rock 'n' rollers like Chuck Berry and Little Richard. Disco came out of black soul music with early hits by Donna Summer and Gloria Gaynor, but by 1977 most white fans thought that the

Bob Marley, the reggae legend.   *Wence Godard*

Australian/British Bee Gees invented disco. Hip-hop started in the Bronx with deejays like Kool Herc and Grandmaster Flash, but over a decade later the Beastie Boys had the first *Billboard* #1 with a rap album (*Licensed to Ill*, 1986).

Jamaica Is the Real Thing

So, even though on one hand I'm suggesting that Bob Marley's music wasn't the same as the rest of Jamaican reggae in the seventies, on the other hand I'm saying that authenticity in the genre is still connected to blackness and Jamaicanness thanks to Bob Marley's domination of reggae in the hearts and minds of fans all over the globe. This has ensured that reggae connected to the black Jamaican experience—such as being produced by Jamaicans in Jamaica—has the most cultural authenticity. There has so far been no Elvis, Eric Clapton, Bee Gees, or Beastie Boys of reggae popular enough to dislodge reggae from the geography and culture of Jamaica. Thank goodness.

Selected Bibliography

Many resources were used to research *Bob Marley FAQ*, including magazines, newspapers, journal articles, websites, liner notes, documentaries, and books. I am indebted to Gerald Hausman for his help in tracking down Bob Marley quotes. Below is a list of many of the sources used in this book, with an emphasis on the full-length books on Bob Marley. There are so many books on him, in fact, that Joe Jurgensen has even published an annotated bibliography that keeps track of them all. There are several entertaining and informative biographies of Bob Marley, in particular Stephen Davis's *Bob Marley: Conquering Lion of Reggae*, from which most subsequent biographies crib heavily. But the world authority on Bob Marley is Roger Steffens, who not only toured with Bob at one point but has also started a reggae radio show (*Reggae Beat*), spearheaded a reggae magazine (*The Beat*), written liner notes, given lectures, and published numerous reggae histories (including an oral history of Bob Marley) and the definitive discography of Bob Marley and the Wailers. It would be a weak Bob Marley project indeed that did not owe a great debt to the tireless work of Roger Steffens in collecting, documenting, and presenting the oral and material culture associated with Jamaican music.

Abu-Jamal, Mumia. "Bob Marley Interview." Philadelphia, Pennsylvania: WHYY, November 1979.

Agentofchange. " Tribute to the Revolutionary Poet Bob Marley." *Beat Knowledge* (blog), May 11, 2011. www.beatknowledge.org/2011/05/11/a-tribute-to-bob -marley-revolutionary-poet/

Anderson, Rick. "Reggae Music: A History and Selective Discography." *Sound Recording Reviews* 61, no. 1, 2004.

Austin-Broos, Diane J. *Jamaica Genesis: Religion and the Politics of Moral Orders.* Chicago: University of Chicago Press, 1997.

Barrat, Patrick. "Bob Marley Interview in Tuff Gong, Jamaica." 1980. www.marley site.com/interview/barrat.htm

Barrow, Steve, and Paul Coot. *Mento Madness.* V2 Records, 2004.

Barrow, Steve, Peter Dalton, and Various. *The Rough Guide to Reggae.* London: Rough Guides, 2004.

Bellanfante, Dwight. "Gov't Will Challenge Any Request to Move Marley." *Jamaica Observer*, February 8, 2005.

Benjamin, Eric. "Bob Marley: Reggae Is Another Bag." July 9, 1975. http://rastafusion .free.fr/bobspeech.htm

Bilby, Kenneth. *Words of Our Mouth, Meditations of Our Heart: Pioneering Musicians of Ska, Rocksteady, Reggae, and Dancehall.* Middletown, Connecticut: Wesleyan, 2016.

Blake-Hannah, Barbara. "Bob Marley and Ethiopia." *Jamaica Observer*, February 26, 2005.

Booker, Cedella Marley, and Anthony C. Winkler. *Bob Marley, My Son.* Taylor Trade Publishing, 2015.

Boyne, Ian. "Bob Marley as National Hero." *Gleaner*, February 8, 2015.

Bradley, Lloyd. *Reggae on CD: The Essential Guide.* Trafalgar Square Publishing, 1995.

Bradley, Lloyd. *This Is Reggae Music: The Story of Jamaica's Music.* New York: Grove Press, 2000.

Burrell, Ian. "Why Bob Marley Can't Rest in Peace." *Independent*, February 1, 2005.

Burton, Richard D. E. *Afro-Creole: Power, Opposition, and Play in the Caribbean.* Ithaca, New York: Cornell University Press, 1997.

Campbell, Horace. *Rasta and Resistance.* London: Hansib Publishing, 2008.

Carnegie, Charles V. "The Dundus and the Nation." *Cultural Anthropology* 11, no. 4, 1996.

Carolyn, Yawney. "Dread Wasteland: Rastafarian Ritual in West Kingston, Jamaica." In Crumrine, N. Ross (ed.), *Ritual Symbolism and Ceremonialism in the Americas: Studies in Symbolic Anthropology.* Occasional Publications in Anthropology: Ethnology Series; no. 33. Greeley, Colorado: Museum of Anthropology, University of Northern Colorado, 1978.

Cathro, Jeff and Eugenia Polos. "Exclusive Bob Marley Interview." *Berkeley Barb*, July 1977.

Chang, Kevin O'Brien, and Wayne Chen. *Reggae Routes: The Story of Jamaican Music.* Philadelphia: Temple University Press, 1998.

Chevannes, Barry. *Rastafari: Roots and Ideology.* Syracuse, New York: Syracuse University Press, 1994.

Clarke, John Henrik (ed.). *Marcus Garvey and the Vision of Africa.* Black Classic Press, 2011.

Coleman, Wanda. "Marley Talks About Jamaica." *Los Angeles Free Press*, December 21, 1973.

Collingwood, Jeremy. *Bob Marley: His Musical Legacy.* London: Cassell, 2008.

Constantine, Alex. *The Covert War Against Rock: What You Don't Know About the Deaths of Jim Morrison, Tupac Shakur, Michael Hutchence, Brian Jones, Jimi Hendrix, Phil Ochs, Bob Marley, Peter Tosh, John Lennon, and the Notorious B.I.G.* Venice: Feral House, 2000.

Cooke, Mel. "'Diseases' Was Never about Polio Outbreak Song Written after Go-Go Club Visit." *Gleaner*, June 19, 2011.

Cooper, Carol. "Tuff Gong: Bob Marley's Unsung Story." *Village Voice*, September 10, 1980.

Cooper, Carolyn. *Sound Clash: Jamaican Dancehall Culture at Large*. Palgrave Macmillan, 2004.

Cronon, E. David. *Black Moses: The Story of Marcus Garvey and the Universal Negro Improvement Association*. Wisconsin: University of Wisconsin Press, 1998.

Cumbo, Fikisha. *Bob Marley and Peter Tosh Get Up! Stand Up! Diary of a Reggaeophile*. Brooklyn, Cace Intl Inc., 2003.

Dallas, Karl. "Bob Marley: 'What We Need Is Some Positive Vibration.'" *Melody Maker*, July 19, 1975.

Davis, Angela. "How Much Do You Know About What Killed Bob Marley?" *Jamaica Observer*, November 19, 2016.

Davis, Stephen. *Bob Marley: Conquering Lion of Reggae*. London: Plexus Publishing, 2008.

Davis, Stephen, and Peter Simon. *Reggae International*. London: Thames and Hudson Ltd., 1983.

Davis, Stephen, Peter Simon, et al. *Reggae Bloodlines: In Search of the Music and Culture of Jamaica*. London: Heinemann International Literature and Textbooks, 1979.

Dawes, Kwame. *Bob Marley: Lyrical Genius*. London: Bobcat Books, 2010.

Douglas, Dave. "Bob Marley and Jacob Miller: 'God Black' Interview." March 21, 1980. https://marleyarkives.wordpress.com/2014/04/20/bob-marley-interview-st-maarten-march-1980/

Dunitz, Mike, and Marc Gregory. "Natty Dread in Babylon: Interview with Bob Marley and the Wailers." *Ann Arbor Sun*, June 20, 1975.

Edmonds, Ennis Barrington. *Rastafari: From Outcasts to Cultural Bearers*. Oxford: Oxford University Press, 2008.

Epstein, Brian. *A Cellarful of Noise*. Souvenir Press, 2011.

Farley, Christopher. *Before the Legend: The Rise of Bob Marley*. New York: Amistad, 2007.

Fergusson, Isaac. "So Much Things to Say: The Journey of Bob Marley." *Village Voice*, May 18, 1982.

Gallardo, Angelica. "Get Up, Stand Up." *Peace Review* 15, no. 2, June 1, 2003.

Garcia, Guy, and E. Thigpen David. "Marley's Ghost." *Time*, September 13, 1993.

Garvey, Amy Jacques. *More Philosophy and Opinions of Marcus Garvey*. London: Routledge, 1977.

Garvey, Julius. "Pardon My Father, Mr. President." CNN Opinion, November 23, 2016. www.cnn.com/2016/11/22/opinions/marcus-garvey-should-have-a-presidential-pardon-garvey/index.html

Garvey, Marcus; Robert A. Hill and Barbara Blair (eds.). *Marcus Garvey Life and Lessons: A Centennial Companion to the Marcus Garvey and Universal Negro Improvement Association Papers.* University of California Press, 1987.

Garvey, Marcus. *Philosophy and Opinions of Marcus Garvey.* Martino Fine Books, 2014.

Gilroy, Paul. "Could You Be Loved? Bob Marley, Anti-Politics and Universal Sufferation." *Critical Quarterly* 47, no. 1–2, July 2005.

Goldman, Vivien. "Bob Marley: In His Own Backyard." *Melody Maker*, August 11, 1979.

Goldman, Vivien. *The Book of Exodus: The Making and Meaning of Bob Marley and the Wailers' Album of the Century.* New York: Three Rivers Press, 2006.

Grant, Colin. *I and I: The Nature Mystics.* London: Jonathan Cape, 2011.

Grass, Randall. *Great Spirits: Portraits of Life-Changing World Music Artists.* Jackson: University Press of Mississippi, 2009.

Greenberg, Alan. *Land of Look Behind.* Subversive Cinema, 2007.

Gross, Terry. "Interview with Curtis Mayfield." *Fresh Air.* NPR, 1993.

Gunst, Laurie. *Born Fi' Dead.* Edinburgh: Canongate Books Ltd, 2003.

Gutzmore, Cecil. "Casting the First Stone!: Policing of Homo/Sexuality in Jamaican Popular Culture." *Interventions* 6, no. 1, April 1, 2004.

Hagerman, Brent. Interview with Aston "Familyman" Barrett, 2003.

Hagerman, Brent. Interview with Imani Carole Anne, 2016.

Hagerman, Brent. Interview with Sly Dunbar, 2006.

Hagerman, Brent. "Ziggy Marley Interview." *Spinner Magazine*, June 6, 2011.

Harris, Trevor. "Reports in Sports 'n' Arts." *Gleaner*, 1987.

Haskins, James. *One Love, One Heart: A History of Reggae.* Jump at the Sun, 2002.

Hatch, John. "Jamaicans See CIA Behind the Bullets." *Chicago Tribune*, June 4, 1976.

Hebdige, Dick. *Cut 'n' Mix: Culture, Identity, and Caribbean Music.* London: Comedia, 1987.

Hebdige, Dick. *Reggae Rastas and Rudies: Style and the Subversion of Form.* Centre for Contemporary Cultural Studies, University of Birmingham, 1974.

Henke, James. *Marley Legend: An Illustrated Life of Bob Marley.* San Francisco: Chronicle Books, 2006.

Henke, James. "Marley Speaks" in *Marley Legend: An Illustrated Life of Bob Marley.* CD. San Francisco: Chronicle Books, 2006.

Hill, Robert A. "Redemption Works: From 'African Redemption' to 'Redemption Song.'" *Review: Literature and Arts of the Americas* 43, no. 2, November 1, 2010.

Hurford, Ray. "History of Version." *The Small Axe People.* Accessed August 6, 2017. www.smallaxepeople.com/History%20Of%20Version.htm

Jaffe, Lee, and Roger Steffens. *One Love: Life with Bob Marley and the Wailers.* New York: W. W. Norton and Company, 2003.

Johnson, Linton Kwesi. "Roots and Rock: The Marley Enigma." *Race Today* 7, no. 10, October 1975.

Johnson, Richard. "Late Reggae Icon's Family Orders Singer to Stop Using Bob's Name." *Jamaica Observer*, May 31, 2014.

Jurgensen, Joe. "Are These Songs Related to Homosexuality?" *Soulrebels* (blog). www.soulrebels.org/dancehall/w_list_songs_maybe_or_not.htm

Katz, David. *People Funny Boy: The Genius of Lee "Scratch" Perry*. London: Omnibus Press, 2006.

Katz, David. *Solid Foundation: An Oral History of Reggae*. London: Jawbone Press, 2012.

Katz, William Loren. "Review of 'Black Power and the Garvey Movement.'" *The Journal of Negro History* 57, no. 1, 1972.

Krebs, Albin. "Jamaican Bandleader Bob Marley Pleads Guilty to Possession of Marijuana." *New York Times*, April 7, 1977.

Kulwicki, Cara. "Yoko Ono: A Feminist Analysis (Introduction: Oh Yoko!)." *The Curvature* (blog), December 15, 2008. https://thecurvature.wordpress.com/2008/12/15/yoko-ono-a-feminist -analysis-introduction-oh-yoko/

LaFont, Suzanne. "Very Straight Sex: The Development of Sexual Mores in Jamaica." *Journal of Colonialism and Colonial History* 2, no. 3, December 26, 2001.

Lee, Hélène, and Stephen Davis. *The First Rasta: Leonard Howell and the Rise of Rastafarianism*. Chicago: Chicago Review Press, 2004.

Lesser, Beth. *Dancehall: The Rise of Jamaican Dancehall Culture*. London: Soul Jazz Books, 2017.

Lindsay, Keisha, and Louis Lindsay. "Bob Marley and the Politics of Subversion." In *Bob Marley—the Man and His Music*, edited by Eleanor Wint and Carolyn Cooper. Kingston, Jamaica: Arawak Publications, 2006.

MacDonald, Kevin. *Marley*. DVD. Magnolia Home Entertainment, 2012.

Manuel, Peter, Kenneth Bilby, and Michael Largey. *Caribbean Currents: Caribbean Music from Rumba to Reggae*. Philadelphia: Temple University Press, 2006.

Marley, Bob, and Gerald Hausman. *The Future Is the Beginning: The Words and Wisdom of Bob Marley*. New York: Crown Archetype, 2012.

Marley, Rita. "Remembering Bob Marley." *Essence*, February 1995.

Marley, Rita, and Hettie Jones. *No Woman No Cry: My Life with Bob Marley*. New York: Hachette Books, 2005.

Marr, Jeremy. *Rebel Music*. Island Def Jam Music Group, 2001.

Masouri, John. *Simmer Down: The Early Wailers Story*. Brighton: Jook Joint Press, 2015.

Masouri, John. *Steppin' Razor: The Life of Peter Tosh*. London: Omnibus Press, 2013.

Masouri, John. *Wailing Blues: The Story of Bob Marley's Wailers*. London: Omnibus Press, 2008.

M'bayo, Tamba E. "W. E. B. Du Bois, Marcus Garvey, and Pan-Africanism in Liberia, 1919–1924." *The Historian* 66, no. 1, March 1, 2004.

McCann, Ian, and Harry Hawke. *Bob Marley: The Complete Guide to His Music*. London: Omnibus Press, 2004.

McCormack, Ed. "Bob Marley with a Bullet." *Rolling Stone*, August 12, 1976.

McDowell, Deborah E. "Lines of Descent/Dissenting Lines." In Hurston, Zora Neale, *Moses, Man of the Mountain*. New York: Harper Perennial, 1991.

Meldrum, Ian. "Interview with Bob Marley." *Nightmoves*. 1979

Mervis, Scott. "Reggae Legend's Final Concert, 30 Years Ago in Pittsburgh, Will Be Remembered with Tribute." *Pittsburgh Post-Gazette*, September 23, 2010.

Mitchell, Anthony. "Ethiopia Reburial for Bob Marley." *Guardian*, January 13, 2005.

Mordecai, Martin, and Pamela Mordecai. *Culture and Customs of Jamaica*. Westport, Connecticut: Greenwood, 2000.

Moskowitz, David V. *Bob Marley: A Biography*. Greenwood Press, 2007.

Parkinson, Mike, and Ray Santilli. *Spiritual Journey*. WHE International, 2003.

Pierson, Leroy Jodie, and Roger Steffens. *Bob Marley and the Wailers: The Definitive Discography*. Cambridge: Rounder Books, 2005.

Raines, Ros. "Master Blaster and the Real Babylon: Bob Marley Talks to Ros Raines."

Richardson, Brian. "Bob Marley: Roots Revolutionary." *Socialist Review*, January 2002.

Rojas, Don. "Bob Marley Breezes Through the Apple with the Kingdom of Jah on His Mind." *New York Amsterdam News*, March 25, 1978.

Roper, Matt. "The Dark Side of the Reggae Superstar: My Husband Bob Marley Raped Me." *Mirror*, March 31, 2004.

Salewicz, Chris. *Bob Marley: The Untold Story*. London: Farrar, Straus and Giroux, 2011.

Salewicz, Chris, and Adrian Boot. *Reggae Explosion*. Urbanimage Media Ltd., 2013.

Schluter, Nancy Hurd. "Marcus Garvey as Theologian." Drew University, 2001.

Schuler, Monica. *Alas, Alas, Kongo: A Social History of Indentured African Immigration into Jamaica, 1841–1865*. Baltimore: Johns Hopkins University Press, 1980.

Senior, Olive. *Encyclopedia of Jamaican Heritage*. Saint Andrew, Jamaica: Twin Guinep Ltd, 2003.

Sheridan, Maureen. *Bob Marley: The Stories Behind Every Song*. London: Carlton, 2011.

Shuker, Roy. *Understanding Popular Music Culture*. London; New York: Routledge, 2016.

Slone, Thomas H. *Rasta Is Cuss: A Dictionary of Rastafarian Cursing*. Oakland, California: Masalai Press, 2003.

Spencer, Neil. "Exclusive Words with Bob Marley: Natural Mystic." *New Musical Express*, April 23, 1977.

Steffens, Roger. *So Much Things to Say: The Oral History of Bob Marley*. New York: W. W. Norton, 2017.

Stern, Marlow. "Ziggy Marley on Legend Bob Marley's Tough Love." *Daily Beast*, June 17, 2011.

Stewart, Dianne M. *Three Eyes for the Journey: African Dimensions of the Jamaican Religious Experience*. Oxford; New York: Oxford University Press, 2004.

Stewart, James B. "Message in the Music: Political Commentary in Black Popular Music from Rhythm and Blues to Early Hip Hop." *The Journal of African American History* 90, no. 3, Summer 2005.

Stolzoff, Norman C. *Wake the Town and Tell the People: Dancehall Culture in Jamaica*. Durham, North Carolina: Duke University Press, 2000.

Taite, Dylan. "Bob Marley Interview." Aotearoa, New Zealand. 1979.

Taylor, Don. *Marley and Me: The Real Bob Marley Story*. New York: Barricade Books, 1995.

Thomas, Jo. "With Pride and Music, Jamaicans Bury Bob Marley." *New York Times*, May 22, 1981.

Toynbee, Jason. *Bob Marley: Herald of a Postcolonial World?* Cambridge: Polity, 2007.

Tudor, Trystan Jones and Genevieve. "World War One: Bob Marley's Father 'Neurotic and Incontinent.'" *BBC News*, August 4, 2014. www.bbc.com/news/uk-england-27426329

Vincent, Rickey. *Funk: The Music, the People, and the Rhythm of the One*. New York: St. Martin's Griffin, 2014.

Wailer, Bunny Livingston. "Wailers Trilogy: Robbery—Conspiracy—Murder." *Wailers Legacy* (blog), November 26, 2011. http://wailerslegacy.blogspot.com

Wailer, Bunny Livingston. "21st Century Jezebel: The Conspiracy on The Wailers Family." *21st Century Jezebel—Rita* (blog), March 30, 2012. http://tuffgongre-cords.blogspot.ca/

Wailer, Bunny Livingston. "Abandoned and a Ban Done! Rita Anderson Jarrett Could Never Be a Marley." *21st Century Jezebel—Rita* (blog), June 24, 2013. http://tuffgongrecords.blogspot.ca/

Wailer, Bunny Livingston. "To The World and Fans of the Wailers." *21st Century Jezebel—Rita* (blog), June 7, 2013. http://tuffgongrecords.blogspot.ca/

Walters, Basil. "Govt, Society Want to Separate Bob Marley from Rasta—Mutabaruka." *Jamaica Observer*, February 22, 2005.

Waters, Anita. "Bob Marley: A Final Interview." September 18, 1980. http://webby.cc.denison.edu/~waters/marley.html

Welch, Chris. *Bob Marley*. Music Book Services Paperbacks, 1996.

White, Jim. "Reggae's New Breed." *Gleaner*, August 13, 1990.

White, Timothy. "Bob Marley | Jamaican Musician." *Encyclopedia Britannica*. www.britannica.com/biography/Bob-Marley

White, Timothy. *Catch a Fire: The Life of Bob Marley*. New York: Holt Paperbacks, 2006.

Whitney, Malika Lee, Dermott Hussey, and Rita Marley. *Bob Marley: Reggae King of the World*. San Francisco: Pomegranate Commun-ications, 1994.

Williams, Andrea. "Interview with Dr. Vernon Carrington: The Beloved Prophet Gad." *Running African*. IRIE FM, 1997.

Williams, Carol J. "Marley Grave Dispute Has Little Peace, Love: Wife Wants Remains Moved to Ethiopia." *Los Angeles Times*, February 6, 2005.

Williams, Joan E. *Original Dancehall Dictionary: Talk Like a Jamaican*. Kingston, Jamaica: Yard Publications, 2015.

Williams, Richard. "The First Genius of Reggae?" *Melody Maker*, February 24, 1973.

Willis, Tom. "From Ragga to Riches." *Sunday Times* (London), April 4, 1993.

Willoughby, Neville. *Bob Marley Interviews: So Much Things to Say*. Ras Records, 1995.

Wolfert, Lee. "Jamaica Gold? That's Bob Marley's Looming Record Sale, Not Just What He Smokes." *People*, April 26, 1976.

———. "Bob Marley's Daughters—Cedella and Karen Marley Talk 'Marley.'" Accessed May 24, 2018. www.youtube.com/watch?v=V8dxNJF8Fbo

———. "Bob Marley Is Not the Greatest Musician—Buju." *Jamaica Observer*, April 27, 2009.

———. "Bob Marley Was Anti-homosexual." www.18karatreggae.com/2015/05/03/bob-marley-was-anti-homosexual/

———. "Interview in Zurich, 1980—Bob Marley | Videos." Accessed May 24, 2018. www.bobmarley.com/media/videos/interviews-docs/interview-zurich-1980/

———. Liner Notes to Bob Marley and the Wailers, *Early Music*. Calla Records, 1977.

———. "Reggae Songs in Anglican Hymnal." *New York Times*, August 7, 2007.

———. "This Man Is Seeing God." *High Times Magazine*, September 1976.

Index

THE FAQ SERIES

AC/DC FAQ
by Susan Masino
Backbeat Books
9781480394506...$24.99

Armageddon Films FAQ
by Dale Sherman
Applause Books
9781617131196.........$24.99

The Band FAQ
by Peter Aaron
Backbeat Books
9781617136139 ....$19.99

Baseball FAQ
by Tom DeMichael
Backbeat Books
9781617136061........$24.99

The Beach Boys FAQ
by Jon Stebbins
Backbeat Books
9780879309879..$22.99

The Beat Generation FAQ
by Rich Weidman
Backbeat Books
9781617136016 ....$19.99

Beer FAQ
by Jeff Cioletti
Backbeat Books
9781617136115 ....$24.99

Black Sabbath FAQ
by Martin Popoff
Backbeat Books
9780879309572....$19.99

Bob Dylan FAQ
by Bruce Pollock
Backbeat Books
9781617136078 ......$19.99

Britcoms FAQ
by Dave Thompson
Applause Books
9781495018992 ....$19.99

Bruce Springsteen FAQ
by John D. Luerssen
Backbeat Books
9781617130939.......$22.99

Buffy the Vampire Slayer FAQ
by David Bushman and Arthur Smith
Applause Books
9781495064722.....$19.99

Cabaret FAQ
by June Sawyers
Applause Books
9781495051449......$19.99

A Chorus Line FAQ
by Tom Rowan
Applause Books
9781480367548 ...$19.99

The Clash FAQ
by Gary J. Jucha
Backbeat Books
9781480364509 ..$19.99

Doctor Who Faq
by Dave Thompson
Applause Books
9781557838544....$22.99

The Doors FAQ
by Rich Weidman
Backbeat Books
9781617130175.......$24.99

Dracula FAQ
by Bruce Scivally
Backbeat Books
9781617136009 .....$19.99

The Eagles FAQ
by Andrew Vaughan
Backbeat Books
9781480385412.....$24.99

Elvis Films FAQ
by Paul Simpson
Applause Books
9781557838582.....$24.99

Elvis Music FAQ
by Mike Eder
Backbeat Books
9781617130496......$22.99

Eric Clapton FAQ
by David Bowling
Backbeat Books
9781617134548 .....$22.99

Fab Four FAQ
by Stuart Shea and Robert Rodriguez
Hal Leonard Books
9781423421382.......$19.99

Fab Four FAQ 2.0
by Robert Rodriguez
Backbeat Books
9780879309688...$19.99

Film Noir FAQ
by David J. Hogan
Applause Books
9781557838551......$22.99

Football FAQ
by Dave Thompson
Backbeat Books
9781495007484...$24.99

Frank Zappa FAQ
by John Corcelli
Backbeat Books
9781617136030.......$19.99

Godzilla FAQ
by Brian Solomon
Applause Books
9781495045684 $19.99

The Grateful Dead FAQ
by Tony Sclafani
Backbeat Books
9781617130861........$24.99

Guns N' Roses FAQ
by Rich Weidman
Backbeat Books
9781495025884 ..$19.99

Haunted America FAQ
by Dave Thompson
Backbeat Books
9781480392625.....$19.99

Horror Films FAQ
by John Kenneth Muir
Applause Books
9781557839503....$22.99

Jack the Ripper FAQ
by Dave Thompson
Applause Books
9781495063084....$19.99

James Bond FAQ
by Tom DeMichael
Backbeat Books
9781557838568.....$22.99

Jimi Hendrix FAQ
by Gary J. Jucha
Backbeat Books
9781617130953.......$22.99

Johnny Cash FAQ
by C. Eric Banister
Backbeat Books
9781480385405..$24.99

KISS FAQ
by Dale Sherman
Backbeat Books
9781617130915........$24.99

Led Zeppelin FAQ
by George Case
Backbeat Books
9781617130250......$22.99

Lucille Ball FAQ
by James Sheridan and Barry Monush
Applause Books
9781617740824.......$19.99

MASH FAQ
by Dale Sherman
Applause Books
9781480355897.....$19.99

Michael Jackson FAQ
by Kit O'Toole
Backbeat Books
9781480371064 ..... $19.99

Modern Sci-Fi Films FAQ
by Tom DeMichael
Applause Books
9781480350618 .... $24.99

Monty Python FAQ
by Chris Barsanti,
Brian Cogan, and Jeff
Massey
Applause Books
9781495049439 .. $19.99

Morrissey FAQ
by D. McKinney
Backbeat Books
9781480394483... $24.99

Neil Young FAQ
by Glen Boyd
Backbeat Books
9781617130373 .... $19.99

Nirvana FAQ
by John D. Luerssen
Backbeat Books
9781617134500 ...... $24.99

Pearl Jam FAQ
by Bernard M. Corbett
and Thomas Edward
Harkins
Backbeat Books
9781617136122 .... $19.99

Pink Floyd FAQ
by Stuart Shea
Backbeat Books
9780879309503... $19.99

Pro Wrestling FAQ
by Brian Solomon
Backbeat Books
9781617135996....... $29.99

Prog Rock FAQ
by Will Romano
Backbeat Books
9781617135873 ...... $24.99

Quentin Tarantino FAQ
by Dale Sherman
Applause Books
9781480355880... $24.99

Rent FAQ
by Tom Rowan
Applause Books
9781495051456...... $19.99

Robin Hood FAQ
by Dave Thompson
Applause Books
9781495048227 ... $19.99

The Rocky Horror Picture Show FAQ
by Dave Thompson
Applause Books
9781495007477 ..... $19.99

Rush FAQ
by Max Mobley
Backbeat Books
9781617134517 .... $19.99

Saturday Night Live FAQ
by Stephen Tropiano
Applause Books
9781557839510...... $24.99

Seinfeld FAQ
by Nicholas Nigro
Applause Books
9781557838575..... $24.99

Sherlock Holmes FAQ
by Dave Thompson
Applause Books
9781480331495..... $24.99

The Smiths FAQ
by John D. Luerssen
Backbeat Books
9781480394490... $24.99

Soccer FAQ
by Dave Thompson
Backbeat Books
9781617135989....... $24.99

The Sound of Music FAQ
by Barry Monush
Applause Books
9781480360433.... $27.99

South Park FAQ
by Dave Thompson
Applause Books
9781480350649... $24.99

Star Trek FAQ (Unofficial and Unauthorized)
by Mark Clark
Applause Books
9781557837929..... $22.99

Star Trek FAQ 2.0 (Unofficial and Unauthorized)
by Mark Clark
Applause Books
9781557837936..... $22.99

Star Wars FAQ
by Mark Clark
Applause Books
9781480360181...... $24.99

Steely Dan FAQ
by Anthony Robustelli
Backbeat Books
9781495025129 .... $19.99

Stephen King Films FAQ
by Scott Von Doviak
Applause Books
9781480355514..... $24.99

Three Stooges FAQ
by David J. Hogan
Applause Books
9781557837882..... $22.99

TV Finales FAQ
by Stephen Tropiano
and
Holly Van Buren
Applause Books
9781480391444..... $19.99

The Twilight Zone FAQ
by Dave Thompson
Applause Books
9781480396180..... $19.99

Twin Peaks FAQ
by David Bushman and
Arthur Smith
Applause Books
9781495015861....... $19.99

U2 FAQ
by John D. Luerssen
Backbeat Books
9780879309978... $19.99

UFO FAQ
by David J. Hogan
Backbeat Books
9781480393851 .... $19.99

Video Games FAQ
by Mark J.P. Wolf
Backbeat Books
9781617136306 ..... $19.99

The X-Files FAQ
by John Kenneth Muir
Applause Books
9781480369740.... $24.99

The Who FAQ
by Mike Segretto
Backbeat Books
9781480361034 .... $24.99

The Wizard of Oz FAQ
by Dave Hogan
Applause Books
9781480350625... $24.99

PERFORMING ARTS
PUBLISHING GROUP

FAQ.halleonardbooks.com

0218